Think Like a Software Engineering Manager

T0289654

Think Like a Software Engineering Manager

AKANKSHA GUPTA

MANNING
SHELTER ISLAND

Manning Publications Co.
20 Baldwin Road
PO Box 761
Shelter Island, NY 11964

Development editor:	Frances Lefkowitz
Technical editor:	Bruce Bergman
Review editor:	Radmila Ercegovac
Production editor:	Andy Marinkovich
Copy editor:	Keir Simpson
Proofreader:	Jason Everett
Technical proofreader:	Srihari Sridharan
Typesetter:	Gordan Salinovic
Cover designer:	Marija Tudor

ISBN 9781633438439
Printed in the United States of America

As I set out on the journey of writing Think Like a Software Engineering Manager, *little did I know that another author was silently contributing her essence to the narrative. Yes, my precious daughter Amaira was conceived during the creation of this book, and with each passing day, her presence became an integral part of its development.*

In the quiet solitude of late-night writing sessions, she was my silent companion, offering unwavering support from within the womb. Her heartbeat, a rhythm that echoed alongside the tapping of keys, served as a constant reminder of the dual roles I was undertaking: author and soon-to-be parent.

Now, as the pages of this book unfold, I proudly declare it to be a collaboration between two authors: me and my daughter. May this book stand as a testament to the harmonious symphony of parenthood and my passion for technology. With immense love and gratitude, I dedicate this book to Amaira.

brief contents

    12 ■ Engineering and operational excellence   247
    13 ■ Organizational change management   273
    14 ■ Time management   290
    15 ■ Beyond this book: Grow yourself   306

contents

2 Individual contributor to engineering manager 28

3 Managing people, teams, and yourself 57

preface

As someone who has always been drawn to software engineering, I have long harbored a keen interest in eventually transitioning from a software engineer role into management, specifically engineering management (EM). This aspiration stemmed from my admiration for my father, who worked in the same field.

Let's start with the reasons why an EM role would be exciting or even desirable for a software engineer. This role combines the principles of engineering and management to lead and deliver engineering projects. As such, the position requires true passion for leadership, strategy, a people-first mindset, and many other management skills. As an EM, you will be put in difficult situations and asked to identify and mitigate risks; make informed decisions, sometimes with limited information; help plan strategies for the organization and company; promote a culture of continuous improvement; handle resource allocations on projects; communicate to leadership; provide transparency; and help people with career development. Whether you're an experienced EM, a newcomer to the role who's stepping into the shoes of a predecessor, or a software engineer who's contemplating moving into an EM role, the position encompasses more than meets the eye. Regardless of the company's scale, the scope of responsibility is extensive.

Fortunately, whenever I made career moves as a software engineer, I found an abundance of books and resources available to educate, support, and aid me in my preparations. After spending several years as a software engineer and becoming serious about exploring a career path in engineering management, I faced a significant challenge. Though numerous resources available on management in general were available (see the following list), I found nothing specifically about making a transition from engineering to engineering management. Here are a few of the books on excelling in management that I read or listened to:

- *The Manager's Path: A Guide for Tech Leaders Navigating Growth and Change*, by Camille Fournier (https://mng.bz/2K1g)
- *97 Things Every Engineering Manager Should Know: Collective Wisdom from the Experts*, by Camille Fournier (https://mng.bz/1GRX)
- *The Mythical Man-Month: Essays on Software Engineering*, by Frederick P. Brooks Jr. (https://mng.bz/PZ7w)
- *Software Engineering at Google: Lessons Learned from Programming Over Time*, by Titus Winters, Tom Manshreck, and Hyrum Wright (https://mng.bz/JZ7o)
- *The Phoenix Project: A Novel About IT, DevOps, and Helping Your Business Win*, by Gene Kim, Kevin Behr, and George Spafford (https://mng.bz/wxAO)
- *Peopleware: Productive Projects and Teams*, by Tom DeMarco and Timothy Lister (https://mng.bz/qOAA)

As you can see, there was a noticeable lack of guidance for someone like me—an engineer seeking to understand what EM entailed and whether it was the right move for my career. Neither was there information on how to transition from an individual contributor (IC; software engineer) to a manager of teams. To my dismay, I discovered that I was the only one in my immediate circle of friends who was considering an EM role, which meant that there were fewer people I could turn to for advice within my online friend network. Consequently, I had to actively expand my network, using platforms such as LinkedIn to connect with individuals who could offer career guidance. My immediate manager also provided valuable support throughout this process.

The challenges and anxieties I experienced during my transition from software engineer to EM were the driving force behind my decision to write this book. Within its pages, you will delve into the EM role, learning about the progression from IC to EM, illustrated by some experiences from my journey as well as anecdotes from industry experts.

acknowledgments

Writing this book demanded significant effort and countless late nights. I want to express my gratitude to numerous individuals for their invaluable assistance throughout this journey.

Foremost, my deepest thanks go to my parents, especially my dad, who bestowed my first computer upon me when I was young, opening the world of software engineering to me. As I navigated the daunting task of writing a book, he believed in my capabilities even when I doubted myself. My parents have consistently inspired me to strive to be a better version of myself.

Next, I want to thank my husband, Gaurav. He always supported me, handling my tantrums when I was overwhelmed by a full-time job, pregnancy, and the book. He always listened to me patiently, helped me plan, reviewed each chapter, and provided candid feedback. He is the one who made me believe that I could do this work. He complements me in the perfect way. I love you, Gaurav.

Furthermore, I would like to express my gratitude to Al Krinker and Frances Lefkowitz, my esteemed editors at Manning. Throughout the process, they offered invaluable guidance and support, contributing significantly to the refinement of this work. A heartfelt thanks to Bruce Bergman and Srihari Sridharan for technical reviews and brainstorming. Thank you for working with me. Working alongside you significantly enhanced the quality of this book for its readers. I would like to also thank Manning's production and marketing teams.

Also, I want to express my thanks to friends and mentors who provided guidance, motivation, and invaluable feedback: Jean Bredeche, Oscar Medina, Sanjay Gupta,

Suyog Barve, Larry Gordan, C.J. Jouhal, Bidisha Das, Sumit Kumar, Saurabh Gandhi, Nathan Bourgoin, Kausik Basu, Nishat Akhter, Richard Frank, Adish Agarwal, Raj Sambasivam, Krishna Behara, Chander Dhall, Mayank Agarwal, Rajesh Subramaniam, and other industry experts quoted in the book who shared their insights. This achievement is the result of a collective effort. Thank you all!

Finally, I would like to thank all our reviewers, who invested their time in reading this book and provided valuable feedback that made a significant difference: To Adail Retamal, Andrea C. Granata, Andres Sacco, Amit Basnak, Arjunkumar Krishnamoorthy, Azizur Rahman, Brandon Rader, Chris Allan, Christopher Forbes, Dave Corun, David Paccoud, Dane Balia, Dirk Gómez, Edin Kapic, Fernando Bernardino, Francisco Rivas, Gary Rosales, Giampiero Granatella, Gilberto Taccari, Gregory A. Lussier, Greta Rossetto, Gustavo Velasco-Hernandez, Harsh Raval, Harshavardhan Mudumba Venkata, Haytham Samad, Ivo Štimac, Jereme Allen, Jeremy Chen, John Guthrie, Jon Choate, Krishna Chaithanya, Mario-Leander Reimer, Michael Lund, Mohammad Zeinali, Muneeb Shaikh, Phil Johnstone, Regan Russell, Saurabh Gandhi, Sergio Gutierrez, Shawn Lam, Sravanthi Pulakurthi, Stephanie Gredell, Steve Hill, Swapneelkumar Deshpande, Tamara Forza, Taylor Dolezal, and Yaz Erkan, you helped make this book better.

about this book

The book aims to help you determine whether the EM role is right for you, guide you in preparing for the position, and provide insights on how to thrive when you assume the role. You will understand what the role entails, explore the challenges that come with being an EM, and introduce frameworks that can be invaluable in your day-to-day responsibilities. I will share factors to keep in mind when making decisions at the company level, especially as most decisions can have consequences that extending far beyond your tenure in the role.

Through thought-provoking exercises at the end of each chapter, you will be encouraged to reflect on how the content resonates with your own job, role, and work. Take time to go through each question and reflect on it. These questions will help you in your current role as well as prepare you for future challenging roles. There are no right or wrong answers—just opportunities to consider and reflect.

Finally, each chapter incorporates the perspectives of other industry leaders who are experts in their field. These provocative quotations are here to enhance your understanding of the topics discussed. Again, there are no right or wrong opinions; these leaders are simply sharing their perspectives and showing how different people think about the situations that confront an EM.

Who should read this book?

First, let's address the fundamental question of who should read this book. If any of the following categories describes you, you have landed in the appropriate book:

- An engineer who is thinking about EM as your next potential career move
- An EM who is new to the role
- An experienced EM who is looking to learn and grow in the role
- An EM who is changing jobs and will be taking over a team from a previous EM
- An EM who will have new EMs under them or will help ICs go through the EM transition

How this book is organized: A road map

This book contains 15 chapters divided into three parts dealing with the fundamentals of the EM role (people, product, and process):

- *Part 1, Start with the people*—This part of the book sets the stage for your journey to being or becoming an EM, focusing on the people aspects of the job.
  - Chapter 1 introduces the basics of management, roles, and responsibilities of an EM, discussing leadership versus management and leadership styles.
  - Chapter 2 is about the differences between ICs and EMs, addressing some common misconceptions about the role, motivations for being an EM, and a three-phased approach for moving from IC to EM.
  - Chapter 3 deals with importance of managing people, your team, and yourself, as well as career development, conflict resolution, and opportunities to learn and grow as an EM.
  - Chapter 4 talks about managing performance, including best practices for performance reviews and managing high performers and underperformers.
  - Chapter 5 dives into the concept of delegation, discussing the differences between delegation, substitution, and allocation. The chapter also provides a framework for applying delegation and teaching it to others to create a multiplier effect.
  - Chapter 6 is about recognition: its role in team development, effective recognition, and how to handle recognition at all levels.
  - Chapter 7 delves into hiring. Topics covered include using a framework for hiring, building teams from scratch versus hiring people for an existing team, hiring externally versus internally, building a hiring pipeline, and creating hiring programs for positive reinforcement.
  - Chapter 8 explores attrition, its effects, and ways to get ahead of it.
- *Part 2, Projects and the cross-functional world*—Here, we explore projects and partnerships.
  - Chapter 9 shows the importance of cross-functional collaboration and discusses common challenges as well as ways to collaborate and communicate effectively in a cross-functional setting.
  - Chapter 10 dives into the project life cycle and the role that EMs play. It covers the stages of a project life cycle: preplanning, planning, execution, and postexecution.

- Chapter 11 deals with the importance of setting and managing expectations, addressing common challenges in expectation management and a framework for managing expectations.
- *Part 3, Learn the process*—In this part, you learn best practices for managing the crucial challenges you'll face.
    - Chapter 12 teaches the importance of engineering and operational excellence for EMs, as well as tools to get you started and help you focus on the iterative process.
    - Chapter 13 shares insights into reorganizations. It provides a framework for organizational change management and shows how to handle changes in leadership.
    - Chapter 14 dives into the importance of time management for EMs, providing tips on planning time and using tools such as the Eisenhower Matrix.
    - Chapter 15 shares insights into continuous learning, offering tips and strategies for nurturing self-development.

You do not have to read all the chapters in a specific order, as some may not immediately apply to your current role. But I strongly suggest going through even those chapters to gain insights into what you can expect in an EM position or see how to deal with situations better if you're already in the role. The book will provide you a comprehensive understanding of the role from various angles, encompassing people, product, and process perspectives. Moreover, by familiarizing yourself with these topics, you will be better prepared to empathize with individuals who are undergoing a similar transition.

liveBook discussion forum

Purchase of *Think Like a Software Engineering Manager* includes free access to liveBook, Manning's online reading platform. Using liveBook's exclusive discussion features, you can attach comments to the book globally or to specific sections or paragraphs. It's a snap to make notes for yourself, ask and answer technical questions, and receive help from the author and other users. To access the forum, go to https://livebook .manning.com/book/think-like-a-software-engineering-manager/discussion. You can also learn more about Manning's forums and the rules of conduct at https://livebook .manning.com/discussion.

Manning's commitment to our readers is to provide a venue where meaningful dialogue between individual readers and between readers and the author can take place. It is not a commitment to any specific amount of participation on the part of the author, whose contribution to the forum remains voluntary (and unpaid). We suggest that you try asking the author some challenging questions lest their interest stray! The forum and the archives of previous discussions will be accessible on the publisher's website as long as the book is in print.

about the author

 **Akanksha Gupta** is an experienced EM who has worked at several big tech firms, including Amazon-AWS, Audible, Microsoft, and Robinhood, where she led full stack teams. She holds a master's degree in computer science from Columbia University in New York. She served as a jury member for several esteemed awards and is an active mentor in the GrowthMentor, Plato, and First Round Fast Track mentorship programs. She has spoken at multiple global tech conferences and is a big advocate for women in technology. To find out more about her, find her on LinkedIn (https://www.linkedin.com/in/akankshaguptamgr).

ABOUT THE TECHNICAL EDITOR

Bruce Bergman is a Senior Software Engineering Manager at Lytx, Inc., with a focus on servant leadership of top-notch software teams, and on best-practice enterprise architecture. He has worked in a variety of industries/verticals, spoken at numerous conferences on many topics, and was a contributing editor to *Embedded Systems Programming* magazine. He holds degrees in Computer Science, Organizational Management, and Audio Engineering/Production.

about the cover illustration

The figure on the cover of *Think Like a Software Engineering Manager* is taken from a book by Louis Curmer published in 1841. Each illustration is finely drawn and colored by hand.

In those days, it was easy to identify where people lived and what their trade or station in life was just by their dress. Manning celebrates the inventiveness and initiative of the computer business with book covers based on the rich diversity of regional culture centuries ago, brought back to life by pictures from collections such as this one.

Part 1

Start with the people

This part of the book sets the stage for your journey to learning, establishing, and becoming an effective software engineering manager, focusing on the people aspect. Beyond spreadsheets and boardroom decisions, the resonance of human connections is what echoes through the corridors of effective engineering management.

In chapter 1, you'll learn about the basics of management, the key roles and responsibilities of an engineering manager (EM), leadership versus management, what differentiates excellent EMs from others, success metrics, and various leadership styles.

Chapter 2 teaches you the differences between an individual contributor (IC) and an EM, common misconceptions about moving from IC to EM, motivations for being an EM, a three-phase approach to IC-to-EM transition, and ways to help others transition into an EM role.

Chapter 3 covers the importance of managing people, teams, and yourself, discussing career conversations; conflict resolution; and the importance of goals, morale, and trust. It also discusses identifying opportunities and acknowledging mistakes to grow as an EM.

Chapter 4 talks about managing performance: best practices, performance reviews, and how to manage high performers and underperformers.

Chapter 5 delves into the intricate dynamics of delegation, meticulously parsing out its distinctions from allocations and substitutions. It navigates the complexities, elucidating the essence of delegation. Furthermore, it furnishes a structured framework that serves as a compass for effective delegation practices.

Chapter 6 talks about recognition and its role in team development, effective recognition, ways to recognize and reward others, and how to handle recognition at various levels.

Chapter 7 highlights the hiring framework, covering the nuances of building a team from scratch versus hiring people for an existing team, hiring externally versus internally, building a hiring pipeline, and creating hiring programs to promote positive reinforcement.

Chapter 8 talks about attrition, including its effects and how to get ahead of it.

When you finish this part of the book, you'll have learned about the people aspect of the EM role and will be ready to embark on your journey to learn about project management, execution, and delivery and how to work with cross-functional partners.

Exploring the engineering manager role

This chapter covers

- The basics of management and the need for it
- Key roles and responsibilities of an engineering manager
- The nuances of leadership versus management
- Traits that differentiate excellent engineering managers
- Success metrics
- Leadership styles

Productivity is most important by engineering management rules, but enjoyment is most important for engineers. One stems from the other.

—Rob Pike

You are the new engineering manager for a team of six engineers. Each engineer is capable of completing 2 tasks per day, for a team total of 12 tasks daily. You, however, think they can do better, and you identify specific opportunities for improvement. Through streamlined code reviews, agile development, and skill-enhancing training sessions, along with cross-training between backend and frontend, the team's productivity increases. With the changes, each developer now accomplishes three tasks a day, resulting in a 50% boost to daily output. Welcome to the world of engineering managers (EMs), the unsung heroes of organizational success!

Effective engineering management is crucial for both the success of the company and the growth of the individual engineers on your team. The job is not just about project execution, but also demands coaching, motivating, delegating, hiring, and firing. As an EM, you play the roles of guardian, navigator, and bridge between your team's brilliant minds and senior leadership's strategic vision. Despite the challenges, including tough decisions and occasional refusals, you guide your team toward greatness. As an EM, you're not just overseeing a team; you're orchestrating a symphony of innovation and collaboration. The job is not about ticking boxes on a managerial checklist, but about creating a thriving ecosystem where everyone leaves work with a sense of accomplishment.

Although fundamental management principles apply to the role, this book is tailored to EMs, emphasizing their pivotal role in the success of tech companies. Whether the task is leading a team in a warehouse or navigating a midlevel position in a tech company, the principles outlined here offer valuable guidance on overseeing people, projects, and processes.

This book provides insights and strategies to guide software engineers who are considering the EM career path, newly installed EMs, or established EMs who want to improve their skills. With example stories, personal insights, and organizational tools and templates, it will put you into every aspect of the job so you can indeed start thinking like an EM. In this first chapter, we explore the role, looking at the scope of responsibilities, the traits that help you navigate the job, and ways to measure your success.

1.1   Demystifying the EM role

EM is a versatile role that combines creativity and expertise, representing a fusion of a software engineer and a manager. An EM oversees the engineering team and also leads collaborations with other teams, known as cross-functional partners. Simply put: Engineering manager = Engineer + Manager.

Titles may vary among companies, and this same role may be called software development manager, senior manager of software engineering, or site reliability engineering (SRE)/DevOps manager, but the core responsibilities and expectations remain consistent. Establishing a new company, especially in the tech sector, requires effective leadership across various domains, such as determining project goals, crafting execution strategies, and managing finances. In the initial phases of a startup, an individual often takes on the multiple responsibilities of engineering management, with engineers reporting directly to the chief technology officer (CTO) in the absence of a formal EM. As the company expands, this approach becomes impractical, leading to the customary introduction of multiple EMs in medium-sized enterprises. A company consisting entirely of engineers without EMs (or where EMs don't do their job well) could lead to friction points such as the following:

- *Lack of leadership*—Without EMs, there may be a lack of leadership roles responsible for guiding and coordinating engineering teams, which can lead to confusion, disorganization, and unclear direction.
- *Communication challenges*—EMs often serve as intermediaries between engineering teams and other departments or stakeholders. Without them, communication channels may become strained, leading to misunderstandings, delays in decision-making, and difficulty in aligning engineering efforts with broader business goals.
- *Unclear prioritization*—EMs typically prioritize tasks and projects based on business objectives, resource availability, and other factors. Without this oversight, engineers may struggle to determine which tasks are most critical, leading to inefficiencies and misallocation of resources.
- *Conflict resolution*—EMs play a crucial role in resolving conflicts within engineering teams or between teams and other departments. Without dedicated EMs, conflicts may escalate.
- *Resource management*—EMs are responsible for managing resources such as budget, time, and personnel within engineering teams. Without them, there may be challenges in allocating resources effectively, leading to bottlenecks, missed deadlines, or overruns.
- *Career development*—An EM can provide mentorship to engineers, managers, and even cross-functional partners. Without this support structure, engineers may feel stagnant in their careers, leading to attrition and talent-retention problems.
- *Engineering excellence*—EMs oversee processes to ensure that engineering deliverables meet the required standards and specifications. Without them, there may be gaps in quality control, leading to product defects, customer dissatisfaction, and reputational damage.

This friction can compromise overall business health. In the dynamic startup world, EMs wear multiple hats, tackling technical problem-solving, team-building, and project management. They navigate challenges such as limited resources, tight deadlines, and the constant need for innovation, emphasizing hands-on problem-solving and effective leadership in uncertain environments.

By contrast, EMs in large corporations face challenges with complex structures, extensive hierarchies, and established processes. The trick here is navigating bureaucracy while fostering innovation and maintaining team efficiency. EMs in large corporations must possess a strategic mindset that aligns technical efforts with business goals and acts as a conduit between technical teams and senior management, emphasizing communication and collaboration.

Regardless of the setting, the role requires a delicate balance of technical prowess and managerial finesse. Although technical expertise is crucial for guiding teams and making informed decisions, managerial skills are equally vital for effective communication, conflict resolution, and overall project execution. In day-to-day operations, EMs seamlessly transition between technical problem-solving and managerial duties such as performance reviews, resource allocation, and strategic planning, ensuring alignment between their projects and the broader organizational objectives. Successful EMs possess qualities that enable them to manage at all levels, demonstrating empathy, soft skills, relationship-building, and effective planning and execution. These skills are refined through experience, particularly in handling ambiguous situations.

EM is a unique position in engineering, and not all developers may be suited for or interested in transitioning to EM roles. Even a highly accomplished engineer may not necessarily excel as an EM, and vice versa. The fact is that career progression doesn't necessarily lead to becoming an EM; alternative paths include remaining a software engineer (such as a solution architect or principal engineer) or exploring parallel roles such as product or project manager, business analyst, and DevOps architect. There's no universal model, and it's not unheard of to be a staff or principal engineer or lead architect while taking on some management responsibilities. Chapter 2 will delve into the career trajectories of software engineers and EMs, exploring commonly used titles and responsibilities associated with these roles. In the next section, we will further explore the nuances of the EM role.

1.1.1 Roles and responsibilities: The core competencies

The role of an EM is complex, as it involves juggling numerous, varied responsibilities and mastering skills such as time management, organization, prioritization, and context-switching. In simplified terms, the EM is responsible for executing the team and the projects. In this section, we will delve into the fundamental competencies that characterize an effective EM.

BUILDING TALENT

One of the primary responsibilities of an EM is to build talent and nurture the skills of the people on the team. This task involves a multipronged approach:

- Understanding the roles and responsibilities the team requires so you can better plan its composition
- Conducting résumé screening, hiring new employees who are aligned with team and company needs, and providing a runway for employees' success
- Engaging in regular one-on-ones and career conversations with engineers (or managers, in the case of a middle manager), and understanding their motivations, aspirations, and blockers
- Coaching and mentoring team members, addressing career gaps, bringing out the best in individuals, supporting career development, and promoting people when they're ready
- Managing performance by assisting both high and low performers and offering constructive feedback
- Facilitating the growth of individuals within the organization and discerning when external hiring is necessary
- Retaining existing talent by keeping them challenged and motivated

EMs achieve a high-performing, self-organizing team by demonstrating empathy, honesty, and emotional intelligence. The overarching goal is to empower team members, unleashing their full potential to achieve collective success. Prioritizing a people-centric culture enhances team engagement and job satisfaction, establishing a robust foundation for overall success within the company. We will dive deep in chapter 3 to learn more about managing people, teams, and yourself as EM.

FOSTERING VISION

For an EM, fostering a clear vision significantly enhances team productivity. It is your responsibility to impart a clear mission statement to your team by translating the organization-wide strategy and vision. This approach ensures that your team understands its purpose as a cohesive unit. Achieving clarity involves the following:

- Clearly defining the team's mission and charter
- Communicating how team goals align with the company's broader vision
- Setting clear and achievable objectives for the team
- Establishing task priorities for engineers so they are clear on their next steps
- Encouraging team members to think big and sharing both short- and long-term visions
- Guiding the team through dynamic tech environments, explaining shifts in strategy, and promoting adaptability

Embracing a visionary role requires mastering effective communication to promote transparency in conveying messages, especially in an era of unprecedented access to information.

LEADING PROJECTS

EMs are integral to leading projects, actively involved from initiation to completion. Responsibilities may vary based on the organization and team structure but could include any of the following:

- Motivating engineers and cross-functional partners to lead projects efficiently
- Making staffing decisions and ensuring that work aligns with individual engineers' career aspirations
- Creating project road maps, running standups, budgeting, and aligning stakeholders
- If the company uses agile methodology, facilitating smooth agile ceremonies in collaboration with the scrum lead and product manager
- Collaborating with peer managers and actively participating in shaping the product
- Presenting the team's vision to stakeholders and translating it into end customer products
- Cultivating a culture of innovation and collaboration
- Resolving conflicts within and outside the team

- Striking a balance between achieving delivery goals and maintaining technical excellence while placing less emphasis solely on coding, which is crucial for the overall success of a project or organization
- Removing roadblocks for the team, using experience and a 50,000-foot view to clear paths
- Ensuring operational stability after the product has been launched into production

The role involves dealing with ambiguity and making decisions with limited knowledge and resources. EMs must know when to delegate, take ownership, and make decisions. It is crucial for EMs to avoid analysis paralysis and own their decisions, whether or not they go well. Transparency and ownership, even in the face of mistakes, foster a positive leadership approach, ensuring continuous improvement. We will learn about leading projects in chapter 10.

> **NOTE** *Extreme Ownership* (https://mng.bz/eoyz) is an interesting read for learning more about the concept of ownership. I found its teachings profound, and two principles especially resonated with me. The first one advocates for leaders to embrace *extreme ownership*, which means taking responsibility not just for the work, but also for every facet affecting the mission. This principle challenges leaders to cultivate a mindset in which accountability has a ripple effect, extending to every step and stage. The second principle is about the nuanced art of leadership, urging leaders to embody humility without succumbing to passivity and to maintain quiet strength without slipping into silence.

As an EM, relying on your experience and skills is crucial. Recognizing the potential costliness of mistakes, you bear responsibility for both your work and your team's work. Maintaining a problem-solving mindset is paramount when leading projects, especially for navigating ambiguity effectively. Your best judgment becomes a guiding force, ensuring thoughtful decision-making and proactive resolution of problems. Embracing challenges with a solution-oriented approach fosters a culture of continuous improvement and resilience, ultimately contributing to the success of projects and the growth of your team.

MASTERING DELEGATION

Effectively juggling multiple projects, facilitating career discussions, aligning stakeholders, and attending numerous meetings solo is simply unfeasible. To expand your capacity, mastering the skill of delegation is essential. This skill involves the following:

- Shifting from a "doer" mentality to a "trust, but verify" (https://hbr.org/2005/05/trust-but-verify) mindset
- Adopting a coaching mindset to empower and guide your team
- Sharing knowledge to create a multiplier effect within the team
- Creating a safe environment for open communication and diverse opinions
- Being organized, managing time efficiently, and prioritizing tasks effectively
- Identifying tasks that can be delegated, determining when and to whom to delegate effectively

Effective delegation not only boosts morale and builds trust with your engineers, but also provides them opportunities to grow that align with their career aspirations. Simultaneously, it allows you to take on additional responsibilities that contribute to your career advancement. Scaling to manage multiple teams is a crucial consideration that is explored further in chapter 5, which is dedicated to the art of delegation.

FOCUSING ON ENGINEERING EXCELLENCE

For EMs, continuous learning and growth are paramount to both personal and team development. You influence the culture of your team. To foster engineering excellence, consider the following steps:

- Understand the existing process and identify constraints.
- Cultivate a culture of process improvements, business excellence, and operational efficiency.
- Improve service performance, reduce infrastructure costs, minimize downtime, and enhance value delivery to customers.
- Raise awareness about technical debt and inspire the team to elevate their standards.
- Implement better documentation, set up guardrails in change management, and establish standard operating procedures (SOPs).
- Elevate the team's operational excellence by actively participating in design discussions, code reviews, bug hunting, and ensuring legal compliance.

These efforts ensure that the team's implementations are optimized for long-term scalability. At the same time, prioritization is the key, as not all tasks are designed for long-term sustainability, especially in dynamic settings where software architectures may change rapidly. Developing the skill to discern opportune moments for transitions is crucial. We will learn in depth about engineering and operational excellence in chapter 12.

1.1.2 *Leadership versus management*

The terms *management* and *leadership* are sometimes used interchangeably, but they have subtle but distinct differences. Whether the title of the role is EM or engineering leader, embodying engineering leadership in practice is crucial. Approaching team management with an engineering-leadership mindset increases the likelihood of success, and the most effective managers seamlessly combine managerial skills with leadership qualities. Table 1.1 highlights the key distinctions.

Although the differences may seem to be nuanced, they often distinguish a successful EM from an unsuccessful one. An engineering leader focuses on team management, as well as providing vision and guidance for holistic problem-solving.

Table 1.1   Differences between leadership and management

Category	Management	Leadership
Role	More a title or tactical role	More a mindset, skill, approach to things, and strategic role
Duties	Management refers to the operational side of things. You help run sprint ceremonies (along with a scrum lead on your team), project deliveries, and more.	Conversely, leadership is a superset of operational plus the emotional aspect of doing things. You help inspire and coach your team in the process.
Outlook	Management focuses on the current situation and keeps the present in mind.	Leadership provides vision, keeping the big picture in mind and considering the present and future.
Value	Management is about increasing developer velocity, striving for stability, and focusing on quantifying the value of the team.	Leadership is about trying new things, challenging the status quo, thinking out of the box, and deciding what creates value rather than just delivers it.
Culture	Endorses the culture of the company	Helps shape the culture of the company

1.1.3   *Traits of a good engineering manager*

An EM holds a pivotal role that's akin to a chief in the military. Their traits can profoundly affect both the team and its projects. In this section, we'll look at key traits that distinguish a good EM.

CARING FOR PEOPLE

The primary responsibility of an EM is to provide unwavering support for and engagement with team members. This responsibility can involve any or all of the following:

- *Facilitating one-on-one discussions*—Engaging in open and constructive conversations with team members.
- *Conducting career conversations and performance reviews*—Supporting career growth through guidance, performance evaluation, coaching, and mentoring. Nurturing team members' development is akin to tending a garden, including fostering mental well-being.
- *Navigating ambiguity*—Providing clear guidance in uncertain situations, ensuring that team members can perform at their best.
- *Enabling team members to perform their best*—Fostering respect, motivation, and challenges.
- *Prioritizing honesty and authenticity*—Establishing a culture of trust, transparency, and genuine interaction.
- *Contributing to team-building activities*—Boosting morale through collaborative and team-centric initiatives.
- *Acting as a patient listener and problem-solver*—Addressing concerns and solving problems to maintain a positive work environment.

- *Maintaining fairness and an unbiased mindset*—Ensuring equal opportunities and providing constructive feedback for growth.
- *Providing protection and support*—Acting as a leader to shield and support team members' well-being and satisfaction.
- *Managing at all levels*—Successfully managing at all levels (your boss, your peers, and your reports), building trust and loyalty even in challenging situations.

In essence, a caring EM not only manages projects and tasks, but also actively supports the personal and professional development of each team member, creating a positive and thriving work environment.

Consider a scenario in which a new engineer, Claire, inadvertently introduces a bug into the software. The reactions of two EMs, Alice and Bob, showcase distinct leadership approaches:

- *Alice's proactive approach:*
  - Swiftly seeks a resolution to address the immediate problem
  - Reminds the team that failures are a natural part of rapid software development
  - Conducts a private discussion with Claire to explore preventive measures for the future
  - Also conducts a team discussion, sharing the message that it's OK to make mistakes because the idea is to learn from them
  - Collaborates with the team to fix the bug, emphasizing a learning opportunity
  - Encourages Claire to view the experience positively, fostering a sense of safety and trust
- *Bob's reactive approach:*
  - Identifies the problem and works on a solution but reprimands Claire for the mistake
  - Deflects some blame to the partner quality assurance (QA) team, focusing on assigning fault
  - While aiming for short-term changes, adversely affects team morale and instills a culture of fear
- *Comparison*—Alice's approach demonstrates effective leadership by addressing the immediate problem, fostering a positive team culture, and turning the incident into a learning opportunity. By contrast, Bob's reactive response may achieve short-term changes but risks damaging team morale and cohesion. His approach leads to hesitancy and reduced effectiveness within the team.
- *Key takeaway*—Effective leadership in challenging situations involves proactive problem-solving, fostering a positive environment, and viewing setbacks as opportunities for growth. Alice's approach highlights the importance of supporting team members through difficulties to ensure long-term productivity and collaboration.

HAVING A CLEAR VISION

An effective EM excels in articulating a compelling mission statement and vision for the team, fostering a shared purpose and encouraging critical thinking. Let's go back to the experiences of Alice and Bob, two EMs who approach this task differently.

- *Alice's proactive approach:*
  - Quickly identifies the team's preference for cross-functional collaboration
  - Actively engages with various stakeholders to gain comprehensive understanding of the company goals
  - Establishes a clear, concise vision for team members, igniting their motivation
  - Sets the team up for success by providing clear goals for the upcoming years
- *Bob's passive approach:*
  - Believes in the team's self-sufficiency and avoids involvement in setting a team vision
  - Tries to engage with partners but faces difficulty in establishing connections with them
  - Experiences frequent pushback on projects and struggles as EM to provide a clear vision
  - Sets the team on a path toward failure despite initial empowerment
- *Comparison*—Alice's proactive approach in setting a clear vision enhances team motivation and strategic clarity, ensuring a path to success. By contrast, Bob's passive stance leads to challenges and frequent pivots, showcasing the importance of having an articulated vision.
- *Key takeaway*—Inspiring a clear vision involves proactive engagement with stakeholders, fostering critical thinking, and providing strategic direction. Alice's approach demonstrates the positive effect of a well-defined vision on team motivation and success, emphasizing the importance of an engaged, visionary EM.

LEADING WITH EMOTIONAL INTELLIGENCE

In the complex and demanding field of engineering management, scenarios often arise that require delicate balancing of project responsibilities with the well-being of team members. Let's look at a hypothetical situation. A crucial project deadline looms while the lead engineer faces a personal tragedy. Key steps for displaying emotional intelligence are

- *Recognizing emotions*—Acknowledge and understand the emotional challenges that team members face. An engineer on the team had a personal tragedy, so as the EM, you need to recognize that engineer's emotions and support them.
- *Granting time and space*—Allow team members the necessary time and space to cope with their personal situations. Demonstrate empathy by showing understanding and support during difficult times.
- *Inquiring and supporting*—Inquire about the lead engineer's needs for support. Offer assistance in accessing resources or support systems that can aid in their recovery.

- *Communicating with stakeholders*—Communicate transparently with stakeholders about the situation and its potential effect on the project deadline. Set realistic expectations, emphasizing the importance of the team member's well-being.

- *Planning for contingencies*—Devise a contingency plan to address potential setbacks in project timelines. Distribute tasks among team members or explore temporary resources to mitigate the effect.

- *Fostering a supportive environment*—Create a psychologically safe environment where team members feel comfortable expressing their challenges. Encourage open communication and ensure that team members know that their well-being is a priority.

- *Providing optimism and productivity*—Foster optimism within the team by highlighting the importance of collective well-being. Cultivate an atmosphere where individuals can freely express their true selves, which contributes to heightened productivity.

When a team member faces a personal tragedy during a critical project, an EM is required to navigate the situation with emotional intelligence. Balancing empathy, effective communication, and strategic contingency planning ensures that the team can weather challenges while maintaining a positive, productive work environment. In such instances, the human-centric approach not only supports the affected team member, but also contributes to the long-term resilience and success of the entire team.

BEING A LEARNER WITH BOTH BUSINESS AND TECHNICAL ACUMEN

An effective EM thrives on continuous learning, recognizing the dynamic nature of technology and business landscapes. Their role requires both business acumen and technical expertise to ensure that they can guide both the business and engineering teams. Doing so requires a continuous-learning mindset, including the following:

- *Admitting limitations*—Proficient EMs are comfortable admitting when they lack answers, demonstrating their commitment to ongoing learning. Strength lies not in *knowing* everything, but in *finding* the right resources and solutions for the team.

- *Providing adaptability and motivation*—Embracing adaptability, EMs adjust quickly to changing circumstances within the tech and business realms. They motivate the team by fostering a culture of learning and improvement.

- *Understanding organizational goals*—Business acumen involves comprehending organizational goals, metrics, financial aspects (capital expenditure), revenue streams, and key performance indicators such objectives and key results (OKRs; https://www.atlassian.com/agile/agile-at-scale/okr).

- *Taking a tech-savvy approach*—Technical acumen requires deep understanding of engineering challenges as well as active participation in code reviews, technical design discussions, and brainstorming sessions.

Maria, a junior engineer on the team, has to decide whether to use in-memory calculations or Elasticache based on data size for an application. She reaches out to the EM for guidance and explains the problem. Alice, the EM, does not know the right choice, so she offers assistance by suggesting relevant online courses and connecting Maria to a tech lead on a sister team. This open-to-learning approach and open communication between the EM and a junior team member fosters confidence in Maria.

On the flip side, a manager like Bob, who leans more toward people management than technical acumen, might redirect the engineer to their team's tech lead without trying to understand the technical problem. For an EM, emphasizing the importance of technical knowledge involves sharing learning resources, encouraging attendance at conferences, and providing time for skill development.

BEING AN EFFECTIVE COMMUNICATOR AND FACILITATOR

Mastering dual communication styles—one tailored to technical audiences and another to nontechnical stakeholders—is crucial for EMs. Effective communication involves written and verbal skills in various contexts, from project documentation to addressing diverse audiences that include higher-level leadership and customers. Constructive feedback and a coaching mindset are part of effective communication and facilitation.

Under Alice's guidance, new engineer Jason overcame initial communication hurdles within the team. Alice took proactive measures to identify and rectify communication gaps by implementing practices that encourage diverse viewpoints. Conversely, Bob's tendency to rely heavily on a senior engineer for decision-making left team members feeling disconnected. Alice's adept communication and facilitation skills nurtured a more inclusive atmosphere, enabling Jason to participate actively in the team's activities.

DELEGATING EFFECTIVELY

Effective delegation for an EM involves understanding team members' career goals and assigning relevant tasks to propel their progress. First, you must recognize the value of empowering individuals; then you must build trust with your team members while avoiding micromanagement. Alice and Bob, our two senior engineers turned EMs, faced initial challenges in delegating tasks and responsibilities. Alice empowered her tech lead to collaborate with other teams, an act that demonstrated her trust in the tech lead's abilities. Conversely, Bob's reluctance to delegate meant that he was the only point of contact with other teams, which confused and frustrated team members and hindered their success.

The initial struggle of new EMs is adapting to delegation. They should identify this gap early and seek mentorship to overcome it. Though the process is not straightforward initially, effective delegation enables EMs to tackle more significant challenges while avoiding the trap of getting lost in technical details. In organizations where EMs also serve as tech leads, balancing engineering and management responsibilities requires coordination with the leadership chain.

LEADING BY EXAMPLE

Demonstrating commitment to doing the work you ask of your team builds confidence and trust. When team members see their leader actively involved, they are motivated to persevere. This approach fosters a culture of trust, motivation, and collective commitment to reaching project goals.

Here is an experience I had while planning a project for a previous employer. The team was tasked with building a new Amazon Web Services (AWS) backend service from scratch. Recognizing the need to familiarize ourselves with the AWS stack, I delved into project details with a senior engineer and decided to pursue AWS developer certification for myself. Collaborating with another senior EM, I initiated group learning sessions on AWS, hoping to encourage other team members to join us. After two months of study, I passed the exam and shared my achievement with the team, inspiring them to prepare to take it themselves. Six of eight engineers obtained AWS certification, contributing to the timely delivery of the project—a significant success for the team that started when I decided to lead by example.

FOSTERING INNOVATION

Optimizing team delivery involves fostering an environment that encourages feedback, new ideas, and innovation. You can create a culture in which everyone feels heard through initiatives such as team hackathons and brainstorming sessions for future backlog ideas. It's crucial for companies to support employees by providing time and resources for such events. Embracing a blameless culture, as outlined in the postmortem approach (https://sre.google/sre-book/postmortem-culture), contributes to a healthy workplace.

A strong EM focuses on learning from failures rather than playing the blame game. Innovation involves a fail-fast mentality: not every idea may make it to production. Treating discarded ideas as learning opportunities and creating a safe environment for healthy mistakes is an integral part of an EM's role. For an EM, it is important to focus on correcting errors, conducting root-cause analysis, and giving team members opportunities to learn and grow.

RECOGNIZING EFFORT AND SUCCESS

Recognizing and appreciating the talent within your team is vital for building trust and motivation. Acknowledging hard work, quick turnarounds, and successful projects sends a positive message, showing that engineering leadership values and supports team members' growth. Effective recognition involves understanding individual motivations, such as public or private praise, rewards of choice projects, or other individual preferences. Here are some methods I have used to recognize my team members:

- Giving the person or team a shout-out on team and leadership channels, sharing the details of the situation and what the team or person did that had a huge effect
- Recognizing people on internal platforms or tools, showing how they met or exceeded the company's leadership-principles standards

- Using monthly meetings to acknowledge all the great work done in the previous period
- Finding opportunities for team members to present their excellent work in all-hands or leadership meetings to help them get visibility

In chapter 6, we'll delve deeper into rewards and recognition.

STAYING ORGANIZED

A skilled engineering leader excels in effective time management, balancing diverse responsibilities such as meetings, staffing planning, one-on-one sessions, project oversight, and senior leadership reporting. Managing time efficiently requires strong organizational skills, strategic thinking, prioritization, and the ability to discern urgency. If an EM continually needs help, distinguishing between personal and team commitments is crucial. Falling behind hampers catching up and addressing various responsibilities. Using project management and organization tools such as Slack, Trello, Jira, and Asana can enhance efficiency.

From caring for people to staying organized, these traits are not exhaustive, but they encapsulate essential qualities that differentiate a strong engineering leader. Continuous refinement of core skills is key for helping both the EM and the engineering team reach their potential. Recognizing growth opportunities and focusing on improvement is crucial, as some skills can be coached and developed.

1.2   *Success metrics as an engineering manager*

Although understanding and practicing the traits we've just discussed is crucial for success as an EM, it's equally important to define objective measures of success. The old saying holds true: "You can't improve what you don't measure." Success can be subjective and can evolve. Metrics provide an assessment to gauge performance against success criteria, aiding you in strategic planning and identifying areas for improvement. Key areas for measuring success in EM roles include the following:

- Optimizing for key business metrics and delivering value
- Increasing team development velocity
- Creating and maintaining healthy team morale, fostering team members' career progress
- Optimizing for operational metrics

These areas are interconnected, and success or failure in one can affect others. Enhancing developer velocity, for example, can influence key business or operational metrics, provided that proper processes are in place. Conversely, persistent failure to affect business metrics can affect team morale. Exploring each area in depth provides comprehensive understanding of success.

1.2.1   Business metrics

The success of an EM can be measured through business metrics that reflect the value the team delivers to the business or customers. Metrics should be realistic and aligned with the company's vision, goals, and strategic direction. Common tech-company metrics include customer satisfaction (https://mng.bz/X1ql), retention rate, and customer feedback. Success is determined by meeting or surpassing metrics set during project initiation.

Shipping a new product that increases customer satisfaction by 20% and reduces escalations by 30%, for example, is considered to be successful when aligned with established metrics. For an EM, collaboration during project initiation helps define success metrics, and meeting set goals indicates project success. Advocate for establishing success metrics if they are not already in place.

Although optimizing for business metrics may appear straightforward on the surface, complexities arise in scenarios involving multiple stakeholders and vendors, as well as accurately pinpointing the root causes of changes in metrics. A 30% reduction in escalations, for example, may result from various factors, and you won't be able to identify them without meticulous analysis. Acknowledging responsibility in case of negative outcomes is also essential, as is avoiding shifting blame to other teams. As you can see, optimizing for business metrics is valuable but can become complex in certain situations.

1.2.2   Development velocity

Measuring the success of an EM involves carefully choosing the metrics based on the work situation and company. Your team's development velocity (https://mng.bz/y8Z7) can help you measure success. DORA metrics (https://codeclimate.com/blog/dora-metrics), proposed by the DevOps Research and Assessment team, is another way to measure the success of your engineering team and your own success. It includes four key metrics:

- *Deployment frequency*—How often services are deployed to production, using continuous integration and continuous deployment
- *Change lead time*—The duration from code change commitment to deployable status
- *Mean time to recovery*—The time it takes to recover services or products in case of an problem
- *Change failure rate*—The frequency at which changes or hotfixes result in failures after deployment

Other metrics beyond DORA that can help are

- *Sprint velocity*—Seeing how many story points your team can deliver in a sprint, including assessing burndown charts
- *Time to complete code reviews*—Ensuring that engineers help review peer code to improve developer velocity as a whole

- *Number of bugs reported and resolved*—Monitoring the number of bugs reported by customers and QA and bringing the count down
- *Failed deployment recovery time*—Monitoring how long it takes to recover from a failed deployment

Indeed, you can explore numerous avenues for improving development velocity, but maintaining focus on quality is crucial. Although we've discussed key metrics, improving development velocity is challenging and requires a longer observation period for fair assessments. Comparing velocity among team members, teams, and projects is also difficult, and we should prioritize value delivered over velocity.

Teams may use story points, but those story points should serve as references for understanding team capacity, task comprehension, and estimation accuracy. Using story points to compare individuals can lead to confusion and unfair assessments when what we really want to know is the overall value delivered by the team.

To drive improvement, it's important to identify high-priority areas where the team is struggling. When improvements are observed, gradually expand focus to other areas. Addressing downtime problems in essential services can significantly affect the team's overall performance; then you can identify the next challenge and optimize for it.

1.2.3   *Team morale*

Team morale is a critical aspect that significantly influences team performance and success. High morale fosters collaboration, open communication, and a positive work culture, which in turn contributes to increased job satisfaction and engagement. Conversely, low morale can lead to negativity, bottlenecks, and potential single points of failure.

Team morale serves as a key success metric, as it affects participation in meetings, job satisfaction, retention rates, levels of trust, and collaboration. Monitoring team morale involves the following:

- Actively participating in and observing meetings and interactions
- Holding one-on-one discussions with team members
- Having candid, informal coffee chats
- Conducting periodic surveys, both companywide and at team level, to gather objective data
- Holding regular team meetings to address concerns openly and find collaborative solutions
- Facilitating upskilling opportunities and ensuring career progression

A successful EM leads a team with high morale, whose members are motivated to go the extra mile for one another, contributing to a conducive learning environment.

1.2.4   *Operational excellence metrics*

Operational excellence and process improvements serve as the backbone of the engineering culture within a company. These metrics reflect the health of services and processes, as well as indicate the team's focus on launching new products versus maintaining existing ones. Key metrics for assessing operational excellence include

- Technical debt on the team (further explored in chapter 12)
- Defects resolution rate (incoming versus resolved)
- Test code coverage (the absence of which can indicate a problem)
- Extensibility and readability of code
- Code maintenance and on-call reports
- Reduced costs and downtime
- Ability to meet defined service-level agreement (SLA) contracts
- Availability of services in production

These metrics offer valuable insights into the state of team services and the codebase. Successful teams actively manage and reduce technical debt while implementing process improvements to enhance their efficiency. Metrics such as the number of lines of code or raw count of user stories closed by a developer can be misleading. The true testament to success lies in the team's ability to operate smoothly even when the EM is on vacation.

Allow me to share an example from my previous team. We noticed a gradual increase in on-call workload—the first line of defense for any problems raised during a designated on-call period. Team members typically rotated and took turns assuming these responsibilities. Upon closer examination, we discovered that our core services deteriorated slowly due to several factors, such as increased technical debt from quick fixes and infrastructure degradation due to missing updates. If left unaddressed, this situation could have had severe consequences for the team in the long run, including reduced developer velocity (as the team was more occupied with resolving problems than delivering new products), decreased team morale, and increased risk of burnout. To tackle this challenge, our team collaborated closely with the site reliability teams to generate ideas and improvements that would enhance the overall health of our services. We prioritized and dedicated a full quarter to working on this endeavor. This exercise was pivotal and ultimately allowed the team to regain its full development capacity.

After you examine diverse success metrics for evaluating an EM's effectiveness, it's apparent that exemplary companies and teams function with seamless efficiency reminiscent of a finely tuned machine. Managing and leading a team effectively requires recognizing different leadership styles and identifying the ones that align best with the team's dynamics.

1.3 Leadership styles

A defined leadership style helps set expectations for your team and yourself. Let's explore six common engineering leadership styles, understanding that each style has its own merits and may be most effective in different situations. The key is adapting and using these styles based on context, team maturity, size, and product.

1.3.1 *Autocratic*

Meet Alissa, an experienced EM who adopts an autocratic leadership style. She takes pride in maintaining control of situations, often being prescriptive and micromanaging her team. Alissa recently mandated that all team members must be present in the office every Thursday, leading to dissatisfaction. Team members feel restricted, but they have no channel through which to provide feedback. Soon, the team experiences declining creativity and innovation. Alissa's rigid approach created a trust deficit and low morale, especially for team members who face personal constraints, such as a new parent who found working from home to be crucial at this stage. If Alissa's leadership style resonates with you, you may

- Prefer full control of situations
- Disregard others' opinions
- Tend to micromanage
- Possess overconfidence in your knowledge
- Embrace a restrictive leadership style
- Adhere strictly to rules and playbooks
- Make decisions without considering others' input
- Potentially prioritize self-interest over team focus

Nonetheless, this leadership style can work effectively in some scenarios. When a project has a tight deadline or a team lacks accountability, an autocratic leader can provide guidance. In general, though, teams do not appreciate an EM who uses this style all the time; it hampers team morale and promotes the feeling that members' needs and concerns are not being heard. Again, depending on the situation, you may or may not decide to use this style.

1.3.2 *Democratic*

Meet Brayden, a relatively new EM with a democratic leadership style. He values building relationships and actively seeks input from his team members in decision-making, even though the final call is his. Brayden recently used a poll along with team discussions to determine the day for sprint grooming, ultimately choosing Monday based on the team's preferences. If Brayden's leadership style resonates with you, you may

- Value ideas from your team members
- Be a good listener
- Embrace innovation and creativity
- Welcome diverse viewpoints
- Be willing to make compromises for team satisfaction and motivation

Although this approach fosters a sense of participation and satisfaction, it has drawbacks. Decision-making can be slow, and collecting timely feedback may be challenging. For crucial decisions, relying solely on democratic methods may hinder strategic direction. Setting clear deadlines or using rapid-feedback tools can address these problems.

1.3.3   *Delegative*

Meet Charlie, an experienced engineering leader with a delegative leadership style. Charlie believes in delegation to manage multiple teams across various geographical areas efficiently. He empowers individuals by giving them decision-making authority and minimal supervision, adopting a hands-off approach that focuses on what needs to be done rather than how. In a recent decision-making scenario, he delegated the load-testing strategy for backend services to his team, emphasizing the importance of outcomes over micromanagement. Identifying with Charlie's leadership style means that you

- Prefer to delegate decision-making to your team
- Trust your team members to make the right decisions
- Adopt a hands-off management approach
- Cultivate a culture of empowerment and leadership within the team

Although Charlie's approach motivates his team and fosters a positive work culture, challenges arise, especially for junior engineers seeking more guidance. Striking the right balance between hands-off and hands-on management is crucial for preventing problems, such as the perception that the leader shows up only for results. Balancing autonomy with support and clear communication is key to achieving optimal outcomes for the team.

For a delegative leader, maintaining effective oversight requires balancing autonomy with team goals and individual capacities. Strategies for achieving this balance include

- Clearly defining expectations and ensuring comprehensive understanding of the big picture
- Clarifying roles, responsibilities, and the support individuals can expect from the leader
- Implementing frequent communication and check-ins to discuss progress, address blockers, and sustain momentum
- Providing necessary training support to enhance individual and team capabilities
- Encouraging feedback and adaptability to foster a collaborative, empowered team environment

The goal is to create an environment in which collaboration thrives and the team feels empowered. We'll discuss delegation in depth in chapter 5.

1.3.4   *Transactional*

Meet Dave, who employs a transactional leadership approach, motivating his team through incentives and consequences. He views work as a gamified experience, fostering healthy competition to bring out the best in individuals. Recognizing hard work, he rewards achievements and provides training to ensure results. Leaders with a transactional style, like Dave, typically

- Incentivize exceptional work with rewards
- Employ consequences for work that doesn't align with expectations
- Cultivate a competitive culture within the organization
- Tend to engage in some level of micromanagement
- Place high value on achieving set goals

Although the transactional leadership style can improve business metrics, it comes with potential drawbacks that affect overall team morale. Unintended consequences of a competitive environment may include unexpected attrition, a noticeable divide between high and low performers, reluctance to share openly, and general disengagement within the team.

1.3.5   *Transformational*

Meet Eric, who embodies a visionary leadership style, prioritizing the company's goals and mission. With a magnetic personality, he passionately drives toward objectives and isn't afraid to make bold decisions. Recently, he inspired his team to transition from a legacy platform to cutting-edge technology—a move that required simultaneous maintenance and resource allocation.

His team members appreciate Eric's forward-thinking approach, considering him to be a strong, visionary leader. But they occasionally feel that finer details are overlooked in the pursuit of bold decisions and that their voices are not always heard during such strategic moves.

If Eric's leadership style resonates with you, you likely possess a transformational leadership approach. This style is characterized by

- Leading through inspiration
- Being considered a visionary leader
- Prioritizing the company's goals and missions
- Uniting the team to achieve goals collectively
- Believing in bold, strategic decision-making

Transformational leaders, often associated with roles such as enterprise architect and DevOps/DevSecOps team, play a crucial role in driving growth and change within a company. Carefully balancing this leadership style with other styles is essential, however, because focusing solely on the future without addressing present needs can lead to unintended consequences. Proposing a complete rearchitecture of a core infrastructure piece, although beneficial for the future, might strain resources and time needed for ongoing operational excellence. If a team is already stretched thin operationally, adding a migration phase to the mix can further burden the team.

The transformational leadership style requires caution. Although this style is valuable for envisioning and driving change, leaders must consider its practical implications and potential strains on existing operations. Striking a balance between future-oriented transformation and current operational needs is key to successful leadership.

1.3.6 *Servant*

Meet Frankie, who identifies as a people manager, prioritizing a people-first mindset to bring out the best in her engineers. She invests time weekly in making individual connections, maintaining career documents to understand team members' strengths, weaknesses, and aspirations. Collaboratively setting goals aligned with career aspirations, Frankie fosters engagement through team-building and constructive feedback. Despite occasional challenges in assertiveness during conflicts, Frankie creates a positive coaching environment, demonstrating emotional intelligence and empathy.

Acknowledging her team's interests, Frankie facilitated a successful transition for one team member from engineering to product management, showcasing her commitment to supporting individual career aspirations. Her team members actively engage in making decisions and contributing ideas, and they express high satisfaction, which contributes to a commendable retention rate. Frankie's genuine investment in her team's career growth fosters trust and empowerment. If your leadership style aligns with Frankie's, you likely

- Prefer a people-first management approach
- Enjoy mentoring and coaching
- View your role as enabling others to succeed
- Seek to understand the motivations and aspirations of your team members
- Provide guidance and feedback to team members
- Believe in the importance of team-building, and go the extra mile for the team's success

This leadership style promotes engagement, motivation, and a sense of belonging among team members. When you advocate for a people-centric approach, however, it's crucial to be assertive in making decisions and resolving conflicts. Playing the devil's advocate when necessary ensures that your team remains focused and driven. Practicing this style with caution can lead to sustained team success while effectively addressing potential challenges.

So which EM do you relate to most: Alissa, Brayden, Charlie, Dave, Eric, or Frankie? Let's see how you can go about choosing your own leadership style.

1.3.7 *Choosing your leadership style*

Choosing your preferred leadership style is crucial, but keep in mind that there's no one-size-fits-all solution. Your leadership approach depends on factors such as your experience, team dynamics, project phase, and company culture. *Flexibility is key.* A hybrid style is OK and often works best because leadership styles depend on multiple factors:

- *You*—Your experience as an engineering leader and your personality significantly shape your approach to leadership.
- *The team*—The size of your team along with the experience levels of your team members, their preferences and aspirations, and how they perceive you influence your leadership style.

- *Project phase*—Different project phases may warrant using different leadership styles.
- *The company*—Several internal and external factors dictate how the company is run, including the company culture, the product strategy, competition, and time constraints.

Choosing a leadership style is highly situational, requiring a unique evaluation of each circumstance. A leader may opt for a particular style or combine several to form a personalized hybrid approach, all while maintaining a positive attitude and a growth mindset that embraces learning opportunities.

When you're faced with a deadline to make a decision without the need for consensus, a combination of autocratic and delegation approaches might be effective. Tough choices, such as downsizing due to market conditions, may demand adapting styles, possibly blending transformational and transactional approaches.

Flexibility is crucial, even when it means unlearning and relearning when an initial leadership style proves to be ineffective. Consider a scenario in which a focus on reducing technical debt inadvertently affects current operations. Swift adaptation, such as organizing a hackathon for revenue growth, illustrates the need to discard the initial plan and embrace a more democratic style based on current circumstances.

In essence, there is no one best leadership style. Leaders must understand the fundamentals, adapt to changing situations, and strive to be effective by responding uniquely to new and unconquered challenges in the engineering field.

What do other leaders have to say?

The most important traits of an engineering leader are focusing on recruiting, motivating, enabling, and retaining the strongest team possible. Think about the team and cross-functional stakeholders as a machine with inputs, outputs, and internal processes; figure out where the bottlenecks are, where there isn't enough backpressure, where adding extra capacity will help, and where adding extra capacity won't help.

—Jean Bredeche, Head of Engineering at Patch,
formerly with Robinhood, Quantopian, and Hubspot

I think this trait is incredibly important in people but especially in leaders: empathy. Mentoring or teaching others is one of the more obvious situations in which this is useful since it can allow a mentor to discuss the relevant subject matter in a way that the mentee understands better. But this extends to all the relationship-building that a leader does as well. An engineering leader often partners with product leaders, creating an information bridge between them and engineers. By understanding the incentives of their coworkers, they can also more effectively assess the structure of an organization (of people) and whether those incentives could be better aligned.

—Richard Frank, Senior Software Engineer
(former manager) at Two Sigma, formerly with Robinhood

The most important trait for an engineering manager is understanding tech and product. As an EM, you work very closely with engineering and product teams, and you can only contribute effectively if you understand both sides of the world. I resonate with democratic leadership. With so much opportunity in the current market for engineering, you need to take your team along with every decision you make.

—Madhur Kathuria, Engineering Leader at Microsoft,
formerly with Moengage, Oracle, and IIT

Though many traits are important to be a good leader, classifying any one as most important will not be completely right. While creativity, curiosity, collaboration, and communication might top the charts, I think empathy is crucial. It is extremely vital to be empathetic towards your team members, your clients, your end users, and everyone you interact with.

—Devika Ahuja, Technology Leader at Strategist

For challenges as EM, in all the companies I've worked with recently, the prevailing leadership perspective was that engineering wasn't delivering enough or was going too slow. This is presented as opinions like "Engineering is lazy" or "Engineering doesn't consider our needs." Yet when you talk with engineers, they consider themselves overworked, frequently putting in nights and weekends to hit deadlines they don't understand. The biggest challenge I have faced in working with these companies is rehabilitating the reputation and trust of engineering teams. The first step has continually been improving the work visibility of engineering efforts. Once you get leadership to internalize that folks are working hard, that they are working on their understanding of priority, and that folks do want to do the best work for the company, it becomes easier to have reasonable conversations around constraints, challenges, etc.

—Nathan Bourgoin, Chief Technology Officer at Alakazam Inc.,
Technical Adviser, and Engineering Leader

The most common issue I've seen EMs face is being able to make prioritization decisions on the move. Most of them struggle with using the right data to make these decisions. I would recommend using the Eisenhower Matrix (https://www.eisenhower.me/ eisenhower-matrix) to put things in perspective quickly. Another way of making quick prioritization decisions is asking yourself "Would this be an easily reversible decision?" If it is, it doesn't need as much scrutiny as a nonreversible decision.

—Adish Agarwal, Director, Software Development at Audible, Inc.

Based on my journey of 15 years of learning as a leader, I'm continuously working to be an authentic leader. I define an authentic leader as a human being whose internal and external personas are aligned. They do not have to act as differently as a leader, they present themselves the same at work as they are at home. In my view, there are three traits of an authentic leader:

1. They are highly self-aware of their strengths, weaknesses, and various emotional states in other words, they have a very high EQ (emotional quotient).
2. They are good human beings with high integrity who want to sincerely help others and make life better for everyone around them.
3. They make time to do new things every day, from learning new things to having fun doing activities they love for physical and mental fitness.

—Sumit Kumar, System Engineering Manager at Cisco

(continued)

To me, the leader of any engineering team or org has to come from a strong technology background. In addition, all the best engineering leaders have a great eye for the future of the industries and trends and stay in touch with the latest. Another key trait is how they treat people and how people respect the leader. I see an engineering leader as a mix of technical acumen, people skills with empathy, and a strong personality to stand for what he or she wants for his organization. I align more with a servant leadership style. As I transitioned from an individual contributor to a manager, it was a natural transition for me to be close to the team and understand the pain points. The EM's role is the mix of technology meets business without impacting people's focus. You are always flirting with those fine lines impacting one of those areas. A successful EM figures out the balancing act.

—Rajakumar Sambasivam, Delivery Manager at Microsoft

An engineering leader should have a good overall understanding of the technology landscape the team is working on, along with people management and leadership skills. They should know when to get into day-to-day execution mode and when to switch to formulating strategy and vision for the team. They should also be able to tune their communication skills according to the group they manage—managing down, up, or sideways.

—Sarin Panambayil, Principal Engineer at Yahoo!

The most important trait of an engineering leader is to deliver the product, and you have to be able to say to the product owners and your bosses that I'm going to deliver these features in this product platform by this date and a new set of features, you know could be phase two, and I am delivering a stable, scalable way by another date, and here's how many engineers I need and the tools I need in the budgets I need to do it.

—Larry Gordan, Managing Director at Emtec, Inc.

1.4   *Stop and think: Practice questions*

1   Who was your favorite manager in your career, and what was different about them?
2   Which manager did you most dislike working with, and what was different about them?
3   In your opinion, what is the most important trait of an engineering leader?
4   If you have been an engineering leader for a while, think about your first role as an EM. What are the best memories from that time?
5   In your opinion, what are your strengths and weaknesses as an engineering leader?
6   Which leadership style resonates with you most?

Summary

- A manager plays a fundamental role in overseeing and supporting employees to enhance their effectiveness and productivity while contributing to the overall business strategy. This role applies across diverse industries, such as technology, customer care, sales, finance, and restaurants.

- Key responsibilities include hiring, performance management, delegation, talent recognition, project delivery, motivation, and enhancing team productivity.
- The engineering manager's role is a blend of art and skill, involving tasks such as resourcing, allocation of engineering resources, conflict resolution, managing expectations, and uplifting the morale of software engineering teams.
- This book is tailored to those who are transitioning from a software developer role to an EM role, newcomers to the role, experienced managers seeking skill refinement, those preparing for job changes, or middle managers anticipating new engineering managers under their supervision.
- For an EM, crucial responsibilities involve developing talent, fostering team clarity, providing project leadership, delegating adeptly, and focusing on engineering excellence. The emphasis is on being an engineering leader, guiding the team with a clear vision and charter.
- Distinguishing traits of effective EMs include a people-first mindset, clear vision, emotional intelligence, technical acumen, proficient delegation, effective communication, honesty, and integrity, as well as leading by example, promoting innovation, recognizing talent, and maintaining authenticity and organization.
- Measuring an EM's success is crucial, focusing on metrics such as business performance, development velocity, team morale, and operational excellence for an objective definition of success.
- Various leadership styles exist, each with a unique effect on team members:
  - The autocratic style works in time-constraint scenarios but is generally poorly received by team members.
  - Democratic style brings everyone together to make consensus decisions, but it can be time-consuming.
  - The delegative style works when the person delegating the work is senior; it might not work when a more prescriptive approach is needed.
  - Transactional style boosts business and development metrics but hampers team collaboration and morale.
  - The transformational style needs to be balanced with other leadership styles, as focusing only on the future can have dire consequences in the present.
  - Servant leadership makes team members feel motivated and engaged.
- You don't have to choose a particular leadership style; instead, you might want to adopt a hybrid style, depending on circumstances.

Individual contributor to engineering manager

2

This chapter covers

- Differences between an individual contributor and an engineering manager
- Common misconceptions when transitioning to engineering manager
- Sharing intentions and motivations for becoming an engineering manager
- A three-phase approach for the transition
- How to help others go from individual contributors to engineering managers

My job is not to be easy on people. My job is to take these great people we have and to push them and make them even better.

—Steve Jobs

In chapter 1, we explored the responsibilities of an engineering manager (EM) and emphasized the importance of managing teams and individuals in this role. As more software engineers consider a move into management, understanding the distinctions between the roles of an individual contributor (IC) and an EM becomes crucial.

ICs contribute to the team and organization without managing others. If you're currently a software engineer, you fall into the IC category. On the other hand, an *EM* supervises and manages other engineers, orchestrating engineering excellence. If you're responsible for a group of software engineers and engage in people management, you are considered an EM; if you do the same for other managers, you are a senior manager.

This chapter delves into the differences between an EM and an IC, including factors to consider when deciding on your career path and strategies for navigating the transition. Whether you're an IC exploring the possibility of transitioning to EM or an experienced EM overseeing ICs transitioning into the role, know that the skills built as an IC are transferrable.

Typically, there are three main reasons for any IC-to-EM transition: having genuine passion for the EM role, being forced to make the move due to organizational needs, or inheriting the role by default. However you get there, pausing to reflect on whether the EM role suits you before you make the transition is worthwhile. To answer this question, we'll explore the differences between the two roles.

2.1 Differences between the IC and EM roles

As you saw in the chapter introduction, you may make the transition from IC to EM by choice or necessity. The IC and EM roles differ in several aspects, including priorities, time commitments, amount of people management, success metrics, specialization, mindset (role versus leader), and so on. To make an informed decision about whether to become an EM, delve into the detailed comparison of the two roles in table 2.1.

Table 2.1 Differences between ICs and EMs

Category	IC	EM
Priority	You value yourself first and then the team, thinking about how to increase your efficiency as a developer. You are task-oriented and typically directed to complete tasks by the team, team lead, product owner, or manager.	The team comes before you. You are always thinking about how to build a high-performing team and increase developer velocity. You are responsive and proactive, flexible and adaptable, and you typically prioritize the needs of others. Rarely do you follow a set or defined task list that includes a personal agenda.
Time allocation	The majority of your time is spent coding and shipping products. You get more focus time to work on tasks.	Coding takes a back seat. You spend most of your time managing people, building teams and strategies, and influencing people around you. You get more meeting time than focus time.
People aspect	You may mentor other engineers but without worrying about the people or career aspects of the mentoring relationship.	You are responsible for the career growth of your team members, as well as not-so-fun human resources and legal matters. You help people get promoted and manage underperformance.

Table 2.1   Differences between ICs and EMs *(continued)*

Category	IC	EM
Success metrics	You have tangible outcomes at the end of the week, such as products shipped and services deployed to production, along with some intangible things, such as learning and development. Hence, measuring success is easy. At the same time, not all metrics are tangible. Some metrics are subjective, such as whether you are learning something or expanding your skills.	Your success is abstract. At the end of the week, you might start questioning your output. You participate in meetings and speak to people but may not have something tangible at the end of the week, as an IC would.
Specialization	You can be a specialist in your area or a subject-matter expert (SME) in your area of technical expertise.	You are a generalist with broad knowledge of technology and an expert on people management.
Role mindset	You have a doer or creator mindset. As an IC, you might be following the examples of others.	You have a delegator or enabler mindset. In many ways, you're also an educator, mentor, and career coach. You lead by example.
Strategy	You tend to think about the what, when, and how of technology. Senior ICs can help contribute to the why aspect.	You must consider the why of a project/technology/business. You must operate at a higher level. Managers fly at the 50,000-foot level, not the 2,000-foot level.
Outcome	Your work produces more immediate results, such as projects shipped, delivery velocity, product/project completion, and DORA metrics.	Your efforts can take time to show outcomes. Successfully leading an organization-wide program does not happen overnight. Your outcomes are far more subjective and include the successes of your people.

In summary, although both roles have significant responsibilities, they have different core competencies that are crucial for success. Your thought process, success metrics, time allocation, and mindset depend on which role you occupy. But merely knowing the general role differences, which may vary slightly between companies, isn't sufficient for making an informed decision. Before making a decision, it's better to gain a 360-degree view so you can address any of your misconceptions or expectations.

2.2   *Common misconceptions*

Let's address some prevalent misconceptions in the tech industry. Surprising as it may seem, these misconceptions are widespread and can affect our understanding of the expectations associated with the EM role.

2.2.1   *IC to EM is not necessarily a promotion*

Contrary to traditional notions, a transition from IC to EM is not always viewed as a promotion in the tech industry. Unlike companies in many other industries, tech companies offer separate career ladders for ICs and EMs. Promotions can occur on each track, allowing individuals to advance in their roles without necessarily moving into management. Major tech companies provide the option to grow as an IC or transition laterally to an EM role after achieving a specific experience level (figure 2.1).

This flexibility extends to moving back from EM to IC, provided that you maintain your coding skills and stay updated on technology. This move is more common on the lower levels of the chart shown in figure 2.1. Although smaller companies may provide varying levels of flexibility, these career ladders offer engineers the freedom to choose and excel in what aligns with their individual preferences and strengths.

2.2.2 EMs do not always write code

Coding skills are valuable for an EM to possess, but they may not be used frequently in the role. The skills you *will* use consistently are people management and your ability to execute the organization's goals and your team's vision.

You must be comfortable with the idea of stepping away from coding as an EM. You can still contribute actively to architectural discussions, staying connected to the product and the code by designing high-level architecture.

In smaller teams, on which technical expertise is vital and coding is expected, you might continue coding until a suitable replacement is found. Expectations regarding coding involvement vary, so make sure that you align your priorities with the requirements and expectations of the particular EM role that you are considering.

First-level managers who recently transitioned from IC to EM may maintain some involvement with coding, provided that they balance their EM responsibilities effectively. But caution is necessary: you

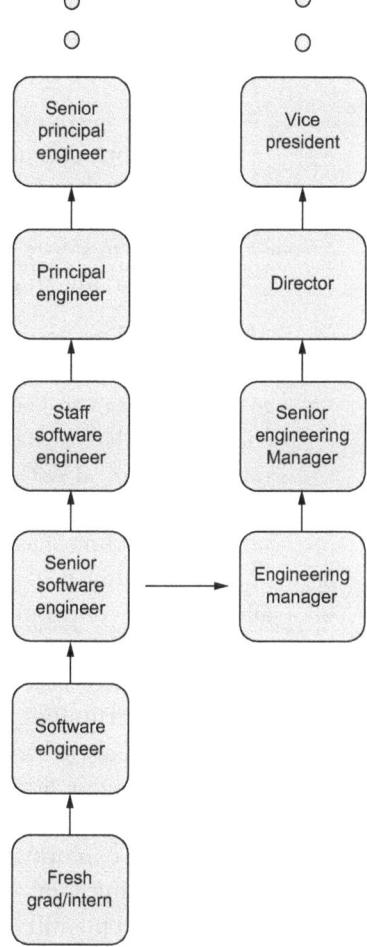

Figure 2.1 This sample career ladder demonstrates the lateral shift between IC and EM roles. As you can see, the transition is not necessarily a promotion; it may be a lateral career-track change.

want to avoid taking on tasks that could create bottlenecks or become single points of failure for the team. Generally, an EM can handle non-mission-critical tasks, such as onboarding a team's service to a tool like SonarQube (https://www.sonarsource.com/products/sonarqube), as needed. But direct involvement in critical project coding might impede progress as you juggle increased managerial responsibilities.

For an EM, finding a balance between people management and technical involvement is crucial. Although participating in code review meetings and technical discussions is beneficial, being too hands-on with technical tasks may hinder your effectiveness in managerial responsibilities. It's essential to prioritize your current role, focusing on people, projects, and processes. Balancing these aspects ensures that you manage effectively without falling behind on technical advancements.

> **TIP** To keep your technical skills current as an EM, engage in coding on the side. Explore opportunities to code for not-for-profit organizations through platforms such as Upwork, Develop for Good, and Taproot Foundation. Additionally, contributing to SourceForge or FOSS projects in your spare time allows you to satisfy your coding interests without hindering your success as a manager or affecting your team's performance.

Although coding as a first-line manager is possible, I strongly advise prioritizing the skills that are crucial for success in your EM role. Attempting to juggle IC and EM responsibilities can lead to burnout. At the same time, don't distance yourself from coding completely. Stay connected to the codebase by actively participating in code reviews, technical system design discussions, and agile ceremonies such as retrospectives. This involvement keeps you aligned with the product and underscores your value in its technical aspects.

Participating in company-wide hackathons or innovation weeks with your team allows you to contribute without becoming a bottleneck and demonstrates your commitment to innovation. Writing scripts for the automation of leadership reports is another valuable task that provides flexibility and avoids creating bottlenecks while offering opportunities to other engineers.

As you become more comfortable in your role, allocate some time for personal coding enjoyment. Striking the right balance allows you to develop necessary EM skills while maintaining a connection to coding when appropriate. Focus less on coding and more on exploring architecture trends in your spare time. Prioritize learning and problem-solving over mere implementation of skills. Understanding emerging architectural concepts will enhance your problem-solving abilities and contribute significantly to your professional development. The distribution of skills between coding and leadership varies based on roles, with ICs focusing primarily on coding and technical expertise and EMs, especially at higher levels, focusing on developing leadership skills (figure 2.2).

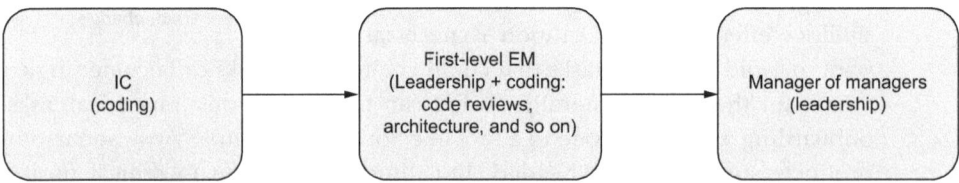

Figure 2.2 Breakdown of coding and leadership skills based on roles. For an IC, the focus is on coding. If you take the EM track and become a manager of managers, you will focus the majority of your time on leadership skills.

For middle managers in the next management tier, coding and code reviews generally are not expected. Their expertise is best used to formulate technical strategies for the company and organization. Because they possess a technical foundation from previous roles, they can still participate in technical discussions when needed. Some senior managers and vice presidents engage in coding for personal growth, staying updated with coding skills and even building fun projects.

The decision to code in this new role is not straightforward; it depends on how you define coding and the intention behind it. Staying connected to the code and contributing to the team without overshadowing development opportunities for engineers is crucial. Coding may not be the primary task; leading the team's technical direction is essential. That role involves more than writing code; it may require developing new skills. Staying involved without undermining the team's trust is vital for an EM.

2.2.3 Coding rounds are not always necessary when changing jobs as an EM

Coding may not be part of the EM role, but some tech companies include coding rounds in their EM job interviews because EMs are expected to excel in system design and fundamentally understand technical tasks, given their previous roles as ICs. The assessment is not about writing code; it's about evaluating a candidate's ability to comprehend and break down coding problems when approached by team members. The goal for EMs is to guide team members toward the appropriate resources or connect them with colleagues who can assist, fostering trust and credibility.

Many companies opt for code-review rounds instead of coding rounds during the interview process, aligning more with what an EM might handle in their daily responsibilities. As you prepare for job interviews, understand the expectations and self-select out of vacancies that don't align with your qualifications.

Discuss key points with interviewers, such as expectations for flawless code writing or reviewing, freedom to use any language you're familiar with, and tolerance for minor mistakes in syntax. Emphasize that your thought process matters more than perfect execution. The examination should focus on understanding concepts, articulating architecture and design, and demonstrating problem-solving skills. You should be able to discuss your thought process in plain English rather than in a programming language. Various resources provide information on preparing for coding rounds, but the key is thinking out loud and sharing your thought process during interviews. Section 2.2.4 addresses a common misconception about selecting the best engineer on the team as the next EM in line.

2.2.4 Not every sound software engineer is a good manager

It's a misconception to assume that the best software engineer in a team will automatically make a great EM. The technical skills of a great IC don't necessarily translate into the skills required for effective people management. It is true that some skills are prerequisites for the role and that others can be developed. But pushing yourself or others into the EM role without considering these aspects may result in turning excellent

IC talent into mediocre EM talent who may act as micromanagers who dive into code, negatively affecting team dynamics.

Did you know?

Google's Project Oxygen, designed to improve business leadership and enhance continuous improvement within the management team, underscores the importance of EMs. The project's research identified eight key characteristics that are crucial for managerial success: putting people first, emphasizing coaching, avoiding micromanagement, being performance-driven, focusing on results, building strategy, fostering career development, and possessing the technical skills to advise the team.

Although some of these characteristics can be developed, others should resonate on a personal level from the beginning. Putting people first, for example, suggests that only some engineers are inherently suited to the EM role. Learn more at https://mng.bz/MZ9E.

NOTE Every sound software engineer differs from a good EM. Both roles overlap from a technical and mentoring standpoint but diverge in terms of the people aspect. As a result, it's essential to look for the right blend of skills to identify the next EM.

Successful IC ≠ Successful EM

For transitioning to an EM role, assessing each engineer's ideal working style is crucial. A friend experienced this situation firsthand. Initially, he set a "no micromanaging" norm on himself, expecting everyone to thrive, but later realized that his top team member struggled without micromanagement. To adapt, my friend conducted one-on-one meetings with each team member, recognizing that not every engineer thrived under the same management style. Some people needed clear task assignments; others preferred autonomy. This experience taught him the importance of tailoring management approaches to individuals.

He found a compromise by assigning tasks to that team member directly while simultaneously coaching them through one-on-one sessions to select tasks from the team backlog that aligned with their interests. That engineer rapidly returned to peak performance. This taught my friend that managing a team requires flexibility, adaptability, and understanding of individual needs, emphasizing open communication and regular one-on-one meetings.

EVALUATING WHETHER AN ENGINEER HAS THE POTENTIAL TO BE AN EM

Evaluating engineers before assigning them to an EM role is vital. When you consider whether the team's technical lead or senior engineer would make a good EM, the first step is understanding what is expected of that engineer in the other role and to make sure that are ready for the new role and its challenges. Following is a four-step framework for assessing engineers that I have used successfully (figure 2.3):

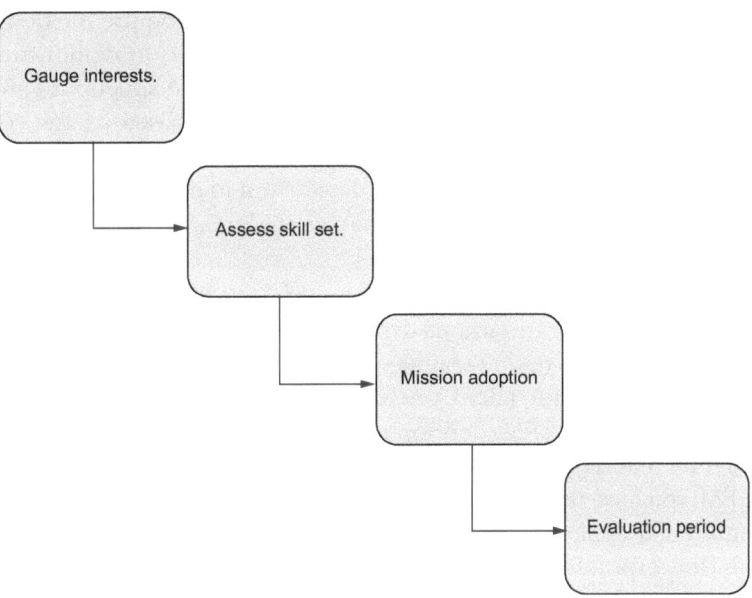

Figure 2.3   Four-step framework for evaluating whether an engineer will make a good EM. At the end of the last stage, you can evaluate based on experience and feedback gathered during the various steps.

1   *Gauge interests.* The first step is determining whether the IC is genuinely interested and passionate about becoming an EM or merely going through the motions, perhaps due to tenure. Understanding a person's underlying intentions and motivations for transitioning to management is crucial. One effective approach is to have the engineer shadow an existing EM to gain firsthand experience and insights into what the job entails.

2   *Assess skill set.* The next step is assessing the IC's skill set for successful EM performance. A few of those skills (not all are always apparent) include
   – Leadership skills
   – Ability to motivate others and identify their strengths and weaknesses
   – Ability to lead by example
   – Authentic qualities of integrity, honesty, and kindness
   – Empathy and emotional intelligence
   – Ability to delegate and avoid the doer mindset
   – Conflict resolution with an unbiased mindset
   – Effective communication
   – Team hiring and culture building
   – A belief in "*we*" over "*I*" and the ability to recognize the work of others
   – Understanding why and learning from errors
   – Patience and openness to feedback

EMs can assess employees' skills by assigning tasks that require the desired competencies. Not all engineers may have had the chance to demonstrate these skills in their current position, so asking about relevant situations can provide insights into their abilities. A gap-analysis document, based on the company's career leveling guide or relevant skills, is a useful tool during this phase; it should be collaborative, objective, and data-driven to minimize subjectivity. This document identifies skill gaps and enables the creation of a plan to address them, as discussed in chapter 3.

3   *Adopt a mission.* To transition to management, individuals must grasp the company's mission and organizational dynamics so that they can craft a precise team charter. They need to define team-level objectives and key results (OKRs) while fostering innovation for talent retention. Understanding the overall business and contributing to strategy development are vital. Developing business acumen becomes increasingly crucial as an engineer moves up the management ladder. As an EM, you have the opportunity to coach team members on business acumen through one-on-one sessions, or you might direct them toward online courses such as the corporate training available on platforms like Udemy.

4   *Have an evaluation period.* The last step gives the candidate the opportunity to experience the role before committing. In section 2.4, we will learn more about the actual transition period. By assessing the outcomes, managers can make thoughtful decisions, ensuring win-win situations for employees and the company.

David, a senior engineer and a team tech lead with more than five years at the company, expressed interest in transitioning to an EM role. In our one-on-one discussions, I discovered his inclination toward EM responsibilities, particularly in mentoring and coaching engineers. To assess his suitability, I evaluated his skills and identified areas for improvement. Although David demonstrated leadership in cross-team projects and operational excellence initiatives, his communication with nontechnical stakeholders sometimes involved technical jargon. I addressed this concern, pairing him with a marketing-manager mentor and recommending relevant LinkedIn courses to enhance his communication skills.

To give David trial experience in the EM role, we created a 90-day plan in which he retained his current role while taking on expanded EM responsibilities. Managing critical projects and working closely with cross-functional partners, he demonstrated leadership. He also conducted effective one-on-one sessions with his peers, which were not easy for him in the beginning. David adeptly navigated the challenge by approaching these sessions with an open mind. He provided opportunities for other engineers to voice their opinions and ensured that they felt heard. He offered valuable coaching and recommended learning resources to his team members, fostering trust and exceeding expectations during his transition to the EM role.

This section addressed prevalent misconceptions in the tech industry and provided insights on how to navigate them. Section 2.3 delves into the key aspects of a successful transition from IC to EM, highlighting the significance of intentions, motivations, and a learning mindset.

2.3   *Intentions and motivations*

Deciding to become an EM involves a deep understanding of motivations—your own and those of others. To determine your readiness for the role, challenge yourself by asking why you want to be an EM at this point in your career.

If your motivation centers on enjoying people dynamics, mentoring, fostering team growth, providing vision, and leading others, you are likely on the path to success. But if your reasons involve seeking control or higher pay, escaping from coding, following a natural growth path, or pursuing titles, you may want to reconsider. Money, titles, and power are valid considerations, but they won't make you an effective manager or leader. If you foresee making a long-term commitment to the EM role, particularly if you're considering an early transition, align it carefully with your career aspirations. Key questions to assess your motivations and intentions include the following:

- Why do I want to be an EM?
- Do I enjoy coaching and mentoring others?
- Am I comfortable handling strategic ambiguous situations and removing roadblocks?
- Can I trust others to do their work and verify their ability at the same time?
- Will I remain honest, authentic, and kind when things go wrong?
- Do I enjoy driving alignment between people in discussions?
- Do I believe in building a positive work culture?
- Am I a strong advocate for equality of opportunity?
- Do I like being available to help others when needed?
- Will I miss coding daily?
- Would I still want to manage people even if I didn't have the manager title?

Reflecting on the answers to these questions ensures clarity. If you answered positively and are open to exploring the rest, you likely possess the positive intentions required for the EM role. "Maybe" responses may indicate a need for further input; consider discussing management interests with your manager. Alternatively, explore other career paths, such as product management or other technical roles, based on what aligns best with your aspirations. Understanding your motivations sets the stage for section 2.4, which explores a three-phase approach for initiating and executing the transition.

2.4   *A three-phase approach for ICs to EMs*

Now that we've delved into the responsibilities and considerations of an EM role, are you ready to give it a try? Making an informed decision about whether this role aligns with your goals is crucial. Instead of requiring an immediate commitment, many tech companies offer you the chance to try out the role. This approach allows both you and the company to assess your compatibility before making a full commitment.

Think of the process as being like a basketball game: you practice and prepare to ensure that you're ready for the challenge. Trying out the role sets you up for success and prevents potential regrets. Preparation before the trial, during the transition, and continuous learning after transition are essential. I've structured the IC-to-EM transition into a three-phased approach, as shown in figure 2.4.

Before you are an EM

• Align with you manager.
• Find mentor(s).
• Start small.
• Talk to more people who have
  made the journey or plan to.

Transition period

• Use company leveling guide.
• Learn about your team members.
• Be an active observer.
• Participate actively.
• Fail fast, learn fast.
• Be a learner.
• Hold a retro at end of transition.

Post-transition period

• Measure success.
• Identify your management style.
• Define whether the outcome is
  as intended.
• Consider change of plans in
  the future.
• Grow in the role.

Figure 2.4   A three-phased approach for going from IC to EM

If you believe that you have a natural inclination to prioritize others and prefer managing people over code, let's explore how you can prepare for the IC-to-EM journey in this three-phase approach.

2.4.1   Phase 1: Before becoming an EM

Transitioning to an EM role may seem daunting, so it's crucial to equip yourself with the right supporting tools. In the initial phase, you prepare proactively, maintaining a growth mindset. Make the most of this opportunity to delve into management and leadership. Invest your time wisely by delving into management literature, participating in conferences, and networking to gain insight into your fit for the EM role. Consider the following ideas to ready yourself for the challenges of being a new EM before you officially step into the role.

ALIGN WITH YOUR MANAGER

Ensuring a healthy and productive working relationship begins with aligning with your manager:

- *State your intentions and set expectations.* State your intentions and set expectations through open, honest communication. Collaborate on a 30-60-90 (days) plan with achievable milestones during your probationary period as an EM. Use this time to assess the role's fit, identify areas for improvement, and address skill gaps. Effective communication and skill in presenting to various stakeholders are crucial for success in the EM role. Working with your manager on these aspects is key to accountability and success.

- *Establish the right timing.* Timing is crucial in transitioning to an EM role. Establish a strong technical foundation, starting as a software engineer and progressing to senior engineer. Share your aspirations with your manager early, allowing alignment and growth toward the EM role. Regularly discuss goals in one-on-one meetings and engage in projects that offer leadership opportunities. This transition requires patience, trust in the process, and a balance between strengthening technical skills and learning leadership aspects. Establish a timeline—typically, around 90 days—for evaluating your adaptation and performance in the new role. Discuss potential outcomes if criteria aren't met, ensuring that you won't be penalized and can continue as an IC if necessary.

FIND MENTORS

Securing mentors during your transition from IC to EM is crucial for success. Seek mentors inside and outside your company who have experience in this transition. Use mentorship platforms such as Plato (https://www.platohq.com), GrowthMentor (https://www.growthmentor.com), and Fast Track (https://fasttrack.firstround.com), or attend local meetups and networking sessions to connect with professionals. Use LinkedIn to reach out for mentorship, aiming to find someone who is invested in your career growth.

Gaining various perspectives is essential at this career stage. Multiple mentors with diverse views on EM roles help you understand different management styles and find those that resonate with you. Acknowledge potential contradictory advice, parse the information, and relate it to your situation. Avoid relying solely on your current manager as a mentor; seek broader understanding. If you struggle to find a mentor, seek help from your manager; also see chapter 15 for some tips on finding a mentor.

Work with your manager to explore different scenarios and real-world examples to stretch your thinking and prepare for the challenges of an EM role. Imagine managing an underperforming employee who stops responding to messages or emails, for example. This exercise helps you practice situational leadership so you can handle unexpected and ambiguous situations. By seeking guidance from mentors and working through scenarios, you'll establish a robust support network and develop the skills needed for successful transition to an EM role.

START SMALL

When you're transitioning from IC to EM, initiating manageable tasks and setting realistic, time-bound milestones are essential. I began by mentoring summer interns and serving as an onboarding buddy for new hires. These tasks not only gave me experience in the people aspect of the manager role, but also showed me that I truly enjoyed helping others grow.

Next, collaborating with my manager, I selected projects involving multiple teams and stakeholders so that I could gain exposure to cross-functional collaboration and stakeholder management. With support and guidance, I identified common pain points and implemented process improvements for operational excellence. Gradually,

I increased my involvement in hiring interviews, exploring my interest in recruitment. Additionally, I shadowed my manager, learning from their observations.

A significant step followed: taking on the role of acting manager during a manager's paternity leave. This experience involved one-on-ones, project execution, and various EM responsibilities. My performance during this period instilled confidence in my leadership team, leading to my official transition to the EM role. Starting small, learning along the way, and gaining experience through practical steps were my keys to success, and I recommend them to you, too.

CONNECT WITH PEOPLE WHO ARE ALREADY IN (OR THINKING ABOUT) THE ROLE

During your exploration period in the EM role, engage with as many relevant individuals as possible—those who are currently in the role, contemplating the move, and even those who transitioned back to IC—to gain a comprehensive perspective. Include potential future peers. Ask questions such as these:

- What are the key responsibilities and challenges of being an EM?
- How can I balance technical expertise with managerial responsibilities effectively?
- What skills and qualities contribute to success as an EM?
- What are your strategies for building and maintaining a strong engineering team?
- How do you ensure effective communication and collaboration with stakeholders?
- What common pitfalls or challenges do EMs face, and how do EMs navigate them?
- Do you have any guidance on setting goals and expectations for team members?
- How do you create a positive, productive work culture within the team?
- How do you support the professional growth of team members?

Tailor these questions to your specific circumstances. The aim is to gather valuable insights from mentors' experiences and expertise to facilitate your transition. Understand that management challenges often involve dealing with unexpected situations. Peers can provide insights into these aspects. If you're reaching out to potential mentors, be clear about your intentions, be transparent about the time commitment, and offer something in return. You might offer to help with projects or tasks within the mentor's area of expertise to demonstrate your appreciation, introduce your mentor to relevant contacts or networking opportunities, or publicly acknowledge your mentor's contributions and expertise through testimonials, social media shout-outs, and professional recommendations. If you get a positive response, great; if not, treat the encounter as a learning experience and move on to the next person. Use the shared ideas to conduct informational interviews, mentally preparing yourself for the transition and gaining wisdom from those who experienced it.

2.4.2 *Phase 2: Transition period*

Having prepared for the transition and gathered information, you clearly understand what to expect. Now you need a well-defined timeline for the transition period, typically ranging from 90 days to 6 months. In this phase, it is important to align your expectations of success in the new role with your manager's and company leaders' expectations.

Sometimes, due to factors such as company size or availability of open vacancies, an IC may have to wait before officially transitioning to an EM role. During this waiting period, it is beneficial to engage in more research and preparation to enhance your readiness for the role when the opportunity arises. The following sections discuss some tools that can assist you during the transition period.

USE THE COMPANY LEVELING GUIDE

In a large company, use the company's leveling guide, which defines roles and responsibilities at different levels. In a startup or a smaller company that does not have such a guide, you can create a similar framework to define roles objectively. Throughout your transition, use this framework to maintain a document that outlines your work and shows how it aligns with expected responsibilities. Creating this document allows you to do two things:

- Clearly understand the expectations and criteria by which you will be measured after the probationary period (typically, 90 days).
- Track your work and its alignment with role expectations. Managing summer interns, for example, may fall under the people-management category.

If the company lacks a clear leveling guide or if the guide is inconsistent, communicate with your manager to ensure your clear understanding of expectations. Document your work, and create a living document validated with your manager. This practice helps you document and align your efforts with expected responsibilities during the transition.

LEARN ABOUT YOUR TEAM MEMBERS

For an EM, establishing rapport with team members is vital and is often achieved through one-on-one meetings. Use this time to get to know team members' motivations and career aspirations. Some team members may be hesitant to share their goals initially, so foster open communication by promoting psychological safety, asking relevant questions, and creating a comfortable environment. In the early stages of your role, do the following:

- Focus on listening more than providing advice.
- Build relationships with cross-functional partners.
- Recognize the transitional nature of this phase for you and your team members, aiming to establish a partnership.
- Focus on learning from errors, fostering empathy, and building trust.

Former ICs who are transitioning to an EM role may find this phase to be challenging. Cultivate an atmosphere of openness and collaboration by being transparent about your own fallibility and demonstrate your commitment to earning the trust of your team members.

BE AN ACTIVE OBSERVER

In the early stages of the EM transition, avoid making assumptions and resist the urge to make immediate changes. Be a patient, active observer without appearing to be disruptive or opposed to different perspectives. Communicate to the team that your intention is not to overhaul everything, but to value input and seek ways for improvement through learning, not just fixing. Here are some guidelines to follow:

- Document your observations and learnings.
- When the time is right, instead of addressing problems directly, pose questions during team meetings to gather feedback on areas that may need improvement.
- Involve team members in the process, making them part of decision-making, and tap into their talent. This approach not only averts a top-down approach, but also secures buy-in from the new team.

PARTICIPATE

In the dynamic landscape of EM roles, maintaining active participation in team sprint meetings, design discussions, and technical forums is essential. As you navigate this new role, it's important to dispel any perception that you chose the EM position to avoid technology. Strike a balance between being hands-on but avoiding micromanagement and hands-off without neglecting team members). Your ability to maintain this balance will evolve as you iterate and refine your management style. Following are some key considerations:

- Continue participating in technical discussions to stay connected with the team's work.
- Find the delicate balance between involvement and autonomy, giving team engineers the space to learn and grow.
- Clearly communicate your expectations regarding your level of participation in the team's technical initiatives.

FAIL FAST AND RECOVER FAST

Embrace the reality that the EM role is new for you and that it's okay to encounter failures along the way. Throughout this journey, actively seek 360-degree constructive feedback from your engineers, manager, and cross-functional partners. Establishing a regular cadence of feedback prevents surprises and enables quicker iterations when things are not working out. This approach provides the time needed to adapt your actions and discover what works best for both you and your team.

BE A LEARNER

Dedicate this period to continuous learning and absorb as much knowledge as possible. Schedule focused learning times on your calendar, taking online courses (on LinkedIn Learning, Pluralsight, YouTube, and so on), reading books such as the ones recommended in the preface to this book and the *Harvard Business Review* series (https://mng.bz/aEmx) or materials provided by your support network (engineering blogs, in-room classroom training, and so on). Consider these key strategies:

- Hone your communication skills.
- Learn effective delegation techniques.
- Use your time wisely to build relationships with partners and stakeholders.
- If you identify gaps or areas for improvement, seek support and training from your manager or mentor. Many companies offer onboarding programs for new EMs.

Don't hesitate to ask for the resources you need, even if they are not part of the onboarding program. Many companies actively support the professional development of new leaders.

MANAGE TEAM RELATIONSHIPS

Navigating team relationships in a management role involves addressing common scenarios within the same company. Effective communication is the key to success, whether you are transitioning to head your own team or a different team or creating a new team from scratch. Let's look at strategies for each of these three scenarios:

- *You are transitioning into an EM role for a different team*—If you're tasked with managing an established team different from your current one, adopt the following approach:
  - *Acknowledge existing dynamics.* Recognize the team's established style, processes, and dynamics. Observe and understand their current setup through one-on-one conversations, team meetings, and feedback surveys.
  - *Introduce changes gradually.* Implement changes in small, gradual steps to avoid disruption. Involve the team in the process, asking relevant questions and making members feel included.
  - *Avoid negative language.* Refrain from pointing fingers or speaking negatively about previous leaders. Focus on positive changes and improvements.
  - *Conduct thorough homework.* Review team documentation and wikis, and speak with the tech lead to understand pain points and desired improvements. Understand both the people and the technical aspects of the team's charter.
  - *Recognize the learning curve.* Acknowledge that there may be a learning curve in understanding both the team and technical aspects.
  - *Engage in team-building activities.* These activities build trust with the team and foster rapport.
  - *Set clear expectations.* Communicate clear expectations, especially if your management style differs from the previous leader's. Solicit feedback from team members on their expectations of you as their new manager.

  If you're transitioning to a new company, the challenge is greater while you familiarize yourself with the business model and culture. Use your manager and support network to plan your first 90 days with clear expectations.

- *You are building a team from scratch*—As a new EM tasked with building a team from scratch, consider the following approach:

- *Set clear scope and mission.* Define a clear scope and mission for the hiring process to give engineers a road map and a sense of how their work adds value to the company. Ensure that engineers see a clear path for their work to prevent frustration and maintain motivation.
- *Use network and recruiters.* Use your network and collaborate with a recruiter to find the best engineers for the team.
- *Seek support and learn from others.* Seek guidance and support from your manager, mentors, and allies. Learn from their experiences to avoid common pitfalls and accelerate your team-building process.
- *Avoid mass hiring.* Resist the temptation to hire a large number of people at the same time. Take gradual steps, regularly assessing the team's needs to maintain efficiency and work lean.
- *Balance excitement and caution.* Acknowledge the excitement, fun, challenges, and risks involved in building teams. Consider building teams later in your management journey, after you gain experience in other EM roles.

Starting with other roles and honing your skills before building a team from scratch can contribute to your growth as an EM.

- *You are transitioning from IC to EM on your current team*—Transitioning into an engineering management role within your current team presents its own challenges and opportunities. Here's a strategic approach:
  - *Build trust gradually.* Patiently build trust before officially assuming the role. Communicate your willingness to learn alongside the team.
  - *Address biases and fair treatment.* Be mindful of biases from your previous IC role. Treat all team members fairly, avoiding favoritism.
  - *Establish unbiased mindset strategies.* Foster self-awareness to recognize and challenge biases. Ensure equal treatment and opportunities based on merit. Practice active listening and open communication.
  - *Continue learning.* Stay informed about unconscious biases. Attend diversity and inclusion workshops. Educate yourself to improve understanding and behavior.
  - *Handle challenges proactively.* Be prepared for potential challenges and skepticism. Address concerns openly and honestly. Set up a candid communication channel for early feedback.
  - *Be open to learning.* Recognize this period as a valuable opportunity to learn leadership skills. Establish open communication with your team for candid feedback. Share your experiences with a mentor to gain insights and balance opinions.

Approach this transition with optimism, view challenges as learning opportunities, and actively seek feedback to refine your leadership skills.

REVIEW YOUR JOURNEY AT THE END OF THE TRANSITION PERIOD

As you approach the end of your transition period, conduct a retrospective to assess your journey. Ask yourself these questions:

- What areas frustrated me as part of this EM transition journey?
- What areas were satisfying for me?
- Do I still feel more connected to code than to people?
- Did I enjoy seeing success through other people's eyes?
- What will my peers and reports say about me?
- Did I do justice to the team members during my transition phase?
- How was the team's morale before and after I took over?
- Did I recognize the talent around me?
- If I were to go back in time, what would I change about my transition period?
- Where are my gaps, and what do I need to address those gaps (perhaps training)?
- Was I honest and authentic with team members when they provided feedback?
- Did I keep my integrity and honesty despite my biases?
- Did I give my best at all times?

Use these reflections to gain clarity, self-awareness, and a deeper understanding of your aspirations. Seek support from peers and mentors, celebrate achievements, and remain open to continuous improvement.

2.4.3 Phase 3: Post-transition period

Phase 3 is the crucial phase in your transition to an EM. Schedule a meeting with your manager to self-evaluate and reflect on your role. Share your experiences during the transition, and gather 360-degree feedback. The objective is to get a clear answer to the question of whether the official transition will proceed. If your manager confirms your transition, establish a timeline and plan for the upcoming period. (The duration will depend on the manager and company policy.) If the answer is no, identify any gaps that you can fill in your quest to become EM. Alternatively, if you prefer to remain an IC, make sure that this option is still open to you.

MEASURING SUCCESS

To gauge success during this phase, assess your experiences in both the pretransition and transition stages by answering a mix of subjective and objective questions, such as the following:

- Did I consistently feel comfortable?
- Were there challenging moments?
- Did I experience instances of satisfaction?
- Can I articulate the mission and vision of my teams?
- Do I feel fulfilled in contributing as a multiplier to the team?
- What percentage of projects did I successfully deliver on time?

- What did peer feedback from engineers and cross-functional partners indicate?
- Did I meet or surpass the team's development velocity goals?
- What was the engineer attrition rate during my tenure as EM?

The aim is to determine whether you will merely survive or thrive if you pursue this role for the next few years. Take a moment to pause and celebrate your journey, acknowledging the challenges of making a career change (temporary or permanent).

IDENTIFYING YOUR MANAGEMENT STYLE

Discovering your management style is a valuable process. Familiarize yourself with various styles, including autocratic, democratic, delegative, transactional, transformational, servant leadership, and hybrid. *Aim for a personalized hybrid style rather than adhering strictly to one.*

During the transition, observe and shadow your manager and mentors to gain practical insights into their style. Reflect on the styles that resonate with your experiences. It's natural for your style to evolve. As you enter the post-transition phase, have a rough idea of your preferred style, but remember that learning and growth are ongoing in this role. Stay open to new ideas, and continue to strive for improvement.

EXPLORING THE OPTIONS IF YOUR TRANSITION DOES NOT GO AS PLANNED

If the transition to EM doesn't go as planned during the transition phase, don't perceive the experience as being a failure: view it as a valuable learning experience that enhances self-awareness and clarifies your preferences. Embrace the opportunity to stay in your current role as an outstanding engineer, reinforcing your capabilities and using the time for learning and growth. Reach out to mentors for support and motivation, maintaining a positive outlook.

Staying an IC is not a demotion; it's a chance to shine and determine your next steps. Explore other career paths that are in the technical domain, such as product manager, technical program manager, or architect. Or continue excelling as an IC, refining your coding skills. Take the time to find the right fit for your career, recognizing that you have control of your journey.

LIKING YOUR CURRENT ROLE BUT KNOWING THAT YOUR PLANS MIGHT CHANGE

Embracing change is crucial, and transitioning between EM and IC roles is a possible option. If you discover that being hands-off from coding bothers you, remember to refine your coding fundamentals regardless of your role. You should view moving into the EM role as a two-way door, though returning to an IC role after an extended period in management might pose challenges. Consider the perceptions tied to job titles and résumés, and be prepared to explain your motivations for the change.

I've seen engineers thrive in EM roles and others choose to return to being an engineer or architect. Having a clear explanation for your decision is important. Whether you prefer providing technical support while leading or exploring different roles, the experience gained from both positions is valuable, enhancing your overall perspective and skill set.

CONTINUING TO GROW IN THE ROLE

Continuing your growth as an EM is essential even after an official appointment. Use company learning platforms, LinkedIn courses, *Harvard Business Review* blogs, and mentorship circles. Engage with local engineering leadership groups or create one if an existing group is unavailable. Maintain a growth mindset and actively seek challenging learning opportunities.

In my first six months as an EM, managing an underperforming team member posed a challenge. Seeking guidance from mentors and my manager, I learned essential processes and approaches to address the problem, which is the benefit of maintaining a learning mindset.

Take advantage of company perks, such as tuition reimbursement and leadership conferences. I've benefited from workshops such as the Confident Club, which focuses on confidence and public speaking. Embrace the "see one, do one, teach one" approach, using your entire mentoring network, and consider mentoring others when you are confident. Expand beyond office work, exploring leadership in diverse contexts such as community service or event organization to develop a well-rounded skill set.

2.5 Challenges of a new engineering manager

Change is often met with resistance, as it brings discomfort and difficulties. As a new EM, your responsibility extends to the success of the team and its members. Embracing this journey, which is filled with bumps, peaks, and valleys, is essential. Transitioning to a management role will be challenging, especially without a formal trial or transitional period.

The initial months will present difficulties, and that situation is normal. The crucial factor is to maintain resilience and a positive mindset. The following sections outline common challenges for a new EM, along with suggested strategies for overcoming them.

2.5.1 Prioritizing coding over people

New EMs may feel drawn to their previous role of coding as an IC. But now their focus extends to team velocity, hiring, and feedback loops, a situation that presents new and overwhelming responsibilities. It's crucial to prioritize understanding and mentoring team members, acknowledging that different individuals have varying growth paces. What can you do? You can do the following things:

- *Prioritize people.* Initially, shift coding to the background. Invest time in one-on-ones to understand team members' aspirations and motivations.
- *Have coffee chats.* Engage in ad hoc coffee chats with team members to build rapport and foster a deeper understanding of individual preferences.
- *Step back from the tech lead role.* Cease being the primary tech lead for the team to allow space for others to step up and grow.
- *Participate in hackathons.* If coding is your passion, participate in hackathons and innovation weeks when your involvement is not a bottleneck.

- *Follow the career leveling guide.* Follow the company's career leveling guide for EMs, aligning your actions with the prescribed framework to guide your energy effectively.
- *Stay updated.* If you fear a technology gap (FOMO), take courses and read technology blogs to stay informed without necessarily coding for work.

2.5.2 Setting clear goals and expectations

As a leader, establishing transparent and clear goals aligned with OKRs is crucial for fostering cohesion and value within the team. Managing ambiguity in competing priorities requires strategic approaches, and using the SMART approach aids in effective career conversations, as outlined in chapter 3. Try the following approaches:

- *Build cross-functional relationships.* Strengthen relations with cross-functional partners and stakeholders to facilitate collaboration and align team goals with broader organizational objectives.
- *Collaborate with leadership.* Work closely with leadership and cross-functional partners to contribute to the formulation and documentation of the team strategy.
- *Shadow in org-level meetings.* Gain insights by shadowing your manager or mentors in organization-level meetings where overarching goals are established.
- *Embrace transparency.* Foster transparency by asking questions and sharing relevant information with your team, providing a shared vision and sense of purpose.
- *Seek support and training.* Be transparent with your manager about challenges, and seek the necessary support or training to enhance your capabilities in the role.

2.5.3 Struggling with delegation

Delegation can be a significant challenge for new EMs who are accustomed to a doer mindset and who desire control. It's essential to recognize the limitations of being omnipresent and avoid micromanagement to build trust within the team. For an EM, scaling efforts and fostering self-organizing teams are key for success. Here are some strategies:

- *Seek guidance.* Engage in discussions about delegation with managers, mentors, and others to glean insights from their experiences.
- *Practice win–win delegation.* Start with delegation by creating win-win situations for both you and the engineer. Trust their capabilities, but verify progress.
- *Have tech discussions.* Instead of engaging in technical tasks directly, learn more about your engineers and participate actively by asking insightful questions. You might inquire about the risks associated with different approaches or how the system handles fault tolerance, for example.

Explore chapter 5 for an in-depth discussion of the importance of delegation and a step-by-step process for overcoming related challenges.

2.5.4 Coping with changing success metrics

Transitioning to an EM role brings a shift in success metrics, emphasizing team achievements over individual accomplishments. The definition of productivity also evolves, and at times, the day may feel less productive because you're spending more time in meetings. Here are some approaches you can try:

- *Build awareness.* Understand and communicate the distinct success metrics in your EM role, recognizing the shift from individual success as an IC.
- *Use support systems.* Rely on the company's leveling guide and your manager for support and guidance in navigating the evolving success metrics.
- *Align with EM metrics.* Measure your success against the metrics defined for EMs and the overall success of your team.
- *Conduct periodic self-assessment.* Regularly assess your performance, identifying areas for improvement. Stay open to adjusting your management style based on what best serves your team and aligns with organizational goals.

2.5.5 Resolving conflict

Conflict resolution is a nuanced aspect of leadership and one of the inherent challenges in managing people instead of coding. Acknowledging and addressing conflicts promptly is critical for preventing potential catastrophic effects. Following are a few strategies:

- *Early identification*—Promptly identify and acknowledge conflicts as they arise.
- *Data-driven approach*—Approach conflicts with an unbiased, data-driven mindset to assess the situation objectively.
- *Active listening*—Be a patient listener to understand the perspectives and motivations of all involved parties.
- *Skill enhancement*—Upskill yourself to handle difficult conversations and navigate conflicts effectively.
- *Collaboration*—Facilitate; don't dictate. Guide the resolution process, but avoid imposing your decision on others. Facilitate a collaborative resolution.
- *Timely action*—Act in a timely manner, avoiding deferral of conflict resolution.

NOTE Conflict management is discussed in detail in chapter 3.

2.5.6 Handling the speed-vs.-quality dilemma

Navigating the tension between speed and quality is a common challenge for EMs, akin to being a ship's captain striving for prompt delivery without compromising quality. This dilemma is compounded by considerations such as tech debt, on-call responsibilities, and aligning engineering goals with business needs. Try these approaches:

- *Adopt data-driven decision-making.* Adopt a data-driven mindset when evaluating tradeoffs between speed and quality, ensuring that decisions are grounded in evidence.

- *Understand business needs.* Gain a comprehensive understanding of business needs, engaging in healthy discussions to scope and set realistic expectations.
- *Promote engineering culture.* Stress the importance of the engineering culture you aim to build, emphasizing values that prioritize quality alongside speed.
- *Align across functions.* Foster alignment by integrating perspectives from product, engineering, and cross-functional teams to ensure that collective goals are met.
- *Lead by example.* Demonstrate the balance between speed and quality through your actions, leading by example to set the standard for the team.
- *Emphasize work–life balance.* Highlight the significance of work-life balance, advocating for the team's well-being and defending against excessive workload demands.

2.5.7 Acknowledging and recognizing others

For an EM, it's crucial to embrace a collaborative mindset, valuing the collective intelligence of the team over individual prowess. Recognizing and appreciating the talent around you contributes to a culture of collaboration and shared success. Here are a few strategies:

- *Reward and recognition*—Actively reward and recognize individuals, including engineers and cross-functional partners, to instill a culture of appreciation and motivation.
- *Positive representation*—Represent the engineering team positively, seeking forums to showcase their achievements. Consider avenues such as demos in organization-wide sessions, shout-outs on communication platforms such as Slack, or using company recognition tools.

2.5.8 Keeping promises made by previous leaders

Addressing promises made by previous leaders poses a common challenge for new EMs, especially when those promises involve promotions or critical projects. It's crucial to navigate these situations with authenticity, honesty, and a realistic understanding of what can be controlled or guaranteed. The following strategies may help:

- *Be authentic and honest.* Instead of imitating the previous leader, be authentic and honest with your team members. Embrace your unique style, bringing your perspectives and ideas to the forefront.
- *Manage expectations.* Avoid making promises that are uncertain or beyond your control, such as guaranteeing no layoffs. Clearly communicate the boundaries of your commitment.
- *Hold three-person handover meetings.* During the handover process, conduct three-person meetings for each team member transitioning below you. Invite yourself, the previous leader, and the team member to the meeting to prevent surprises and facilitate a smooth transition.

2.5.9 *Managing people and performance*

Managing people and performance is a key responsibility for EMs, involving supervising work, holding career conversations, and addressing both high performers and underperformers. The role may encompass recruitment, training, feedback, and handling human resources problems, tasks that require strong people skills. (Chapters 3 and 4 dive deeper into these topics.) Continuous improvement in people management is crucial, and following are some strategies to enhance these skills:

- *Regular check-ins*—Schedule regular check-ins with your team to discuss concerns, expectations, and feedback, building rapport and addressing problems proactively.
- *Empathy and compassion*—Manage with empathy and compassion by understanding and supporting employees' needs. Foster an open work environment through active listening and demonstrate genuine care for team members.
- *Timely and constructive feedback*—Provide timely, \constructive feedback aligned with individuals' goals, promoting clear goal-setting and personal/professional growth opportunities for improved productivity and trust.
- *Filtered information*—In the role of an EM, be mindful of sensitive information, learning to filter as necessary. Maintain confidentiality where required and discern what can and cannot be shared to uphold trust and strong relationships.

2.5.10 *Managing time*

Effectively managing time is an essential skill for EMs, who often find themselves pulled in multiple directions. Context switching, coupled with challenges such as lack of domain knowledge and technical debt, can lead to feelings of unproductivity. Try these strategies:

- *Prioritized to-do list*—Maintain a to-do list, prioritizing tasks to gain control of your calendar. Use systems that help you manage priorities and organize ideas.
- *Blocked focus time*—Block focus time slots on your calendar to dedicate uninterrupted periods for deep work and concentration.
- *No-meetings day*—Consider promoting a no-meetings day, especially for engineers, and adhere to it yourself to allow for focused, uninterrupted work.
- *Time-management tools*—Employ time management tools such as Clockwise to stay organized. Protect your calendar, ensuring that breaks and focus-time blocks are preserved.
- *Self-reflection*—Take time for self-reflection to understand your managerial strengths and weaknesses. Work on enhancing your strengths and addressing areas that need improvement.

NOTE Further tools and techniques for time management are explored in detail in chapter 14.

2.5.11 Documenting

As a coder, you write code and technical design documents. As an EM, you will be transitioning from writing code to writing various documents, from strategy papers to promotion packets. Document writing can be challenging, especially when you're dealing with language differences. Here are some helpful strategies:

- *Audience-centric writing*—Keep the audience in mind while writing. Avoid using technical jargon for nontechnical audiences, and ensure clarity in communication.
- *Clear purpose*—Clearly state the purpose of the document, incorporating a TL;DR (too long; didn't read) summary at the beginning to alert readers to its significance.
- *Deep work*—Embrace the concept of deep work, from the book of the same name by Cal Newport (https://mng.bz/gv7Z), to plan uninterrupted, focused writing sessions.
- *Direct and objective language*—Avoid unnecessary complexity and subjectivity. Keep the document objective and data-driven. I recommended reading *HBR Guide to Better Business Writing* (https://mng.bz/677G).
- *Proofreading*—Read the document at least twice to ensure clarity, grammatical correctness, and relevance to the intended audience.
- *Continuous skill development*—Take online courses to enhance written communication skills. Seek feedback from a small group or proofreader before sharing the document with a larger audience.

2.5.12 Communicating

Effective communication is paramount for EMs, who spend a significant amount of time in meetings. New EMs may struggle with balancing technical details and conveying the essence of discussions. Focusing on both written and verbal communication skills is essential for success and career progression. The following strategies may help:

- *Develop the art of communication.* Hone the art of effective communication, ensuring clarity and relevance in your messages.
- *Know your audience.* Learn to understand and cater to the needs of your audience, tailoring your communication style accordingly.
- *Practice public speaking.* Engage in public speaking opportunities, whether internal meetings or external conferences. Consider joining a Toastmasters group or local meetup to enhance your presentation skills.
- *Write regularly.* Dedicate time each day to writing. Create blog posts or journal entries to articulate your thoughts. This practice serves as a valuable tool for communication and long-term benefits as an EM.

Acknowledge the multifaceted challenges of the EM role and focus on continuous improvement in communication skills to navigate these complexities. In section 2.6, we'll explore strategies to support others in transitioning from ICs to EMs.

2.6   *Assisting the IC-to-EM transition*

Assisting others in transitioning from IC to EM is a crucial aspect of your role as an established EM. Use this framework to support their success:

- *Understand motivations and assess strengths and weaknesses.* Conduct one-on-one conversations and use gap analysis to understand their aspirations, motivations, strengths, and weaknesses. Channel your efforts based on this understanding.

- *Set achievable and time-boxed goals.* Collaborate on creating achievable and time-bound goals for the transition. Assist in building a 30-60-90 (day) plan, sharing personal examples and experiences to guide them effectively.

- *Help them build a network.* Emphasize the importance of teamwork and collaboration. I always ask my ICs who are going through the transition or new EMs hired in the role to do the following:
  - Write the names of all the engineers you will manage on a piece of paper.
  - Set up a one-on-one meeting with each engineer on this list.
  - Ask them about the pain points in the team and what is working well. Next, ask them to give you the names of at least three people you should talk to. If those people aren't currently on your list of people to talk to, add them and then continue.
  - Upon completion of this exercise, you will have engaged with a significant portion of your team, cross-functional partners, and stakeholders. Through this interaction, you'll gain a detailed understanding of the team's strengths and areas for improvement.

- *Open a communication channel with feedback and recognition.* Establish a bidirectional communication channel. Meet regularly to share progress on milestones, recognize achievements, and provide constructive feedback. Foster an environment where open communication is encouraged and valued.

Supporting the IC-to-EM transition involves taking a holistic approach, considering individual motivations, setting goals, building a network, and fostering effective communication.

What do other leaders have to say?

I first moved into an EM role (managing a couple of teams) at a small startup where I was in the first EM role the CTO had created. Before that, he had directly managed all the engineers. It was a learning experience for me, and very much learning while on the job since we didn't have much formal training. I think the empathy and TLM (technical lead/manager) pieces came naturally to me, and the new aspects (end-of-year reviews, compensation, attrition, etc.) easily filled up many of my conversations with my manager, essentially just in time when the need arose. I often felt a bit nervous and somewhat out of my depth during that time, but I also felt like my manager (and cross-functional partners) had my back, which typically eased my concerns.

—Richard Frank, Senior Software Engineer
(former manager) at Two Sigma, formerly with Robinhood

(continued)

I have always been a people person. I believe in the system of Model, Coach, and Care, which I feel is a core part of management. If my senior engineer shows interest in being an EM, I would first understand the motivation behind the same. If they are in for the right reasons, I would support their choices with the right coaching.

—Madhur Kathuria, Engineering Leader at Microsoft,
formerly with Moengage, Oracle, and IIT

Coding is not a primary skill, but it is something that EM should be able to do when required. I do code reviews, troubleshoot problems, and sometimes do code. A solid understanding of system architecture, data structures, and programming language has always helped me communicate with my developers, understand their challenges, and take an appropriate mitigation plan. EM should focus on developing a wide range of technical and interpersonal competencies.

I am an avid reader, so I have a daily routine to read books, blogs, articles, etc, to keep myself updated. My favorites are Medium, Reddit, GeeksforGeeks, List Apart, Google Developers, and Dzone. Other than that, I have registered on platforms like ClassCentral, Coursera, Udemy, and LinkedIn, learning to keep myself updated with the latest tools and technology.

—Devika Ahuja, Technology Leader at Strategist

I had great EM role models during my career, and I looked up to them for all sorts of guidance, not just work-related. This initial fascination with the role led me to research more about it and understand how critical the role is towards the success of an organization. It is common knowledge that engineers leave managers, not companies, and I wanted to be the reason talent stayed with my organization rather than going elsewhere. Moving to a different role always feels like stepping outside one's comfort zone. Deciding to move from an individual contributor to an EM role felt the same way to me. I was uncertain if I could leverage skills acquired as an IC in this new role. My manager helped me overcome these inhibitions by creating a plan for the transition. I was also mentored by experienced EMs who provided invaluable input. Apart from all the people who helped me make the switch, my company's policy regarding trying out career opportunities without facing any backlash minimized the uncertainty involved in this process, which helped propel me to success as a transitioning EM.

—Adish Agarwal, Director, Software Development at Audible, Inc.

If my senior engineer comes to me to be an EM, I will celebrate that they've identified a goal for themselves that we can work towards. I would also discuss why they want to be an EM. My goal would be to help them assess how their interests match the EM role or whether they see it as the only path beyond senior engineering. I would acknowledge that the role needs to be a match between the company and the individual filling that role, so we should: assess what behaviors or skills lie in the gap between that tech lead's current demonstrated abilities and the EM role, identify goals/tasks to close that gap; keep our eyes open for an available EM opportunity (if it's not already present).

—Richard Frank, Senior Software Engineer (former manager),
at Two Sigma, formerly with Robinhood

As a senior leader, there are a few ways I stay up to date with coding and technical skills, such as doing code reviews for my team and asking nonblocking questions when I don't understand something. This gives a side effect of allowing engineers to educate their managers and is great for team building. I tinker at home on personal coding projects. None of these have launched, but scoping them adjacent to my team's technology helps me keep up to date. I can't enumerate the number of times that I have solved a problem in a personal project that has become relevant a month later in my "real job." My entire web experience was built this way, and now I'm coding full-stack features for my team between meetings. What I could improve at is keeping up with the newest news about all the frameworks, languages, etc. While I casually read tech news and frequently have moments of "Oh, that's cool," I've never been a "technology for technology's sake" kind of engineer. The best I do is file those snippets away so that when I have a problem that could use that solution, hopefully, it is remembered.

—Nathan Bourgoin, Chief Technology Officer of Alakazam, Inc., Technical Adviser, and Engineering Leader

EMs coding depends on the team and organization. But I feel they should be close to the code and continue coding at least on their own as garage projects. I keep myself updated by taking online learning and training. I try participating in hackathons, brown bag sessions, and design workshops. I also monitor the support and escalation threads to identify quality problems and health monitoring.

The choice to make the transition was organic. But the transition itself was challenging. Getting out of the habit of jumping into solutions and design versus delegating was the hardest. Delegating is not a natural one for me, so I had to force myself to stop advising while letting the team figure it out.

—Rajakumar Sambasivam, Delivery Manager at Microsoft

To succeed as an EM, you essentially are working for your team. Your people are always your #1 priority, you must ensure you provide them opportunities and resources to be their best in the role. Every team member has a unique definition of success. I lead the Pre Sales Engineering Team in the Networking industry, so I am often asked if the EM would have to be hands-on, and the answer is No. Your role as EM is to help the business needs into technology if you can do that without being hands-on, you are good. I'm not completely denying the need for it, but in my view, it is not a mandatory need. It is more of a good practice that increases the chances of success if used rightly. There are two pitfalls you have to consider:

1. It will take time that you can spend on key activities for your role as a leader.
2. Would the quality of your technical work create comparison and disturb the emotional dynamics of the team?

I would rather spend time bringing in new ideas and awareness of new technologies in the team instead than demonstrating my hands-on technical skills.

—Sumit Kumar, System Engineering Manager at Cisco

Read, read, read! If you're not coding daily, you should stay abreast of emerging trends and technologies, look at best practices, explore new architectures and ideas, and learn from your peers. In addition, the best way to keep your skills up is to teach what you know: speak at conferences, panels, seminars, and meetups. Even within your own department, if nothing else.

—Bruce Bergman, Manager at Lytx

2.7   *Stop and think: Practice questions*

- What brought you to management?
- Why did you make/or want to make a change from IC to EM, and how does it align with your long-term goals?
- Share your experience of doing the IC-to-EM transition.
- What skills do you look for when growing ICs into EM roles?
- What are your criteria for success as an EM?
- Do any constraints in your current role stop you from transitioning? If so, do you plan to combat them?
- What new problems or opportunities are you looking for in your new role as EM?

Summary

- IC and EM are distinct career tracks requiring specific skill sets.
- ICs contribute directly to the team and organization, whereas EMs manage other engineers. EMs may also oversee managers in middle-management roles.
- Misconceptions include viewing the IC-to-EM transition as a promotion rather than a lateral move and questioning whether EMs can code. It's essential to debunk these myths and understand that career changes are not one-way doors.
- Successful EMs need more than technical skills; attributes such as empathy, organizational skill, and a passion for people management are crucial. Prioritize personal and professional growth to succeed in the role.
- Adopt a three-phased approach (pretransition, transition, and post-transition) to understand the role, align expectations, and evaluate the experience against personal and professional goals.
- New EMs encounter various challenges, such as prioritizing code over people, setting clear goals, struggling with delegation, resolving conflict, coping with changes in success metrics, and managing expectations.
- Assist individuals transitioning from IC to EM by understanding their motivations, setting achievable goals, helping build a network, and fostering open communication channels with feedback and recognition.
- Building networks, supporting others through transitions, and fostering communication create a multiplier effect, benefiting both individuals and the organization.
- The journey from IC to EM involves continuous learning, adaptation, and focus on both technical and interpersonal skills to thrive in the dynamic role of EM.

Managing people, teams, and yourself

This chapter covers

- The importance of managing people, teams, and yourself
- Career conversations, support, and conflict resolution
- Focus on goals, morale, and trust
- How to manage yourself to identify opportunities and acknowledge mistakes

It's not about money. It's about the people you have and how you're led.

—Steve Jobs, Co-Founder, Apple, Inc.

To excel in management, you must thoroughly understand what you oversee. Just as a successful army comprehends its strengths and adversaries in order to strategize, effective management involves understanding and leading three distinct entities: individuals, teams, and oneself. This understanding entails grasping motivations, providing support, and fostering growth, which in turn enhance trust, engagement, and productivity. By matching individual strengths with responsibilities, managers maximize team potential, which leads to higher employee satisfaction, productivity, and retention rates.

Managing a team involves defining goals, boosting morale, setting expectations, building trust, ensuring accountability, and evaluating success. Good management of a team fosters collaboration, innovation, and positive behavior, enhancing performance and enabling the team to achieve its goals. Strong team dynamics also encourage knowledge sharing and mutual support.

Self-management is also part of effective leadership. Prioritizing self-care, time management, and skill development enables managers to perform at their best, set a positive example, and inspire others. Effective self-management gives you the time and the mindset to make informed decisions, adapt to challenges, and grow both personally and professionally. When you manage all three aspects well, you create a positive work environment, nurture talent, and contribute to long-term success for your team members, your company, and yourself.

3.1 Managing people

Mastering the art of managing people involves being present, understanding motivation, maintaining communication, fostering growth, and resolving conflicts. Holding team members accountable through candid communication is essential for preventing unfairness and fostering a positive culture. Each team member contributes uniquely to building a strong team and achieving success, and it's important to work with the traits and goals of each individual.

3.1.1 Having one-on-one conversations

One-on-one conversations are private meetings between a manager and an employee to discuss various topics, such as information sharing (company goals, processes, training, and so on), social connection (connecting on a personal level and understanding to support them), career growth, and feedback. These conversations provide an opportunity to discuss project highlights and challenges, and they foster open communication and mutual growth. The goal is to empower employees to find solutions by asking the right questions and actively listening to their thoughts and priorities. Starting with a question like "What's top of mind for you?" sets the stage for a candid, supportive dialogue that can build trust between the two of you and allow you to address concerns effectively. Sometimes, you can switch things up with questions like "How was your weekend?" to connect on a personal level.

One-on-one meetings also serve as a platform for discussing career opportunities and giving team members actionable feedback for growth. Although not every meeting focuses on career, having these conversations should be a regular practice. An effective framework for discussing career goals is the SMART framework, which can be adapted to suit individual needs. Rather than presenting it as a rigid guide, introduce it as a flexible starting point and tailor it to each employee's unique path. This personalized approach ensures that goals are meaningful, relevant, and achievable.

Did you know?

The SMART framework is a common structure for setting clear, achievable goals for a project or product launch. It helps keep assumptions to the side and sets clear guidelines for reaching goals. It can also be adapted for identifying career goals. SMART stands for

- *Specific*—The goal needs to be specific regarding what needs to be performed, who will perform it, what steps will be taken, and what support will be provided for achieving it.
- *Measurable*—The goal needs to be quantifiable and measurable. If we would like to reduce the number of trouble tickets or customer escalations, a measurable goal could be to reduce trouble tickets by 20%.
- *Achievable*—You want to ensure that the goal is realistic and achievable in the desired time frame and with the resources provided. For a project to be delivered, it is important to note whether the deadline is in two months or six months and whether you are investing $10,000 or $1 million. Now the goal can be set up to be achieved in the given time frame, which is a true reality check.
- *Relevant*—Why are we doing it? We must understand the intention and why the team and company are spending those resources on the goal or project.
- *Time-bound*—To ensure project success, we need to clarify the time boundaries of the project. When will the team start working on the project, and what is the anticipated end date? This clarification helps us create and track timelines to ensure that the team completes the work by the end date.

The SMART framework can help set both short-term and long-term goals and identify the motivations and context of the goals. Let's apply the SMART framework to track a career-progression goal for software engineer Alex, who is one of the engineers on your team responsible for building machine learning models for the company's streaming recommendation system. You set up a one-on-one conversation with Alex to discuss career goals as follows:

- *Specific*—Increase proficiency in machine-learning models, particularly those that recommend content to users
- *Measurable*—Efficiency should increase by at least 20% in the main model. Also, complete two online courses on advanced machine learning algorithms within the next six months.
- *Achievable*—Attend at least one machine learning conference or workshop within the next year.
   As a manager, you provide relevant training resources, budget, and time off for the employee to attend the conference/workshop and encourage participation in relevant industry events, keeping in mind the company's education policy. Also, you schedule regular check-ins every two weeks to monitor Alex's progress and provide support.
- *Relevant*—Apply the knowledge gained as part of the project to improve other models. The knowledge gained from learning how to increase efficiency in this model is relevant because Alex can apply that knowledge to improve other models.
- *Time-bound*—Help improve the efficiency in the main model in the next six months. Also, develop a portfolio showcasing machine learning projects completed by the end of the year.

These career conversations can ensure that high performers are challenged appropriately and tasked with advanced work that keeps their interest. For low performers, these meetings are a chance to provide support to help them improve. A *gap analysis document*, also known as a *career growth document*, is an effective tool to help team members evaluate their performance and identify areas for improvement. This document typically follows a row-column format, with rows detailing competencies required for the role and columns illustrating situations that demonstrate these competencies, using the Situation-Behavior-Impact (SBI) format.

Did you know?

SBI (https://mng.bz/oeeN) is a format for expressing an overall scenario to provide detailed context. *Situation* refers to the overall outline of the conditions that existed, *behavior* refers to the set of actions taken by team members, and *impact* refers to the outcome of the overall behavior in the situation. The format is clear, contextual, and factual; no one has to guesstimate. Let's look at a sample SBI scenario:

- *Situation*—As part of a new-product launch, multiple promotion capabilities were requested so that the company could offer the best discounts to customers. There was no existing promotion capability or tool.
- *Behavior*—Xavier stepped up and deep-dived into the details of the situation. Then he analyzed the various industry tools that could be used, identifying their pros and cons. Next, he ensured that each engineer understood the full scope of the project and worked on the technical design. Time and again, he collaborated well with the cross-functional partners to ensure the timely delivery of the project.
- *Impact*—Xavier's contributions led to a 10% increase in company revenue and a timely delivery of the new product. Further, it helped reduce customer escalations by more than 50%.

Documents like the gap analysis help identify gaps between intent and impact. It's important to note that sometimes, the competency list will not align with day-to-day work realities. As an engineering manager (EM), ensure consistency across the list for all employees at each level and clarify distinctions between role capabilities and expectations. A competency matrix, which lists competencies, how they're demonstrated, and progress made against them, helps analyze individual gaps. Create a template that works for you and that you can easily reuse across team members to identify and address gaps. Table 3.1 shows a sample competency matrix that represents a gap analysis document template.

Engaging in career conversations presents an excellent opportunity to discuss individuals' goals and find potential internal mobility positions, as well as avenues for skill expansion. It's also a suitable time to explore training opportunities and resources to refine abilities further. Facilitating connections between mentors and mentees fosters learning and personal development. Additionally, career conversations provide a platform to ensure the well-being of team members and address any concerns they may

Table 3.1 A competency matrix representing a sample gap analysis document

Competency	How do you demonstrate it?	Status (To do, In progress, Done)
Technical skills. Employee should be adept at coding and system design and have experience with large-scale system designs.	*Situation 1*—Dave was tasked with delivering a project to build a continuous data streaming service due to the missing mechanism. *Behavior*—Dave stepped up to understand the problem statement and did a deep dive into the architecture design. He worked with senior engineers on the team and developed a technical design document detailing the pros and cons of each approach. Next, he implemented the project under a tight deadline. *Impact*—His efforts led to a timely launch of the streaming service and helped reduce message latency by more than 80%. *Situation 2*—<> *Behavior*—<> *Impact*—<>	Done
Participation in technical events.	*Situation 1*—<> *Behavior*—<> *Impact*—<>	In progress
Sharing learnings and expertise with cross-functional partners and having influence across teams.	*Situation 1*—<> *Behavior*—<> *Impact*—<>	In progress
Helping to improve operational excellence metrics for the team.	*Situation 1*—<> *Behavior*—<> *Impact*—<>	To do

have, including general life updates and personal matters. As an EM, be prepared for one-on-ones, but prioritize allowing employees to speak more. These sessions are crucial for employees; it's their time to shine and be heard. Checking project status is best done through project status meetings, stand-ups, or progress meetings, not one-on-ones.

Did you know?

Skills Framework for the Information Age (SFIA; https://skillstx.com/about-sfia) serves as a universal language that helps you identify the skills necessary to advance to the next stage of your career. Companies use the SFIA framework for resource management and recruitment. SFIA is beneficial for

- Standardizing job roles
- Providing clear skill descriptions and levels of responsibility
- Establishing a common language for defining expertise
- Serving as a baseline for capabilities

You can use SFIA to structure career conversations by

- Clearly identifying current skills and competencies based on the role.
- Measuring proficiency against each competency and interpreting whether that proficiency is a strength or an opportunity.

(continued)

- When opportunities are identified, focusing on them and how to strengthen them. Here is where you, as EM, will provide resources (training, mentors, self-paced courses, and so on) to help the employee develop needed skills.
- Ensuring that opportunities and skills align with the organization's broader goals.
- Throughout the process, providing regular constructive feedback.
- Being approachable and open to adjustments as you see fit.

The SFIA framework can enhance the quality and effectiveness of one-on-one career conversations by providing a structured approach to skill assessment, goal setting, progress tracking, and career planning.

3.1.2   *Supporting junior versus senior engineers*

As an EM, you will manage a diverse team whose members have varying skills and tenures in software engineering. Because career advancement is a key factor in employee retention, providing a clear growth path for both junior and senior engineers can keep valuable team members at the company longer. Because there is no one-size-fits-all approach for managing these two groups, personalized support is essential.

Junior engineers, being early in their careers, are often energetic and passionate but may require more guidance and coaching to develop their skills. They benefit from prescriptive guidance and support in tackling new challenges. You might provide resources and encouragement for them to pursue certifications and then share their knowledge through technical sessions. Additionally, pairing them with mentors for technical guidance can accelerate their development and set them up for success in their career. Junior engineers can be likened to blank sheets; as an EM, you play a pivotal role in shaping their career trajectory by providing them the necessary guidance and support to succeed.

Senior engineers, having extensive experience in the technology sector, may exhibit rigidity and stronger opinions while desiring more autonomy and complex challenges to stay motivated. For their growth, it's important to provide mentorship opportunities and encourage them to guide mentees.

In one instance, I tasked a senior engineer with addressing a critical organizational challenge related to configuration management for our backend services. This challenge involved implementing a kill-switch feature and developing a centralized visualization tool to enhance control and visibility over configurations. This deficiency posed significant hurdles during testing phases and necessitated painstakingly coordinated rollouts, particularly when deployments went awry or while coordinating launches across multiple marketplaces. In the event of failure, executing a rollback was equally complex and time-consuming. I empowered the senior engineer with resources, including documentation on the problem statement, a history of problems that teams faced with this problem, and access to a principal engineer who had solved a similar problem in their organization. The engineer embraced the challenge with enthusiasm and determination, successfully overcoming the daunting obstacles faced by our team. This experience highlighted the importance of entrusting senior engineers with ownership of complex problems and providing necessary support for them to excel.

There is a stark difference between the type of support and the type of problems that can excite a junior engineer versus a senior engineer. Juniors are at 1,000 feet, mid-level engineers are at 5,000 feet, seniors are at 10,000 feet, and staff are at 20,000 feet. As engineers progress in their careers, their perspective shifts from the micro to the macro, and they become more adept at handling widely dispersed, complex problems. Although individual preferences and circumstances may vary, understanding this progression can help EMs tailor their support for the specific needs of each team member.

3.1.3 Resolving conflicts between team members

Team conflict is a natural occurrence in collaborative environments, and if properly managed, it can foster healthy competition, motivating team members to excel. Diverse perspectives often lead to varying viewpoints and occasional conflicts. As an EM, it's your responsibility to recognize and address these conflicts, guiding team members through the resolution process.

In the midst of launching a revamped version of a promotion capability, a significant conflict arose between two of my engineers, Jack and Jamie, regarding the technical design discussions. Jack advocated for building a new user interface and tool for setting up promotions, emphasizing increased control and backend management. Conversely, Jamie proposed using an existing internal tool from a sister team, citing familiarity and quicker onboarding for sales teams.

Initially, I adopted a hands-off approach, allowing both engineers to articulate their perspectives and letting them figure out the solution on their own. The impasse persisted, however. As their EM, I intervened to address the escalating conflict, recognizing the potential erosion of trust. I ensured that discussions remained data-driven and free of dominance by one member on another, and I facilitated an environment where each voice was heard. I initiated one-on-one sessions with each engineer to provide a safe space for expression and to coach them on considering broader implications. Through probing questions regarding effort, timelines, reusability, and resource allocation, I encouraged holistic thinking.

As a result, the engineer who advocated for a new tool acknowledged the associated challenges and infrastructure costs, leading to a convergence of ideas and a consensus on the solution. This resolution not only resolved the conflict, but also strengthened collaboration and trust within the team. Reflecting on this experience, I recognized the importance of transparency in decision-making and prioritization. To enhance team understanding, I organized lunch-and-learn sessions with the product manager to share insights on planning and prioritization factors, fostering a culture of informed decision-making and collaboration. Here are some things you can do for conflict resolution:

- *Observe from the sidelines.* Start by observing the conflict from the sidelines. Give time to team members to resolve the conflict. If the deadlock continues, move to the next step.
- *Initiate open conversations.* Start with open conversations to comprehend various perspectives and allow sufficient time and space for opinions.
- *Hold individual discussions.* Have individual discussions with conflicting parties to understand their viewpoints thoroughly, getting a clearer picture of the underlying problem.
- *Host group discussions with a data-driven approach.* Bring conflicting parties together for another discussion, incorporating a data-driven approach to decision-making.
- *Involve a neutral third party.* In some cases, involve a neutral third party, such as another senior engineer, to provide feedback and contribute to conflict resolution (figure 3.1).
- *Ensure that all opinions are heard.* Allow space for input, work toward consensus without full agreement, and ensure that all opinions are considered.
- *Break deadlocks.* If conflicts persist, convene a meeting to explain moving forward with consensus, breaking any deadlock.
- *Follow the Disagree and Commit principle.* This famous management principle (also an Amazon leadership principle) plays a critical role during conflict resolution. Its main goal is to keep the team from falling into a consensus trap that ends with deadlock if no consensus is reached. Encourage the Disagree and Commit principle, allowing healthy debate but emphasizing commitment to the agreed-upon decision for project success.

Figure 3.1   Bring a neutral party to help build alignment in times of conflict.

By adopting these strategies, conflicts can be effectively managed, ensuring a collaborative environment for the team members. I also suggest reading some books on conflict resolution, including these:

- *The Anatomy of Peace: Resolving the Heart of Conflict,* by The Arbinger Institute (https://mng.bz/nggv)
- *Crucial Conversations: Tools for Talking When Stakes Are High,* by Joseph Grenny, Kerry Patterson, Ron McMillan, Al Switzler, and Emily Gregory (https://mng.bz/v88x)
- *Never Split the Difference: Negotiating As If Your Life Depended on It,* by Chris Voss and Tahl Raz (https://mng.bz/4JJB)
- *Difficult Conversations: How to Discuss What Matters Most,* by Douglas Stone, Bruce Patton, and Sheila Heen (https://mng.bz/QZZm)

3.1.4 *Challenging team members*

Working with diverse individuals can be challenging at times. Managing difficult team members provides valuable learning experiences that cannot be obtained from educational materials alone. In my journey as an EM, I encountered a significant challenge with a senior engineer on my team. Let's call him Dave. Despite his strong technical skills, Dave's dismissive behavior toward ideas from junior team members was causing friction within the team. During discussions on backend service throttling options, for example, Dave was absent from meetings and had disagreements with James, a junior engineer who had conducted thorough research and presented his findings.

Addressing this interpersonal conflict fell on my shoulders. I initiated a one-on-one conversation with Dave, seeking to understand his absenteeism and discussing the effect of his behavior on team morale. Using specific examples, I explained how his actions could also impede his own career growth. To tackle the adversarial situation, I decided to try to change the dynamic by putting Dave and James in a mentor–mentee relationship instead, in the hopes of fostering an exchange of knowledge and experience. Despite the challenges, my coaching efforts led to positive changes in Dave's behavior, including increased engagement in meetings and active involvement in mentoring even more engineers.

To ensure the effectiveness of the mentorship, I established specific goals and conducted regular check-ins to monitor progress. This proactive approach not only facilitated personal and professional growth for both Dave and James, but also fostered a more cohesive and collaborative team environment.

For a first-time EM, it's normal to struggle with difficult situations. Seeking support from other EMs, managers, or human resources is essential for handling such situations effectively. EMs can also encounter nontechnical challenges within their teams.

Suppose that your engineers attend a training organized by your workplace on diversity, inclusion, and equality (https://mng.bz/X11Y) to learn to be more respectful and inclusive toward the other team members around them. Right after the training, one of your engineers makes an insensitive comment in a group setting. In this scenario, your intervention as EM becomes necessary. You need to raise awareness and coach the individual in a one-on-one setting on the effect of their remark while also organizing inclusion training for the team to prevent future incidents. In serious cases, involving the human resources department may be required to address sensitive matters effectively.

3.1.5 *Leading by example*

Leading by example, also known as walking the talk, involves setting expectations with team members by demonstrating behaviors rather than just talking about them. Leading by example is about showing how things are done to guide others toward the same goalpost. When managers lead by example, they build trust with their team members, who are more likely to follow their lead and emulate their actions.

Suppose that an EM named Jayden preaches the importance of punctuality to his team, but he himself is habitually late to team meetings and often arrives flustered and unprepared. In the organization-wide all-hands meeting, Jayden is invited to serve as a panelist to encourage team members. He tells the audience that his success recipe is valuing time management and punctuality. He emphasizes the need for everyone to be on time and respect everyone else's time. During the talk, however, he realizes that he's running late for another meeting and abruptly ends his talk, rushing out the door without even acknowledging his own lateness.

In this scenario, Jayden is failing to walk the talk. He's talking about the importance of punctuality, but his actions don't align with his words, undermining his credibility and the message he's trying to convey to his team. (We learned in detail about this trait, which is important for a good EM, in chapter 1.)

In this section, we learned about managing people, which is a core competency for an EM. In section 3.2, let's look at handling the members who make up a team.

3.2   Managing teams

As an EM leading team, you must recognize each member's unique qualities that contribute to collective success. You serve as the captain of the ship, guiding the team toward goals, which are particularly crucial in managing distributed teams due to remote work. Effective team management boosts individual performance, nurtures pride and loyalty, and fosters long-term retention. *Management is not just about organizational outcomes, but also about fostering purpose, mastery, and joy for team members, leading to meaningful outcomes in their professional and personal lives.*

Did you know?

A Gemba Walk (https://mng.bz/y88J) is a structured workplace observation designed for understanding team members' tasks and identifying opportunities for productivity improvement. Originating from Toyota's process improvement strategies, the term *Gemba* translates to "the real place" in Japanese, emphasizing the importance of observing work in its actual setting.

During a Gemba Walk, leaders engage with employees, inquire about their tasks, and observe workflow processes. This direct observation enables leaders to bridge the gap between perceived and actual work practices, fostering a culture of continuous improvement. By interacting with team members, leaders gain valuable insights that inform strategic decisions and help them manage teams better.

But clarifying what a Gemba Walk is *not* is essential: it is not an opportunity to criticize or blame employees, implement changes hastily, or disregard employee input. Instead, it is a collaborative endeavor focused on gathering information and fostering open communication.

By prioritizing observation, active listening, and thoughtful reflection after a Gemba Walk, leaders cultivate a cooperative atmosphere within their organization. This approach mitigates the fear of punitive measures and encourages employees to share their insights and experiences openly. Ultimately, Gemba Walks serve as an important tool for EMs to bring in positive change, driving organizational success and employee engagement.

3.2.1 *Defining team goals, vision, and strategy*

As an EM, one of your most crucial responsibilities is to establish the team's tenets, vision, goals, and strategy, uniting team members under a shared mission. This process may involve using methodologies such as objectives and key results (OKRs) or setting half-yearly and yearly goals, depending on the organization's planning approach. Regardless of the method, it's essential to define goals with a clear understanding of why they are pursued and how they will be achieved. Considerations such as cost, development effort, timelines, feasibility analysis, and dependencies must be taken into account. Collaboration with cross-functional teams is key to ensuring alignment and fostering collective ownership of the team's objectives. Here's how to approach team management:

- *Understand organizational objectives.* Start by aligning team goals with the broader objectives of the organization. Understand the company's mission, vision, and strategic priorities to ensure that team goals contribute meaningfully to the overall success of the organization.
- *Practice collaborative goal setting.* Engage team members in the goal-setting process to foster ownership and buy-in. Hold collaborative discussions to identify key areas of focus; prioritize objectives; and establish clear, measurable goals that align with both team and organizational objectives. Team meetings and sprint planning sessions are great forums for discussing team goals. An EM should also ensure that the goals set for their team do not conflict with or undermine the goals of other teams. It's crucial that these goals align with those of other teams and EMs within the company.
- *Establish vision and success criteria.* Define a compelling vision for the team that inspires and motivates members to strive for excellence. Articulate the team's long-term aspirations and desired outcomes, painting a vivid picture of what success looks like and how it aligns with the organization's mission. Ensure that everyone understands their role in achieving the vision. (We will learn more about defining roles in chapter 9.)
- *Develop a road map.* Outline a strategic road map that outlines how the team will achieve its goals and realize its vision. Identify key initiatives, milestones, and action plans necessary to execute the strategy effectively. Consider factors such as resource allocation, timeline, and potential risks and challenges. Work with cross-functional partners to understand dependency management and get buy-in from leadership.
- *Communicate effectively.* Communicate team goals, vision, and strategy clearly and consistently to all stakeholders. Ensure that team members understand their roles and responsibilities in achieving the team's objectives. Foster open communication channels to solicit feedback, address concerns, and celebrate successes along the way. (We will learn about the communication framework in chapter 9, so stay tuned.)

- *Use tools and technologies.* Use appropriate tools and technologies to facilitate goal setting, collaboration, and tracking progress. Project management tools such as Jira, Asana, and Trello can help in setting and tracking goals, assigning tasks, and monitoring progress. Communication platforms such as Slack and Microsoft Teams can facilitate team collaboration and information sharing.
- *Review and adapt.* Regularly review progress toward team goals and strategy and make adjustments as needed based on feedback, changing priorities, or external factors. Encourage a culture of continuous improvement and adaptation to ensure that the team remains agile and responsive to evolving challenges and opportunities. You can use sprint end demos, retrospectives, and regular team meetings to keep everyone on the team on the same page.

We will explore clarifying and aligning goals further in chapter 9. Additionally, we'll delve into scope definitions and alignment on roles and responsibilities in chapter 10.

3.2.2 Handling morale problems

Managing team morale is vital for team success and individual happiness. Low morale can harm productivity, performance, and team culture. It leads to negative work environments with decreased motivation and communication, affecting team dynamics and causing missed deadlines and poor-quality work. As an EM, identify morale problems early and acknowledge their existence. Look for indicators such as decreased motivation and communication within the team. Addressing morale problems promptly is crucial. Some signs that can help identify potential morale problems on the team include

- Members consistently missing meetings
- Members showing disinterest or disengagement
- Members having emotional outbursts
- High turnover rates
- Declining productivity
- Lack of accountability among team members
- Signs of burnout
- Reduced communication and innovation
- Noticeable signs of stress among team members
- Feedback from team surveys that reflect morale problems

After you identify morale problems, here are some steps to address them:

- Organize team-building events such as painting events, year-end holiday parties, and milestone celebration events. I have used various third-party vendors to help organize such parties for my team when I had budget approvals. For a low-budget event, I've organized online happy hours in which everyone joins the call, talks, and chills.

- Promote shout-outs and other recognition of team members. We will learn in detail about this topic in chapter 6, and we will also learn various methods for public and private recognition.

- Use one-on-one forums to identify motivation and coach team members. These forums can be frank discussions in which folks can speak up. Just be careful that a forum does not become a dumping ground.

- If people are stressed, work with them to identify the root cause, and help with balancing workload or provide support a flexible work schedules. Also create open communication channels with team members to promote transparency and address employees' pain points.

- Work with your human resources business partner to understand the reasons for attrition and take steps to mitigate them.

- If an employee feels less challenged, find interesting, challenging opportunities for them to keep them engaged; give them more autonomy if they desire it.

- Ensure that team members have good work–life balance.

- Use forums like team meetings to gather feedback and brainstorm ideas.

- A critical responsibility of an EM is diagnosing problems and identifying opportunities for process improvements, which involves finding ways to give developers more time, help them avoid repeating mistakes, and reduce their workload burdens.

These steps can help you navigate morale problems and keep employees motivated. Next, we'll explore building trust and transparency within teams.

3.2.3 *Building trust and transparency*

Creating a positive work environment with psychological safety so team members feel that they can be themselves is the key to team success. Promptly address bad behavior, and be consistent with all employees. Building trust and transparency involves the following:

- Engaging in candid conversations with employees through one-on-ones and team meetings to know them on a personal level and understand their goals, areas of expertise, and challenges.

- Providing clarity on teamwork and team charters to foster a sense of belonging.

- Leading by example. Do not ask employees to do something that you wouldn't be comfortable doing.

- Communicating honestly about the company's direction, project updates, and any relevant changes that could affect the team's work. *Communicate clearly and consistently*, providing regular updates on project status, milestones, and any obstacles encountered along the way.

- Facilitating knowledge sharing through lunch-and-learning sessions or technical talks.

- Encouraging learning from mistakes and solving problems constructively.

- Being a patient listener.
- Soliciting feedback through regular surveys, sometimes anonymously, ensuring that everyone has a voice in the decision-making process.

As an EM, you hold dual responsibility for facilitating information flow and safeguarding sensitive data within the team. It's crucial to discern what information is pertinent and necessary for the team's operations. Divulging the specifics of compensation band definitions or individual rankings within those bands isn't conducive to team dynamics or morale. Therefore, as an EM, it's essential to exercise discretion and classify information appropriately, ensuring that you share only relevant and appropriate details with the team. Chapter 9 provides further insights on trust and transparency within cross-functional teams. Collaborating with other teams to adjust road maps is crucial for effective team management.

3.2.4 *Convincing teams about dependencies in the team road map*

Having control of your team's technical road map and charter is essential but not always sufficient. In some instances, you must persuade other teams to adjust their road map to accommodate dependencies between teams. As an EM, you need to understand what's best for the company, not only your team. You always need to see the bigger picture and understand where the most effect and value will be made, sometimes adjusting your team's road map. Effective preparation is crucial in these situations. Clearly communicate your needs and the importance of the work to convince the other party of its significance as well.

Let's imagine a scenario. You, as the EM, are overseeing the platform team for a car rental company. Your responsibilities involve modernizing the company's outdated promotion capabilities. Currently, online promotions involve customers entering a code to receive a free car accessory, with royalties paid to the accessory providers. As you embark on the revamp, however, it becomes evident that separating the royalty functionality from the promotion system and integrating it into a dedicated royalty system would be more efficient. Given your team's lack of expertise in royalties, collaboration with the royalty team and the data warehouse team became essential.

Initially encountering resistance from the royalty team, you take the initiative to organize a kickoff meeting between the royalty team and your team to explore potential synergies and align road maps. During this meeting, it becomes apparent that the top priority for the royalty team is revamping the royalty calculation system and transitioning to a third-party tool. Recognizing this common ground, you craft a concise business-value document outlining the urgency of integrating your use case into their road map. Highlighting the financial strain of maintaining the current infrastructure, you propose incorporating your royalty calculation requirements into the ongoing revamp efforts.

Moreover, you present various collaborative options, underscoring the benefits and cost savings of addressing both initiatives together. Seeing the value of tackling these projects simultaneously, the royalty team agrees to include your use case in its technical road map. To solidify your commitment to collaboration, you offer one of our engineers to assist with the development work. By pooling the expertise of both teams and aligning efforts, your aim is to streamline the promotion and royalty systems, reduce maintenance costs, and enhance overall efficiency for the company.

To expedite progress, you negotiate a phased approach, focusing on a trimmed-down version for phase one to unblock your team and lay the groundwork for a full-fledged feature in phase two. This approach not only unblocks your team, but also effectively removes royalty dependencies from the promotion system, paving the way for smoother operations and future enhancements.

As you can see from this example, navigating scenarios in which you need to convince other teams to adjust their road map requires four elements:

- Earning trust and building rapport with cross-functional partners by listening patiently and understanding their motivations
- Leading by example and piloting new guidelines within your own team before asking others to follow suit
- Providing metrics and effect to demonstrate the benefits
- Rewarding and recognizing members of cross-functional teams to foster collaboration and appreciation

With these strategies in mind, let's shift our focus to understanding how to manage remote teams effectively.

3.2.5 Managing remote teams

Managing remote teams, including hybrid setups with both in-office and remote employees, has become increasingly common post-pandemic. In these settings, it is especially important to have clear team norms, vision, and purpose. Otherwise, subjective interpretations take over and prevent effective collaboration.

On fully remote teams, members are often dispersed across various countries, whereas hybrid teams may comprise individuals from the same country who work in-office part-time. In both situations, managing across different time zones and assessing individuals' well-being without their physical presence pose notable challenges. Additionally, both setups require monitoring productivity diligently and offering support to team members who are facing declines in performance, all while recognizing the nuanced effect of lacking physical presence.

Lack of productivity is a clear indicator that underlying problems on the team need to be examined and addressed. Remote teams, however, have the advantage of accessing global talent without geographical constraints. Remote teams also benefit from reduced office expenses. To manage remote or hybrid teams effectively, consider the following strategies:

- *Provide infrastructure support.* Provide functional work-from-home environments with necessary equipment and internet connectivity while ensuring compliance with security protocols. Some companies have adopted a hoteling model, in which desks are not assigned but which employees can book when they plan to be in the office. As an EM, you can facilitate opportunities for team members to sit together or have lunch meetings, fostering a sense of togetherness and collaboration.

- *Have regular check-ins.* Conduct frequent one-on-one meetings and team check-ins to understand members' motivations and promote social connectivity while avoiding micromanagement.

- *Activate video.* Use video in meetings to foster human connection and engagement, as visual cues enhance virtual interactions.

- *Avoid multitasking.* Dedicate full attention to conversations during meetings, refraining from multitasking such as checking emails while talking to maintain transparency and focus.

- *Hold team events.* Organize virtual team-building activities and occasional in-person gatherings to boost morale and foster a sense of belonging. Some team event ideas that you can try are virtual escape rooms, food-making/noodle-making classes, sip-and-paint events, remote lunches, or even regular happy hours, all of which can help boost team morale. Virtual hackathons are another great way to unite team members to promote innovation and thinking outside the box. At the same time, once in a while—maybe every quarter or half-year—try to get team members together physically in one location so people can connect in person, striking a good balance between the virtual and physical worlds.

- *Set clear work boundaries.* Establishing clear work boundaries is crucial in remote work settings, where the lines between work and personal life can easily blur. Unlike physical offices, where leaving your desk signals the end of the workday, virtual environments lack this visual cue. Communication occurs primarily through chat messages and calls, with notifications being the primary means of contact. To address this challenge, it's essential to communicate and set expectations regarding working hours.

  If team members are collaborating across time zones, consider adding official working hours to communication tools. It's equally important that team members not feel obligated to respond outside those hours. Encourage discussions among team members to determine how they prefer to share work hours. Avoiding constant attention to messages outside work hours helps prevent burnout. Many communication tools offer features to set working hours and mute notifications, facilitating a healthy work-life balance. Transparency about working hours and effective use of communication tools can establish clear boundaries, and promote sustainable remote work routines.

- *Make meetings effective.* In a remote or hybrid setting, individuals often experience FOMO (fear of missing out) when they miss meetings, particularly if recordings or minutes aren't provided later. To mitigate this problem, it's crucial to organize meetings effectively. Establish agendas and clear objectives;

encourage prereading where necessary; invite only essential participants; and share outcomes, recordings, or minutes with the entire team afterward. Ensure that people do not talk over each other. Discover way to involve individuals in discussions and encourage their participation, mirroring the inclusivity of face-to-face interactions.

- *Emphasize documentation.* Prioritize robust documentation such as troubleshooting runbooks to facilitate learning and reduce dependency on others, especially in virtual environments.

- *Provide ongoing training.* Provide resources and support for ongoing training and development, particularly for remote onboarding and skill enhancement. Make sure to give new team members the time, support, and space they need to learn and come up to speed as they join your team. Provide access to internal company resources, as well as training courses from organizations such as Coursera (https://www.coursera.org), Pluralsight (https://www.pluralsight.com), LinkedIn Learning (https://www.linkedin.com/learning-login), and Udemy (https://www.udemy.com).

- *Promote flexibility.* Supporting flexibility in work arrangements is one way to accommodate the diverse needs of your team members. If a team member needs to pick up their children from day care daily at 5 p.m., it's important to respect and accommodate this non-negotiable commitment. Adjusting meeting schedules to avoid conflicts with personal obligations demonstrates empathy and fosters a supportive work environment. Similarly, recognizing and accommodating time-zone differences and cultural considerations is crucial for promoting inclusivity and setting the right team culture. For offshore teams, aim for a balanced overlap of working hours each day to facilitate effective collaboration. By empathizing with your team members' individual needs and providing necessary support, you can create a flexible work environment that promotes work–life balance and enhances productivity.

- *Provide mental health support.* Prioritizing mental health is essential for overall well-being and productivity. Mental health problems can significantly affect personal and professional life, highlighting the importance of proactive support from companies. Many companies are now offering mental health support resources and implementing practices such as mental health days. These days, teams and team members are allowed to take a collective day off to focus on their individual well-being. Alternatively, team members may choose to take off the day in the month or quarter that suits them best. Regardless of the approach, it's crucial to recognize the significance of mental health in fostering a healthier lifestyle. For companies that do not permit mental health days, an alternative is to designate internal team mental health days. You might consider implementing a system that gives team members the flexibility to allocate two designated days and allows each member to choose one day to prioritize their mental well-being. This approach ensures that the team remains operational while accommodating individual needs for self-care. Also, implementing "no-meetings Fridays" can give team members dedicated time to focus on tasks and alleviate meeting fatigue, contributing to their overall mental well-being.

- *Offer recognition.* Acknowledge and appreciate the work of team members to affirm their contributions and encourage growth. We will learn more about reward and recognition in chapter 6, so stay tuned.

3.2.6 *Accepting responsibility for your decisions*

When it comes to making decisions, it's best to take ownership of your decisions, be transparent about them, and explain your reasoning. Commit to and implement your decisions, but also learn to navigate scenarios in which the consequences do not come out as intended.

Imagine this scenario. You meticulously crafted a road map for your team for the current quarter, but a sudden shift in priorities at the executive level demands your team's immediate support for a project that cannot be delayed. Despite not being part of the original plan, the project's significance necessitates assigning one engineer to it full time for the next three months.

To minimize disruption to the team's road map, you identify a senior engineer who is currently working on a task related to operational excellence, which isn't a high-priority item for the quarter. Despite the engineer's limited experience with the codebase of the service that's being updated, you communicate the urgency and opportunity of the project to them, ensuring their confidence in taking on the challenge. You perceive this situation as being an opportunity for the engineer to contribute to a high-visibility project and deepen their understanding of the codebase within the project's time frame. Proactively seeking feedback from cross-functional partners, you aim to address any potential challenges early.

Despite your calculated risk, however, negative feedback surfaces regarding the engineer's reliance on guidance, lack of ownership in completing tasks, and defensiveness during technical discussions. This feedback highlights a gap between your expectations and the engineer's performance, prompting you to view this situation as a coaching opportunity.

In one-on-one sessions, you create a safe environment for open discussion and share the peer feedback with the engineer. They express their struggles with the service codebase, which contributed to their missing the first milestone deadline for the project. To support their improvement, you offer practical advice such as reviewing training materials, watching recorded sessions by subject-matter experts (SMEs), and emphasizing the importance of ownership and thorough consideration before responding defensively.

To address the gaps in knowledge, you assign another senior engineer, an SME on the service, to assist with implementation and mentor the struggling engineer. Though missing the first milestone had repercussions, the team adapted by temporarily allocating another engineer to the project for two weeks. As a follow-up, you collaborate with the engineer to create a gap analysis document, identifying areas for improvement and pairing them with a mentor to address these deficiencies.

After two months, another round of peer feedback shows significant improvement, reflecting the effectiveness of the corrective measures you implemented. Reflecting on this experience, you delve into the onboarding process for the engineer and ensure that technical documentation for all services your team manages is comprehensive and up to date. You also review the onboarding plan to identify potential enhancements, such as providing access to recorded technical talks that could aid engineers in similar situations in the future. In conclusion, by taking ownership of your decisions and learning from mistakes, you build trust with your team and position yourself and your team for success in future endeavors.

3.2.7 *Evaluating metrics for the team*

Evaluating team success is crucial for identifying gaps and celebrating achievements. Here are some key metrics to consider:

- *Establish clear baselines*. Define metrics, vision, and boundaries for the team, focusing on data-driven evaluation. Metrics may include meeting project timelines, service-level agreements such as threshold promised, OKRs achieved, project delivery success rate, and management of technical debt. If blockers arise, people can resolve them and move forward quickly.
- *Gauge employee satisfaction*. Gauge team morale and empowerment through surveys and feedback, assessing trust, ownership, and accountability.
- *Get 360-degree feedback*. Collect feedback from peers, subordinates, superiors, and cross-functional partners to understand sentiments and identify growth opportunities, reflecting communication effectiveness.
- *Measure the team development rate*. Measure team members' focus on career opportunities, upskilling, and personal well-being, leading to promotions and knowledge sharing to prevent single points of failure.
- *Review engineering metrics*. Consider developer velocity (https://mng.bz/MZZ2) and success metrics related to customer value proposition, adoption rates, and use patterns to evaluate team success and inform future strategies. Another interesting read is the McKinsey report at https://mng.bz/aEEJ. Also read Dan North's opinion on developer velocity (https://dannorth.net/mckinsey-review) and Gergely Orosz and Kent Beck's response (https://mng.bz/gvvR) to the report.

Ultimately, the success of an EM is tied to the success of their team. Providing support and fostering an environment for team success are paramount.

3.2.8 *Avoiding burnout*

Avoiding burnout is crucial, especially in virtual work environments where clear boundaries may be lacking. Burnout can occur due to various factors such as excessive workload, lack of motivation, and personal problems. Here are some strategies to prevent burnout on your team:

- *Set realistic goals.* Set achievable project deadlines and goals to reduce stress and prevent burnout.
- *Balance the workload.* Ensure a fair distribution of workload among team members to avoid overburdening individuals. Monitor capacity planning in agile ceremonies, and address any signs of burnout promptly.
- *Support open communication.* Foster a culture of open communication where team members feel comfortable discussing their concerns. Involve them in finding solutions to the challenges they face.
- *Promote work–life balance.* Encourage work–life balance by respecting personal time and boundaries. Discourage overtime work except in exceptional circumstances, and provide opportunities for relaxation and rejuvenation through team activities. Having clear work boundaries, not reaching out to individuals who are on vacation, and giving people space during sick or bereavement times are some of the ways you can give time and space to others. Lead by example by demonstrating your own work–life balance.
- *Avoid cognitive bias, and celebrate success.* Promote critical thinking and diverse perspectives to minimize cognitive biases. Celebrate team successes and recognize individual contributions to foster a culture of appreciation and reduce burnout. We will learn about this topic in more detail in chapter 6.

As an EM, I found myself amid a high-performing software engineering team tackling complex projects with tight deadlines. We were pushing boundaries and achieving milestones, but as time progressed, signs of burnout began to surface. Burnout started subtly, with missed deadlines, decreased productivity, and a noticeable decline in team morale. Initially, I attributed the situation to the natural ebb and flow of workload. But as the symptoms persisted and conversations with team members revealed underlying stress and exhaustion, I realized that we were facing a significant challenge.

Acknowledging the problem was the first step. I organized a team meeting where we candidly discussed our experiences and concerns. The meeting was a sobering moment when everyone acknowledged feeling overwhelmed and fatigued. I initiated regular one-on-one meetings with team members to provide a safe space for them to express their feelings and share any challenges they were facing. This approach allowed me to gain deeper insights into their individual situations and tailor support accordingly. One key strategy we implemented was prioritizing workload and setting realistic expectations. We revisited project timelines and deadlines, making necessary adjustments to ensure that they were achievable without sacrificing quality or overburdening the team.

Additionally, I encouraged a culture of open communication and collaboration within the team. We introduced regular check-ins where team members could share progress, discuss roadblocks, and support one another. This approach not only fostered a sense of camaraderie, but also enabled us to problem-solve collectively and alleviate individual burdens.

Recognizing the importance of work–life balance, I encouraged team members to take regular breaks and prioritize self-care. We implemented flexible working hours and encouraged unplugging from work outside designated hours. Moreover, I took proactive steps to address underlying systemic problems contributing to burnout, including advocating for additional resources, streamlining processes, and providing opportunities for skill development and career growth.

Over time, the efforts paid off. Team morale improved, productivity increased, and signs of burnout gradually diminished. The effort was a collective one, and witnessing the positive effect reaffirmed the necessity of addressing burnout proactively. Reflecting on the experience, I realized the importance of realistic goal-setting, communication, and proactive leadership in navigating challenging situations such as burnout.

In summary, cultivating a healthy work environment is essential for the team's growth and success. A positive atmosphere encourages productivity, innovation, and excellence. I'm proud to share my experience with a team that initially faced challenges but ultimately thrived.

When I began managing this team, members struggled with critical legacy services, causing frequent customer problems. But they rallied, supporting one another during root-cause analysis and improving our on-call experience. They actively shared knowledge on Slack and organized lunch-and-learn sessions. Teamwork was exemplified when a member fell ill close to a project deadline; two engineers stepped up to share the workload.

The team embraced failures as learning opportunities rather than assigned blame, which contributed to personal and professional growth. During conflicts, I provided support and encouraged open technical discussions to reach resolutions. We celebrated successes together and prioritized keeping the team motivated, fostering a shared vision, identifying career development opportunities, and providing coaching when needed.

Working with this team taught me the importance of bringing out the best in each member and collaborating toward common goals. Together, we transformed into a dream team.

3.3 *Managing yourself*

In addition to managing individuals and the teams, it's essential for EMs to prioritize self-management. This often-overlooked aspect is crucial for personal and professional growth. As an EM, you set the tone for the team and play a pivotal role in establishing its culture. If you're not well, you can't perform at your best in the workplace or support and coach others effectively. To excel as an EM, it's essential to prioritize self-care and allocate time for personal well-being, which enables you to collaborate and lead your team effectively.

By exemplifying traits such as organization, motivation, and valuing innovation, you instill trust and confidence in your team. Leading by example allows team members to bring their authentic selves to the table. Effective self-management enhances productivity, enabling you to focus on strategic goals for the team. These practices contribute to both personal development and credibility with your team, peers, and leadership. Recognizing the importance of self-management empowers EMs to lead and manage others effectively.

In the midst of my journey as an EM at a large technical firm, I found myself navigating multiple roles simultaneously: professional leader, expectant mother, and aspiring author working on the very book you're reading. It was an exhilarating yet daunting time. Balancing the demands of work, impending motherhood, and personal aspirations seemed like an insurmountable challenge at times. Yet I quickly learned that neglecting my own well-being would not only affect me, but also ripple through to my team. It became evident that to lead effectively, I needed to prioritize self-care, set boundaries, and manage my emotions and workload efficiently.

In those moments of feeling overwhelmed, I leaned heavily on the strategies I outline in this section (especially section 3.3.4,) to manage my emotions and well-being. I prioritized tasks and communicated openly with my team about my circumstances. I also made time for self-reflection, ensuring that I remained grounded and focused amid the chaos. Managing myself wasn't just about personal survival; it was also about maintaining the integrity of my leadership and the well-being of my team. By prioritizing self-care, I was better equipped to make sound decisions, provide support to my colleagues, and maintain a positive work environment. My experience taught me that as EMs, we must recognize the symbiotic relationship between our own well-being and the success of our teams.

3.3.1   *Identifying opportunities*

Identifying opportunities for growth is essential for achieving your goals and career aspirations. Self-awareness is key to understanding your strengths and weaknesses, enabling you to develop your skills effectively.

During EM interviews, a common question is '"What would your reports say about your strengths and weaknesses?" This question aims to gauge your level of self-awareness. EMs often highlight strengths such as organization and time management skills, as well as strategic-thinking abilities. Your strengths can help inspire, motivate, and guide the team effectively. But many EMs struggle to identify growth opportunities, which are just as important. If your weaknesses are poor communication or micromanagement, you can hinder the ability of your team members to trust and collaborate.

EMs' strengths and weaknesses shape their leadership style and approach. Strong technical skills might be balanced with weak interpersonal abilities, affecting team dynamics. Recognizing areas for improvement allows EMs to focus on honing their managerial skills. To identify growth opportunities, you can

- Conduct one-on-one meetings to seek feedback from team members, peers, and leaders.
- Send anonymous surveys to the team to encourage candid feedback.
- Consider the team's morale score, reflecting confidence in the EM and the work culture.

As an EM, I found myself at a crossroads when I decided to implement core working hours for my team. The idea was simple enough: designate specific hours when everyone (including me) would be present in the office and available for meetings. I believed that the plan would streamline communication and foster a more cohesive work environment. Little did I know that this seemingly innocuous decision would uncover a significant growth opportunity for me.

The feedback came during my routine one-on-one meetings with members of my team. Some of them expressed concerns about the rigid structure of the core working hours. One of the engineers mentioned personal obligations that clashed with the designated times, and another highlighted the importance of flexibility in managing their workload. It became clear that my well-intentioned initiative was inadvertently limiting their autonomy and causing unnecessary stress.

Admitting my oversight was humbling, but I quickly realized that this moment was pivotal for growth and improvement. Instead of brushing aside the concerns or becoming defensive, I chose to embrace the feedback as an opportunity to course-correct and foster a more inclusive work environment. I took a few steps to correct the problem at hand:

1 I called for a team meeting to discuss the problem openly. I expressed gratitude for their honesty and shared my commitment to addressing their concerns.

2 Next, I brainstormed with them potential solutions that would balance the need for structured communication with the importance of flexibility. This process helped make them part of decision making. We ultimately decided to revise the policy on core working hours to allow more flexibility while still ensuring adequate overlap for collaboration and meetings.

3 I decided to lead by example by adjusting my own schedule to accommodate the new policy, making it clear that flexibility was not only acceptable, but also encouraged.

4 I made myself more accessible outside the designated hours, reassuring my team that their needs and preferences mattered.

In time, team morale improved and productivity soared as team members felt empowered to manage their workload in a way that suited their individual needs. Looking back, I'm grateful for the feedback that prompted this growth opportunity, which reminded me of the importance of humility, open communication, and adaptability in leadership. This experience enabled me to create a more inclusive and supportive work environment for my team.

3.3.2 Succeeding as a manager

Success in a managerial role differs significantly from success as an individual contributor. As an EM, your success revolves around prioritizing the needs of others. As an EM, you succeed if your team succeeds. If your team is able to deliver what was agreed on time and with quality built in, that's your success. Ideally, this success will also add value to the company (in cooperation with a product). In terms of people, your success as a manager is often measured by the growth and promotion of your team members.

In my first managerial role, I was entrusted with guiding a college intern through her summer internship with our company. From the outset, I made it my mission to recognize and nurture the intern's potential. I took the time to understand her unique strengths and weaknesses, tailoring my guidance to suit her individual needs. By fostering an environment of trust and support, I created a safe space for her to explore and grow. As her manager, I didn't focus only on the technical aspects of her role; I also invested in her personal and professional development by carving out time for her to take self-paced courses through LinkedIn Learning and Udemy. I provided constructive feedback, encouraged her to take on new challenges, and celebrated her successes along the way.

Witnessing her transformation from a novice intern to a skilled software engineer was nothing short of inspiring. With each milestone she reached, I felt a profound sense of pride and accomplishment. Ultimately, her journey didn't end with her role as a software engineer. She continued to excel in her career, eventually ascending to the position of senior software engineer. Knowing that I played a part in her success remains one of the most fulfilling experiences of my managerial career.

From a project perspective, success as an EM involves adapting to changing requirements, proactively identifying dependencies and risks during development, avoiding single points of failure within the team, and cultivating a positive work environment. From a product perspective, an EM needs to understand the business context, the why of what their team is asked to build, and what success looks like. The art is achieving this success with your team, ideally without no burnout and with people growing on the job. It's important to acknowledge that success metrics now revolve more around the achievements of others than around personal accomplishments or code-related achievements.

3.3.3 *Recognizing that everyone makes mistakes*

It's crucial to recognize that everyone, including EMs, makes mistakes. Rather than being the smartest people in the room, EMs should surround themselves with intelligent individuals who can contribute to sound decision-making. Finding the balance between humility and assertiveness is key, especially in leading a team.

One significant mistake I made was becoming overly friendly with some team members I supervised, influenced by my previous role as a software engineer on the same team. Failing to establish clear boundaries led to two team members not taking my constructive feedback seriously. This situation affected project deadlines, as one engineer didn't respond promptly to my request for assistance. Acknowledging my error, I held a one-on-one meeting to clarify expectations and emphasized the importance of separating friendship from professional responsibilities.

Additionally, serious mistakes can occur on the project front, such as assuming that solutions will work without conducting proof of concept or failing to allocate resources effectively. As EMs, we must ensure the right balance of skills and experience on projects, with senior engineers overseeing complex tasks. Although mistakes are inevitable, learning from them and making informed decisions based on available data is crucial for personal and team growth.

3.3.4   Managing emotions and well-being

For an EM, it's vital to manage both the team's well-being and your own. When you leave a challenging meeting, it's crucial to regulate your mood to prevent it from affecting others, highlighting the importance of self-management, which requires handling stress effectively and avoiding overcommitment. Here are some strategies for managing well-being:

- *Prioritize self-care.* Take time off when necessary, and encourage your team to do the same. Engage in activities that promote peace of mind, such as mindfulness sessions or hobbies.
- *Establish boundaries.* Avoid sending work-related emails late at night, as this practice may set unrealistic expectations for your team. Although it may be possible for you to find time at night when others in your household are asleep, it is courteous to indicate in the email subject line that the message should be read the following day, such as adding <Read next day> or a similar indication. Use email features like Send Later to respect others' working hours.
- *Dedicate time to enjoyable activities.* Set aside time for hobbies or relaxation. During one-on-one meetings, discuss weekend activities with your team to foster a positive work–life balance.
- *Practice self-reflection.* Set aside regular time for introspection, reflecting on accomplishments and future goals.
- *Manage emotions.* Address challenging situations such as managing underperformance or conflicts within the team with empathy while ensuring that emotions don't cloud judgment. Base decisions on objective data, and allocate time to prioritize well-being.

By prioritizing self-care, setting boundaries, engaging in enjoyable activities, and managing emotions effectively, EMs can maintain well-being while fulfilling their responsibilities.

As an EM, you're tasked with overseeing the comprehensive landscape around you, encompassing individual team members, multiple teams, and your own role. Although you can influence behaviors, ultimately, the team's response to these influences shapes outcomes. Sometimes, your attempts to foster certain behaviors yield unintended results. Hence, it's crucial to consider the implications of your actions and policies carefully. Navigating this complexity involves leading individuals toward shared objectives, fostering collaboration among teams, and continually enhancing your own leadership skills. This multifaceted role demands a holistic approach to managing the diverse elements that contribute to the team's and organization's success.

What do other leaders have to say?

The biggest challenge when managing people is that every person is unique in terms of their motivations and learnings. As a leader, you are always on a mission to help them to become the best version of themselves so a good manager has to spend time and effort on effective methods of recognizing and motivating each of the team members and also find the most effective ways of providing feedback. My one-on-one effort is to ask the right questions to empower them to find solutions to grow personally and professionally. These also allow us to know team members outside the work, enabling us to build trusted relationships.

—Sumit Kumar, System Engineering Manager at Cisco

One-on-ones with your team should never be about their work but about them and your understanding of them. Always go in with the right set of questions to ask them. I have seen mostly engineers come unprepared in their one-on-ones, and you need to guide them towards the right direction to identify what is that works or doesn't work for them.

—Madhur Kathuria, Engineering Leader at Microsoft,
formerly with Moengage, Oracle, and IIT

The one-on-one is mostly for the employee rather than for the manager. My goal is to hear how they are doing and what's on their mind (both what they want to share and maybe to tease out other important things that they didn't mention) and to hear what they need. If there are course corrections or advice I need to give, then I will deliver that information.

—Jean Bredeche, Head of Engineering at Patch,
formerly with Robinhood, Quantopian, and Hubspot

For the biggest challenge to manage people, it is very easy to conflate team productivity with individual performance. Don't. A team doesn't have "performance"; a team has productivity. Team productivity is not a sum of the individual performance of members of that team. Individual performance is how well an individual operates in the context of the team and company dynamics. One of your jobs as a manager is to own team dynamics and externalities for your team and to work toward them being more favorable.

The best way I have found to break this connection is not to assign work to individuals and instead have individuals opt into taking the highest-priority work from the backlog. Having a team organized around "How do we deliver this important work?" takes the bullseye off individuals and shifts it to the team. Individual performance becomes a management retrospective, where I (their manager) can inspect the work someone did after the fact and how they operated within that team-owned plan.

—Nathan Bourgoin, Chief Technology Officer at Alakazam, Inc.,
Technical Adviser, and Engineering Leader

As an EM, resolving conflicts and getting alignment across a broad spectrum of people becomes part of your job description. No two people have the same perspective, and finding common ground is crucial to progressing in this plethora of views. The most common conflicts I see are software ownership when working on projects across multiple software teams.

I recommend not keeping ownership as a primary factor for solutions. It plays a part in long-term maintenance but should not make technical designs more complex/convoluted. I have found that setting design tenets helps teams focus on what's important. For some, performance might be higher than availability or security. For others, cost or maintainability might be a bigger concern. Look for what matters to your team and use that to inform your decisions.

—Adish Agarwal, Director, Software Development at Audible, Inc.

Managing a team in itself is a challenge, and it becomes more complex when you have virtual teams and furthermore complicated when the teams are in different time zones. The biggest challenge in my career was managing people in different time zones. First and foremost, identifying all your challenges early is the key. If there are many, prioritize them and tackle the most critical ones first. Once your final list is ready, you can spend the rest of the time developing a strategy. The best part is you don't have to find the resolution alone. In my situation, we had to figure out how to collaborate, review the code, and conduct meetings among the many. To combat it, I've invited the whole team to brainstorming sessions and engaged the team to pitch in their ideas, share their opinions, hear them out & weigh in on each option. I created virtual polls to gather everyone's inputs, and eventually a consensus was reached among the team with little guidance and facilitation.

—Vindhya Avvari, Cloud Integration Manager, University of Southern California

Regarding managing people, since they come from various backgrounds, the biggest challenge is to understand their roots so you can assess the situations and ask with proper context. One way I always try to approach this is first getting a level of connection with the people and trying to put myself in their shoes. I have tried various approaches for one-on-ones. The recent one is to have the teammate set the agenda for the meeting and not you as a manager driving the meeting. Of course, you can add your topics, but one-on-one is for and about them.

—Rajakumar Sambasivam, Delivery Manager at Microsoft

For managing people, the biggest challenge is to assign the right person to the right job; then most of the other challenges will be taken care of by the individual employee. Being a mentor and coach to the employee will speed up productivity and reduce conflicts. For successful one-on-ones, keep track of action items, provide status to the employee on the action item, even if you did not make progress, let the employee talk, ask a more open-ended question, and balance it with all the aspects like job/career/team health/job satisfaction/new ideas. Basically, it is not just career coaching. And don't get into teaching/preaching mode.

—Saravanan Subramanian, Senior Manager at Amazon Web Services,
formerly with Capital One, Citi, and Cisco

When moving from an IC which works mostly with machines to EM, one striking difference is, unlike systems which are mostly molded in similar dies, people are way different from each other. Each person's motivation, drive, fear, etc., are very different, particularly in a well-balanced team with diverse backgrounds. Navigating through this may be the biggest challenge.

—Sarin Panambayil, Principal Engineer at Yahoo!

3.4   *Stop and think: Practice questions*

1 As a manager, what is one of the most difficult management situations you have been in? Why was it difficult?

2 What is your manager's expectation when it comes to career conversations? Do you practice what you expect?

3 What is the biggest challenge you've faced when working in a remote environment?

4 What are your success criteria? How do you measure them?

5 What is the biggest mistake you have made at the workplace? If you could change one thing about it, what would that be?

6 As an EM, how do you plan to build rapport and establish trust with your team?

7 As a first-time EM, how do you plan to support the professional growth of your team members?

8 How do you plan to maintain a healthy work–life balance as a manager?

9 What strategies do you have in place for managing stress and avoiding burnout?

Summary

- To excel as a software EM, you need a deep understanding of your team, effective communication, and a commitment to personal and professional growth, which includes setting clear goals, addressing morale problems, building trust, managing remote teams, and evaluating success.
- Leading by example is crucial; showing rather than just telling sets expectations for the team.
- Handling conflicts and challenging team members are inevitable but valuable learning experiences.
- Defining team goals and strategies fosters unity and direction.
- Maintaining morale, trust, and transparency is essential for team cohesion and productivity.
- Persuading other teams to accommodate dependencies requires clear communication and mutual understanding.
- Managing remote teams demands balance between in-person and virtual interactions.
- Taking responsibility for decisions and evaluating team metrics ensures accountability and progress.
- Preventing burnout and prioritizing self-management are vital for personal and team well-being.
- Identifying opportunities and tracking progress fosters continuous growth as a manager.

- Success in management is about prioritizing others' needs and learning from mistakes.
- Balancing team care and personal well-being is essential for effective leadership.
- As an EM, you navigate complex dynamics, foster collaboration, and prioritize growth for both your team and yourself.

Managing performance

4

Performance management involves embracing employees' strengths and being open to innovative ideas—even ones that change the status quo.

—Steve Jobs, Co-Founder, Apple, Inc.

As a new engineering manager (EM) overseeing critical product features for a team, you have one engineer, David, who consistently meets deadlines and takes on additional stretch work. Jason, another strong engineer, focuses on streamlining technical processes but misses key deliverables due to this extra effort. Although Jason's contributions have long-term benefits, his time management affects project timelines.

Managing performance involves understanding team motivations and providing continuous feedback to foster growth and trust. In David's case, he meets expectations, but Jason's situation requires coaching on balancing priorities and timely communication. Effective performance management involves recognizing and rewarding high performance while providing guidance to address deviations. By intervening and mentoring Jason, you, as EM, can optimize team productivity and project outcomes.

4.1   Importance of managing performance

A well-implemented performance management system fosters employees' development and maximizes their potential by setting clear goals and objectives. Collaborating with employees on career planning enhances individual and team performance. Benefits of an effective system include

- Sustained productivity
- Career planning support
- Proactive feedback
- Goal alignment
- Improved retention rates
- Informed leadership for future hiring needs

Effective performance management cultivates continuous improvement, engagement, accountability, and competitiveness, all of which are vital for achieving business goals.

4.1.1   Sustained productivity

Performance management is essential for tracking expectations and employee performance, fostering trust, and demonstrating investment in growth. A performance management system creates a sense of safety and purpose, boosting productivity and engagement while enhancing team trust and internal promotion opportunities. It reinforces the importance of staying on track for all performers and allows leadership to reward high performance and address underperformance promptly.

In our example, David consistently met expectations and aligned with management, showcasing sustained productivity. But Jason struggled to balance productivity, exceeding expectations on stretch goals but missing critical project deliverables. Performance conversations could have helped Jason realign his efforts.

4.1.2   Career planning

A company-wide performance management system, including performance reviews and planning tools, aids in career planning and identifying growth opportunities. Continuous one-on-one discussions allow managers to understand employees' strengths and motivations, facilitating candid conversations and crafting short-, mid-, and long-term career plans. This approach fosters work satisfaction and timely performance improvements.

On our team, both David and Jason underwent career planning. David progressed according to plan, but Jason got sidetracked by project management, which caused him to miss deliverables and fall short of his goals. For an EM, failing to refocus Jason risks rewarding the wrong behavior.

4.1.3   Proactive feedback

Continuous performance management empowers engineering leaders to offer proactive feedback rather than react to problems after they arise. Although there's a reactive element to addressing incidents or patterns, the focus is on providing regular feedback through frequent one-on-ones and career discussions. This approach enables timely course corrections for employees who may have diverged or underperformed, fostering a two-way dialogue between individuals and managers.

In the case of Jason's missed project deadlines, proactive communication could have prevented negative consequences, allowing the manager to provide guidance and ensure that crucial deliverables were met, thus safeguarding the team's success.

4.1.4   Alignment on strategic goals

Performance management fosters alignment of individual, team, and business goals through regular check-ins. Clear goal-setting and measurement methods ensure that individuals contribute to team and company objectives. Continuous reviews help identify and address risks or blockers early, ensuring that everyone works toward shared strategic goals.

In our example, regular performance check-ins could have alerted the team to Jason's missed project deliverable sooner, preventing last-minute problems. Had there been frequent goal checks, Jason's progress could have been monitored and supported earlier in the process.

4.1.5   Better retention chances

A job that supports career growth and development, offers learning opportunities with the latest technology, and provides clarity on performance expectations is desirable to most employees. Employers that are invested in career development have better chances of hiring and retaining talent, reducing attrition costs and onboarding time. In the incident with David and Jason, David is more likely to stay and feel valued, whereas Jason may feel resentful and disengaged. You, as EM, could get Jason refocused on the project at hand so he does not feel resentful but feels confident in his contributions. A robust performance management system can significantly influence outcomes in such situations.

4.1.6   Plans for future hiring and training programs

A robust performance management system aids leadership and human resources in planning future hiring and training programs by identifying performance patterns and the fiscal effects of promotions. It also ensures that compensation is aligned with industry standards through market reviews. Planning for training initiatives allows employees to develop skills, such as system design, with resources like courses and conferences. EMs can use planning phases to identify training needs and support employee growth. Additionally, an EM can plan diversity, equity, and inclusion initiatives for a positive work environment. Overall, a robust system enables real-time progress tracking as well as intervention to prevent problems later, all benefiting individuals, teams, and the organization as a whole.

4.2 Best practices for managing performance

Performance management is a multifaceted process that necessitates ongoing attention to various factors. It's not a single event but a continuous endeavor supporting the growth and enhancement of every employee. Given its substantial effect on individuals' perception of their role and how well they are fulfilling it, adhering to industry-standard best practices is paramount for fostering employee development. It's crucial to recognize that although applying best practices is important, true excellence lies in understanding individuals' unique circumstances and facilitating their progress accordingly. This recognition doesn't necessarily imply poor performance; rather, it acknowledges that our standardized approaches may not apply to every situation. Although intuition and adaptability play significant roles, let's delve into some essential best practices for managing performance.

4.2.1 Promoting transparency

Promoting transparency is crucial for organizational growth, with psychological safety serving as its foundation. This environment allows employees to take interpersonal risks without fear of reprisal, thereby fostering trust, open communication, and inclusivity. Transparency doesn't mean divulging every detail; finding the right balance is key. Shielding teams from organizational chaos enables focus on execution, for example, and sharing feedback without revealing sources maintains clear channels for development. For an engineering leader, being transparent about mission, goals, and expectations is vital. Setting clear SMART goals (chapter 3) ensures that feedback aligns with individual development. One-on-one meetings are the best places to deliver this feedback. This transparent approach to feedback and performance management cultivates a culture that reflects both organizational objectives and your and your company's commitment to performance.

4.2.2 Ensuring fairness

Ensuring fairness and avoiding personal bias and favoritism are crucial in maintaining a productive workplace environment. You should establish consistent behavior and equitable distribution of work and recognition to prevent recency bias. Many companies use leveling guides to define performance standards objectively, promoting fair assessment and reducing subjective bias. Advocating for the creation of a leveling guide, if one is not already in place, can help you achieve this goal. Fairness initiatives—including diversity, equity, and inclusion programs—reinforce the importance of treating every individual with respect. Raising awareness, providing training, and implementing data-driven discussions are essential steps in promoting fairness and combating bias. Additionally, establishing mechanisms for employees to address perceived unfair treatment and facilitating a fair appeal process enhances workplace fairness. Consistency is key in maintaining fairness, ensuring that employees are consistently held to the standards outlined in the leveling guide.

In the case of David and Jason, both employees should be evaluated against the company's leveling guide to ensure consistency in performance expectations. When exceptions arise such as accommodating employees with personal obligations—an employee who takes care of an elderly parent at home or an expectant mother who is not quite as productive as usual, for example—you should provide empathy and support. Encouraging teamwork and using a divide-and-conquer strategy can mitigate any effect from absent team members.

4.2.3   Avoiding the Halo and Horns Effect

Avoiding the Halo and Horns Effect is crucial in fair performance evaluation. The Halo Effect occurs when employees are overly praised based on a few positive traits, whereas the Horns Effect unfairly focuses on negative attributes, overshadowing other contributions. These biases can lead to distorted perceptions and hinder employee development.

Idolizing a key contributor may overlook areas for improvement, for example, and unfairly critiquing someone for a single mistake can undermine their overall performance. To counter these biases, conversations and reviews should be data-driven, incorporating factual evidence and peer feedback to provide a holistic assessment. For engineering leaders, it's essential to steer clear of such biases to foster a supportive, inclusive work environment.

4.2.4   Providing recognition

Recognition plays a vital role in fostering employee confidence, motivation, and sense of value, which contributes to higher retention rates. Acknowledging individuals who consistently exceed expectations encourages positive behavior and boosts productivity. As you manage performance, it's important to identify and appreciate employees who use their strengths and go the extra mile. But rewards and recognition should be based on objective criteria, maintaining professionalism and avoiding biases. You can find further insights on using recognition to enhance employee engagement in chapter 6.

4.2.5   Communicating effectively

Effective communication is a crucial tool in managing performance, ensuring that both parties feel fully engaged and understood. It involves open and candid dialogue, with the team member and the leader actively listening to each other's perspectives. Effective communication facilitates discussing past actions and areas for improvement, as well as setting clear expectations and goals. It also involves providing feedback and recognition based on individual communication styles, whether you're appreciating high performers or addressing instances of underperformance. Tailoring communication approaches ensures receptivity and fosters productive conversations between leaders and team members.

4.2.6 Providing training

Training is essential for fostering skill development and addressing performance gaps within the team. For a manager and engineering leader, it's crucial to collaborate with team members to identify areas that need improvement and to provide necessary resources and support. If a senior employee struggles with delegation, you can guide them through training resources such as LinkedIn Learning, leadership seminars, or conferences. Pairing them with an experienced mentor or sharing personal experiences can also aid in skill development. By offering support tailored to individual needs, you build trust, making team members better equipped for success.

4.2.7 Performing continuous performance management

Continuous performance management is an agile and ongoing process that prioritizes consistency in planning, coaching, and supporting employee growth. Regular check-ins and clear road maps are essential for monitoring progress and ensuring employee engagement. Standardized processes across the company make performance management lightweight and fair, addressing problems early to prevent larger problems. This approach has proved to be effective in improving performance and supporting underperformers through early feedback and necessary support.

4.3 Performance reviews

Performance reviews (also known as the talent cycle) are conducted regularly to assess individual achievements, motivations, performance against company standards, and talent trends. These reviews serve as crucial inputs for compensation changes, although the frequency of reviews must be balanced to prevent human resources and managerial burden. At the same time, not all reviews involve the compensation-changes component. Compensation adjustments typically reflect performance ratings, with top performers receiving higher pay increases.

Despite being perceived as time-consuming, performance reviews are essential for career development and employee engagement. Human resources oversees this process to ensure fairness and address employee concerns, serving as a platform to identify resource gaps for employee success. Effective preparation for performance reviews entails identifying the performance-review cadence and striking a balance between organizational requirements and team dynamics.

4.3.1 Evaluating performance

In the evaluation stage of performance reviews, individual performance against company expectations is assessed, considering potential for the upcoming year. It's crucial for new EMs to evaluate engineers based on a career growth framework to minimize bias and ensure consistency across evaluations. Data collection involves gathering feedback from sources including managers, other employees, and peers, along with revisiting established goals and project deliverables. Impartiality and consideration for the employee's motivations are key during this process. Managers assign potential ratings, finalized during calibration, using either a bell curve or a rating scale. Identifying and correcting any performance gaps promptly is essential for aligning personal and professional goals and supporting employee growth. Involvement in hiring initiatives can provide valuable development opportunities, with managers offering necessary tools, training, and mentoring support. For new EMs, this process can be time-consuming. Planning early to avoid last-minute rushes can significantly alleviate this burden.

Did you know?

A widely used evaluation/performance management technique in various industries is the nine-box ranking approach. An employee is categorized into one of nine boxes based on their current performance and future potential, as shown in the following figure. This method ensures consistent talent evaluation and facilitates the identification of high performers and underperformers who require attention.

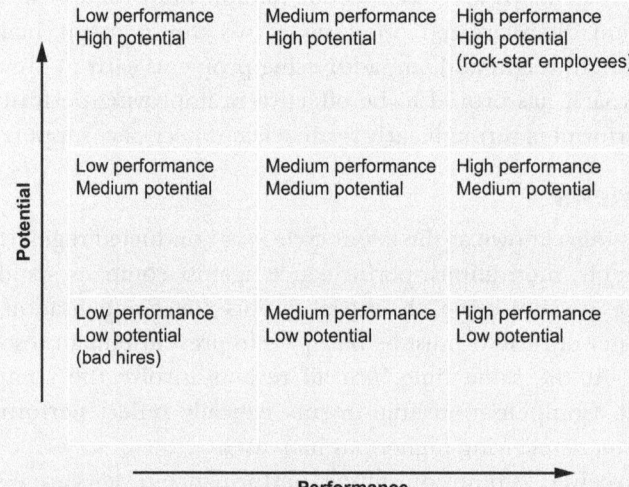

The nine-box ranking approach that takes into consideration performance and potential

This approach offers leadership insight into current talent and aids future talent planning. Using a data-driven approach to categorize employees in one of nine buckets helps mitigate biases, enabling the identification of opportunities for high performers and training and support for underperformers.

COLLECTING FEEDBACK

Collecting feedback involves gathering input from multiple sources, including your own observations, the employee's self-assessment, and peer feedback. For an EM, using notes from the past period facilitates providing comprehensive feedback. Self-assessment encourages employees to reflect on their performance and identify areas for growth. *Peer feedback*, also known as *360-degree feedback*, offers valuable insights from colleagues across various teams, aiding in identifying growth opportunities and understanding others' perceptions of their work. Approaching feedback positively and seeking input from engineers, peers, and leadership ensures a well-rounded perspective.

To gather comprehensive feedback as an EM, it's crucial to be explicit in your request, specifying the time frame to be considered for feedback, which could involve asking whether the feedback should encompass the past six months, one year, or another relevant period. Additionally, ensure that peers have ample time to provide feedback, encouraging them to detail both strengths and areas for improvement. Following are some questions you can ask peers as part of the feedback request:

- What strengths have you observed in this individual's work?
- In what areas do you see opportunities for growth or development for this individual?
- Would you like to share any other feedback or insights about this individual's performance that weren't covered by the previous questions?
- What added value does this individual bring to our team/company?
- What would make this individual more effective in their role?

Integrating feedback from peers into performance reviews enhances the objectivity and comprehensiveness of evaluations. It's essential, however, to establish a culture where peer feedback is constructive and not misused. For an EM, fostering such a culture promotes continuous improvement and learning from past experiences. Additional resources on providing effective feedback, such as the *Harvard Business Review* article at https://mng.bz/eooJ and the blog post at https://mng.bz/pppP, can further support this endeavor.

ADJUSTING EXPECTATIONS

Adjusted expectations involve considering any unique circumstances that may have affected an employee's performance during the year, such as role changes, external factors, or leaves of absence. This approach doesn't mean lowering the performance bar; it means ensuring fairness in evaluations. If an employee took maternity leave, you should assess their performance based on the time they were available and their potential for the future, rather than compare them to someone who worked the entire year. Instead of comparing employees, calibrate them against the career growth plan, using a gap analysis document (chapter 3). Managers can offer options such as flexible hours or reduced-capacity programs to support employees, following human resources regulations. For an employee like David who transitioned from an individual contributor to a manager midyear, evaluations should consider the new role's expectations.

4.3.2   *Calibrating across teams/organizations*

After individual evaluations, the next step is calibrating employees across teams and organizations, a task typically led by directors and vice presidents. Managers present strengths, weaknesses, and growth opportunities, sharing potential ratings. Although EMs may not attend these sessions, their notes are used for calibration. Open discussions ensure alignment with company leveling guides, promoting fairness and uncovering any favoritism or harassment. Human resources business partners participate to ensure consistency and fairness.

These sessions offer insights into organizational performance and facilitate discussions on attrition, retention, and promotion opportunities. Underperforming employees are identified for improvement, and final ratings are determined based on discussions. Effective time management and thorough preparation during the evaluation phase are crucial for successful calibration sessions.

> **TIP** You can find further resources on best practices for calibration meetings can be found in the Lucid chart blog post at https://mng.bz/OZZP and the LeadDev blog post at https://mng.bz/JZRK.

4.3.3 *Preparing and conducting performance reviews*

After evaluations and calibration are done across the organization, the next step is preparing and conducting performance reviews in one-on-one meetings with employees. Managers should schedule the meeting, ensuring buffer time for questions, and arrive prepared with a data-driven write-up that reflects the individual's effect and feedback from team members. The aim is to provide holistic feedback and support growth. Managers should allow employees time to process feedback and then discuss strengths and growth opportunities for the next year. During the conversation, it's essential to do the following:

- Be a patient listener.
- Evaluate individual progress and achievements of individual members of the team as part of performance reviews that allow for reflection on the past x months' worth of work. Performance reviews acknowledge growth and excellence while identifying areas for improvement and understanding the reasons for any lack of progress.
- Figure out what's next for the employee by talking about their goals and understanding what motivates them. A resource you can refer to is the book *Why Motivating People Doesn't Work . . . and What Does* (https://mng.bz/Y777).
- Foster transparency and drive consensus.
- Meet in a noise-free environment for both in-person and virtual meetings. Facial expressions should be visible in video calls.
- Use the right phrases, providing praise, and discussing financial matters such as promotions and compensation.
- Be prepared to make difficult discussions and seek training on compensation structures. You can prepare a list of frequently asked questions (FAQs) or resources to address common questions.

These meetings are opportunities to celebrate achievements, discuss improvement areas, and plan a career road map with employees. You should treat career conversations not as a one-time chore, but a continuous opportunity to work with individuals and help them plan a career road map.

4.3.4   Handling pushback on the feedback

Anticipate challenges in conversations with team members, especially when addressing areas needing improvement. Employees may push back due to fear of incompetence or job insecurity. For EMs, handling such scenarios requires tact to build trust. Here are key points to consider:

- Listen closely! Reports may push back because they feel undervalued or overlooked. Sometimes, they overestimate their capabilities; at other times, they seek quicker advancement. Understanding their reasons for pushing back is crucial before addressing their concerns effectively.
- Provide clear, data-backed feedback on strengths and areas for improvement, referencing specific instances such as effective problem-solving or production problems.
- Ensure that performance reviews align with previous one-on-one discussions, preventing surprises. Encourage active participation from team members.
- Avoid giving false praise, watering down critiques, or comparing employees. Evaluate employees against company standards, not one another.
- Practice humility and patience, using career growth frameworks and emotional intelligence skills.
- Share support and a road map for improvement, offering resources such as mentoring and coaching.
- Follow up regularly to ensure progress and offer assistance if needed. Be assertive when necessary, relying on data for tough discussions.

> **TIP**   Some suggested books to read for giving effective feedback are *Crucial Conversations* (https://mng.bz/GZZN), *Difficult Conversations* (https://mng.bz/z88Z), and *Fierce Conversations* (https://mng.bz/0GGz).

4.3.5   Using a performance review template

Companies often use different formats or templates for performance reviews, with some lacking standardization, especially in smaller startups and midsize companies. Here's a sample template to cover the basics: evaluating individual work, reflecting on achievements and growth opportunities, and aligning for the next performance cycle. Let's consider Alice's performance review, shown in table 4.1.

Table 4.1   A sample template for performance review cycle

Employee name	Alice
Employee ID	1242221
Department	Software Development
Review period	Jan 2021–Dec 2021
Manager name	David M.

Table 4.1   A sample template for performance review cycle (*continued*)

Manager evaluation rating	Top Tier
Rating scale	1 (assuming a rating scale from 1–3, with 1 being top tier and 3 the lowest)

What are some of the ways this individual created the most effect in the review period?
(Make use of company leadership principles and career leveling guide.)

Employee evaluation	Manager evaluation
In the first half of the year, I worked on the delivery of project ABC, which involved creating a complex categorizer engine. I collaborated with cross-functional partners and helped increase the test coverage from 30% to 70%.	I agree with what Alice shared. On top of it, I will add that Alice has shown customer obsession by helping resolve a mission-critical customer bug (within 2 hours of the incident) that had a blast radius of 20,000 customers. Further, she showed a bias for action by documenting her learnings and creating an operational run book for troubleshooting production deployment problems for on-calls.

What are some of the ways this individual can increase effect/opportunities going forward (areas of improvement/growth opportunities)?

Employee evaluation	Manager evaluation
Focus on depth of knowledge in services and infrastructure	Alice has an opportunity to help with hiring initiatives for the company. She can help with interviewing and helping onboard new hires to the team. For this task, her manager has paired her with a mentor to coach her on hiring and mentoring other junior engineers.

Any additional comments/notes?

N/A

Employee	Manager
Aligned, accepted	Aligned, accepted

Using such a template acknowledges Alice's hard work while highlighting areas for improvement and providing focus points for the future. During reviews, ensure data-driven input to keep conversations on track. When the review is delivered, both parties align and accept it, moving it to a terminal state.

4.4   Managing high performance

EMs often overlook managing high performance because they prioritize addressing problems with underperformers. But neglecting high performers due to assumptions of self-sufficiency can be detrimental. High performers are invaluable assets to retain, considering the significant cost of replacing them. Identifying the characteristics of high performers is essential for effective management.

4.4.1   Identifying high performance

Identifying high performers is crucial, as they consistently exceed expectations, boost team velocity, and inspire others. They are sought after in the job market and serve as go-to resources within the team. Recognizing their traits also helps set a benchmark for hiring top talent. Let's explore these traits further:

- *Proactive rather than reactive*—High performers are proactive, anticipating and addressing problems before they arise. During a period of rapid company growth, one of my engineers created a tool to streamline the process of adding new configuration files for each marketplace. This tool automated the process, reducing deployment time from days to hours and showcasing the team member's commitment to efficiency.

- *Growth mindset*—High performers embrace a growth mindset, seeking not only immediate tasks, but also big challenges and long-term company growth. Envisioning the future needs of a movie provider app, they may advocate for a server-driven architecture. This approach enables easy updates without extensive mobile deployment cycles, demonstrating innovative thinking and foresight.

- *Go-to quality*—High performers are reliable go-to resources for debugging and technical support, embodying a coaching mindset by sharing their expertise with others. One standout team member not only assisted with backend technical problems within the team, but also offered weekly office hours for engineers seeking guidance. Their genuine interest in others' success distinguished them and made them indispensable to the team.

- *Extreme ownership*—High performers value accountability, preferring to work autonomously with minimal intervention. They exhibit a strong work ethic, reliability, and a proactive approach to driving projects to completion.

- *Self-motivation*—High performers are self-motivated, self-aware individuals who excel at self-organization. This trait enables them to maximize their potential and inspire others. One engineer on my team demonstrated self-motivation by focusing on operational excellence and reducing technical debt. Through proactive actions such as sharing proof of concepts and raising awareness in team meetings, she fostered a culture where every engineer contributed to operational excellence tasks.

These traits distinguish high performers as approachable role models who actively support their team members. It's crucial to demonstrate appreciation and value for high performers. As EMs, we have several ways to support them.

4.4.2 Supporting high performers

High performers significantly affect productivity and company culture. Despite often being overlooked, with the right opportunities and support from leadership, they can propel the organization forward. Let's explore common ways we can support high performers for demonstrating sustained performance.

AUTONOMY AND AUTHORITY

High performers excel with autonomy, thriving when given space to learn and grow without micromanagement. EMs should delegate tasks to them to foster their development. It's essential, however, to ensure they don't become single points of failure for the team. Consider the Bus Factor, which highlights the importance of distributing knowledge and responsibilities among team members to mitigate risks of critical knowledge loss. As an EM, you should support high performers while encouraging them to mentor others to prevent becoming bottlenecks.

GROWTH OPPORTUNITIES

To nurture high performers and facilitate their success, it's vital to provide growth opportunities. This task includes assigning challenging projects, connecting them with mentors for career development, and opening doors to opportunities beyond their current team or organization. The objective is to foster their skills and unleash their full potential.

A friend of mine, a senior software engineer and top performer, expressed a desire to transition to product management, which aligned with his strengths. Recognizing his potential, his manager facilitated his move within the same team. Now thriving as a successful product manager, he further enhanced his skills through a mentorship program. This example illustrates the significance of engineering leaders who prioritize growth opportunities, even if it involves transitioning to roles outside the immediate team or organization.

FORMAL RECOGNITION

High performers often seek formal recognition as a way to feel valued. This recognition can include giving them shout-outs in team and leadership channels and acknowledgment across the company's leadership principles, as well as sharing their achievements in all-hands meetings for visibility. But it's essential to consider that some high performers may prefer private recognition, especially if they are introverted. Chapter 6 explores different forms of acknowledgment and strategies for implementing them effectively.

COMPENSATION

Compensation is a key way to demonstrate appreciation for high performers. Performance reviews in most organizations typically result in increased annual compensation or spot bonuses for exceeding expectations. Given the high demand for top talent in the technical industry, it's crucial to compensate high performers competitively to align with industry standards and retain their valuable contributions.

CONSTRUCTIVE FEEDBACK

Constructive feedback entails offering data-driven insights with positive intentions to help individuals recognize strengths and areas for improvement. Supporting high performers through such feedback enables them to enhance their skills and access resources for growth. I suggest reading the book *Radical Candor* (https://www.radicalcandor.com) to learn more about giving effective feedback.

I once assisted a high performer on a team that was struggling with delegation by coaching in one-on-ones, providing specific examples and suggesting training resources and mentorship opportunities. Through timely feedback and support, the team members successfully improved their delegation skills.

CHALLENGES

High performers thrive when they're challenged with exciting projects that align with their growth and understanding of the bigger picture. EMs should provide such opportunities while being mindful of preventing burnout by setting realistic goals and ensuring adequate support. Regular check-ins help maintain a sustainable workload. I once collaborated with a high performer to address an organization-wide problem of a missing mentorship program for backend engineers, setting challenging yet achievable goals.

Managing and supporting high performers is essential for EMs. Let me share two examples. Alice, an expert backend engineer, improved her team-oriented attitude through persistent discussions, eventually earning a promotion. By contrast, Bob, a skilled engineer with strong teamwork and leadership qualities, received a promotion due to his effective collaboration and cross-functional partnerships.

4.5 *Managing low performance and underperformance*

Underperformance refers to falling below the expected standards for a job role, whether in meeting project timelines, delivering quality work, or exhibiting appropriate behavior. It negatively affects team morale and overall performance. Managing underperformance is as crucial as nurturing high performers. Timely identification allows employees to course-correct with support while enabling the organization to plan effectively. Let's delve into a framework for managing underperformance, drawing from my personal managerial experiences.

4.5.1 *Managing underperformance*

Addressing underperformance necessitates thorough root-cause analysis to support both the individual and the business unit. For EMs, it's vital to advocate for the importance of managing underperformance. This information should not be a surprise to the individual, as forums such as one-on-one sessions and performance reviews offer continuous actionable feedback. Now let's explore an easy-to-use framework for managing underperformance in challenging situations.

IDENTIFY THE UNDERPERFORMANCE

The initial step in managing underperformance is identifying its cause within your team. Despite EMs' inclination to believe that everything is running smoothly, it's essential to remain observant and recognize indicators such as changes in work quality, missed deadlines, or decreased engagement.

Upon joining my team as the new EM, I observed consistent disengagement and missed deadlines by John, a junior software engineer. Despite positive feedback from the previous EM, John provided excuses for delays, exhibited a lack of attention to detail, and demonstrated lower productivity compared to his peers. Recognizing these signs, I promptly initiated an investigation to uncover the root cause of his behavior.

ANALYZE THE ROOT CAUSE

When addressing underperformance, it's essential to conduct a thorough root-cause analysis, free from personal biases. Several factors could contribute to underperformance, including the following:

- Lack of technical skill sets
- Personal reasons such as health problems or family concerns that affect emotional and physical well-being
- Poor role fit (the employee's skills don't align well with their current position)
- Insufficient tools and resources for success
- Lack of clarity about role expectations and scope
- Shift in interests, with the employee becoming more interested in other roles or responsibilities

In John's case, I approached the situation objectively during a candid one-on-one meeting, inquiring about any personal problems affecting his work. But he cited no compelling reasons and appeared simply to be avoiding tasks. Consequently, I shared consolidated feedback with him to discuss the effect of his work. For first-time EMs, navigating this situation can pose challenges. It's important to avoid making assumptions; instead, rely on a data-driven approach through one-on-one conversations.

SHARE CONSOLIDATED FEEDBACK

Sharing consolidated feedback is a crucial step that involves conveying information objectively while maintaining a data-driven mindset. This approach entails gathering 360-degree feedback from peer engineers, cross-functional partners, and other EMs who have collaborated with the individual. The goal is to gain a comprehensive perspective on the employee's work and behavior, highlighting both strengths and areas for improvement. During this conversation with the team member, the focus should be on discussing behavior, its effect, and the consequences and helping the individual understand the gaps in their knowledge and the areas where they need improvement.

In John's case, I shared the consolidated feedback with him, maintaining a data-driven approach. Here's how I went about it:

1 I referenced a paper trail for clarity. For all my one-on-ones with the employee, I maintain a paper trail, which is simply a document with the date and outcomes in our one-on-ones. I showed John the specific instances during the year when we discussed his underperformance; then I offered coaching and suggested next-action items for him.

2 I used 360-degree peer feedback that provided insights into how others perceived his work. I highlighted both his successes, such as serving as the scrum lead, and areas that needed improvement, such as missing project deadlines and delivering subpar code quality. For code quality, a good metric is the comments made by peer engineers on the code reviews and the amount of revisions a code review goes through before it lands in production. Our team used an in-house tool for collecting feedback. You can also tools such as Lattice

(https://lattice.com) if your company doesn't have an existing mechanism for feedback collection.

3 I referenced the company's leveling guide to conduct a gap analysis. (Chapter 3 provides a sample template of a gap analysis document.) This analysis identified disparities between performance expectations and reality, serving as a foundation for a plan to support John's success moving forward.

CREATE A COACHING PLAN

Following the consolidation of feedback, the next crucial step is establishing a structured coaching plan. This plan translates feedback into actionable items with clear timelines, typically spanning 60 or 90 days, to ensure adherence to time constraints. Transparent communication with the employee, such as John, is essential for outlining areas for improvement, how progress will be measured, and what support the EM will provide.

John and I established a timeline and a list of achievable tasks with specific competencies. As part of the coaching plan, I shifted from biweekly to weekly one-on-one meetings to provide faster support and feedback. Each session focused on clearly defined goals for the upcoming week and reviewing progress made. Furthermore, I facilitated access to learning resources, including internal videos and technical documents, and suggested courses on platforms such as Udemy to enhance his technical skills. We set the expectation that John would engage with these materials during designated time periods outside his regular work hours. This plan could include allocating specific blocks of time during the workday for learning or setting aside time before or after work to ensure that learning activities did not interfere with his primary responsibilities and deadlines.

Additionally, it was important to communicate transparently the consequences of not meeting expectations. In this case, I conveyed that John's failure to meet expectations would result in his being moved to a Performance Improvement Plan, discussed later in this chapter.

MONITOR AND REVIEW

After providing feedback, it's crucial to monitor progress regularly. Weekly one-on-one meetings are effective for sharing progress and offering feedback. In John's case, progress was discussed in these meetings, and documentation was maintained via email, including progress updates and feedback. Despite my efforts to align expectations to the company leveling guide and provide coaching, John continued to struggle with meeting deadlines. As a result, I had to take further steps to address his underperformance.

IMPLEMENT A PERFORMANCE IMPROVEMENT PLAN

When an employee fails to meet expectations despite the coaching plan, the next step is implementing a Performance Improvement Plan (PIP), also known as a Performance Empowerment Plan. This process should be approached with careful consideration, as it serves as a final opportunity for the employee to improve before potential termination. A PIP is similar to a coaching plan in that it outlines actionable items with estimated timelines to ensure that time constraints are respected. But PIP is more formal and time-bound. It often involves more direct action items and robust documentation, and human resources is typically involved in the process. Furthermore, the plan is shorter than the initial coaching phase. Also, the consequences of a PIP are more serious: failing to improve after a PIP might lead to termination.

Given John's lack of improvement through coaching, we initiated a 90-day PIP in collaboration with human resources. (PIPs of 30, 45, and 60 days are also common.) The plan included setting specific SMART goals and clear expectations, including the following:

- *Code reviews*—Address comments within two business days and minimize code revisions.
- *Timelines/delivery*—Meet sprint goals unless technical blockers arise.
- *Documentation/knowledge sharing*—Contribute to team documentation and trouble tickets.

The keys to a successful PIP are clear communication of expectations and support to achieve them. I provided a structured plan for John's improvement and set expectations for him. I also took further actions to support him:

- Maintained approachability and empathy, being available to John except during meetings or off-hours
- Paired John with a buddy on the team for technical guidance and support, enabling activities such as pair programming and additional code review
- Created a Slack channel for John, the buddy, and me to enable quicker communication and answers to questions

NOTE In instances of misconduct, it's crucial to involve human resources early in the process. This involvement is especially important because legislation regarding employment and labor laws can vary significantly between countries and regions. By engaging human resources promptly, you ensure that the appropriate protocols and procedures are followed in accordance with local laws and regulations. Keep detailed records of all communication, especially if it involves non-performance or compliance problems. Depending on the severity, a coaching plan or PIP may not be necessary, as human resources typically handles cases of misdemeanor or misconduct directly.

Unfortunately, John exhibited minimal improvement during the PIP and was uncooperative, resorting to crying during calls. Although I was empathetic, I adhered to the company's leveling guide. Human resources keeps a copy of the PIP documentation in the employee's file. PIP serves as a precursor to potential termination if improvement is not seen.

MAKE THE FINAL CALL

The final step involves evaluating the individual's progress on the PIP and making a decision. If the employee successfully meets the defined expectations within the PIP time frame, the outcome is positive. If they continue to underperform, tough conversations are necessary. You may need to meet with human resources to discuss options, such as offering severance. If the employee chooses severance, they receive a salary for a set period and leave the company to pursue other opportunities. To handle the exit of the terminated employee smoothly and mitigate the effect on the team, refer to chapter 8, which outlines an action plan for seamless transition.

In John's case, because he couldn't meet expectations, human resources and I had to have a difficult conversation with him, ultimately leading to his decision to take severance and leave the company.

4.5.2 You win some, you lose some

Dealing with underperforming employees can require tough decisions, but not all cases end in termination. In one instance, a software engineer II showed signs of disengagement and missed deliverables. After identifying a shift in their interests toward project delivery, I suggested that they explore the role of a technical program manager (TPM). Through shadowing and mentorship, the employee successfully transitioned to the TPM role within three months, excelling on critical projects. Another engineer with gaps in technical skills was provided mentorship and training, ultimately improving within a time-boxed coaching plan of 60 days.

4.5.3 Communicating the outcome to the rest of the team

Communicating the outcome of employee performance problems to the team requires sensitivity and adherence to confidentiality agreements. Coordination with the human resources and legal departments is essential to ensure compliance with company regulations. Here are some key points to remember:

- Hold a meeting to inform team members of the employee's departure while respecting confidentiality guidelines and legal constraints.
- Expect questions but refrain from divulging specific details. Involve the human resources or legal teams if necessary.
- Remind the team of the company's values, goals, and expectations for behavior and performance. Emphasize the importance of moving forward and focusing on the team's current objectives.
- Reassure team members of their job security and clarify any changes in workload distribution.
- Emphasize the importance of professionalism and confidentiality in discussing the matter.
- Keep an open-door policy for team members to address any concerns or questions.
- Acknowledge the effect of the change on workload redistribution and ensure transparency in communication.
- Keep an eye on any instances where the terminated employee's influence is still present and address them promptly. Redirect conversations or decisions back to the current team dynamics and leadership.

4.5.4   *Managing an underperforming team*

Managing an underperforming team can be challenging, especially for new leaders who are still familiarizing themselves with team dynamics. Although there's no one-size-fits-all solution, a systematic approach can help address underperformance. Start by identifying the root causes, which can include ineffective leadership, skill gaps, or lack of motivation. Seek secondary input to gain different perspectives and identify potential mismatches in team dynamics. Look out for behaviors that may be influencing team performance negatively, such as task spillovers in sprints.

On one team I managed, repeated task spillovers indicated underperformance. Upon investigation, I found that communication problems led to duplicate efforts and missed deadlines. Two engineers inadvertently worked on the same task, and another went on vacation without proper communication, causing delays. Additionally, feedback from one-on-ones highlighted prolonged code review times due to lack of collaboration. Addressing these problems required improved communication and collaboration within the team.

For a manager, establishing clear communication channels and fostering teamwork can mitigate underperformance and improve productivity. When you're handling and turning around an underperforming team, these tasks are key:

- *Observe and learn.* Begin by observing the team dynamics and listening to team members' perspectives without rushing to intervene or urging a doer mindset.
- *Set clear expectations.* Communicate identified gaps and expectations clearly, fostering an environment where team members feel comfortable speaking up. Use tools such as anonymous surveys if necessary and ensure clarity on team goals and timelines. Identify and address inefficient processes that hinder team productivity, which could include lengthy pipelines, unreliable tests, time constraints due to tech debt, or ineffective communication channels with other teams. Simply setting clear expectations isn't sufficient; you must actively work to improve processes and remove blockers to ensure team effectiveness.
- *Provide support.* Provide necessary tools, resources, and mentorship to help team members improve their performance and skills.
- *Monitor performance and provide feedback.* Keep track of team performance, offer constructive feedback, and identify areas for individual growth. Trust your team but verify to avoid surprises later.
- *Hold crucial conversations.* If some team members continue to underperform despite support and feedback, be prepared to make tough decisions to address the problem promptly without upsetting team effectiveness.

In addressing one of my underperforming teams, I began by acknowledging the problems and facilitating a data-driven discussion during a team meeting. I encouraged input from team members and cross-functional partners, involving them in finding solutions. Together, we implemented measures such as the following:

- Using Slack for communication
- Updating the Jira board in real time
- Proactively addressing vacation schedules in stand-ups
- Introducing extra catch-up time for open discussions

These measures, combined with individual coaching during one-on-ones, led to improved productivity and turnaround for the team. When addressing underperformance, it's crucial to focus on incremental changes and use data-driven measurements to assess success. With practice and experience, engineering leaders can effectively navigate such challenges by following these fundamental principles.

Although much attention is often given to high and low performers, it's also essential to recognize the importance of average performers to the team. These individuals consistently meet expectations, ensuring that work flows smoothly and acting as a cohesive force for the team. They may not stand out, but their reliability is invaluable.

Furthermore, it's crucial to acknowledge that everyone experiences different phases in their personal and professional lives. Some periods may see individuals excel and strive for growth; other times may see them maintain current performance levels due to life circumstances or personal challenges.

For average performers, similar strategies apply, including setting clear goals, providing regular feedback, and offering positive reinforcement. The emphasis may differ, however, with less focus on autonomy and authority and a greater emphasis on manageable challenges to ensure that they can handle their workload effectively.

What do other leaders have to say?

Performance reviews are an important part of being an EM and should be approached with utmost responsibility. I always look for outcomes achieved by an individual rather than the activities which he is doing. Being outcome-driven to rate someone is the right model as it serves good for both employees and the business. A typical performance review should talk about outcomes in the tenure, areas of improvement, and peer perspective.

—Madhur Kathuria, Engineering Leader at Microsoft,
formerly with Moengage, Oracle, and IIT

Managing people is very different from managing projects and deliverables. People have different needs and expectations that change with time. Keeping high performers engaged requires understanding their needs and expectations at different stages of their careers and being able to help them fulfill them. Some things high performers on my team generally appreciate are visibility and acknowledgment for their work, the opportunity to solve complex problems, and being able to learn and teach new trends and technologies. Some other expectations I have entertained include accommodating different working hours for a limited period, remote/in-office working requests, and nomination to extracurricular activities and conferences.

—Adish Agarwal, Director, Software Development at Audible, Inc.

(continued)

To grow managers, in many organizations, new managers are high-performing ICs who either are pressed into it organizationally (that's the only way to continue growing) or are looking to see if it is a fit for them. I consider team leaders and squad leads in this grouping. Frequently, IC skills do not translate directly to management skills. As a result, new managers need patience.

For more senior managers, I use manager growth as a mechanism to also demonstrate my career growth. By delegating tasks to managers above their role and helping them manage through those tasks, you increasingly demonstrate that they are growing into the next role and that you can grow folks into that role. In the past, this has included demonstrating that a manager working for me was ready for my role, and since I was able to grow into that, so was I.

—Nathan Bourgoin, Chief Technology Officer at Alakazam, Inc., Technical Adviser, and Engineering Leader

Many first-time managers (myself included!) don't realize how different it is to manage versus being an IC. Your job is no longer to produce work but to build the team that produces the work. I help my managers frame their efforts and measurement in the three axes of people, process, and product.

—Jean Bredeche, Head of Engineering at Patch, formerly with Robinhood, Quantopian, and Hubspot

For managing performance, providing feedback early and often if important. No sugarcoating low performance and providing constructive feedback is the key. Data collection and preparation of the message are key. Getting feedback from teammates and other external stakeholders helps to get a full picture.

—Rajakumar Sambasivam, Delivery Manager at Microsoft

For managing performance, we must continuously observe our team member's performance and provide in-time coaching and feedback. My top three practices are set clear KPIs for the role, provide in-time coaching and feedback aligned with their goals, and recognize small wins.

—Sumit Kumar, System Engineering Manager at Cisco

To grow managers, let people run with things, get them training, and use one-on-ones to learn about them.

—Larry Gordan, Managing Director at Emtec, Inc.

Performance review discussions should never come as a surprise to either party. As time passes, email yourself notes and collect tidbits of information about personal successes and efforts, challenges, acknowledgment from others, and areas where growth was noticed for each of your direct reports. These will help you when it comes time for crafting an accurate and SMART review that will help your employee improve and grow.

—Bruce Bergman, Manager at Lytx

4.6   *Stop and think: Practice questions*

1   Does my company value the importance of performance management?

2   Are my engineers aware of the roles and responsibilities expected of them at their job level?

3   What are some of the best practices I have seen other managers exhibit when it comes to managing performance?

4   Does my organization identify leaders from within the organization and help develop them?

5   Does my organization help provide the right support and training resources for individuals to grow?

6   What is one of the most difficult conversations I have had with an employee?

7   Why was that conversation difficult for me? If I were to go back in time, what would I change about the conversation?

8   How can I recognize my team members for their good work?

9   Are there any gaps in the current performance management system in my organization?

Summary

- Managing performance is a nuanced art that involves understanding team members' motivations, providing coaching and feedback, and fostering growth. It's an ongoing cycle that requires transparency, fairness, and continuous review.

- Performance management offers benefits such as career planning, feedback alignment with company goals, and improved retention rates.

- Performance reviews involve evaluation, calibration, and conducting reviews with data-driven preparation.

- High performers are valuable assets and require autonomy, appreciation, and challenge to be managed effectively.

- Conversely, managing underperformers involves identifying root causes, providing coaching through a coaching plan, and potentially implementing a PIP if performance does not improve.

- For EMs, simply setting clear expectations isn't sufficient; we must actively work with the team to improve processes and remove blockers to ensure team effectiveness.

- Managing team performance requires similar approaches, including setting clear expectations and offering support through one-on-one interactions.

- Communication and planning are crucial, especially in managing employees, to balance confidentiality and team stability.

Delegation: Learn to let go

> *Don't be a bottleneck. If a matter is not a decision for the president or you, delegate it. Force responsibility down and out. Find problem areas, add structure, and delegate. The pressure is to do the reverse. Resist it.*
>
> —Donald Rumsfeld, former U.S. Secretary of Defense

It's Monday morning, and you're gearing up for a busy week when, on top of everything else, an urgent email lands in your inbox, requesting a new operational dashboard. With deadlines looming and performance reviews on the agenda, you're feeling stretched thin.

Delegation comes to your rescue. Delegation is the key to managing overwhelming tasks. By entrusting responsibilities to others, you can alleviate pressure and foster team collaboration. Effective delegation involves trusting others' abilities, removing bottlenecks, promoting communication, and looking at the bigger picture (systems thinking). It's not about passing off work arbitrarily, but about empowering others to contribute meaningfully.

The concept of delegation can be categorized into two types: planned and unplanned. Planned delegation involves strategic collaboration with individuals ahead of time, using tasks or projects as opportunities for growth. Conversely, unplanned delegation occurs when tasks arise unexpectedly, potentially leading to effective delegation if handled properly but often rushed through.

In this chapter, we'll explore the principles of effective delegation and address common questions about when, why, to whom, and how to delegate. We'll also introduce a practical framework for delegation to help navigate daily challenges and empower others to delegate effectively.

5.1 The art of delegation

Delegation is an art that requires you to move away from doer mentality and step into coaching mentality. It enables career growth and leadership development for your team members. Effective leaders use delegation to amplify their effect, extending their influence through others' actions. When you empower team members, tasks are completed efficiently, and each receives the necessary attention. Despite the many benefits of delegation, however, some engineering managers (EMs) may hesitate to practice it. Let's look at some of the reasons for their hesitation.

5.1.1 Avoid the do-it-yourself attitude

As humans, we lean toward doing tasks ourselves, especially if we're familiar with them. Teaching someone else can seem time-consuming initially, but the long-term benefits are substantial. Relying on past methods may seem efficient, but it can stifle innovation and lead to bottlenecks.

Let's consider a basic example: completing ten similar tasks. Doing them individually takes ten days. Let's say you decide to delegate and teach another person, which requires a three-day knowledge transfer session and an additional day when you show the other person how to do the work and they shadow you, leading to a total of four days (figure 5.1).

After these four days, however, you have the task delegated, and you saved six days' worth of your work. Although there's a natural inclination to handle familiar tasks ourselves, delegating these tasks can be a valuable opportunity for team members to learn and for managers to develop their coaching skills.

1 task = 1 day worth of effort
10 tasks = 10*1 = 10 days

With delegation:

Knowledge transfer = 3 days
Shadow task = 1 day
Total days spent = 3+1 = 4 days

Figure 5.1 Days of work with and without delegation

5.1.2 Don't be the sole knowledge bearer

Improper delegation can lead to a single person's becoming the sole holder of knowledge, creating a bottleneck for the team. Some new EMs may resist involving others, fearing loss of control. This resistance deprives team members of growth opportunities, however, and sends the wrong message about trust and   collaboration.

Consider a scenario in which a senior engineer, now an EM, relies heavily on personal knowledge rather than documentation. This approach can lead to what's called *tribal knowledge* because it remains undocumented, making it difficult for other engineers to fill knowledge gaps. Dependence on the EM as the sole source of expertise can hinder team scalability, especially during periods of increased workload. If the team is suddenly tasked with numerous important deliverables due to a shift in company priorities, the EM may struggle to address all knowledge gaps, resulting in delays and inefficiencies. To mitigate these risks, it's crucial to spread knowledge throughout the team and avoid relying solely on one individual.

LACKING TRUST

New EMs in particular may struggle with trust, leading to controlling behavior that affects team performance and morale. This lack of trust often arises from doubts about team members' judgment. If a senior engineer displays punctuality and knowledge-sharing problems, the EM may begin distrusting all team members, resulting in micromanagement and excessive reminders. In addition, this lack of trust and generalization can confuse team members and lower morale. Alternatively, providing feedback and corrective measures directly to the senior engineer can address the problem more effectively. Micromanagement not only consumes the EM's time, but also reflects a desire for perfectionism and a reluctance to trust the team.

FEELING GUILTY ABOUT OFFLOADING WORK TO OTHERS

EMs may experience guilt when delegating tasks originally planned for themselves, but it's crucial to understand that delegating tasks empowers others and contributes to their growth. Instead of feeling guilty, EMs should view delegation as a positive step. Furthermore, delegation doesn't absolve EMs of accountability. Although not all tasks need to be done exclusively by EMs, the managers remain accountable for ensuring that tasks are completed on time and accurately. It's essential to discern which tasks require the EM's involvement, particularly in people management, and which can be delegated appropriately. When new tasks arise, delegating them to an engineer can affect team velocity and focus. In such cases, the EM may take on the task temporarily to prevent immediate bottlenecks. The goal is to foster shared responsibility, provide growth opportunities, and manage time effectively.

If an EM is already overloaded with five crucial tasks, feelings of guilt may be valid if they simply offload two tasks to a senior engineer without thinking them through properly. But by following a systematic process of identifying suitable tasks for delegation, selecting the right person, and highlighting the value and career growth potential in taking up those tasks, the EM gives the senior engineer an opportunity to learn and grow. This approach creates a win–win situation, enabling the EM to scale their workload while offering meaningful development opportunities to team members.

Without delegation, EMs and leaders may become overwhelmed and unable to focus on the tasks that require their attention. But it's important to empower employees to succeed, which means giving them space to take ownership of delegated tasks while remaining accountable for the process. Therefore, being strategic about when, why, what, to whom, and how to delegate is crucial. In section 5.2, we'll explore the nuances between delegation and allocation, as well as how they differ from substitution.

5.2 *Delegation vs. allocation vs. substitution*

Now that we've explored delegation, let's see how it differs from allocation and substitution. Although all three concepts involve sharing work responsibility to achieve goals, the key distinction lies in execution and the level of support provided by the *delegator* (the person who delegates the task) to the *delegatee* (the person to whom the task is delegated).

5.2.1 *Delegation vs. allocation*

Distinguishing delegation from task allocation is crucial for ensuring appropriate task and personnel selection. Many people mistakenly view delegation and allocation as interchangeable, a misunderstanding that can lead to potential challenges. These approaches are distinct and have differing outcomes.

Consider the task of tracking project metrics. With task allocation, a software engineer is assigned responsibility for preparing and sharing project reports within a deadline, focusing solely on task completion.

By contrast, effective delegation starts with identifying an engineer who has interest or expertise in operational excellence—perhaps the team's operational excellence lead. You collaborate with them to set expectations, develop strategies, and provide support and autonomy for ongoing task completion. You also assure them of your approachability and readiness to assist when needed. This approach fosters trust, learning, and support, emphasizing the engineer's growth and development rather than just task completion.

Understanding the nuances between delegation and task allocation is pivotal in fostering a culture of continuous learning, empowering team members, and enhancing their long-term skill sets through effective delegation. How tasks are assigned or taught makes all the difference. In table 5.1, you can see more details on the differences between the two approaches.

Table 5.1 Differences between allocation and delegation

Aspect	Allocation	Delegation
Skills	We use allocation when we simply want the work to be done. That's it.	We use delegation when we want the work to be done but are also looking for some learning of skills that will continue beyond the immediate task.
Process	Allocation is an instruction-based method in which the person follows instructions to complete the work.	In this coaching-/mentoring-based approach, the person is told what to but not how to do it. The individual is given responsibility and ownership to execute the tasks.

Table 5.1   Differences between allocation and delegation *(continued)*

Aspect	Allocation	Delegation
Approach	This approach is "assign and forget." In allocation, ownership is with the new person who's working on the task: after you assign it, you can forget about it.	Delegation is also assigned, but you are part of the process along the way, doing check-ins, feedback, and the retrospective. This process is more continuous. With delegation, the EM still has complete ownership and accountability for the task, even though it's being performed by a delegatee under their supervision.
Authority	Here, the authority is handed over to the new person, and they are accountable for completing the task.	Here, the person delegating the task provides authority to the delegatee that is essential for the completion of the task. But the delegator keeps the rest of the authority, as ultimately, they are solely responsible for the task.
Long-term opportunities	As part of allocation, we focus on getting the work done without necessarily considering long-term growth opportunities.	One outcome of delegation is to help the person who is delegated a task to grow in the job and get a boost in their morale and trust.

As highlighted in the table, how tasks are conveyed and executed to others can determine whether the results are short-term or enduring.

5.2.2   *Delegation vs. substitution*

In delegation, the delegator maintains full accountability for the task while empowering the delegatee to execute it. Although the delegatee is *responsible* for task completion, the delegator remains ultimately *accountable* for the outcome and should provide guidance and oversight to ensure success. Delegation involves entrusting someone with authority and autonomy to complete the task, fostering their growth in the process.

On the other hand, substitution occurs when someone is entirely replaced and is no longer accountable for the tasks at hand. Substitution is appropriate when the individual will not resume the task in the future.

Suppose that you, as a manager, plan to be away from the office for six weeks due to travel plans. To cover your absence, you identify a senior engineer who is interested in becoming a manager over the long term and delegate your day-to-day tasks to them. This process involves providing support and guidance as needed, following a delegation framework.

By contrast, consider a scenario in which you established a new team from scratch at another company. Your role was to set up the team and ensure its smooth operation until a new manager was hired. When the team was stable, you hired a new manager to oversee the team's long-term management, effectively substituting another person for yourself. You were no longer responsible for the project.

Another classic example of substitution is grooming a high-performing engineer for promotion. As an EM, you may involve them in cross-functional partner meetings, initially shadowing you, and gradually taking on more active roles until they fully replace you in those meetings.

5.3 The when, why, what, who, and how of delegation

Delegation involves more than simply assigning tasks. Asking someone to attend a meeting on your behalf may not be delegation unless it aligns with that person's career development goals and aspirations. Let's unravel the intricacies of effective delegation and learn to maximize its benefits.

5.3.1 When and why to delegate

We cannot handle everything independently, especially in senior roles or leadership positions, which necessitates the delegation of tasks. Delegation becomes essential in several situations:

- *Maximizing available capacity and time*—In a fast-paced environment with approaching deadlines and competing priorities, delegation is crucial. By delegating tasks, we free our time to focus on critical tasks that require immediate attention, thereby achieving more and aligning with strategic goals. This approach also helps us maintain a healthy work–life balance and prevent burnout by averting overextension.
- *Grooming team members*—For EMs, prioritizing the growth and upskilling of team members is paramount. Delegating tasks that contribute to employees' career advancement creates new opportunities and fosters commitment. Setting stretch goals and providing necessary support allows team members to grow and balance their workloads effectively.
- *Using subject-matter experts (SMEs)*—SMEs play a crucial role in teams, akin to a conductor leading an orchestra. By delegating decision-making authority to SMEs, we allow them to lead in their areas of expertise, leading to more informed and more effective outcomes. If a decision is needed on the throttling strategy for backend services, an in-house expert or passionate engineer could lead the initiative. Delegating decision-making authority to the lead software engineer empowers them to analyze requirements, assess technical feasibility, and choose the most appropriate technologies and methodologies. This approach not only uses the expertise of team members, but also cultivates a sense of ownership and accountability, fostering professional growth and development. Ultimately, delegation to SMEs leads to better decisions and enhances team performance.
- *Delegating on behalf of others*—Delegation can also occur on behalf of others, such as when a team member is unavailable. Assigning tasks to other team members with additional information helps ensure smooth workflow and identifies potential bottlenecks or single points of failure.

When you are considering delegation, these questions can help you decide whether it is the right choice:

- Are the tasks I'm working on repeatable and easily transferable?
- Do I have SMEs on the team to make critical technical decisions?
- Will delegating some of my tasks create more opportunities for my engineers?
- Am I spending significant time on tasks that are less critical and can be delegated?
- Am I experiencing signs of burnout?
- Do my team members and I have a healthy work–life balance?

Although this list is not exhaustive, it serves as a helpful starting point for identifying situations in which delegation can be beneficial. Delegation is a multiple-step process that demonstrates investment in team growth, fosters a supportive environment, and enhances trust and confidence within the team.

5.3.2   *What task to delegate*

Not every task is suitable for delegation. Tasks with high criticality, such as reports shared with the C suite or performance reviews, should be handled by EMs and leaders due to their close involvement and confidentiality. Similarly, sensitive human resources matters should remain within a closed group.

Tasks approaching critical deadlines should be evaluated carefully before delegation, especially if the team is understaffed, to prevent burnout. But tasks such as progress reports on operational excellence can be delegated to on-call team members or an operational-excellence ambassador.

Additionally, you should avoid delegating tasks that require your unique perspective. It's crucial to select tasks that set the delegatee up for success. Consider breaking tasks into smaller subtasks for better tracking and delegation, assigning smaller tasks to new team members and allowing experienced members to handle more extensive tasks independently. By choosing the right tasks for delegation, you maximize efficiency and ensure successful outcomes.

Repetitive tasks such as providing quarterly summaries of team progress to leadership often burden EMs. Templatizing such reports allows you to coach senior engineers to create them, offering career visibility for them while freeing EM time for you. This approach involves conducting knowledge transfer sessions and demonstrations to equip team members with the necessary skills and knowledge. Despite task repeatability, ongoing supervision ensures support and direction, matching task delegation to suitable team members. Complex reports suit senior engineers, whereas simpler tasks may be delegated elsewhere. In my experience, delegating operational-excellence review meetings to a senior engineer not only liberated my time for strategic initiatives, but also aligned with their career aspirations. That's effective delegation.

On my recent team, I delegated responsibility for organizing and leading operational-excellence review meetings to a senior engineer. This delegation not only allowed me to allocate more time to focus on other strategic initiatives, but also gave the senior engineer valuable opportunities to lead and facilitate meetings. Additionally, it enabled them to gain insight into critical team tasks, particularly regarding technical debt, aligning with the career aspirations we discussed during our one-on-one meetings. When you're considering delegation, these questions can help you choose the right tasks:

- Have I chosen the appropriate task for delegation?
- Is the task repetitive?
- Do more pressing tasks require my immediate attention?
- Is the task suitable for delegation?
- Do I have the time to train someone else to complete the task?
- What are the potential consequences if the delegation is unsuccessful?
- Do any sensitive problems or requirements prohibit delegation?

When the task has been selected for delegation, the next step is identifying the right person to execute it. Several core factors can aid in this decision-making process.

5.3.3 *Whom to delegate to*

When the task to delegate is identified, the subsequent step is pinpointing the appropriate individual (delegatee) to perform it. Sometimes, you want to identify multiple individuals to delegate tasks to, facilitating a divide-and-conquer approach and ensuring that tasks are aligned with each person's abilities. The objective is to match the right individuals with the right responsibilities.

Solid reasoning should underlie the selection of someone for a delegated task. Understanding their motivations, strengths, weaknesses, and sources of inspiration can aid in this regard. Effective one-on-one meetings serve as a tool for learning about these aspects of team members. By delegating tasks that align with their learning and career aspirations, we pass on the task and also create opportunities for personal growth in the long term.

When deciding whom to delegate tasks to, fairness is essential. Tasks should not always be assigned to top-performing employees; aim to create equal opportunities for all team members.

A situation from my early career as a senior software engineer highlights the effectiveness of planned delegation. My manager, aware of my aspiration to transition to a management role, collaborated with me on a time-limited plan. As part of this plan, I was delegated the task of managing an intern for the summer. This task involved setting up their project, providing guidance throughout the summer, and conducting weekly one-on-one meetings. Proper documentation was essential for the intern's end-of-internship debrief. This delegation aligned perfectly with my career goal, providing me an early opportunity to explore mentoring and management responsibilities and to assess my interest in such roles before officially transitioning.

Delegation isn't limited to your direct team members. It's essential to consider delegating tasks to individuals outside your team's traditional scope, such as business users, product managers, and members of cross-functional teams if their roles align better with the task at hand.

On our team, we used to assign responsibility for providing biweekly progress reports on various projects and programs to project tech leads (engineers). I recognized, however, that this responsibility diverted valuable time from engineers who were already providing updates during team stand-ups and project meetings. Instead, this task was more suitable for someone who was managing at a program level but did not have deep engineering expertise.

In our organization, we had a technical program manager who attended our stand-ups but focused primarily on consolidating reports at the organizational level. To address this situation, I scheduled a one-on-one meeting with the program manager and proposed that they take ownership of the granular team-level and consolidated reports. This approach allowed them to stay closely connected to the team's products and facilitated easier creation of the consolidated report. Additionally, it enabled them to go above and beyond their regular duties, build relationships with engineers and EMs from various subteams, and strengthen their work. We discussed and agreed on a plan of execution for this delegation, clarifying how the process would work. When you're considering delegation, these questions will help you select the appropriate person to whom to delegate a project:

- Is the person capable of handling the task?
- How will this task benefit the individual?
- Is someone else better suited for the task?
- Who is eager to take on new responsibilities and learn?
- Whose career aspirations align with the task?

When we've delegated a task, our job isn't done. We must ensure a win–win situation by providing necessary support and resources for the individual to succeed. The distinction between allocation and delegation is crucial, as effective delegation involves providing support throughout the task.

5.3.4   *How to delegate and support*

When it comes to actual delegation, involving other team members is vital for success. It's important to share the vision, reasoning, and context that explain why the chosen individual is best suited for the task. By explaining how the task aligns with organizational goals, team objectives, and the individual's career aspirations, we add a personal touch and motivate them to excel. Delegation isn't just about assigning work; it's also about fostering learning and growth, creating a multiplier effect within the team. This situation is an opportunity to demonstrate trust in the individual's abilities and empower them as the rightful owner of the task. Such actions boost teamwide morale and cultivate stronger long-term relationships.

During delegation, timing and conditions are critical. Even if you have identified the right tasks and the ideal person to delegate to, external factors such as tight deadlines can impede success. You must set realistic expectations, whether by adjusting scope or involving more team members for parallel work. Clear communication of timelines from the outset is essential for preventing confusion. Planning for delegation should account for external factors from the start, ensuring a successful outcome.

When you first meet with a team member to discuss delegating a task to them, think of the meeting as a sales call to the employee in which you share job prospects and team details, as well as gauge their interest and commitment. Communicate tasks effectively so that they feel like part of the decision-making process. You can do this communication in a one-on-one meeting, allowing you to address any questions they may have.

An effective exercise is to create a list of tasks and survey team members to gauge interest, with the caveat that you'll match tasks to interests as much as possible. This approach keeps communication open, considers team members' aspirations and choices, and boosts team engagement. Understanding the when, what, why, to whom, and how of delegation helps leaders make informed decisions when assigning tasks and selecting individuals.

5.4   *Framework for delegation*

Let's summarize the delegation framework:

1   *Understand the why.* Assess the situation and recognize the benefits of delegation for engineers.
2   *Identify tasks.* Determine transferable tasks, assess time and energy availability, and evaluate potential risks.
3   *Choose the right person.* Match tasks to individual strengths and abilities, highlighting long-term benefits and personal development opportunities.
4   *Implement effective delegation:*
    – Provide necessary support and focus on what needs to be accomplished.
    – Clearly outline tasks, goals, and performance criteria for clarity.
    – Be available for support and feedback, or assign a buddy if you're unavailable.
    – Equip individuals with tools and resources for success.
    – Foster ownership and accountability to enhance job satisfaction.
    – Offer constructive feedback to recognize effort and identify growth opportunities.

Figure 5.2 shows the details of this framework. This simple yet effective framework can streamline the delegation process and keep team members engaged and motivated.

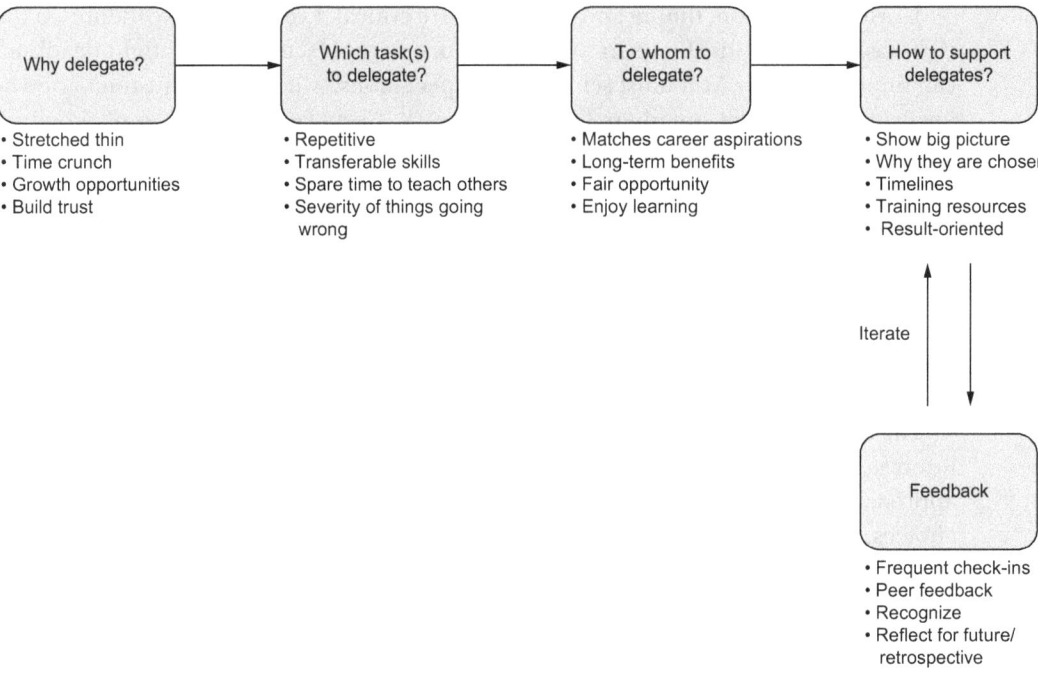

Figure 5.2   Framework for delegation of tasks. We start with why we should delegate; then we identify the task(s) to delegate, identify the person(s) to whom to delegate, and decide how to delegate and support them.

5.4.1   *Supporting delegation*

To ensure successful delegation, it's essential to communicate the support available to the team member and create a win–win situation. This communication includes providing necessary information and resources for success. Effective delegation involves understanding the team member's skill set and the skills required for the task and then addressing any gaps to set them up for success. Following are key things to consider, but given a specific situation, they can vary:

- *Communication*—Clear communication is essential for successful delegation. When assigning tasks, explain why you chose this person, highlight the benefits, and clarify your support as their manager. Maintain an open-door policy and seek early feedback by having them repeat and explain the task to ensure understanding. Effective delegation hinges on clear two-way communication, which involves not only conveying task expectations and goals, but also actively listening to feedback and questions from the delegatee. You'll read more about the communication framework in chapter 9.

- *Mutual expectations and agreement*—When you're delegating tasks, clarify the desired outcome and establish agreed-upon timelines and processes. This process includes aligning on the task's start time, frequency of check-ins, coordination methods, key delivery milestones, and the final outcome. Communicate the task's priority, any problems, blockers, or risks, preferred communication channels and response times, and whether documentation is required for future reference and knowledge transfer. Transparency is key, so discuss these details up front. Additionally, agree on contingency plans to prevent surprises if the task exceeds the established timelines. Emphasize the importance of documentation to ensure transparency and clarity for all parties involved.

- *Training and resources*—When you've identified skill gaps between what's needed for the task and the individual's current skills, conduct a gap analysis and determine resources to bridge those gaps. This task may involve pair-programming sessions, knowledge transfer, demos, and learning resources from platforms such as YouTube or LinkedIn. Be cautious, however: if the knowledge/skill gap is too significant for the person to perform the task effectively, you may be overstretching them and hindering their success. In such a case, reassess whether that person is the right fit for the task.

- *Focus on outcome and results*—Avoid assuming previous knowledge and clearly communicate the desired outcomes and results of the task. Focus on the what and who rather than the how, steering clear of micromanagement and rigid approaches. Strive for a balance between being hands-on and hands-off, granting ownership, accountability, and autonomy to foster innovation. When you're assigning an engineer to create an engineering metrics report, for example, provide inputs and expectations without prescribing specific tools. Granting autonomy encourages fresh ideas and builds trust.

- *Feedback/follow-up mechanism*—Delegation goes beyond simple task allocation, involving continuous follow-up and commitment to ongoing learning. Feedback is essential in this process, helping identify areas for improvement. As EMs, we should focus on positive reinforcement, acknowledging what is going well and sharing positive feedback from peers or cross-functional partners to boost morale. Recognizing and rewarding hard work strengthens manager–employee relationships. Additionally, feedback gives you an opportunity to reflect on the delegation process, learn from it, and identify future opportunities. Constructive feedback facilitates improvement and strengthens the delegation process within the team.

Mutually agree with the individual on the cadence and method for progress sharing to avoid relying solely on one big check-in and follow-ups. This approach ensures accountability for checkpoints and prevents slippage of task-delivery timelines while providing support to the person who will perform the delegated task. Afterward, conduct a retrospective meeting with the person to identify common learnings and improve future processes. As depicted in figure 5.3, key elements of supporting delegation include communicating, setting mutual expectations, providing training and resources, focusing on outcomes, and establishing a feedback mechanism.

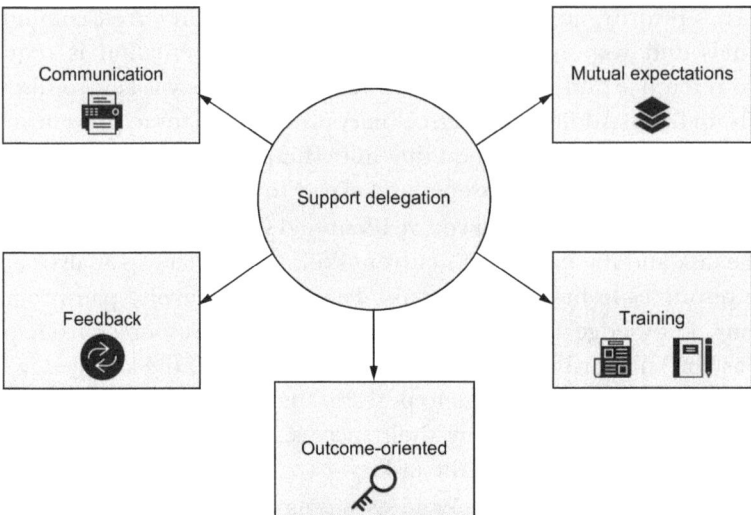

Figure 5.3   Supporting delegation is crucial for success. Providing the right resources ensures that individuals are set up for success.

When you're considering delegation, these questions will help you to do it effectively:

- Have you clearly communicated the desired outcome of the delegation?
- Have you delegated the appropriate level of authority needed to accomplish the task?
- Have you communicated the success criteria for the job?
- Does the team member feel supported in carrying out the delegated task?
- Are regular follow-ups conducted based on mutually agreed-on milestones?
- Is constructive feedback provided to improve performance?
- Is recognition given for team members' hard work?
- What practices should be continued, stopped, or started for improvement?

5.4.2   *Tracking delegation*

We've discussed delegation, but eventually, we want to scale. Today, we manage a single team, but six months from now, we will manage three teams. How do we manage and track all our delegations and scale over time?

Table 5.2 is a basic delegation-tracker template that you can use to streamline multiple delegations. You can also use scalable project management tools such as Jira and Azure DevOps for more comprehensive tracking of delegations and tasks. These tools offer features such as task assignment, due-date tracking, and progress monitoring, which can help reduce confusion and keep you on top of all delegated tasks even as you scale your management responsibilities across multiple teams.

Table 5.2   Sample delegation tracker

Task description	Delegated to	Why delegated	Timelines	Latest progress	Status	Notes/comments/feedback
Preparation of an operational dashboard to measure incoming trouble tickets	Alice	Alice is the team's operational-excellence (OE) ambassador. She is passionate about operational excellence (OE), which is one of her key focus areas.	Two weeks. Estimated time of delivery (ETD): Sept. 11	Requirements have been gathered. Alice is working on setting up the Looker dashboard.	In progress	Alice is working with Charlie on overall coordination of the template for the OE dashboard.
Onboarding new hires to the team	Bob	Bob's long-term goal is to transition to an EM role. He enjoys the people aspect of the role and would like to gain experience on this front.	Two months. ETD: Oct. 30	Bob has filled out the onboarding template for the new hire. Next, he will identify an onboarding task for them.	In progress	The joining date of the new hire is Sept. 5.

This delegation tracker facilitates easy, seamless planning and tracking of delegated tasks. Sharing the tracker with team members promotes transparency and accountability. Although the provided template serves as a foundation, feel free to customize it according to your specific needs. You can opt to track overall task status rather than granular details, for example, while monitoring any risks that may cause delays.

With the core fundamentals of delegation understood, let's move on. In section 5.5, we will explore how to create a multiplier effect by sharing our experiences and teaching delegation to others.

5.5   *Teaching delegation to others*

Now that we've grasped the essence of delegation, we understand that as we advance in our roles, we'll encounter situations in which we both delegate tasks and need to train our team members to become proficient delegators themselves. Consider a scenario: a staff engineer on your team is overwhelmed with critical projects. They need time to refine their delegation skills by entrusting tasks to other senior engineers to maintain motivation. Your role as a leader is to identify such opportunities and take responsibility for teaching delegation to others within your team. Drawing on your own experiences and stories will help reassure and comfort those you're training, effectively passing down your learnings and creating a multiplier effect by empowering those around you (figure 5.4).

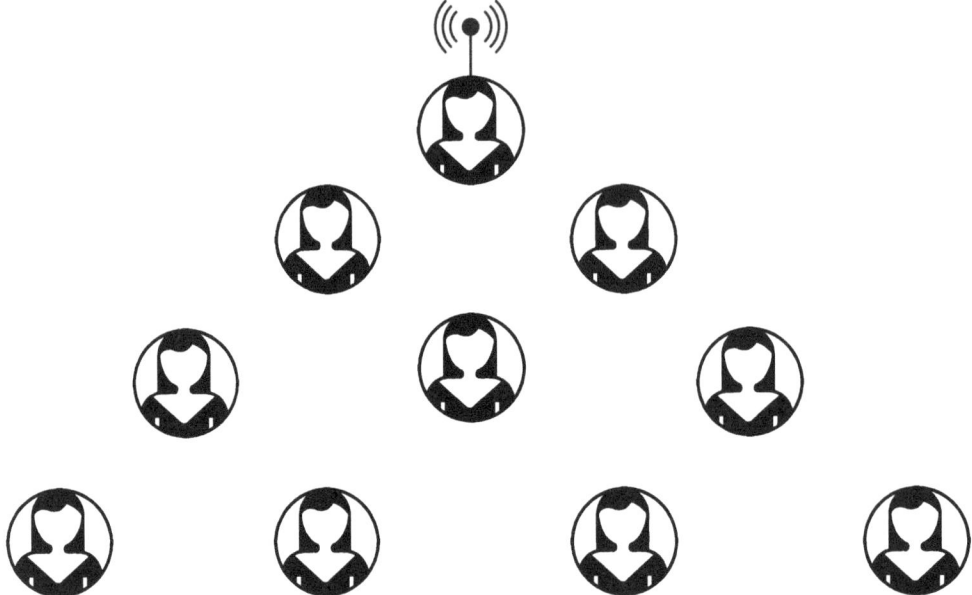

Figure 5.4   Teaching delegation to others creates a multiplier effect.

Here are some actionable steps you can take as you teach others the art of delegation:

- Conduct one-on-one sessions to explain the importance of delegation and its benefits.
- Share your personal experiences and lessons learned from your own journey of learning to delegate, fostering an organic relationship.
- Assist in identifying tasks that team members can delegate and provide opportunities for them to practice delegation.
- Offer resources and express your support throughout the process, serving as a sounding board for any challenges or obstacles they may encounter.
- Maintain a coaching mindset by encouraging them to brainstorm solutions to difficult situations rather than simply providing answers.
- Recognize and acknowledge their efforts while providing constructive feedback to aid mutual growth and improvement.

I recently mentored a staff software engineer on my team who was feeling overwhelmed after being promoted from senior engineer. In our one-on-one discussion, she stated that she was struggling to balance her previous responsibilities with her new ones. Recognizing the need for delegation,

I shared the benefits and recounted my own challenges in transitioning to a managerial role. I emphasized the fact that delegation is a skill that requires practice and learning. Together, we identified specific scenarios in which delegation would be appropriate. She could delegate responsibility for running project meetings to a senior engineer, for example, allowing them to develop communication skills and gain visibility with cross-functional partners.

Additionally, I recommended some reading material (https://mng.bz/9dd8) and outlined my vision for the delegation process. I encouraged her to use a delegation tracker as she expanded her responsibilities. Two months later, she successfully embraced delegation, strategically selecting tasks and providing coaching to other engineers to foster growth opportunities.

This case exemplifies successful delegation. Not all instances will proceed smoothly, however. In section 5.6, we'll explore scenarios in which delegation may fail due to ineffective practices or external factors, along with strategies to address the problems.

5.6   When delegation goes wrong

Delegation is a powerful management tool, but if it's not used carefully, it can lead to adverse consequences for the company and individuals involved. Selecting the wrong person for a delegated task can result in wasted time and hinder personal growth and development. In such cases, it may be necessary to rescind the delegation, although this action doesn't equate to failure; instead, it may require exploring alternative approaches to achieve the desired outcomes. Here are some common reasons why delegation can go wrong:

- *Lack of clarity*—Vague instructions or unclear goals can lead to misunderstandings and subpar results.
- *Overdelegation*—Delegating too much too soon or to the wrong person can overwhelm team members, leading to stress, burnout, and decreased productivity. Assigning tasks to a new junior engineer who may need more guidance due to their newness in the role can be problematic. In such cases, it's crucial to find the right balance between providing guidance and allowing autonomy for successful task completion. EMs must embrace mistakes and view them as learning opportunities rather than shy away from delegation. Instead of resorting to upward delegation, in which you take tasks back under your control, it's better to collaborate with team members to address problems and develop a path forward. When you and your team work together to solve problems and foster a strong partnership, delegation can lead to success. As in playing chess, training and positioning the right pieces (team members) are key.

- *Micromanagement*—Excessive oversight after delegation can stifle creativity and autonomy. Constantly checking in, second-guessing decisions, or requiring frequent updates undermines trust and demotivates team members, negating the benefits of delegation.
- *Missed development opportunities*—Delegating only routine or low-impact tasks may save time initially, but you miss the chance to develop employees' skills and confidence. It's essential to balance delegation with opportunities for growth and challenge to foster professional development.
- *Failure to provide support*—Delegation requires ongoing support and guidance through necessary resources, training, or assistance. Failing to provide support can lead to frustration and errors.
- *Ignored feedback*—When you don't seek input or feedback from team members, you may overlook valuable insights and alternative approaches.
- *Failure to require accountability*—Delegating without accountability can result in a lack of ownership and responsibility for tasks.

Early in my career as an EM, I embraced delegation, but one situation taught me a crucial lesson. I assigned a critical project to a relatively new junior engineer without providing adequate details or guidance. Excited to entrust responsibility, I gave the engineer only a brief overview of the project objectives and timeline. Unfortunately, I failed to provide clear expectations on the milestones, which would unblock sister teams as development continued; I assumed that the engineer would figure out the milestones independently.

As the project progressed, it became clear that my approach had backfired. The engineer struggled, missing deadlines for the milestones and delivering subpar work, causing frustration for both of us. Also, the project was delayed by a few weeks as the sister teams failed to start the integration work with our backend service. Realizing my mistake, I scheduled a meeting with the engineer to discuss challenges and offer support. I openly admitted my error, apologized, and listened to their concerns. Together, we identified communication gaps and devised a plan. I provided clear instructions, outlined the milestones and expected timelines, and offered ongoing support. I also paired them with a seasoned engineer for technical advice. I scheduled regular check-ins to monitor progress, provide feedback, and address concerns promptly. From this experience, I learned the importance of effective communication in delegation. I committed to approaching delegation with greater care and an attitude of continuous learning.

In summary, delegation is a vital skill for leaders who aim to expand their roles and manage broader teams effectively. Mastering delegation helps prevent burnout and frees time for higher-priority tasks. It enables EMs to think strategically and gain a comprehensive view of their teams and projects. Delegating tasks also demonstrates trust and investment in the growth of team members, fostering confidence, accountability, and motivation.

For those who are new to delegation, starting with small tasks and gradually progressing to more significant responsibilities is key. Embracing a shared-responsibility mindset strengthens team culture, boosts motivation, enhances employee retention, and ultimately leads to effective delegation practices.

What do other leaders have to say?

Not only is delegating work crucial, but equally vital is providing the necessary support for individuals to accomplish their tasks. This approach should foster a learning experience, enabling them to grasp the fundamentals thoroughly. Consequently, if they need to repeat the task, they will have acquired the groundwork and be able to handle it independently next time.

—Sanjay Gupta, General Manager at HCL Technologies

Be lazy after you have delegated. That means trusting them to take their own calls and correct them only if needed. Let them own their choices and outcomes.

—Madhur Kathuria, Engineering Leader at Microsoft,
formerly with Moengage, Oracle, and IIT

For me, the biggest challenge for delegation is becoming comfortable with solutions different from how I would accomplish something. I practice this daily by asking my team to ask me questions like "Here is how I am thinking about doing XYZ" rather than "How should I do this thing?" I then try to hold myself accountable by asking myself "Will this have the intended outcome?" instead of "Is this how I would do it?"

—Nathan Bourgoin, Chief Technology Officer at Alakazam, Inc.,
Technical Adviser, and Engineering Leader

The most important aspect of delegation is trust. You have to trust people to do the work that you don't have time to do. At the minimum, you must trust that they will execute it well. In the best case, you trust they will do it better than you could because of their experience or perspective in the area.

—Jean Bredeche, Head of Engineering at Patch,
formerly with Robinhood, Quantopian, and Hubspot

Delegation goes wrong when the person does not understand the request or is not the right person for the task. I delegated a task to one of my architects to manage a customer request. As the architect is technology-focused and did not entirely understand the business effect, the output fell short of the business needs.

—Rajakumar Sambasivam, Delivery Manager at Microsoft

There was a time when delegation went wrong. I had an engineer back me up in an escalation. However, I didn't spend enough time with this person to prepare for customers' expectations and politics. The lack of preparation annoyed the customer, and we almost lost their trust by the end of the call, which took several more weeks of effort to restore.

—Sumit Kumar, System Engineering Manager at Cisco

(continued)
Delegating is the art of letting go. I consider it an art because it's part of trust, empowerment, and growth (for both parties). You're describing a "painting" for your delegate on what needs to be done, giving them permission to achieve it as they see fit, and trusting them to accomplish the task on your behalf. Sometimes, the picture can surprise you and need touch-ups and maybe even repainting. Other times, it can be a masterpiece showing that everyone worked together towards the same end vision. Over time, delegation becomes easier and easier, and the results more reliable and repeatable.

—Bruce Bergman, Manager at Lytx

5.7   Stop and think: Practice questions

1 Give an example of a time when you had to delegate a task.
2 How did you go about choosing the right person for the task?
3 Give an example of a time when the delegation went wrong.
4 What would you do differently if you had a time machine and could reverse the situation?
5 Is someone on my team better suited to do a particular task than me?
6 Will this work occur again in the future, and is it a good candidate for delegation?

Summary

- Effective delegation is a crucial leadership skill that involves entrusting tasks to promote learning, growth, and development. It necessitates adopting a coaching mindset rather than a doer mentality.
- When executed well, delegation benefits both leaders and team members, allowing leaders to focus on strategic goals while providing growth opportunities for team members.
- Reluctance to delegate may stem from various factors, such as control problems or lack of trust in team members.
- Understanding the differences among delegation, allocation, and substitution can guide informed decisions about task management.
- A delegation framework provides structure for identifying suitable tasks, selecting delegatees, and supporting the delegation process effectively.
- Using a delegation tracker helps monitor progress and provide support as needed.
- Effective delegation aligns tasks with individual team members' growth and fosters long-term benefits.

- Feedback is critical for introspection and iteration in the delegation process.
- Teaching delegation to others cultivates collaboration and trust, leading to enhanced performance and satisfaction.
- Although mishandling delegation can hinder its benefits, learning from mistakes and continuously improving delegation practices empowers teams and drives success.

Rewards and recognition

This chapter covers

- The importance of recognizing your team's development
- Aspects of effective recognition
- Ways to recognize and reward others
- Nuances of handling recognition at different levels

> *To win in the marketplace, you must first win in the workplace.*
>
> —Doug Conant, former President and CEO, Campbell Soup Co.

Early in my career, as I reflected on my first six months of being an engineering manager (EM), I realized that I had overlooked a crucial aspect of leadership: rewards and recognition. Despite my team members' dedication, I hadn't acknowledged their contributions. Through research and discussions, I discovered the transformative power of recognition in boosting job satisfaction and fostering collaboration. I learned that recognition isn't just about rewarding achievements but also about nurturing a sense of belonging and purpose within the team.

Armed with this understanding, I started to acknowledge my team members through various strategies that I will share shortly, including personalized thank-you notes and team outings, yielding remarkable results. This chapter underscores the importance of rewards and recognition in empowering teams.

Recognizing and rewarding employees is vital, especially for engineering leaders in tech companies. The engineering talent pool is a valuable resource, and motivated engineers contribute to faster development and shape future product iterations. Studies such as one conducted by Quantum Workplace (https://mng.bz/ppKG) highlight recognition as a top driver for increasing employee engagement. It fosters a sense of value, trust, and high morale, which are crucial for team dynamics. Effective recognition is essential for creating a positive culture, addressing factors that may make employees feel unappreciated, and steering the team toward success. It aids retention, supports personal and professional development, and fosters an environment that's conducive to learning. Well-appreciated employees exhibit a higher sense of belonging and motivation, contributing to the company's positive culture and growth. Before delving into effective recognition strategies, let's start with understanding distinct types of recognition.

6.1 Recognition levels

Recognition within a professional setting occurs at all levels, involving team members, peers, and leadership. The key is to express appreciation for others' efforts and convey a positive affirmation message. Let's explore the three common levels of recognition.

6.1.1 Top-down

Top-down recognition may come from an immediate manager or someone higher in the hierarchy. It can be conveyed publicly or privately. Here's an example illustrates effective top-down recognition. Ryan, a software engineer, receives acknowledgment from his manager, Bob, for resolving a complex technical problem. Bob highlights Ryan's efforts to a broader audience, including senior leadership, through an email that details the problem, Ryan's approach, and the effect of his work. This public recognition not only shows appreciation for Ryan's hard work but also motivates him to tackle challenging problems in the future. The choice of recognition mechanism depends on factors discussed in section 6.3. The key is for leaders like Bob to acknowledge and highlight the extra effort that team members contribute.

6.1.2 Peer

Peer recognition is acknowledgment received from colleagues while collaborating on various projects. Over the years, peer feedback has become integral in evaluating employee performance. Although feedback from bosses and management is crucial, recognition from peers holds unique significance. In the scenario with Ryan, his peer and collaborator, David, sent written feedback to their manager, Bob, praising Ryan's contributions. This feedback, detailing Ryan's efforts and the significance of solving the problem, motivated Ryan to collaborate more effectively with team members.

Similar to top-down recognition, peer recognition can take various forms and doesn't necessarily come from immediate team members. It can also originate from cross-functional partners, both within and outside the engineering domain. Furthermore, peer recognition doesn't always require managerial involvement. Companies often use tools that allow direct peer-to-peer recognition, bypassing the management chain. This kind of recognition, whether from immediate peers or cross-functional partners, significantly influences team dynamics. A culture rich in recognizing outstanding work contributes to the success of a high-functioning team, and this area is where an engineering leader can excel.

6.1.3   *360-degree*

360-degree recognition, which integrates top-down and peer acknowledgment, offers employees a comprehensive understanding of how their work is valued. It enables employees to grasp the effect of their work through feedback from peers and cross-team partners within the company. Gathering feedback from various sources provides valuable perspectives. For 360-degree feedback to be effective, an open and honest environment, free of repercussions, is essential so that staff members feel free to provide their true opinions. In a supportive atmosphere, where feedback is anonymous and geared toward improvement and positive recognition, 360-degree feedback is highly beneficial.

Additionally, 360-degree feedback serves to uncover problems that are not immediately apparent. In one of my past jobs, despite a developer's successful project deliveries, 360-degree feedback revealed communication challenges highlighted by two cross-functional partners. This feedback signaled a need to delve deeper, understand the root cause and effect, and provide actionable feedback to the engineer.

6.2   *Effective recognition principles*

Creating a recognition-rich culture hinges on understanding effective recognition principles. When evaluating your recognition process, consider the following building blocks for mastering the art of recognition and fostering a healthy work culture.

6.2.1   *Timely*

A small, timely gesture of acknowledgment has more effect than a delayed, more significant recognition. Consider Ryan's situation. If praise for his challenging project came only during end-of-year evaluations, he would have missed out on motivation throughout the year. Well-timed recognition is vital for boosting team morale and should be a priority when you're striving to create a positive work culture.

6.2.2   *Frequent*

Frequent recognition is often overlooked but plays a vital role in keeping the team engaged. Although it's natural to celebrate significant achievements, it's equally important to pay attention to and celebrate small victories. Encouraging team members to recognize one another's accomplishments fosters a culture of shared celebration. Establishing a process for peer recognition not only promotes a positive atmosphere but also provides an opportunity for positive reinforcement by rewarding the recognition-giver. It's crucial to build and endorse a culture of recognizing achievements within your team. Even a simple conversation with your team members can ensure that everyone feels free and comfortable to acknowledge and celebrate successes.

Cultural shifts within teams take time, but implementing small, straightforward processes can expedite this transition. An example is Jason, an EM who is establishing a monthly internal post to recognize engineers who excel in completing test tasks. This small gesture motivates junior engineers, contributing to team onboarding and addressing technical debt. Acknowledging small wins is crucial, as they often lead to significant achievements. If you are looking for ways to institute more frequent recognition, ask yourself questions like these:

- Did anyone recently finish onboarding?
- Has anyone started a project?
- Has anyone achieved a significant milestone?
- Did anyone deliver an important project?
- Has anyone reached a work anniversary?

Although frequent recognition is valuable, don't overdo it, which may diminish its effect. Employees can see through insincerity, which can in turn lead to reduced motivation.

6.2.3 *Specific*

Being specific in recognition is crucial. Recognition is not about completing a list of check boxes but genuinely acknowledging contributions. It involves acknowledging details, articulating the work's effect, explaining its necessity to the team, and linking it to the company's objectives. Specific recognition fosters a sense of belonging and helps employees understand the effect of their actions on the goals of the team and the company. By contrast, generalized feedback risks sounding ambiguous and hollow. A simple "Thank you for the work you did" is general and could be said to anyone. Instead, effective feedback that recognizes particular achievements is more like this: "Thank you for your hard work on Project X. Your swift implementation of the categorizer engine, especially under tight deadlines, is crucial for our company's goal of increasing customer engagement by 1.1%. Your focus on load testing ensures a robust system for our customers." When you write a note like this, the engineer knows that you truly notice what they are adding to the team.

6.2.4 *Visible*

Private and public appreciation serve distinct purposes. Private recognition fosters a personal sense of appreciation, whereas public recognition magnifies the effect achieved by an individual or team. Public acknowledgment through an announcement or company-wide email not only brings visibility to great work but also opens opportunities for collaboration and highlights innovative solutions that may otherwise be overlooked. It sets expectations for others, fostering engagement and motivating valuable discussions.

An example from my early career illustrates the power of visibility. My manager publicly praised a senior engineer's work, articulating the problem, the challenges, and the engineer's efforts. This praise showcased effective work and also served as a benchmark for excellence, guiding improvement for other team members.

Although public recognition is a valuable tool, in some scenarios, keeping acknowledgments private is preferable. We'll dive into that topic in section 6.3.2.

6.2.5   *Fair*

Fairness is a cornerstone in effective recognition, emphasizing a leader's responsibility to cultivate a team culture based on prosperity and integrity. Creating an environment that recognizes both conscious and unconscious biases is essential. Leaders should reflect on existing recognition practices to ensure equity across different roles, levels, and contributions. Strategies to reduce bias and enhance fairness include

- *Using data*—Establish clear, well-defined criteria for recognition based on data, avoiding favoritism and promoting transparency. Data can help you recognize valuable but less flashy work, such as addressing technical debt.
- *Using peer involvement*—Encourage inclusivity by involving everyone in the decision-making process, using employee surveys, peer awards through nominations, and other inclusive approaches. Peer affirmation adds motivation and diversity to recognition.
- *Retrospectively examining bias*—Periodically review recognitions delivered to identify unconscious bias retrospectively. This review helps you adapt and reduce biases in future recognition practices.

There's no one-size-fits-all solution for reducing bias, but being aware of biases is more important than debating specific approaches. Being cognizant of biases and continuously working toward minimizing them is a significant step. Personal awareness of unconscious biases led to the adoption of various strategies to reduce bias in the tech industry.

6.3   *Forms of recognition*

Recognition can manifest in various ways, and it's essential to tailor it based on whether you're acknowledging an individual or a group. Regardless, you should keep several considerations in mind. Let's begin by exploring ways to recognize the achievements of a group of people.

6.3.1   *Group recognition*

Group recognitions serve as a means to collectively celebrate team milestones. Involving the entire group in commemorating achievements not only boosts morale for those directly involved but also fosters team cohesion. Celebrating both small and significant accomplishments as a team promotes unity and serves as a stress reliever for hard-working teams striving toward common goals.

Here are a few suggestions to consider as effective starting points for group recognition efforts. Note that companies differ in budget and celebration policies, so pick what fits your situation best.

CELEBRATIONS AND LAUNCH PARTIES

Celebrating project deliverables or launch parties is an excellent way to recognize a team's achievements, such as completing a significant milestone or launching a minimal viable product. Acknowledging the collective effort of individuals, both inside and outside the team, is crucial, especially for larger initiatives that require collaboration with multiple cross-teams. Although there may be opportunities for individual recognition, celebrating the project delivery as a team reinforces the value that the company places on each team member's contributions.

Launch parties don't need to be extravagant, and budget constraints may limit the scale of the event. Regardless, the emphasis should be on acknowledging the team's recent accomplishments. Even with a small budget, you can gather the working team in a room, offering snacks, food, or drinks as a gesture of celebration. The key is to recognize the team's efforts. Including all project collaborators, including cross-functional engineering and business partners, is always good practice.

TEAM OFFSITES

Team offsite meetings provide an excellent opportunity to celebrate project wins and foster team camaraderie. Typically occurring every quarter, half, or year, these events offer a break from daily work, prevent burnout, and contribute to team engagement and happiness. Beyond relaxation, team offsites can serve as a platform for reflection and recognition.

Before every offsite, reflecting on the team's achievements since the previous event helps you identify any recent recognition misses. Creating a forum to highlight project achievements and acknowledging the team's efforts becomes a powerful motivator. Using this time gives you flexibility in organizing the offsite, such as starting with thank-you notes for different subteams.

When you're planning offsite events, inclusivity is crucial. Consider accommodating employees who are unable to attend after-hours events due to personal commitments and those who work remotely. Detailed considerations on inclusivity are discussed in section 6.3.2.

PROJECT/TEAM SWAG

Team swag, or Stuff We All Get (SWAG), including team-branded items such as T-shirts and water bottles, fosters a sense of pride and connection among team members. Incorporating team or project swag is a fantastic way to celebrate accomplishments and recognize hard work. Despite potential budget constraints, using opportunities for recognition through these items is crucial.

During a year-long initiative involving seven engineering teams collaborating on a new framework, a 50-member virtual team was formed due to pandemic-induced remote and hybrid work arrangements. To overcome challenges in connecting outside a professional setting, the team created project-specific swag items, distributing them to all involved. This thoughtful gesture effectively acknowledged contributions and highlighted the team's achievements.

Another noteworthy example is the use of challenge coins, particularly for large projects. These inexpensive tokens, reminiscent of military rewards for mission accomplishments, can be presented to team members as project phases are complete,. Challenge coins serve as memorable tokens of appreciation, fostering pride and providing an opportunity for team members to share their achievements when displayed. Customized thank-you cards and other forms of memorabilia can serve similar purposes.

Although these strategies are effective in a traditional setting, adapting recognition approaches for hybrid or remote teams presents challenges. Let's explore strategies to ensure that remote workers are not left out of recognition efforts.

HYBRID/REMOTE WORK

The shift to hybrid/remote work in the tech industry has become prevalent, offering flexibility but (as studies show) presenting challenges for team connection. So we have to adapt recognition strategies for diverse work profiles. Some strategies, such as sending project swag to dispersed teams, translate well; others, such as team offsites, require thoughtful planning.

To ensure that remote employees feel included in celebrations such as project launches or team offsites, EMs should organize remote-friendly events. Virtual options—including dinners, escape rooms, workshops, classes, and treasure hunts—can be facilitated through specialized event-management companies. Simple remote activities, such as virtual lunches with games, are effective within budget constraints. Recognizing the achievements of remote employees during these events is crucial for fostering a sense of belonging.

Special shout-out channels of communication channels for release notes are common tools for recognizing individual contributions. Recently, we threw a virtual launch party for our team. The celebration included awards of DoorDash coupons for food and drinks, a presentation showcasing the team's project achievements, and a team-building treasure hunt organized by an external provider. This approach prioritized inclusivity and involvement for all team members and emphasized the importance of recognizing accomplishments, especially for remote employees. Next, let's explore ways to appreciate individual talent.

6.3.2 *Individual recognition*

Although group recognition is effective for acknowledging collective efforts, it lacks the personal touch needed to fuel an employee's motivation. Recognizing the specific contributions of an individual provides direct feedback, eliminating ambiguity and addressing impostor-syndrome concerns. Different team members may require varied levels of validation; some are confident in their roles, and others need reassurance. For an EM, being mindful of these differences and offering both direct feedback and recognition is essential. Don't forget to track and preserve recognized achievements for future performance reviews.

There are two platforms for individual recognition. Employees may prefer private recognition or a mix of public and private acknowledgment. Understanding individual preferences is vital, and early discussions, such as during initial one-on-one meetings, can help tailor recognition to each team member's liking. This approach ensures that recognition is meaningful and relatable for each individual.

PUBLIC RECOGNITION

Public recognition is a powerful method to acknowledge and showcase an employee's achievements. It not only positively affects the individual being recognized but also raises awareness about their qualities and the substance of their work among peers. This form of recognition fosters connections and networks, which is particularly beneficial for new employees seeking broader visibility. The ripple effect of public recognition can lead to collaborative opportunities, as demonstrated by an engineer on our team who, after publicizing a successful testing infrastructure, received collaboration requests from multiple teams, resulting in mutually beneficial scenarios.

Using internal communication channels such as Slack shout-outs and formal recognition tools such as Lattice (https://lattice.com), Applauz (https://www.applauz.me), Nectar (https://nectarhr.com), and Kudos (https://www.kudos.com) gives you control of transparency and visibility for various audiences. Tailoring messages to different groups, such as engineers, leaders, and product partners, provides flexibility in highlighting achievements. Beyond digital platforms, recognition can be extended in various forums, including all-hands meetings, team gatherings, retrospectives, offsite events, and nonprofessional occasions. Company portals or dashboards such as Mango (https://www.mangoapps.com), SharePoint (https://mng.bz/z82a), Teams (https://mng.bz/0Gzx), and Workplace Chat (https://mng.bz/KZwK) serve as excellent spaces for highlighting public recognition.

Although public recognition is a potent motivator, it's crucial to exercise caution so that you don't overuse or misuse it. Public acknowledgment sometimes leads to questions of fairness, triggering insecurities among team members who feel overlooked. Additionally, some individuals may not be comfortable with public recognition, requiring sensitivity to their preferences. After all, the ultimate goal of the recognition process is to motivate employees.

Overusing public recognition can lead to negative consequences, such as fostering resentment and feelings of exclusion among team members. To address these concerns, involve the team in the recognition process by using surveys or nomination systems to identify outstanding contributions. This approach ensures a well-rounded perspective and allows those who nominated a colleague to recognize their work publicly. By incorporating peer feedback and involving team members in the recognition process, you promote fairness and transparency, ultimately enhancing the effectiveness of public acknowledgment.

PRIVATE RECOGNITION

Unlike public recognition, the private approach involves acknowledging an individual's work in a private setting, providing a more personal touch. Although private recognition eliminates concerns about managing others' feelings, it requires careful consideration to ensure fair and accurate judgments. Personally recognizing someone's efforts reinforces their belief that their work is appreciated and highlights your investment in their growth.

Continuous feedback and recognition through private acknowledgments contribute to ongoing employee growth, irrespective of their current performance level. Tracking these recognitions throughout the year and revisiting them during performance reviews enhances the feedback process and directly supports professional development. This record also proves beneficial during promotions reviews, showcasing why an employee is ready for advancement.

It's essential to note that public and private recognition aren't mutually exclusive and can be used together effectively. Most scenarios benefit from a combination, catering to employees who appreciate varied approaches. Although there are numerous ways to reward others, let's explore a few strategies.

MONETARY REWARDS

Monetary rewards, a highly effective way to recognize and motivate employees, come in various forms, such as increased compensation, spot bonuses, and award programs. Although you may be constrained by budget limitations and organizational processes, being proactive in creating budget flexibility for high-performing individuals enhances the success of recognition and rewards. Some companies use external tools to gamify their reward systems, partnering with providers that use a point-based system. Points earned based on the effect of contributions can be redeemed for company swag, gift cards, or other items. Gamification, such as organizing a testathon event with points for writing tests, enhances engagement and results. Additionally, exploring partnerships with learning providers such as Pluralsight and Coursera for subscriptions as rewards contributes to employee recognition and future success.

NONMONETARY REWARDS

Nonmonetary rewards offer a flexible, accessible way to recognize and motivate employees. They eliminate budgeting constraints and approval processes, making them a practical choice in many scenarios. Crowdsourcing recognition becomes simpler with nonmonetary rewards.

Privately recognizing someone through forums such as one-on-ones with clear and succinct feedback, designating them as an expert or a subject-matter expert (SME), providing increased responsibilities, and opportunities to represent the team in meetings are effective nonmonetary rewards. The focus is not always on material rewards.

Employees seeking promotion, for example, may find joy in affirmation of their growth rather than a small monetary gift.

Engaging the leadership chain to recognize recent accomplishments amplifies the effect. Sending an email acknowledging someone's work and copying managers and leaders not only boosts the employee's confidence but also bridges the gap between employees and leadership. Regardless of the approach, generosity in praise is fundamental. Being clear and concise in recognizing achievements without underselling them establishes a strong foundation for effective employee management.

Mastering the art of rewards and recognition is not just about offering tangible incentives; it's also about understanding and appreciating the unique motivations of each team member. Whether through monetary or nonmonetary means, the key lies in fostering a culture where acknowledgment is genuine, frequent, and tailored to individual preferences. Striking the right balance between public and private recognition, using leadership support, and embracing a culture of continuous feedback not only uplift team morale but also paves the way for sustained growth and success. For software EMs, recognizing that every contribution matters and every individual thrives on different forms of acknowledgment is the key to building a motivated and high-performing team.

What do other leaders have to say?

Take the time to comprehend what drives the individual, as this will reveal the most effective ways to recognize their efforts and facilitate their career growth and overall happiness.

—Sanjay Gupta, General Manager at HCL Technologies

A few ways I ensure people feel valued are publicly celebrating wins, making sure everyone is empowered to speak up because good ideas come from everywhere, and making sure that if someone needs something, they get it. If in a one-on-one someone asks me for something, I make sure I do it, to build trust.

—Jean Bredeche, Head of Engineering at Patch,
formerly with Robinhood, Quantopian, and Hubspot

Feeling valued is not just determined by their rewards but by their day-to-day experience with the company and team. As a manager, I try to make sure that they have meaningful work which aligns with their skill growth.

—Madhur Kathuria, Engineering Leader at Microsoft,
formerly with Moengage, Oracle, and IIT

Value and recognition pairs well with work visibility. Once a team's work is visible across the organization and we have cross-company alignment to deliver the most important work, connecting that to individual recognition becomes much easier.

—Nathan Bourgoin, Chief Technology Officer at Alakazam, Inc.,
Technical Adviser, and Engineering Leader

(continued)

Getting rewarded or recognized for your efforts is one of the most common needs for all individuals. I believe in regularly identifying, recognizing, and rewarding high performance/contribution in my team, whether it is a simple "Good job done" in morning meetings to relying on employee-of-the-month programs to ensuring rewards like merit increases or promotions to the most deserving team members. I also strongly believe that building an environment within the team where each team member feels comfortable in bringing their best. And actively contributing to each other's success is the key to overall success because in our world, teamwork would always triumph over individual brilliance, and hence I constantly reward and recognize the overall team along with the individual performance.

—Devika Ahuja, Technology Leader at Strategist

We do not provide enough recognition for people that they deserve. So I intentionally create environments where people get recognized by their colleagues and leaders. A key component of good recognition is to add the evidence of good behavior; otherwise, it looks phony. I always highlight the behavior as evidence of why a person deserves the recognition.

—Sumit Kumar, System Engineering Manager at Cisco

Along with pay, give your team meaningful work so you know that their ideas are implemented, their skills are appreciated, and they have a say in the product they're building. This ensures people are aligned in what they're trying to build.

—Larry Gordan, Managing Director at Emtec, Inc.

6.4 Stop and think: Practice questions

1. Do I value recognition of my team?
2. Does my team/company have a culture of recognizing and rewarding employees? If not, can I build it within my own team?
3. When was the last time I recognized someone on my team? How did they take it?
4. How often are your team members recognized for their work?
5. Do I feel valued when I am recognized for my efforts?
6. What type of recognition do you value most?
7. How do my team members individually like to be recognized and rewarded?
8. Do you feel that employees are treated fairly when they're rewarded? Why or why not?
9. Do you have recommendations for leadership to recognize the good work around you?

Summary

- To excel as an EM, recognizing the efforts of your team is paramount. Adhering to effective recognition principles is crucial for gauging your proficiency in acknowledging others' work.

- Practicing the tenets of effective recognition will make you better at realizing whether you are doing a good job of recognizing others. Effective recognition should be timely, frequent, specific, visible, and fair.

- There are several ways to recognize employees. Before starting this process, though, understand the difference between how you would recognize a group of individuals versus one person.

- For group recognition, if you have the budget, use different milestones in the project to celebrate with your team and highlight the work they have done up until now. Post-project delivery and launch parties are great ways to recognize others.

- Use team offsite meetings to create another platform for recognizing teamwork.

- Keep your recognitions inclusive, accounting for hybrid or remote employees you may have on your team.

- For individual recognition, use public recognition as a key resource to spread the message about the work they have done. Provide clear and concise feedback for private recognition, and consider monetary rewards for high performers.

- Acknowledging individuals as SMEs or go-to people for certain areas of ownership or for representing you or the team in different meetings is another way to recognize the work that employees have dome.

- Irrespective of context, always be generous with your praise to foster a positive and motivating work environment.

Hiring 7

> *It doesn't make sense to hire smart people and then tell them what to do; we hire smart people so they can tell us what to do.*
>
> —Steve Jobs, Co-Founder, Apple, Inc.

In the soft glow of the early-morning light, you find yourself surrounded by a multitude of open browser tabs containing the résumés of candidates for your software engineering team. The weight of responsibility rests on your shoulders—responsibility for sculpting the future of your team, a decision that will affect not just your team but also the success of your organization.

Hiring is an art. It means delicately crafting a team on which each member becomes a vital piece in the intricate puzzle of innovation. Whether you are tasked with developing a product or pioneering the next tech breakthrough, you need a robust team of software engineers, managers, and cross-functional partners. As we've learned, your success as an engineering manager (EM) is intricately tied to the success of your team(s).

Navigating the hiring landscape demands perseverance, motivation, and a hiring strategy. That strategy is composed of your understanding of the company's growth direction, the hiring budget, the estimated effort for upcoming initiatives, and the hiring process details, all of which will be explored in this chapter.

But first, it's essential to understand that hiring is significantly more costly than retaining talent. Reports by Employee Benefit News (https://mng.bz/OZBn) estimate that hiring a replacement consumes approximately 33% of an employee's annual salary—a substantial investment. Your goal, and the goal of everyone in the hiring pipeline, should be hiring for the long term.

At the same time, today's mobile labor market means you need to treat hiring not as an episodic event but as a continuous, iterative process. Beyond focusing on near-term needs and open head counts, view hiring as an ongoing planning process at all organizational levels. This process entails proactive engagement in tech forums, meet-ups, and conferences, showcasing your team and company. You should see hiring as an opportunity for mutual assessment, with candidates also evaluating your company.

This chapter unravels the intricacies of hiring, providing a comprehensive framework, insights on staffing your team, considerations for hiring externally versus internally, and guidance on constructing a robust hiring pipeline. Let the expedition begin.

7.1 Following a hiring framework

We'll kick things off with a structured hiring framework. This framework breaks the hiring process into clear, step-by-step actions to follow.

7.1.1 Identifying the need for hiring

The initial and crucial step in the hiring process is recognizing the need for additional staffing. This step means assessing the current and future needs of the company and addressing questions such as "Why hire?", "Who do we hire?", "When do we hire?", "How long do we need new hires?" The next step is looking at the company's budget and analyzing job market trends. In a growing company, you'll want to identify where investments will be made and how these decisions will affect staffing requirements in specific areas. After you address these questions, conduct your research, and decide that you need some new hires, it's time to communicate the following to leadership:

- Why do we need additional staff? Is it because
  - The company is growing rapidly?
  - The company plans to start one or many new initiatives?
  - Your team requires additional support to continue existing initiatives?
  - You want to backfill existing head count because of natural attrition?

- Why we should consider external hiring over internal growth for the role?
- Should any specific skill sets be targeted?
- What would the effect of not hiring be?

The answers to these questions will serve an input for the job description that gets advertised to candidates, including details on the company and the role, what you as the manager are looking for, location, salary, benefits, and the application process. A well-crafted job description serves as a valuable tool for attracting top talent and ensuring alignment between candidates' abilities and organizational needs. Read more about writing an effective job description at https://mng.bz/Y7DN.

At times, the company may need to hire, but leadership wants you to maximize existing workforce efficiency instead. Don't shy away from these discussions. Instead, use a data-driven approach to demonstrate your team's capacity and how resources are distributed. This approach will help ensure that your team functions at its best. When hiring more personnel truly is not feasible, at least you can work with leadership to identify the initiatives they want the current staff to prioritize.

Addressing tough questions also involves outlining the consequences of not hiring. By presenting both sides of the coin, you empower everyone involved to assess risks and explore ways to mitigate them. Clearly communicate whether not hiring might lead to project delays, cause burnout in existing teams, or pose other challenges. Remember that you can always seek guidance on this task from your manager or mentor.

7.1.2   *Sourcing potential candidates*

The next phase in the hiring process is sourcing suitable candidates. By *suitable*, I mean individuals who align with the company's values and goals, possess the necessary skills and experience, and perhaps held equivalent roles or worked at similar companies. Employee transitions between companies, often driven by a pursuit of improved work–life balance and benefits, are not uncommon, leading to a dynamic recruitment landscape. Following are some key guidelines to observe when sourcing candidates.

TAPPING INTO DIVERSE TALENT POOLS

A diverse workforce contributes significantly to organizational success by fostering creativity, innovation, and a thriving work culture. Explore opportunities to promote your company and available roles through various channels, including conferences such as Grace Hopper, local meetups, impact groups, and university internship programs. You can also use online platforms such as Glassdoor and LinkedIn to reach a broad audience, ensuring a diverse pool of candidates with unique perspectives and ideas. I suggest reading the McKinsey report on why diversity matters (https://mng.bz/GZeq).

USING GENDER-NEUTRAL LANGUAGE

It may seem like a nuance, but gender-neutral language can go a long way toward creating an inclusive environment and mitigating unconscious biases. Gender-neutral language can be more or less customary, depending on your country or area of the world. Being gender-neutral means using language that is unbiased toward any particular gender or social group and does not assume which gender the potential hire would belong to. So when referring to candidates, use neutral terms. Another tip is to extend the gender-neutral approach to job descriptions and interview feedback, using terms such as *they* and *them*, referencing the initials of the candidate's name rather than guessing the person's gender, or using generic terms such as *candidate*, *person*, and *individual*.

One cool hackathon idea that an engineer in our company implemented was creating a script that ran over filled-in interview feedback on the hiring tool and suggested words that should be updated to be gender-neutral. This hackathon project helped the company's initiative to create a more inclusive and diverse hiring pipeline.

COLLABORATING WITH RECRUITING PARTNERS AND COORDINATORS

Recruiting partners and coordinators are pivotal in the hiring process. These partners can be internal recruiting functions, external agencies and placement organizations, or a combination. It's important to assess any agreements or contracts that are in place with external agencies and the associated rules or policies. Collaborate closely with recruiting coordinators to manage tasks such as résumé collection, initial screening, and coordination of interviews, fostering a streamlined hiring process. Also ensure that you have a written hiring process to clarify the steps and who owns each step. This approach allows recruiting partners to pinpoint candidates who not only meet the basic requirements but also have skill sets that align well with the current job role.

When candidates are identified, the recruiter collaborates with you, the hiring team, and the candidate to schedule interview loops and provide relevant information to the interviewing team. If you decide to move forward with a candidate and extend an offer, recruiting partners typically communicate offer-related details. During offer negotiations, you collaborate with your budgeting team and recruiting partner to determine the best approach. With multiple touchpoints in play, establish a strong working relationship with your recruiting partners and coordinators for a successful hiring process.

KEEPING LONG-TERM NEEDS IN MIND

It is important to align hiring decisions with the company's long-term goals, avoiding compromises for short-term gains. You need to evaluate candidates not only for immediate team fit but also for their potential contribution to other teams within the organization. Ensure that candidates possess qualities that make them adaptable and valuable across various teams, supporting the company's seamless internal transfer opportunities. Ask yourself this question: if they come on board and want to switch teams six months or a year down the line, would they be just as useful on the new team?

Organizations may also set hiring objectives that target underrepresented groups (URG), aiming for a specific percentage of hires from these groups. Considering these company-wide goals in your hiring process is crucial for effective planning. One of my past companies had a URG goal for hiring by year-end. To achieve this objective, I worked with a team to analyze the hiring processes of the past six months. We suggested several actions, including boosting onsite interviews for URGs; reaching out to groups such as the Hispanic Alliance for Career Enhancement, the National Society of Hispanic MBAs, and local chapters of the Latino Professionals Association; and incorporating inclusion training into our hiring protocols.

It's also essential to weigh the pros and cons of small versus large teams. Large teams offer benefits such as increased shared resources, task specialization, reduced risk of a single point of failure, division of labor, and strong group identification. On the flip side, smaller teams provide advantages such as effective communication, higher individual ownership of work, ease of information sharing, and recognition of individual contributions. There's no one-size-fits-all solution; the hiring strategy should be based on the specific use case and organizational goals.

UNDERSTANDING THE SOURCING WORKFLOW

Several steps will occur before a candidate comes up for an interview. The recruiter may contact certain candidates and filter some out before sending them to the EM. Then you, as EM, will see the résumés of all the candidates who applied for the position and make the decision on résumé screens. When a candidate makes it into consideration, ask yourself these questions:

- Do they have to take a test or an online assessment?
- If so, does the online assessment cover technical and personality assessments?
- Are you using some external companies for these online assessments?
- Will some candidates get an exemption from these online assessments? (A candidate may have interviewed recently for a similar role in a different department, for example, and received an inclined offer. You have the interview loop notes to consider.) What is company policy regarding these exemptions?

The workflow structure and the answers to these questions depend on your company policy, existing hiring processes, and current situation. Candidates can't be expected to attend interviews without specific workflows.

Now you've sourced candidates. The next step is organizing hiring interview rounds for these candidates.

7.1.3 *Setting up hiring rounds and the loop*

The next step is setting up the interview loop, with multiple rounds assessing specific skill sets. A junior engineer role might have three to five rounds focusing on technical skills (such as problem-solving, understanding of algorithms, system scalability, and technical design) and soft skills (such as collaboration, openness to feedback, and adaptability). An effective interview loop is challenging but aims to be fair, unbiased, and diverse, reflecting the company's commitment to inclusion and inviting a wide range of perspectives in the hiring process. Some key skills and qualities to look for in potential candidates are

- Self-motivation
- Collaborative nature
- Team-player mindset
- Easygoing but driven attitude

- Technical and/or business acumen relevant to the job
- Eagerness to learn and accept challenges
- Ability to thrive in ambiguity
- Passion for the product and company culture
- Strong culture and team fit
- Ability to work across multiple areas

Here are some red flags to watch out for:

- Not a team player
- Negative remarks made about previous team members or managers
- Resistance to ambiguity
- Superficial answers to questions and inability to provide concrete examples
- Signs of distrust or dishonesty
- Defensive attitude
- Getting lost in details and forgetting the bigger picture
- Inability to communicate concepts or thought processes clearly
- Unwillingness to admit not knowing an answer, instead fighting to prove a point

Although these lists are generic things that I look for in a candidate at any level, other resources that are specific to the company can be helpful in following a consistent, scalable and maintainable hiring process. Following are some best practices that were used on my teams at Microsoft, Amazon, and Robinhood:

- *Leveling guide*—The levels in a role are cross-referenced against the expected competencies at that level for consistent hiring practices.
- *Interview question bank for standardized assessments*—With a set number of questions that are well calibrated with several engineers and managers within the company, an interview question bank provides an opportunity to maximize value and efficiency in making great hiring decisions. It also helps in the hiring calibration process, determining ratings such as "strong hire," "hire," "neutral," "weak hire," and "no hire." The calibrated question bank often includes criteria for a strong hire response distinct from the hire or neutral category.
- *Adaptive testing*—Adaptive testing involves adjusting questions based on a candidate's experience, such as coding-language preference. Suppose that your company primarily uses Java, but you are interviewing a candidate who has experience only with the Go language. In such a situation, it's crucial to pose relevant questions to the candidate, adjusting your interview to grasp their thought process, and consequently gain new insights. Keep in mind that
  - The interview focuses on assessing the candidate's claimed knowledge.
  - Interviewers should avoid questioning recent learning or personal interests.
  - Interviewers need to adopt the mindset that they are instruments in the process, acknowledging that the final decision rests with the organization or the team involved in the hiring process.

- *Training on interviewing and inclusion*—This training is designed to create an aware interviewer, reduce biases including unconscious bias (https://mng.bz/z8Za), and create awareness of the company's commitment to inclusion and diversity. This training helps interviewers understand what information they can disclose and what should be kept confidential during interviews, ensuring the integrity of job-related confidentiality.

- *Proper ending of interviews*—Thank candidates and outline next steps. This step also helps set a positive example for potential employees by creating a positive candidate experience for them. Also make sure to leave some time for the candidate to ask questions.

- *Handling split loops*—*Split loops* are interview rounds in which some interviewers consider the candidate suitable for hire and others assess the candidate as unsuitable. Divergent experiences among interviewers can arise during the interview process. A candidate might excel in the coding round but struggle in the architecture-design round, for example. Split loops are common during the debrief session, when the team gathers to synthesize feedback gathered from various rounds of interviews. Such situations call for following the leveling guide strictly and putting competencies in buckets ("raises bar" versus "lowers bar"), evaluating coachability, and seeking additional clarification through extra rounds if necessary. This objective approach to the hiring process helps eliminate bad hires. (If you end up with a bad hire, which happens in the real world, you'll have to spend more time and effort managing performance than you initially thought.) You may also encounter some individuals who are extremely proficient technically and maybe better than most people on your team, but if they are hard to work with, it is almost impossible to count this person as anything but a bad hire. A person who is one of the best coders in the world but has a disparaging attitude toward others will create more problems than they solve.

- *Conduct rounds without sharing feedback in between*—Yes, do all the necessary rounds of interviews before rejecting a candidate. This approach provides a holistic view of performance across rounds, and chances are that the candidate may have some unique skill set your team can benefit from. Also, between rounds, do not let interviewers share feedback with those who are doing subsequent rounds to prevent bias from creeping in.

Candidates who do not meet the hiring bar should be informed politely with help from recruiting partners (who are well trained in this area) to maintain transparency, with reasons of outcome provided based on company policies. When a candidate meets our hiring standards and we're prepared to extend an offer, let's conduct a persuasive sales call to present the benefits and opportunities of joining our company.

7.1.4 Conducting the sales call

The *sales call* is a crucial step in the hiring process for software EMs. In this call, you, the hiring manager, directly discuss job details with the candidate, going beyond what the recruiting coordinator covered. The conversation provides clarity on day-to-day responsibilities, the 30/60/90 (day) onboarding plan, growth opportunities, and insights into your team's culture and technical road map. This process is not just about selling the role but also about creating space for the candidate to assess their fit and avoid surprises upon joining.

Once, my team was considering a senior software engineer who had multiple job offers in hand, so the sales call became an opportunity for me to discuss the engineer's special interests. It turned out that he was passionate about cloud technologies, particularly Amazon Web Services (AWS), and had completed multiple AWS certifications. I talked about the related projects my team was working on and would be picking up in the next quarter. This personalized discussion played a pivotal role in the candidate's choosing the company.

Sales calls also offer a chance to discuss additional company benefits within the bounds of company policies. Understanding the candidate's preferences, such as a focus on continuous learning, shapes discussions of available benefits. As an EM, your role is to provide a realistic representation of the job, emphasizing opportunities and potential effects. Encouraging candidates to talk to various members of your team and sister or partner teams and cross-functional partners gives them a comprehensive view of your team dynamics.

Expressing gratitude for the candidate's time is crucial, regardless of their decision. Recognizing that candidates are not just potential employees but also potential customers, maintaining a positive experience is vital. Keeping doors open for future collaborations is essential even if a candidate decides not to join your team. Disgruntled candidates can share their experiences on platforms such as Glassdoor and Fishbowl, influencing industry perceptions.

7.1.5 Creating an onboarding plan

The hiring process doesn't conclude with the candidate's accepting the offer, because the onboarding phase can help determine the new hire's success. To ensure success, develop a comprehensive onboarding plan, typically structured around a 30-60-90 (day) time frame. To facilitate a seamless transition, assign an existing engineer from your team as an onboarding buddy, mentor, or co-pilot; schedule frequent one-on-one meetings; and provide access to pertinent training materials. The time invested in crafting a well-thought-out onboarding plan is undoubtedly time well spent. To further assist you, figure 7.1 shows a sample onboarding-plan template.

Now that we have a hiring framework in mind and can follow a step-by-step process to hire the best and maintain our hiring bar, let's look at hiring decisions that involve staffing from scratch versus hiring for an existing team with an established charter.

<Sample>Onboarding Plan for Alice

Hello, Alice!

We are excited to have you on the team.

Team overview and details:
<Other description of company, mission, team and tenets>

Onboarding buddy: Bob
Onboarding buddy contact information: <Slack Handle>, <Email> (Whatever communication channel your team prefers)

Key people to meet:
<Here, you suggest names of key people the new employee should meet. This can be set of peer software engineers they will work with or cross-functional partners like product, technical program managers, UX, QA, and other leaders in the chain>

Tasks/Activities:
<This section explains the desired courses, training, or logistic paperwork that needs to be completed in the coming weeks>

Task #	Task description	Target finish week	Status (to do, in progress, completed)
1	Complete onboarding training bootcamp	Week 1	In progress
2	New-hire paperwork	Week 1	To do
3	...	...	...

Key projects/deliverables:
<This section goes into further details of the plan for next 30, 60 and 90 days. This can be combined with the above section or kept separate to describe the projects and key deliverables to own in the upcoming three months.>

First 30 days:
- Understand the landscape of services and infrastructure.
- Meet critical stakeholders.

First 60 days:
- Take ownership of core services and prepare for launch of project XYZ.

First 90 days:
- Prepare to go on call for team's weekly operational on-call rotation.
- Help launch the core pricing service.
- Help prepare a robust run book for ABC feature.

Figure 7.1 Sample onboarding plan for new hires

7.2   *Staffing from scratch versus hiring for existing teams*

There are two primary scenarios for hiring:

- *Staffing from scratch*
  - *Context*—Relevant when setting up a new team from entirely new hires.
  - *Trigger*—Prompted by a new strategic initiative the company is investing in or an expansion of responsibilities that requires a dedicated team.
  - *Considerations*—For an EM, addressing the purpose and vision of the new team is crucial. Defining the number and types of roles needed to accomplish the work is a key aspect. Communicating this vision is vital for attracting potential candidates to join this new team.

- *Hiring for an existing team*
  - *Context*—Pertains to situations in which the team already exists but with a defined purpose and direction.
  - *Trigger*—Hiring additional members due to increased workload, expanded responsibilities, or backfilling roles after recent attrition.
  - *Considerations*—In this scenario, the nature of the work that potential candidates will be involved in is clearer. But ensuring that new hires can integrate seamlessly with existing team members is a critical consideration. Team dynamics and cohesion are essential factors in the hiring decision.

To facilitate a more informed staffing decision, let's delve into the detailed differences between these two scenarios.

7.2.1 Purpose

When you're building a team from scratch, you must clearly articulate the purpose and guiding principles. Developing an organizational chart and outlining the team's mission in broad strokes provide a foundational vision. This clarity is crucial for making informed decisions throughout the hiring and staffing process. Additionally, having a well-defined vision enables effective communication with potential candidates, who in turn are evaluating the alignment of the team's purpose with their career aspirations. This transparency enhances your chances of attracting candidates who resonate with the team's objectives.

Conversely, when you're hiring for an existing team, the purpose, direction, and tenets are typically well established unless the team is undergoing a reorganization or a charter change. In such cases, you should communicate the existing layout and objectives of the team, as well as the team's structure and deliverables, to potential candidates.

7.2.2 Sizing

When you are staffing a team from scratch, it is crucial to carefully estimate the team size and head counts needed over a 1/3/5 (year) time frame. The charter serves as a guide for determining the initial number of engineers required. Although you may have flexibility to hire more engineers as needed, the key is avoiding initial overhiring. Overstaffing may lead to insufficient work for team members, potentially resulting in attrition.

When you're augmenting an existing team, the need for head count is based on immediate requirements, making team sizing less complex. By the time the decision to hire is made, the importance of the role is well established, providing clarity on the specific requirements for the candidate who will fill that role. Keep in mind the widely accepted principle that a scrum team should not exceed the size of a two-pizza team, consisting of six to eight engineers, to ensure a manageable and efficient team structure. This rule of thumb applies to both scenarios: staffing from scratch and hiring for an existing team.

As an EM overseeing pricing and promotions strategy, I once encountered a significant milestone when my manager approached me with the idea of establishing a new team dedicated to payment handling. Because I was already leading a team of around eight engineers, this idea presented a remarkable opportunity to expand my leadership responsibilities. The challenge extended beyond mere resourcing, however; it also entailed strategically sizing both teams effectively. The existing team already leaned toward the higher end of the two-pizza-team concept. To address this situation, I initiated a transparent discussion within my team, presenting the prospect of the new payments team. Two engineers expressed keen interest in contributing to the setup of the payments team and also embracing a growth opportunity that would push them beyond their comfort zones. With this internal alignment, I crafted a comprehensive plan that outlined the need for additional head counts: two to fill the void left by team members transitioning to the payments team and two more to establish and bolster the new payments-focused team. This strategic approach aimed to maintain equilibrium across both teams while fostering career development and seizing the potential for innovation in the payments domain.

7.2.3   *Specialization of skills and experience*

When you are establishing a team from scratch, look for diversity in technical skills and years of experience. A spectrum of technical skills contributes to forming a well-rounded, full-stack team or individuals who are capable of adapting and introducing fresh ideas. It is also better to have a mix of junior and senior engineers on the team. Junior engineers bring curiosity and willingness to learn, making them adaptable to the company's strengths and needs. Senior engineers bring a wealth of experiences, including working with large-scale distributed systems, and offer mentorship to junior team members. There is no one-size-fits-all ratio for junior, midlevel, and senior engineers on a team; the ratio depends on the project, the work environment, and other factors.

For existing teams, filling roles based on skills and experience is more straightforward, given the existing team composition. If the team has four junior engineers and an open role, hiring a senior engineer makes sense; that person can provide mentorship and guidance to the junior members. Similarly, if the team consists primarily of iOS and web developers in a frontend-focused team, hiring an Android engineer for an open role aligns with maintaining a balanced ratio of software engineers across different experiences. Your objective is to sustain a well-calibrated mix of software engineers, ranging from those early in their careers to seasoned veterans, ensuring a dynamic and collaborative team environment.

7.2.4   *Diversity*

Prioritizing diversity in hiring not only aligns with most organizational values but also addresses the needs of a diverse customer base. A team that mirrors the diversity of the target audience enables a deeper understanding of a broad range of customer needs, ultimately enhancing customer satisfaction, loyalty, and overall business success. To integrate diversity considerations into the hiring process seamlessly, you can do the following:

- Use diverse candidate-sourcing channels.
- Implement blind résumé reviews.
- Incorporate inclusive language into job descriptions.
- Provide diversity training for interviewers and decision-makers.

Beyond hiring, establishing inclusive policies and practices is crucial for supporting and retaining a diverse workforce. Strategic planning is essential when you're aiming for diversity in a team built from scratch. This process involves defining the desired diversity in skill sets and backgrounds, allowing for intentional hiring based on specific criteria. For existing teams, use what you know about current team members and tap into diversity programs to maintain a balanced, diverse team. Additionally, conducting inclusion training for team members fosters allyship and contributes to a healthy work environment, reinforcing commitment to diversity throughout the team's life cycle.

In a leadership role, I faced the challenge of leading a team of engineers on which I happened to be the only female member. Recognizing the importance of diversity, I proactively used available resources such as the Women in Tech network and local New Jersey meetups to advocate for both my team and the company. Though it took some time and effort, this initiative was successful in securing two diverse candidates who were well aligned with the team's goals and brought valuable perspectives to our collaborative efforts.

7.2.5 Team dynamics

Team dynamics are a foundational consideration in assembling a team, though the role of team dynamics is less pronounced initially, as there is no established team culture. Team dynamics becomes crucial over time, however as the team evolves with new hires. You should set clear expectations for each team member to prevent confusion and potential conflicts. Clearly defining roles on the team, such as designating a tech lead, helps prevent unhealthy competition.

For an existing team, it is imperative to ensure that new hires can integrate seamlessly with the existing team's mission and culture. Mutual acceptance and openness to collaboration are key aspects that contribute to a positive team dynamic. If the prevailing team culture emphasizes collaborative planning, introducing a new member who does not align with a team-oriented approach could adversely affect your team culture and morale. The emphasis, therefore, is on fostering a harmonious and collaborative team environment, whether you are establishing a new team or integrating a new member into an existing one.

7.2.6 Tale from the trenches

In one situation, I was tasked with establishing a sister team from scratch to focus on payment portfolios in global markets. Before delving into the hiring process, I thoroughly understood the team's vision, mission, and tenets. A key tenet was to provide a seamless payment-transactions experience, ensuring extensibility for future use cases. Defining success criteria for the team set the foundation for hiring. With six open positions, I interviewed individuals who had diverse skill sets to ensure the team's success. I also promoted the opportunities internally in the organization and received internal interest. This approach led to the successful transition of two existing team members to the sister team. Because the existing team members who transitioned were senior engineers, to maintain a sustainable ratio of senior and junior engineers, I focused my external hiring on engineers early in their careers.

In another scenario, I was tasked with hiring for an existing team of six members with four open spots. Careful planning based on existing team skill sets and diversity guided the hiring strategy. Adhering to the agile two-pizza rule was essential for avoiding disruption while ensuring effective communication. The goal was to maintain team dynamics and prevent any disruptions caused by new hires.

As highlighted in the preceding sections, various factors influence team staffing and hiring strategies. Given the irreversible nature of hiring decisions, it's crucial to take a gradual and iterative approach, as opposed to a big-bang hiring approach. In section 7.3, we will explore the fundamental differences between external hiring and internal growth, offering insights into shaping team culture.

7.3 Hiring externally versus growing internal talent

The perpetual dilemma that many EMs face revolves around the choice between hiring externally or nurturing internal talent within the organization. Both approaches come with advantages and disadvantages, and there's no definitive right or wrong approach. Striking a balance and adopting a tailored approach based on the circumstances at hand is the key to navigating this decision-making process. Let's explore various scenarios in which one approach may be more fitting than the other.

7.3.1 Hiring externally

External hiring injects fresh perspectives and enriched experiences into teams, as candidates bring knowledge and insights from their diverse backgrounds, whether in large corporations or startups. This diversity enhances thought processes, challenges assumptions, and cultivates an innovative culture. It also introduces industry-wide best practices, skill sets, and cutting-edge technologies, accelerating innovation and maintaining competitiveness in the swiftly evolving tech landscape. External hiring is beneficial when you are looking to achieve certain goals, such as the following:

- *Addressing skill gaps*—If a team lacks certain skills, such as machine learning expertise, hiring an individual with that background can significantly benefit the team.
- *Achieving a balanced seniority level within the team*—If a junior Android engineer would benefit from mentorship, hiring a senior Android engineer can bridge the gap and ensure a balanced Android experience.
- *Overcoming tunnel-vision syndrome*—External hires bring in fresh perspectives, revealing and addressing inefficiencies that are not easily noticeable from within.

Remember that external hires may face a learning curve in understanding the technology stack and company culture, leading to lower productivity initially. Allowing your new hires ample time to ramp up contributes to the team's long-term growth.

Recently, a new engineer on my team pointed out improvements in our current technical-design review process based on their previous company's practices. Their insights led to a complete overhaul of the review process, introducing a new technical-design template that brought consistency and efficiency to reviews. The revised process not only streamlined reviews but also prompted document writers to consider critical design aspects that they might have overlooked.

7.3.2 Growing talent internally

As an EM, one of your core responsibilities is to guide your team members in planning their career development, ensuring that they excel in their current roles and are also prepared for future advancements. Facilitating the growth of internal talent to fill open roles not only reinforces positive sentiments but also communicates a vested interest in their professional evolution. Overrelying on external hires without nurturing internal talent comes at a substantial cost to the company. If the perception emerges that internal growth is not an option, your employees may seek opportunities elsewhere, resulting in a sudden loss of valuable contextual knowledge—a resource that is difficult to build and easy to lose. An EM who is actively invested in their team's growth fosters engagement, trust, and motivation. This approach contributes to higher retention rates, sending a positive signal to employees. Additionally, individuals who are familiar with the technical stack and processes require less ramp-up time, mitigating the cost associated with onboarding new hires.

Although internal growth is advantageous, relying on it exclusively can lead to a narrow vision for the team. Without external hires, you risk missing out on new skills and diverse experiences that individuals from different backgrounds and companies bring. Startups, facing time constraints, sometimes opt to hire trained engineers with existing skills rather than invest in internal growth. Striking a balance between external hires and internal growth is crucial. Creating opportunities for existing team members to step into new roles and grow is beneficial, but recognizing situations that necessitate external hires is equally important.

Consider Bob's interest in becoming a product manager after the recent departure of the team's product manager. Bob was a senior developer on a few critical products and worked closely with the departing product manager to learn the know-hows. He was also actively mentored by the sister team's product manager to transition to the role eventually. This situation presents an ideal opportunity to support Bob's career aspirations, using his familiarity with the company for a smooth transition. On the other hand, with the departure of the data scientist on the team, Alice's desire to become a data scientist is evident. Because she lacks the necessary skills, however, the strategic move is to hire an external data scientist who can fulfill immediate needs and mentor Alice over time. By thoughtfully considering the career aspirations of employees, the specific needs of the team, and external hiring opportunities, you can make informed decisions that drive professional growth and ensure the team's success.

7.4   *Developing the hiring pipeline*

In the evolving landscape of software engineering, where innovation is the key to success, establishing a robust hiring pipeline transcends being a mere task; it becomes a strategic imperative. Envision a dynamic ecosystem where talent flows seamlessly—a continuous stream of exceptional individuals eager to contribute their skills to the collective brilliance of your team. How cool, right?

In the competitive realm of hiring, the latest trend emphasizes a proactive approach, treating hiring not as a reaction to immediate needs but as a strategic move. This forward-thinking approach ensures agility, efficient hiring practices, and a competitive edge over rivals. Building a talent pipeline necessitates aligning with the strategic direction of the company, enabling the planning and construction of a road map to connect with potential candidates effectively. Let's explore the steps that organizations (and you) can take to distinguish themselves in this process:

- *Branding*—Crafting a company's brand marks the initial impression for potential candidates. Branding is an opportunity to tell the company's story, showcase its vision and mission, and communicate the desired skill sets. Using various platforms such as the career page, advertisements, social media, and networking events enhances the company's brand, allowing candidates to align with its values and envision a role within the company. As an EM, you can work with your recruiting partner to share successful stories from your engineers on various platforms.
- *Streamlined hiring process*—A well-thought-out hiring process is crucial, channeling candidates through the right avenues. For this purpose, you can reach out to experts in relevant fields on platforms such as LinkedIn (https://www.linkedin.com), using gender-neutral language in job advertisements, establishing fair interview loops with trained interviewers to avoid biases, and employing effective tools to centralize the hiring process. For niche roles, tapping specialized forums or attending relevant conferences can help target the right talent pool.
- *Personalized reach*—Throughout the interview process, personalization is key to making candidates feel valued. From the initial outreach on platforms such as LinkedIn to the culmination of the hiring process, personal engagement is a significant factor in attracting top talent. This personalized approach extends to passive candidates, and targeting vetted individuals from previous applications or referrals increases the likelihood of success. If sending a cold message to a potential candidate can help you hire them, why wait?
- *Completing the circle*—Nurturing potential candidates involves maintaining communication, regardless of the hiring outcome. Closing the loop with candidates, whether or not they receive an offer, ensures transparency and a positive candidate experience. Timely responses and expressions of gratitude for candidates' time contribute to a favorable impression, fostering goodwill for future interactions. Usually, recruitment teams convey the final responses to the candidate; your job as an EM is to follow up and ensure that the circle is complete.

As remote interviews become more prevalent, clarifying the setup and paying attention to verbal communication and candidate engagement become crucial. Developing a consistent hiring pipeline requires effort initially, but it proves invaluable for streamlining the hiring process, planning for attrition, and maintaining a data-driven approach for continuous improvement. Successful companies master the art of cultivating a hiring pipeline, ensuring a constant influx of talent and strategic planning for the future.

7.5 Employing hiring programs for positive reinforcement

Navigating the intricacies of the hiring process reveals that it's a multifaceted challenge. The question to keep in mind is how you can elevate your hiring approach. Can you do more than just fill vacancies? One approach is to work with hiring programs, designed not only to acquire talent but also to serve as powerful instruments of positive reinforcement. Your goal is to attract exceptional individuals and retain and nourish their potential for the long run. Let's explore some of the channels that can help you build a healthy and diverse talent pipeline.

7.5.1 Internship/campus hiring programs

Are you looking for someone with fresh perspectives who can bring academic learning to practice? Is some of the work at your workplace coachable for a new hire fresh out of college?

Internships, co-ops, and campus hiring programs are ideal for engaging with young talent and recent graduates. Campus hires, early in their careers, can be shaped to fit job requirements. They also bring passion for learning, minimal biases, and readiness to grow. With this talent, you can bring fresh eyes and new perspectives to your team. Focus on team and company fit, not just specific programming languages. Further, with the help of your existing team, you can train these new hires in required skills and create a mutually beneficial situation. Campus hires can also help shape the company's brand as they seek to understand its values, culture, and perks.

Companies of all sizes often use campus events and career fairs to build brand awareness and tap alumni networks. If you have employees who are alumni of a particular university, have them conduct a few on-campus awareness sessions at the same university. Sharing their success stories will show current students the benefits and growth opportunities at your company and increase the chances that they will consider full-time opportunities in your company. This strategy also allows you to collect résumés, address questions, and provide a contact point for further inquiries.

Virtual career fairs, spurred by the pandemic, offer the advantage of reaching talent globally. Although this strategy widens the pool, it lacks the personal touch of in-person interactions. I've successfully recruited interns and employees from Canada and Europe to collaborate with my U.S.-based teams. It is personally satisfying to see college hires joining as full-time employees and eventually reaching great heights.

7.5.2 *Returnship programs*

Many prominent companies recognize that life is unpredictable and that employees may take breaks from their careers due to various life situations, such as the following:

- Caring for elderly relatives
- Caring for children
- Taking a part-time role as they support a family member
- Relocating for family reasons
- Search for a remote role only

Companies such as Amazon (https://mng.bz/lMP8), Meta (https://pathforward.org/your-path-forward-at-meta), and Thoughtworks (https://mng.bz/KZGK) have established returnship programs to help individuals restart their careers after a break of one year or more. The idea is to help these individuals by ensuring that they have the basic qualifications for the job and a structured environment, training them on the job with the latest technology and providing a probation test period in which they can work more like interns. Based on the work and the company hiring bar, the employer can decide to extend a full-time offer for hire. Here are some benefits of instilling a returnship program:

- *Skillful contributions*—By offering a platform for individuals to refresh their skills, these programs bring in valuable experience. This influx of expertise introduces new ideas and fresh perspectives to enhance problem-solving and innovation.
- *Revitalized diversity*—Given that women have been likely to take breaks from their careers, returnship programs play a crucial role in reinvigorating diversity within the workforce. These initiatives provide equal opportunity for individuals to upskill themselves, breaking down barriers and fostering a more inclusive workplace.
- *Positive company branding*—Beyond their immediate advantages, returnship programs contribute to building a positive company brand. By demonstrating their commitment to welcome individuals back into the workforce, organizations affirm their investment in the professional development and success of their employees. This commitment becomes a compelling factor in attracting top-tier talent.

During my tenure at Audible, I witnessed numerous instances of returnship candidates succeeding with the aid of coaching and ramp-up programs. Their ability to integrate into the workforce swiftly and transition to full-time employment underscored the effectiveness of such initiatives. Evidently, this approach not only proves instrumental in attracting diverse talent but also contributes significantly to enhancing the company's overall brand.

7.5.3 *Diversity, equity, and inclusion programs*

Diversity, equity, and inclusion (DEI) programs encompass a workforce with diverse backgrounds, ideas, faiths, experiences, age groups, genders, sexual orientations, and walks of life. This variety brings a unique flavor to the company's culture. Equity ensures that individuals with equal skill sets and experience are compensated equally, regardless of other factors.

As an EM and leader, you must champion diversity and inclusion both to attract new talent and retain existing team members. Companies deploy a range of initiatives to foster a diverse workforce, such as groups for working mothers, Latinos, women, members of the LGBTQ+ community, veterans, individuals with disabilities, and employees of color. These programs often incorporate fireside chats, awareness weeks, and reminders highlighting the importance of diversity to cultivate a positive workplace environment. Additionally, offering flexibility in the work environment and demonstrating accommodation and empathy contribute to creating a psychologically safe workplace.

Allow me to share an example from my experience with an allyship program. This initiative brought together like-minded individuals committed to becoming better allies, promoting awareness of diversity and inclusion. The program involved working groups on how to be a better ally, open discussions on relevant topics related to DEI, joint viewing of inclusion videos, and mandatory inclusion training. These efforts not only strengthened bonds within the organization but also deepened understanding, openness, and empathy toward the diverse situations and perspectives of others.

It's crucial to recognize that DEI extends beyond mere hiring or program introduction; it embodies a continuous improvement process and a mindset. Striking the right balance ensures that DEI principles permeate every aspect of the company's operations, transcending policy documents to become ingrained in the company culture. As engineering leaders, it falls on us to not only endorse positive reinforcement in hiring and growth but also amplify this message within our teams and consistently practice what we preach.

What do other leaders have to say?

As a leader, I'm always scouting for talent, even when I do not have a head count. Talented people can help us achieve success, and they can be found everywhere. So I make it a point to stay connected with talented people I meet.

—Sumit Kumar, System Engineering Manager at Cisco

My hiring philosophy is to hire for the attitude, and you can always train for skills. To elaborate skills in the technology world go through many changes, and every professional must regularly update and upgrade themselves. However, the inherent character of an individual is what makes them successful. The attributes I look for are the ability to learn, work in a team, problem-solving skills, and last but not least, can-do attitude. In today's world of various tools like GitHub, Stack Overflow, and the latest ChatGPT, we all are expected to do well on tech competencies; however, none of these tools will ever teach a person to be a great team player, which in a tech world is probably the single biggest need from every individual.

(continued)

When deciding to hire externally versus internally, I prefer developing my own team members for the new positions or even hiring from the larger organization internally; however, there are many circumstances one has to hire externally too. First is the growth scenario when I want to grow my team for various business needs; second, if there are immediate short-term requirements that cannot be fulfilled within the team; and last, if there are special skills required which are difficult to train or if you want to build new competencies in the team. Sometimes, it helps to hire new team members externally as they bring a fresh perspective and newer ideas, which helps the overall team.

—Devika Ahuja, Technology Leader at Strategist

When deciding to hire externally versus internally, some of my considerations tend to be

1. *Has an existing staff member expressed career interest in this need?*
2. *Is this need incremental to an existing staff member, or is it net new skills for the team/organization?*
3. *What is the effect of moving an individual into this role/need on their existing team? Does it shift the skill gap to a new place, or does it fill the skill gap?*
4. *Is an existing staff member looking to demonstrate growth to help solidify a promotion or improvement in performance?*
5. *Is it easy/cost-effective to hire someone with this skill?*

—Nathan Bourgoin, Chief Technology Officer, Alakazam, Inc., Technical Adviser, and Engineering Leader

When hiring people, I look for the growth rate. I don't mind as much where someone is right now, but I want to get enough data points to understand their trajectory. A high growth rate usually means they can learn fast, adapt, work hard, etc. (Obviously, there are ways to fake this, and this is not the only relevant data point.) I also look for grit. How will this candidate handle adversity?

—Jean Bredeche, Head of Engineering at Patch, formerly with Robinhood, Quantopian, and Hubspot

For closing senior engineers, creating an environment of trust and transparency is key! Earning trust is a two-way street; a manager has an equally important responsibility to earn the trust of engineers to be in lock-step in all team matters. Transparency [means] providing well articulated and actionable feedback, sharing opportunities for growth, and improving along with acceptable behaviors.

—Saurabh Gandhi, Senior Director, Software Development at Audible, formerly with American Express

Hire for team fit first and technical skills second. You can teach (and learn) new technologies, new languages, and new skills. If you find someone that is a good fit for your team and your company and matches your corporate culture, you'll have a much more successful time working toward the right technical fit. On the contrary, if you hire for technical skills first and you don't have a good team fit, you're negatively affecting not only your new hire and yourself but your existing team as well.

—Bruce Bergman, Manager at Lytx

7.6 *Stop and think: Practice questions*

1 How many open roles do I have in my organization?
2 What kind of open roles do I have in my organization, and is there a need to backfill them?
3 Is my organization consistently meeting the annual hiring goals?
4 Do we encourage team members to use referrals to attract talent?
5 How are referrals processed, what incentives are given to employees, and what is the success rate of referred candidates?
6 How are referrals treated or considered at my company?
7 What is the ratio of offers extended to accepted?
8 What is the retention rate of employees?

Summary

- The hiring process is a meticulous and time-intensive endeavor that demands meticulous planning and attention to detail. It involves identifying necessary skills, sourcing candidates, reviewing résumés, and conducting interviews to find an ideal match.
- Success in hiring requires a proactive and well-organized approach, encapsulated in a five-step framework that includes identifying hiring needs, sourcing high-potential candidates, setting up fair interview rounds, making sales calls to candidates, and conducting a smooth onboarding process.
- Different considerations apply when hiring for a new team from scratch or an existing team. Building a team from scratch offers flexibility but requires alignment with broader organizational goals. Hiring for an existing team involves considering fit with the team dynamic and culture, ensuring that the new hire contributes to overall success.
- Deciding between external hiring and internal promotion involves weighing pros and cons. External hiring brings in new perspectives, whereas internal promotion shows commitment to employee growth. The choice depends on the specific needs and goals of the company.
- Maintaining a healthy hiring pipeline is crucial for successful talent acquisition. Focus on the company brand, streamline the hiring process, and make personal connections with potential candidates.
- Initiatives such as returnship programs and DEI efforts contribute to attracting and retaining a diverse and talented workforce, fostering a positive work environment and increasing employee satisfaction and retention.

Handling attrition

> *When you ask someone to leave where they are or ask them to join you, you are asking them to make a commitment. I take the commitment seriously.*
>
> Myra Norton, President, Company Arena

Imagine a gentle ping on your phone from the Blind app (https://www.teamblind .com), a portal into the tech world where people seamlessly double their compensation by switching companies. You're intrigued, scanning the latest job trends flooding digital channels. Recruiters, like diligent messengers on LinkedIn, bring tempting job offers with perks ranging from gourmet meals to higher pay. Perhaps you've brushed aside previous offers, but now doubt creeps in. Are you in the right role in the right place?

This scenario reflects the allure of attrition—a force capable of breaking professional ties. *Attrition* is gradual workforce reduction due to talent loss or intentional departures (figure 8.1). It's not just a numerical drop; it also signifies a knowledge drain, leaving employers grappling with the aftermath of departing expertise.

Figure 8.1 **When an employee feels frustrated, you're in danger of losing someone to attrition.**

8.1 *Attrition is inevitable*

Achieving a near-zero attrition rate may be an ideal goal for companies, but the reality often diverges. In many ways, attrition is an inevitable phenomenon that demands adaptability and proactive planning. Suppose that Dennis, a valued team member, decides to leave. Finding a replacement isn't straightforward. After Dennis's departure, several time-consuming procedures must take place:

- The engineering team juggles and balances workload until a new hire or *backfill* (replacement) role is identified.
- The recruiting team lists the vacancy while the accounting team handles settlements.
- Information security secures accounts and revokes access for the departing employee.
- The hiring team navigates candidate identification, interviews, and onboarding, providing ample time for the new hire to learn about the team and the role.

Even if an employee doesn't quit immediately, their contribution diminishes as they consider leaving or conducting a job search. All in all, filling a vacant position incurs substantial costs, including financial costs, with studies suggesting figures close to 1.5 to 2 times the employee's annual salary (https://mng.bz/9dYl).

Cost of backfill = Cost of hiring + cost of onboarding and training + cost of learning and skill development + cost of unfilled time and much more

Although it's essential to maintain a satisfied workforce, some turnover can be advantageous. Eliminating underperformers supports organizational rejuvenation and expansion. By reframing attrition as a chance for favorable transformation rather than merely a hurdle, companies can embrace renewal and ongoing enhancement.

Although turnover isn't always negative, silent departure, marked by declining employee engagement, can indeed be detrimental. Regarding attrition as an opportunity for positive transformation enables companies to cultivate a culture of continual improvement. In section 8.2, we'll delve into the factors that influence an employee's departure decision, enhancing our comprehension of this complex phenomenon.

8.2   Reasons people leave

In the traditional employment landscape, long-term careers with a single employer were common, especially in government and defense roles. Loyalty was fostered over decades through factors such as pension plans, job security, and security clearances. But the modern professional terrain, particularly in the dynamic technology sector, has shifted toward frequent company transitions driven by enhanced compensation, enticing perks, and more fulfilling work experiences.

Today, people leave employers for various reasons, ranging from voluntary choices to involuntary circumstances, creating a spectrum of departure scenarios. The line between voluntary and involuntary attrition can be nebulous, influenced by external factors that shape an individual's decision. External factors can include market conditions such as recession, company restructuring, and lack of workplace flexibility.

In many instances, managers may have some inkling that an employee may be planning to leave. Here are some early signs of impending employee attrition:

- An employee begins to miss deadlines.
- An employee misses work without mentioning the reasons why.
- You see sudden changes in the quality of an employee's work.
- An employee is less engaged in team meetings and is distancing from other team members.
- An employee is less candid in one-on-ones, and if they speak, they are pessimistic about the company's vision.
- Regular surveys on employee morale seem to show some negative trends, though because the surveys are anonymous, it is difficult to find out whether a particular team member is unhappy or whether the problem is broader.
- An employee does not use personal time off, and their vacation lapses.
- Your team has a single point of failure, and this expert on your team might be overwhelmed with work.
- Rarely, an employee is keen to know the company policy on vacation benefits upon departure.
- An employee's friend or mentor in the company recently took a new role in another company.
- An employee starts showing a general negative attitude in the workplace.

Navigating attrition requires foresight and strategies to be explored in section 8.4. Now let's delve into the reasons why people leave their jobs.

8.2.1   Voluntary reasons

In most cases, attrition results from voluntary choices made by employees. Let's explore some of these voluntary reasons.

MISALIGNMENT WITH COMPANY VISION AND PRINCIPLES

Consider Alice, an employee of Company A, dedicated to crafting a premier social networking platform. As a devoted mother of two, she perceives dissonance between the company's mission and her values. The social network becomes a distraction for her children, prompting her to seek employment at Company X, where her values align better.

In this scenario, Alice's choice stems from misalignment of personal beliefs with the company's values. Such situations arise when employees clash with leadership or management practices. Company visions can evolve due to shifts in direction or leadership changes. As an EM with an employee who has misalignment problems, you can do the following:

- *Conduct transparent discussion*—Initiate a one-on-one meeting to understand concerns and communicate your perspective transparently.
- *Collaborate with senior leadership and human resources*—Engage with senior leadership and human resources to explore alternative teams within the organization that align better with the employee's values.
- *Consider amicable departure*—If misalignment persists, parting ways amicably allows the employee to find a more suitable environment while you and the company maintain organizational alignment.

The dynamic nature of company visions underscores the importance of continuous communication and adaptability. Recognizing misalignment early can lead to constructive outcomes for both the employee and the organization.

DISSATISFIED WITH THE ROLE

Let's explore the story of Santiago, an employee of Company B, which is a retail organization. Driven by a passion for innovation, Santiago joined the company with aspirations to contribute to unique product creation. Over two years, however, limited opportunities for innovation and product development became a recurring challenge for him. A chance encounter with a friend who worked at a company with dedicated time for innovation projects fueled Santiago's curiosity. Convinced that his passion for innovation could find a more fertile ground elsewhere, Santiago decided to explore options and ultimately chose to depart.

Following are some situations that may lead employees to seek alternatives:

- *Work–life balance challenges*—Long hours, extensive commutes, virtual-meeting fatigue, or online-presence expectations
- *Monotonous maintenance activities*—Dominance of routine maintenance activities overshadowing excitement about feature development or innovation
- *Tech debt and operational burden*—Wrestling with substantial technical debt and operational challenges, making the coding experience arduous
- *Restricted internal mobility*—Lack of support for internal mobility hindering team transitions and opportunities on other products.

- *Slow career advancement*—Long promotion queues, limited growth opportunities, or company preferences for external hires impeding career progression
- *Learning and growth constraints*—Insufficient resources or time constraints hindering skill acquisition and professional growth

Addressing employee dissatisfaction requires a nuanced approach. For an EM, understanding and empathizing with concerns is crucial; it involves having open conversations, identifying solutions, and aligning them with individual and team needs. EMs must acknowledge, however, that not every problem is within their immediate control. Some challenges require higher-level interventions; others, such as work–life balance, can be managed proactively through load balancing, motivational events, and flexible work hours. Recognizing the nuances of each situation allows you to navigate employee-satisfaction challenges effectively.

COMPENSATION AND BENEFITS

Meet Chris, a seasoned employee of the retail giant X. After five years with minimal promotions, Chris discovers a stark contrast in his earnings compared with market standards during a conversation with a friend who works at a rival company. Inspired, Chris researches salary landscapes on platforms such as Glassdoor (https://www.glassdoor .com/index.htm) and Levels.fyi (https://mng.bz/jXpx), deciding to explore opportunities beyond those at his current employer.

Chris's story reflects a common trend in which individuals actively seek compensation benchmarks by using online platforms, while recruiters play a pivotal role in enticing employees with promises of higher pay and perks. In a competitive job market, the allure of better compensation intensifies, creating a tug-of-war between companies poaching talent with lucrative packages, as shown in figure 8.2.

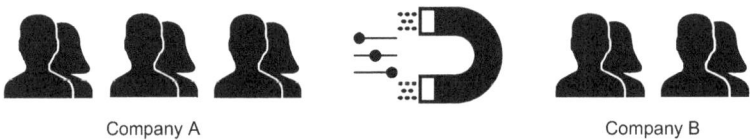

Company A   Company B

Figure 8.2   Online salary databases and recruiter enticements make it easy to poach employees of other companies.

As an EM, your influence in shaping compensation bands may vary based on the company's size. In small organizations, EMs actively contribute to defining these bands, considering team dynamics and individual contributions. In large corporations, compensation structures often originate from higher organizational echelons. Regardless of company size, EMs play a pivotal role in advocating for equitable and competitive compensation packages. This role requires a nuanced understanding of industry benchmarks, individual performance metrics, and organizational strategy. You serve as both a guardian and advocate, navigating compensation negotiations to ensure fair and motivating rewards for your engineering teams.

COMPANY CULTURE AND POLICIES

Company Z, once known for camaraderie and positivity in social networking, faces discontent under new leadership due to changes labeled as unrealistic by the majority of employees. These changes include the following:

- A mandatory work-from-office policy with little to no flexibility to work from home
- Removal of the spot-bonuses award, which was given monthly to employees who went above and beyond in their work
- Lack of collaboration and transparency among team members
- Lack of 360-degree peer feedback
- Incompetent performance management system, especially to handle underperformers
- Ineffective communication with leadership, with lack of communication or top-to-bottom flow of information with a strict hierarchy in place

Will you expect the same set of people to be happy? Probably not! Employee satisfaction varies, as what may be tolerable for one person can be a deal-breaker for another. Mandated office returns may suit those who live close to the office but pose challenges for those who relocated during the pandemic. Company culture and policies on work flexibility, parental leave, community engagement, and alignment with the mission statement contribute significantly to employee satisfaction.

As an EM, you must recognize that not every aspect of the work environment is within your control. Although fostering transparency and collaboration is possible, certain policies may be beyond your immediate influence. Striking a balance between advocating for positive changes and adapting to constraints requires a comprehensive understanding of the organization and its culture and the diverse workforce's needs.

PERSONAL REASONS

The intricacies of personal matters intertwine seamlessly with our professional lives, profoundly shaping our decisions and career paths. Consider a team member who is expecting a child—a situation that demands acknowledgment and genuine support. On a past team, we tailored our approach to accommodate the needs of an expectant mother, from avoiding late meetings to collectively handling on-call duties as her delivery date approached. This approach not only fostered a positive work environment but also minimized attrition risks by ensuring that she felt welcomed and supported.

Various personal reasons may prompt individuals to consider a change in their professional landscape:

- *Family reasons*—Relocating due to a spouse's job transfer or taking a career break for family care
- *Higher studies*—Pursuing academic qualifications such as a master's degree or PhD, leading to a temporary transition to an academic setting

- *Burnout/sabbatical*—Feeling burned out or seeking new ventures
- *Work stability*—Prioritizing job stability over perks during an economic downturn, especially for those on work visas
- *Retirement*—Reaching a point where the desire to retire and spend time with loved ones becomes a driving force
- *Sector change*—Wanting to shift industries, driven by fascination with a different sector or a longing for startup dynamics after working in large corporations

As engineering leaders, it's our responsibility to comprehend these personal motivations, tailor our approach, and provide necessary support to team members who have challenging personal situations that are within our sphere of influence.

8.2.2   *Involuntary reasons*

Now let's look at some of the reasons that may not directly be under an employee's control and can lead to *involuntary attrition*, in which the company terminates the employee.

LAYOFFS

Layoffs are common during downturns, such as the COVID-19 pandemic, as companies align operational costs with revenue. These decisions stem from financial reviews showing an inability to meet targets for EBITDA (earnings before interest, taxes, depreciation, and amortization, which measures core corporate profitability). Poor EBITDA reports may lead to the challenging choice to reduce staff. In startups, financial constraints may force workforce reduction. Layoffs can also be triggered by stock-market panics, organizational restructuring, or discontinuation of unviable products.

Factors such as performance, organizational shutdowns, and role terminations determine whom to let go during layoffs. Layoffs can create a ripple effect, with more individuals leaving due to heightened job-stability concerns. *Unregretted attrition* (letting individuals go due to underperformance) requires delicate conversations. In the prepandemic era, companies such as Airbnb, eBay, and Yahoo! underwent layoffs for financial stability amid increased competition. During the pandemic, high-value technology companies downsized due to previous overhiring, intensifying competition in the job market.

As an EM, your role varies with the company's size, and you may not have a say in staffing decisions. But your responsibilities do include the following:

- *Clear communication*—Align communication with the broader message from leadership. Be transparent about the situation and the reasons behind it.
- *Accessibility*—Keep your doors open and let team members know how they can reach out for support (Slack messages, meeting invites, and so on).
- *Empathy*—Recognize the emotional toll of layoffs and be empathetic toward all employees.

- *Support for remaining members*—Address concerns about project reprioritization, workload balance, responsibility changes, and adjusted expectations for those who remain.
- *Comfort and transparency*—Comfort the team regarding job-stability concerns. Avoid making promises unless you're certain you can keep them, and provide transparent reasoning for layoffs.
- *Morale boost*—Engage in team activities to boost morale and publicly recognize hard work.
- *Support for those affected*—Assist those who are affected by layoffs by connecting them with your peer network, aiding job searches, offering networking and career guidance, and providing recommendations for their work.

Despite your best efforts, more employees may leave. Use this situation as a learning opportunity. Be mentally prepared and professional, actively working on rebuilding a postlayoff team. The situation is undoubtedly challenging for everyone involved.

RETURN TO OFFICE

The pandemic prompted a shift to remote work, but some companies later mandated a return to the office. This mandate may not align with all employees' preferences, potentially leading to counterproductivity, especially for those with long commutes or personal constraints. Hybrid and remote roles have become expectations, and a forced return policy can drive employees to seek opportunities elsewhere. One of my team members relocated from New Jersey to Philadelphia, drastically increasing their commute time from 30 minutes to 2 hours. With the implementation of the return-to-office policy, the team member encountered difficulties and subsequently transitioned to a new role with less stringent return-to-office requirements.

Factors such as commute time, increased expenses, health concerns, and personal beliefs contribute to reluctance to return to the office, which may result in resignations and create a "you're in or you're out" situation. A one-size-fits-all approach risks losing valuable talent, emphasizing the need for flexible arrangements to accommodate individual needs and preferences.

ACQUISITION AND MERGER

Acquisitions and mergers frequently lead to employee departures, especially to eliminate redundant roles. They can also lead to people quitting, as organizational changes create uncertainty about leadership shifts, job responsibilities, cultural differences, and job security. These factors collectively drive employees to explore opportunities outside the company.

COMPETITIVE MARKET

In a competitive job market, attrition rates tend to climb. Take Bob, who might be casually exploring opportunities. He could find himself participating in numerous interviews and securing offers. In a thriving job market, Bob's sought-after skills put him in a strong position to negotiate with companies eager to hire top talent. This dynamic often leads individuals to consider leaving their current employer in search of better career prospects and benefits. Although the competitive job market itself is beyond the control of the employee, when enticing opportunities arise, the decision to leave becomes voluntary, driven by the desire for personal and professional growth.

8.3   *Effect of attrition*

Attrition has cascading effects throughout an organization, affecting individuals at all levels. For operational frontline engineers and managers, it often results in increased workload, heightened stress, demotivation, burnout, and dissatisfaction due to limited resources. For an EM, taking proactive measures is crucial to alleviate the strain on the team. These measures might include pushback when necessary, meticulous workload balancing, and task prioritization.

The emotional toll on the team is significant as well. Losing key players can negatively affect morale and cohesion. Middle management faces added pressure to maintain output with constrained resources. At the executive level, challenges include coping with increasing customer demands, managing low team morale, and dealing with the stress of losing business opportunities. The company's reputation is also affected, making hiring and attracting new talent difficult.

The cost of replacing an employee extends beyond knowledge loss, encompassing expenses for finding replacements, hiring, and onboarding. Temporary dependency on a single team member can pose challenges, with that single member acting as a potential point of failure for the team. Overall, attrition's repercussions extend to many facets of the workplace, affecting individuals, team dynamics, workload distribution, and the overall health of the organization.

8.3.1   *Low team morale*

Attrition directly affects team morale, especially when a high-performing team member departs. This departure can lead to declining work quality, reduced motivation, and a negative atmosphere among the remaining employees, resulting in decreased productivity and developer velocity. Departures for higher-paying jobs can create a ripple effect, causing missed meetings, deadlines, and lower engagement.

For an EM, transparent communication is crucial for addressing such situations. Communicate the departure process clearly, and outline steps for knowledge transfer, task reprioritization, and the hiring process to alleviate strain on the team's morale.

Once, I was working at a company when a key team member was laid off. This layoff created a sense of survivor's guilt for those of us who remained. Because we had no communication from higher up, we walked around wondering whether we would be next to lose our jobs. The effect on team morale was tangible, particularly for those on work visas, for whom job security is closely tied to overall life stability. These challenges highlighted the need for effective communication and support strategies during difficult times.

8.3.2 Loss of knowledge

Every departure from a team creates a knowledge and context gap that requires attention. On a team of five engineers, each of whom is a subject-matter expert (SME), the exit of one team member necessitates rebuilding domain knowledge and creating meticulous documentation. Avoiding single points of failure on teams is crucial for mitigating the effect of knowledge loss, which can lead to an additional workload on remaining team members and extended task-completion times until expertise is rebuilt. This delay can significantly affect business operations, potentially hindering timely customer service.

Consider a company that is downsizing nearly half its workforce due to market conditions. The remaining employees may lack knowledge about how half the systems work, posing risks. The loss and transfer of knowledge become critical concerns, with the departing individual ideally transferring specific knowledge to the team. This process can be time-consuming, however, leading to significant loss of productive time for the team. The challenge is determining the most critical information to transfer—a decision that is typically left to the departing individual, who may already be mentally disengaged. Section 8.4.3 talks about how to navigate a transition when an employee leaves.

8.3.3 High hiring and backfill cost

The hiring process is intricate and resource-intensive, involving stages such as candidate identification, interview loops, debriefing, offer sharing, and onboarding. These steps demand significant time and financial investment and cannot be handled by a single individual. In competitive markets, the challenges of hiring become more pronounced. Conducting interviews and making offers only to realize a limited acceptance rate can be frustrating and resource-draining (although if we have a successful hire, the process was worthwhile). Additionally, if the top candidate rejects the offer, the hiring process starts anew, presenting a dilemma: compromise on standards or risk losing more time searching for the ideal candidate.

The effects of attrition on existing employees, teams, and the business are substantial. Filling open roles involves substantial costs, potentially reaching 1.5 to 2 times an employee's annual salary. These costs include not only recruitment expenses but also investment in onboarding and training.

Let's do some quick basic math to understand the concept. Suppose that we want to calculate the total cost to backfill an open role for a software engineer with a $100,000 annual salary:

- *Hiring cost*—Includes recruiter cost and engineering team cost
    - *Recruiter cost*—Suppose that the annual salary is $60,000, and the recruiter spent 40 hours' (1 week's) worth of effort. These criteria make monthly salary $60,000/12 = $5,000. For simplicity, let's say that each month has 4 weeks, so 1 week of effort = $1,250.

- *Engineering team cost*—This cost involves *interview loops*, which are calls with potential candidates to do a sale call. Let's assume that each engineer makes roughly $100,000 and that 4 engineer loops are done for 10 potential candidates before the prime candidate is found. Roughly, each engineer spent 2 hours per candidate, so 4 engineers* 10 candidates*2 hours = 80 hours = 2 weeks, or $8,300/2 = $4,150.
  - *Total*—The costs in this scenario add up to $1,250 + $4,150 = $5,400.
- *Onboarding cost*—Includes training cost
  - *Training cost*—Suppose that we used an internal/external trainer for 2 days who charged $5,000 for the training.
  - *Ramp-up-period cost*—The engineer was given 60 days to ramp up to the new technology stack and the company culture, at a cost of $100,000*(2/12) = $16,600.
  - *Total*—The costs in this scenario add up to $5,000 + $16,600 = $21,600.
- *Miscellaneous costs*—Cost of putting up job ads, using tools to filter through résumés, and so on = $3,000
- *Grand total*—All the above costs result in a total $30,000 in backfill cost.

Now compare this grand total with the hypothetical cost of retaining the existing employee, estimated at $10,000 (maybe to match the new job offer they got or to invest in their training). The retention cost is significantly lower—only a third of the expense associated with hiring a new employee. Moreover, the loss of institutional knowledge and productivity when an existing employee leaves adds further intangible costs.

Recognizing the financial implications underlines the importance of investing in existing employees and implementing effective retention strategies. Proactively addressing attrition challenges becomes crucial for sustainable workforce management.

8.4   Getting ahead of attrition

Attrition is an inevitable aspect of any workforce, but as engineering leaders, our responsibility is to plan strategically to mitigate its effect. This strategy involves a combination of proactive, reactive, and transitional measures. Additionally, it's crucial to collaborate with human resources and benefits teams to implement company-wide strategies. Attrition can manifest in various scenarios, some predictable and others sudden. Let's deep-dive into some steps you can take, depending on the situation you are tasked with.

8.4.1   Proactive measures

If employees feel safe and valued, they are bound to stay at a company for extended periods. Proactive measures help leaders get ahead of attrition and plan for it. You, as the leader, must continuously iterate and look for ways to improve the workplace so that people love where they work. The following sections discuss some standard proactive measures.

OPTIMIZE HIRING

Developing effective hiring strategies is essential for attracting top talent in the industry, prioritizing a blend of technical expertise and cultural alignment. To maximize success in hiring, it's important to concentrate on both acquiring new talent and retaining existing employees. One effective method is to encourage referral-based hiring: recruiting new employees through recommendations by existing employees within the organization or from their personal networks. Referral-based hiring can significantly boost positive word-of-mouth recommendations.

PROMOTE INTERNAL MOBILITY AND DEVELOPMENT PROGRAMS

Promoting employee development is crucial for both short-term satisfaction and long-term retention. Regular one-on-ones and career discussions, coupled with stretch goals aligned with individual aspirations, contribute to continuous learning and growth. Robust onboarding programs and initiatives such as comprehensive training in emerging technologies not only build foundational knowledge but also upskill employees continuously.

At my previous company, we initiated a comprehensive training program in introductory machine learning for all team members. This initiative had dual benefits: it enabled our team to prepare for upcoming challenges and allowed members to enhance their technical skills. Simultaneously, we actively encouraged scenarios where employees sought role changes, such as transitioning from a software engineer to a product manager or vice versa. Internal opportunities within the company were promoted, fostering an environment where individuals could explore diverse roles. One of the senior engineers on my team, who was proficient in project delivery and execution, expressed waning interest in coding exclusively. As their manager, I identified the root cause of their dissatisfaction and facilitated a transition to a role better aligned with their aspirations: shifting from a senior software engineer to a senior technical program manager. Identifying and addressing such needs proactively can prevent talent loss.

RECOGNIZE EMPLOYEES

In chapter 6, we explored the significance of rewards and recognition in maintaining workforce motivation. Frequent and objective acknowledgment of employees is crucial for appreciating their excellent work, fostering positive sentiments, and providing motivation.

CREATE A CONDUCIVE WORK CULTURE

Ensuring a positive working environment is essential for fostering employee satisfaction and motivation. Here are some key practices to achieve this goal:

- Maintain open and transparent communication channels to facilitate a bidirectional flow of information, ensuring that employees feel heard and valued.
- Clearly communicate team visions and goals, aligning them with the company's mission and vision to promote a sense of purpose and inclusiveness.

- Emphasize innovation by providing avenues for employees to contribute ideas, potentially through hackathons or innovation challenges, fostering a culture of creativity and involvement.
- Build a diverse and inclusive workforce, creating an environment where people from various backgrounds feel safe, valued, and encouraged to share their perspectives.
- Offer flexibility in work arrangements, including work-from-home support, rampback programs, and initiatives to support individuals with specific needs (specially abled, working mothers, and so on), fostering adaptability in the hybrid working mode. In the new paradigm of hybrid work, the team may have a no-meeting day that team members use to work on their independent tasks and protect their time spent in meetings.
- Provide training programs for leaders to enhance their skills in managing performance and conducting career growth discussions, including opportunities to attend and participate in technical conferences and conventions.
- Balance work and play by organizing fun holiday events and team-building activities to strengthen relationships among team members. Remember that all work and no play makes Jack a dull boy.

ESTABLISH PERIODIC FEEDBACK MECHANISM

Periodic surveys and feedback mechanisms are vital for maintaining open communication and addressing concerns proactively. These surveys can cover aspects such as developer tools, processes, work-from-home support, career growth, and leadership. Engaging employees in this manner allows the company to understand their concerns and work toward resolving them promptly.

An approachable leadership style encourages employees to express dissatisfaction or potential departure in advance, fostering a candid relationship. But it's crucial to handle this information responsibly and involve human resources in brainstorming solutions. The goal is to stay ahead of attrition.

Insights from surveys guide the company in prioritizing critical areas for improvement, enabling the effective allocation of resources. Anonymity in surveys encourages honest feedback, creating an environment where employees can express thoughts freely. At companies I've been part of, survey results are thoroughly examined at all levels, prompting leadership to take actionable steps for continuous improvement while maintaining professionalism and ethical boundaries.

8.4.2   *Reactive measures*

When an employee's resignation is anticipated or unexpected surprises arise, managers can take actions to retain that employee, such as considering job-role adjustments or offering compensation changes. In some circumstances, however, retention may not be feasible, such as when an employee needs to relocate for personal reasons. The crucial aspect is to respond promptly upon becoming aware of the situation and implement appropriate measures. It's essential to learn from these experiences to prevent similar occurrences in the future.

UNDERSTAND THE ROOT CAUSE

If David from the team decides to resign, the first step is identifying the reason, such as work-related dissatisfaction, flexibility problems, personal considerations, or compensation concerns. Self-reflection is crucial for discerning whether any of your actions led to an employee's decision to leave. If some factors are within your control—if David is leaving due to project-related problems, for example—you can take proactive steps such as offering support or exploring project changes. When some factors are uncontrollable, such as a family-related relocation, acceptance is key. I once had a team member who left due to his family's relocation to the West Coast, where the company had no presence. In such cases, as a manager, you should wish the departing employee well and leave the door open for a potential return if circumstances change.

LAST RESORT TO KEEP THE EMPLOYEE

When a valuable employee is contemplating leaving, both the employer and the manager should engage in a "dive and save" approach, exerting extra efforts to retain the employee given their significance to the company. It's essential to determine whether the decision is final or whether there's room to address the employee's concerns. In one case, one of my team members who had a PhD in machine learning expressed dissatisfaction and considered opportunities elsewhere. Recognizing their value, I proactively connected them with relevant teams within the company, identifying a role that aligned better with their expertise and goals. This effort successfully retained the employee's skills, emphasizing the importance of internal mobility and commitment to retaining valuable talent.

8.4.3 Point of no return

Sections 8.4.1 and 8.4.2 explored proactive and reactive measures to prevent attrition, retain employees, and secure a better fit within the company. In some instances, however, the decision to leave is irreversible. I encountered this situation when an employee received competitive offers with significantly higher pay. Despite our efforts to negotiate with the compensation department and human resources, the vast pay gap rendered those attempts unsuccessful. In such a situation, the focus shifts to planning the employee's departure.

ACTION PLAN FOR A SEAMLESS TRANSITION

As the engineering leader, your primary objective is to facilitate a smooth departure and transition for both your team and the departing employee, minimizing disruptions. When a key engineer decides to leave—particularly one with expertise in a critical service—knowledge distribution within the team becomes crucial. Implement measures such as lunch-and-learn sessions, technical talks, and thorough documentation to prevent a single point of failure and maintain a balanced workload.

Additionally, prioritize creating a positive experience for the departing employee. Plan for a seamless transition and express gratitude through gestures such as a thoughtful thank-you card signed by the team. Treating departing employees with respect not only ensures a positive transition but also reflects positively on the team's culture. Also, maintaining communication with departing engineers, particularly those who demonstrated strong performance, has proved to be advantageous for me. Continuing to stay connected with former team members yields numerous benefits—notably, facilitating a valuable network for future hiring needs. Because I nurture these relationships, when the time comes to recruit new engineers, I can readily tap this pool of talented individuals to see whether any of my past reports are suitable for the role. Figure 8.3 is a sample offboarding list that can guide a seamless transition.

	Action plan	Status
☐	Provide robust documentation on the projects being worked on and their state/outstanding tasks	
☐	Document the important system designs and the processes. If the documentation already exists, make sure it's useful, relevant, and up to date.	
☐	Hold technical talks or lunch-and-learn sessions that are recorded, and cover the essential details of the systems and projects they've worked on in their time at the company.	
☐	Do pair programming sessions with team members for critical components as needed, especially to share troubleshooting mechanisms for common production issues, ensuring that they are well documented.	
☐	Review any access permissions, and revoke all access to critical systems, infrastructure, and so on for the departing employee.	
☐	Retrieve important contacts for cross-functional partners per project/points of contact.	
☐	Do a manager-level exit interview.	
☐	Provide a thank-you note for the employee from the team.	

Figure 8.3   A sample offboarding checklist to use for a seamless transition when an employee departs the team

Every attrition experience serves as a valuable learning opportunity, shaping future retention strategies. Keep existing employees motivated and engaged through team-building activities, clear communication of the team's vision, and regular one-on-one conversations to better understand their goals and aspirations.

FEEDBACK MECHANISM

Use each departure as a learning opportunity to gather feedback for process improvement. Debrief the departing employee to understand the root cause; then follow up with an exit interview through human resources for additional insights. This feedback loop helps identify trends, such as employees leaving for compensation reasons. Addressing these trends in human resources and company-wide is essential.

During the postdeparture phase, engage with remaining employees to address their concerns and collaborate on strategies to mitigate the effect. Learning from attrition experiences is crucial in a competitive job market. Despite the challenges, implementing small measures and gaining insights from each departure contribute to creating a positive work environment and attracting top talent.

What do other leaders have to say?

In some kind of dystopian ideal world, everyone is fungible, and attrition leads us simply to rearrange our resources (team members) according to project priorities and meanwhile to hire back a new resource. But in reality, everyone is unique, i.e., not fungible; they have different interests and skills gained from different experiences over different careers. This means that we can't quite so easily replace someone.

We expect some constant (hopefully low) attrition rate and have enough of a pipeline of team members moving up in tenure and expertise such that when folks leave, others can fill in (temporarily or permanently). I think it's rare that we have that pipeline fully fleshed out, but we can try to mitigate it through documentation and other knowledge sharing. All the while, we should be training our team up.

—Richard Frank, Senior Software Engineer (former manager) at Two Sigma,
formerly with Robinhood

Some reasons for attrition:

- *Growth mismatch—Companies need to grow at some pace for their employees to feel like they are also growing (there are professional opportunities to grow, like promotions, more responsibilities, and so on). If there is a mismatch between the company growth rate and the employee growth rate, then attrition is expected.*

- *Systematic compensation problems—If lots of people are leaving due to compensation problems, then we need to fix that. I've fortunately never been in this situation.*

- *One-off cases—It's natural for people to pursue other opportunities, hopefully because they are running to something new, not running away from their current situation. (If so, the company needs to examine what happened).*

In all cases, it's important to maintain trust with the remaining team. Share what you can share about the attrition, explain the backfill plans, have one-on-ones with anyone you're worried about, etc. In terms of getting ahead of attrition, assuming compensation is not the problem; it's all about matching what an employee wants (their goals, what fulfills them, etc.) with the responsibilities they are being given. An EM should know what their teammates' goals are and ensure (as much as possible) that they are being met or else being up front with them and sharing how they might be met later on.

—Jean Bredeche, Head of Engineering at Patch,
formerly with Robinhood, Quantopian, and Hubspot

Very recently, I had an employee who decided to put down papers primarily because of pay differences. I started by showing him the career path we had planned for him and the opportunities he would have if he continued with the team. I also shared his path toward becoming a senior and how that would take him closer to the offer he had from outside. Even though he still took the outside opportunity, that showed how much we cared for our employees, keeping an option of returnship.

—Madhur Kathuria, Engineering Leader at Microsoft,
formerly with Moengage, Oracle, and IIT

(continued)

The first time someone on my team told me they were leaving, they were visibly emotional about it. I imagine feeling guilty and potentially uncertain about my reaction; it was their first time leaving a job. Given my own short tenure in my role, I felt somewhat emotional myself. I felt like I'd let them down, that their leaving was my failure, even though they were leaving for a role more aligned with their interests. They had originally joined our company to pursue a particular focus (NLP), but our team did not move in that direction. My next step was to discuss with my manager how to proceed. We talked about immediate tactics (which I don't recall much anymore), and he reassured me that I wasn't the cause and reminded me of the inevitability of employees changing companies. I remember walking to calm down and letting the information sink in.

—Richard Frank, Senior Software Engineer (former manager) at Two Sigma,
formerly with Robinhood

My philosophy to handle attrition is that the personal relationship effect of attrition is unavoidable. People will leave what others like, and you can do nothing about it. The best way I have found to manage this is to make sure that when someone does leave, they aren't also leaving the team with a skill gap. Cross-train and remove skill silos to reduce the team risk when someone does leave proactively.

—Nathan Bourgoin, Chief Technology Officer at Alakazam, Inc.,
Technical Adviser, and Engineering Leader

To handle attrition: Ensure the team is motivated and has enough challenges and consistent opportunities to learn & grow, Work on building the bench strength and encourage knowledge sharing, Employees often want to try new things, and as EM, it's important to find those opportunities as short-term/long-term assignments even if they are outside of your org.

—Saurabh Gandhi, Senior Director, Software Development at Audible,
formerly with American Express

Always maintain an open and honest line of communication with your employees about how they're doing, whether they are happy in their role, and whether they feel respected and appreciated. Encourage them to come to you first when they are unhappy so that you can work with them to either improve their condition, transition to a new role elsewhere in the company or work towards helping them find their happy place somewhere else. An EM's first response to such a conversation should be "How can I help?"

—Bruce Bergman, Manager at Lytx

8.5   Stop and think: Practice questions

1   Do I feel motivated to go to work? Does my company promote innovation?
2   What top three things are essential for me at the workplace?
3   Does my company value giving recognition for good work?
4   Is anyone other than me involved in my career development process?
5   Am I aligned with the mission and vision of the company I work for?
6   Do I feel supported by my leadership and the company culture?

Summary

- Attrition, defined as reduction in the workforce, can stem from various factors, including the employer's ability to retain talent, personal circumstances, layoffs, or performance problems.
- The departure of an employee generates significant costs involving recruiting, engineering, and leadership, affecting customers and project deliverables.
- People move on for two major categories of reasons:
  - *Voluntary*—This category can encompass a variety of reasons. Maybe the employee is not aligned with the mission statement of the company or is dissatisfied with their role (may be looking for an opportunity to innovate but isn't getting it) or compensation. Or the company culture may not be conducive to the employee's growth. Also, family reasons may be involved.
  - *Involuntary*—Sometimes, factors that lead to departure are outside the employee's control, such as layoffs, termination due to underperformance, an enforced office return that is unsuitable for the employee, a merger or acquisition, or a competitive job market.
- Attrition negatively affects employee morale. It also results in a loss of contextual knowledge and increases the burden of technical operations on existing employees temporarily. Additionally, the cost and effort involved in hiring and filling the vacant role can disrupt the team's immediate plans.
- Engineering leaders can get ahead of attrition by taking measures such as the following:
  - *Proactive measures*—These measures include optimizing the hiring process, creating career development opportunities, promoting internal mobility, fostering a reward-and-recognition culture, establishing a supportive work environment where employees feel safe and valued, and implementing regular feedback mechanisms to prevent unexpected problems.
  - *Reactive measures*—If you're informed about an employee's decision to leave, it is important to undertake specific measures such as identifying the root cause and, if necessary, discussing compensation concerns with human resources. Additionally, exploring alternative roles within the company that align with the employee's skills and interests can help you retain them.
  - *Point of no return*—When an employee is resolute in their decision to leave, it is important for the leader to prioritize a smooth transition for both the departing employee and the remaining team members. It is also valuable to view this situation as a learning opportunity, identifying any gaps that can be addressed within the team.
- Navigating attrition is a multifaceted endeavor that involves understanding diverse reasons for employee departures, implementing strategic measures, and fostering a workplace culture that values and retains talent.

Part 2

Projects and the cross-functional world

Having delved into the human aspects that form the bedrock of effective engineering management, now you set sail into the realm of projects and partnerships. As an engineering manager (EM), you are responsible for conducting projects and navigating the complexities of timelines, resources, and objectives. In the chapters that follow, you will learn about strategies for leading projects and handling cross-functional partnerships.

Chapter 9 talks about the importance of effective cross-functional collaboration, common challenges, effective collaboration, and communication in a cross-functional setting.

Chapter 10 walks you through the project life-cycle phases and your role as an EM, as well as the stages of the project life cycle, such as preplanning, planning, execution, and postexecution.

Chapter 11 discusses the importance of setting and managing expectations, as well as common challenges, and presents a framework for managing expectations.

As you navigate the intricate web of projects and partnerships, you'll emerge equipped with the tools you need to lead your team across the evolving terrain of technological innovation. So let's dive right in.

Working with cross-functional partners

Talent wins games, but teamwork and intelligence win championships.

—Michael Jordan

David, an engineering manager (EM) at Musica, is vital to integrating music recommendation platforms across the company's products. Despite ambitious goals, his team faces productivity challenges, mainly in cross-functional collaboration. One primary challenge is communication breakdowns, where information and priorities may not be effectively communicated between teams, leading to misunderstandings

181

or delays in project execution. Additionally, differing priorities and objectives among cross-functional teams can result in conflicting agendas, making it challenging to align efforts toward common goals. Moreover, varying work styles and approaches to problem-solving across different functions can create friction and hinder smooth collaboration. The decline in productivity raises a critical question: how can David address and rectify this problem?

Cross-functional collaboration, in which multiple teams work collectively toward a shared goal, is a common challenge for an EM. This collaboration may involve teams such as product management, engineering, design, quality assurance, user experience (UX), and legal, all aligning efforts to achieve success by harnessing specialized skills and yielding exceptional product experiences. Figure 9.1 illustrates this collaboration, showcasing the integration of various functions. Projects requiring cross-team collaboration also facilitate networking, which helps EMs develop leadership skills.

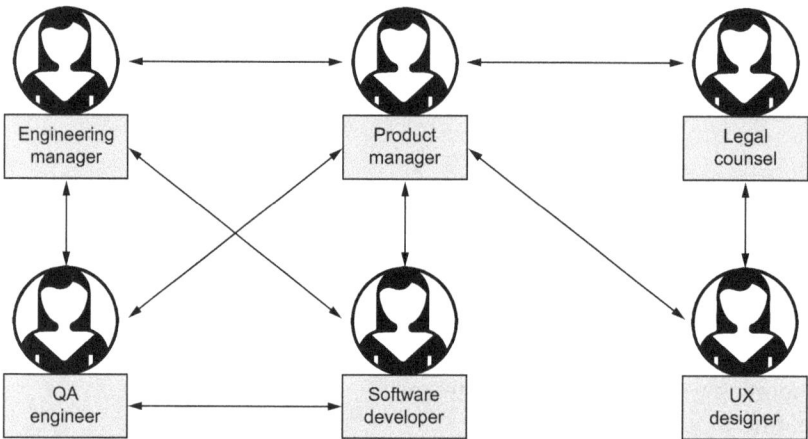

Figure 9.1   Sample interdependency of cross-functional partners. At minimum, the EM communicates with product managers, software developers, and QA engineers.

A *Harvard Business Review* study (https://mng.bz/WE20) reveals that nearly 75% of cross-functional teams exhibit dysfunction. Often, leadership's lack of a structured approach to problem-solving contributes to this dysfunction. Clear guidance and precise governance are essential for efficient cross-team collaboration, as is having a collaborative ecosystem in place. Let's explore common problems that hinder effective collaboration.

9.1   *Dealing with common challenges*

Imagine leading a greenfield development to enhance your product's profile page, collaborating with various teams such as marketing, UX, and engineering. As the feature nears completion, critical questions arise on the marketing team. Attempts to align with the product manager (PM), however, result in conflicting priorities and busy schedules, causing a weeklong delay in contact. Limited availability of the PM leads to no definitive next steps, leaving the project feature in limbo and the launch postponed.

Such challenges are common in the technical industry, illustrating difficulties in cross-functional collaboration. Despite good intentions, conflicting priorities and overloaded schedules often hinder project success. This scenario reflects many of the recurring problems an EM faces when overseeing collaboration.

9.1.1 Competing priorities across different teams

Competing priorities among teams significantly hinder effective collaboration in cross-functional projects. A delay in delivering product features arises from conflicting goals across organizational teams, each pursuing its own objectives. When you're working on projects with multiple cross-functional partners, aligning individual team goals with the overall project objective becomes crucial.

In a case study, our team aimed to enhance customer engagement metrics for a mobile app, a shared goal with cross-functional partners. But the core infrastructure team, handling various features for multiple product teams, had competing priorities. Aligning the customer engagement goal with their priorities proved challenging. Despite continuous efforts, the core infrastructure team's investment fell short, leading to delays and compromises on project requirements.

This example highlights how misaligned goals can disrupt cross-functional collaboration. Another common scenario involves platform teams and their dependencies. Incorrect abstractions in platform development can lead to conflicting directions, necessitating early risk identification and collaboration with leadership. Establishing a consistent company-wide prioritization of projects can align all teams and foster collaboration. Challenges arise when project goals themselves are poorly defined; explore section 9.1.2 for further insights.

9.1.2 Ill-defined goals

Poorly defined goals contribute to ineffective cross-functional collaboration. Teams may be assigned vague projects targeting a general problem statement that lacks clarity or concrete objectives. Teams might lack specific metrics for improvement, leading to aimless pursuit of poorly understood problems.

Consider David, an EM at a small social media company, tasked with addressing deteriorating customer sentiment on the website. The problem statement lacks concrete backing, making it challenging to determine customer sentiment holistically across various engagement points. The project appears to be prioritized ad-hoc, lacking involvement from the data science or data engineering teams to measure customer sentiments accurately. To avoid such pitfalls, it's crucial for the EM to define project goals in depth, strategically identify the minimum required teams, and ensure effective communication and coordination for clarity.

9.1.3   *Inefficient coordination and communication*

Communication breakdowns are common in cross-functional projects, arising from varied communication protocols among teams. Some teams may follow weekly stand-ups, whereas others prefer daily check-ins, and these differences may lead to irregular communication. Engineers on cross-functional teams may neglect updates due to unfamiliarity with established processes, causing inefficiencies and breakdowns. Resistance to adapting to new working methods can further contribute to communication challenges.

Involving more teams increases the likelihood of inefficient coordination and communication. Team leaders may have personal reasons, such as resistance to changing standup frequencies, that can hinder effective communication. Adjusting communication methods based on project urgency, such as transitioning to daily standups during critical phases, can alleviate collaboration problems.

9.1.4   *Unclear roles and responsibilities*

Unclear roles and responsibilities can also hinder cross-partner collaboration. Consider Rajesh, an EM leading a project to enhance customer growth through machine learning infrastructure. In collaborating with Ian's team, Rajesh's team initially agreed on using an existing framework, with research scientists handling machine learning and Rajesh's team working on ranking APIs.

Midway through the project, however, critical aspects for deploying the machine learning model in production were not assigned to either team, causing confusion, churn, and delays. Vague responsibilities impeded progress, causing the teams to miss the opportunity to enhance customer experience sooner. The late realization led one team to backtrack on commitments. Clearly defining the roles and responsibilities of each team at the outset could have made the project more successful.

Although it's natural to overlook certain aspects, it's crucial to maintain adaptability and delegate tasks even after a project has commenced. Perfection is elusive, but our plans are not set in stone. Embracing an agile approach demands openness to adjustments as circumstances evolve.

9.1.5   *Conflicts*

When conflicts arise between teams, the project's success can be at risk. Excessive discord, stemming from factors such as competitiveness among technical leaders or personal conflicts between team members, can create unfavorable working conditions. Power dynamics become tricky, especially with varying seniority levels. Unresolved feedback dismissals and nonprofessional reasons such as personality differences can fuel conflicts between team members. Effective EMs should avoid destructive behaviors and manage conflicts to refocus everyone on the common goal.

Conflicts about the technical aspects of the project may also surface, as in a recent project where two senior engineers had conflicting ideas on system design. Striving for consensus is crucial, but individual preferences can cause disagreements. The key to avoiding these disruptions and streamlining decision-making during conflicts is to designate a project authority figure early. Appointing a final authority from the project's outset not only mitigates conflict but also simplifies decision-making and enhances project execution.

9.1.6 Geographical constraints

The recent shift toward remote work, accelerated by the COVID-19 pandemic, has led to teams being spread across different time zones, posing a challenge to effective cross-functional collaboration. Even before the pandemic, many companies operated offices worldwide, making this kind of collaboration a common occurrence.

During one of my projects, I encountered significant scheduling difficulties due to the diverse locations of the teams involved. With teams spanning the United Kingdom, India, Australia, and the United States, coordinating meetings became a complex task. Aligning schedules with the London team, which had only a six-hour time difference from my office in the United States, was somewhat manageable. Coordinating with teams in India and Australia presented more significant challenges. To address this situation, I prioritized establishing strong working relationships and clear communication protocols beforehand. This process involved scheduling regular check-ins with each team to discuss progress, address concerns, and align priorities across time zones. Additionally, I implemented tools and platforms that facilitated real-time collaboration, such as videoconferencing and shared project management software. To specifically tackle scheduling technical design sessions, we clearly defined meeting times, agendas, and roles. Further, I used asynchronous communication channels, such as detailed documentation and recorded meetings, to ensure that team members in different time zones could stay updated and contribute to technical designs even outside scheduled meetings. Overall, proactive communication, strong relationships, and efficient use of technology were key to overcoming the scheduling challenges inherent in cross-partner collaboration.

> **TIP** Some suggested reading materials on this topic are The Remote Playbook (https://mng.bz/8wOP) and the Medium blog post at https://mng.bz/EZaJ.

9.1.7 Missing support/underperforming partners

Insufficient support from or underperformance by a cross-functional partner can significantly impede certain projects. Debugging and resolving this challenge becomes complex, especially when you lack direct managerial authority over those employees. Underperformance may result from personal problems, pursuit of other job opportunities, or general disengagement, complicating matters further. Identifying underperformance early is crucial, requiring validation through soft feedback from other team members.

When you recognize underperformance, providing guidance and robust support is essential. Immediate actions can include pointing to internal resources, suggesting mentors, and collaborating with the underperforming partner's manager to establish concrete goals. Another factor contributing to underperformance may be the complexity of projects with numerous moving parts, which section 9.1.8 explores in detail. For a deeper dive into managing performance, refer to chapter 4.

9.1.8   *Overwhelming work*

Cross-functional collaboration involves numerous interconnected components, and for an engineer who's accustomed to a focused coding environment, this situation can be overwhelming. On a previous team of mine, a new engineer from a core infrastructure background faced challenges in initiating a major project: PMs lacked transparency, engineers struggled with requirements, and UX considerations were overlooked. Investigating the project's stagnation revealed that the root cause was that the engineer felt overwhelmed. Collaborating with a senior engineer on the team for support could have jump-started the project and facilitated progress. This example emphasizes the need for additional support on projects that require cross-functional collaboration.

9.2   *Building a cross-functional team*

Building a cross-functional team that consists of engineers, designers, analysts, and more is a pivotal task for any software EM, requiring a thoughtful and strategic approach. The following sections discuss actionable steps for constructing a cohesive, high-performing cross-functional team.

Did you know?

A common but old strategy for group team development is the Forming, Storming, Norming, and Performing model (https://mng.bz/NR1D), first proposed by Bruce Tuckman. This model, shown in the accompanying figure, facilitates the cultivation of high-performing teams by harnessing the optimal potential of each team member.

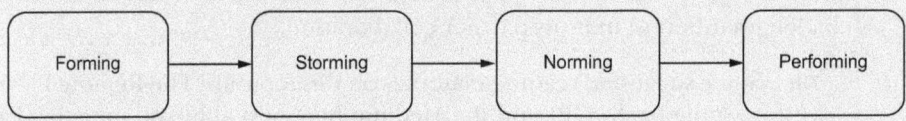

The Forming-Storming-Norming-Performing model for team development

The four stages of the model are

- *Forming*—This initial stage focuses on team formation, involving meetings and networking sessions in which team members can acquaint themselves. It includes discussions and agreements on crucial aspects such as the preferred agile approach, team ceremonies, and individual roles in the development process. As the EM, your role is to collaborate with cross-functional partners, fostering team cohesion, establishing a clear direction, and defining the team's mission. This phase marks a shift from casual conversation to laying the groundwork for a sustained working relationship.

- *Storming*—As previously mentioned, not everything unfolds as anticipated, and conflicts are inevitable. The storming stage encapsulates these disagreements, emphasizing the importance of empathy, understanding perspectives, identifying common ground, and navigating through what works and what doesn't. Effective conflict management and collaborative problem-solving are central to gaining team buy-in. Empowering the team to decide on their working methods autonomously is crucial. Recognize the uniqueness of each team and allow teams to discover their own approaches and resolutions.
- *Norming*—When the team has figured out difficult situations through storming, it is reasonable for them to find a working relationship and make it a norm. This does not mean everyone is always thinking the same; it means that open discussions and negotiations help bring them to a joint resolution. Getting to normal might not be an easy walk and will take time and energy, sometimes iterating over a few ways of working to find the right sweet spot for the team.
- *Performing*—In this rewarding stage, the team has matured, achieving a harmonious synergy that characterizes a high-performing team. As the EM, your role is continuing to support team members, identifying areas where additional assistance and resources can enhance their success. Acknowledging individual contributions becomes crucial at this juncture to bolster confidence. It's essential to note that not every team reaches this phase. Failure to navigate the preceding stages effectively can impede progress, preventing the team from attaining high-performance status.

The model helps team members build trust and transparency and work together toward a common mission.

9.2.1   Clarifying and aligning on goals

Competing priorities and unclear, misaligned goals are key factors contributing to dysfunction on cross-functional teams. To foster success, it's crucial to address competing priorities and align on clear objectives. Communication challenges may arise, especially in fast-paced start-ups, making it essential for engineering leaders to define well-aligned goals and mission statements from the outset. A common problem is misalignment between UX and engineering teams, often resolved by appointing an engineering point of contact for collaboration and breaking efforts into milestones.

Did you know?

Nemawashi (https://safetyculture.com/topics/nemawashi), a Japanese business practice, involves discreetly preparing for a proposed change or project by engaging with relevant stakeholders, gathering their support and feedback before making a formal announcement. This process is another way to ensure that concerned people are in alignment and to set the foundation before the central formal meeting. It also gives people space to discuss their questions and concerns outside the broader audience.

Here are some things you can do as an EM:

- Adapt on the fly to enable teams to deliver results efficiently and iterate on improvements for a better UX.
- Share a clear vision and robust documentation on team charter and ownership with the team members.
- Outline what is in scope and what is not.
- Establish dedicated communication channels, and align on the frequency of communication. Create specific channels or groups for different purposes, such as technical-design discussions and general support. Encourage team members to use these channels, fostering inclusivity and a sense of belonging. Simultaneously, exercise caution against overextending communication channels, which risks diluting the core message and purpose. It's essential to strike a balance to maintain clarity and focus during the collaborative process.
- Periodically, create anonymous platforms for raising concerns, empowering team members to ask challenging questions.
- Use project tracking tools such as Jira (https://www.atlassian.com/software/jira) or alternatives such as Asana (https://asana.com) or Trello (https://trello.com) for transparent collaboration, allowing team members to monitor task status and enhance communication.

9.2.2 *Identifying key skills and roles*

For an EM, it's essential to assess project requirements and identify key skills and roles for success. Build a diverse team that includes developers, designers, a technical program manager, QA testers, and domain experts, ensuring a well-rounded staff.

RACI, which stands for Responsible, Accountable, Consulted, and Informed (https://www.forbes.com/advisor/business/raci-chart), is a responsibility assignment matrix that helps you define clear roles and responsibilities for each member who is part of the project. This tool helps set involvement and expectations for each member, as well as remove blurred lines about the roles and what is expected of them. Additionally, the model delineates specific activities and project deliverables, assigning ownership to respective team members. This framework serves as a comprehensive tool for tracking progress both during and after the project launch. Figure 9.2 shows a sample RACI matrix.

Implementing a RACI model helps you defining roles and responsibilities, preventing duplication of work and fostering accountability within the cross-functional team. When dealing you're with consultants or third-party vendors, coordinate regular meetings to discuss progress, align with company policies, and establish expectations for deliverables and quality standards. Collaborate closely with your legal team; assign a team member to work closely with external partners, facilitating knowledge transfer and building expertise.

RACI Matrix

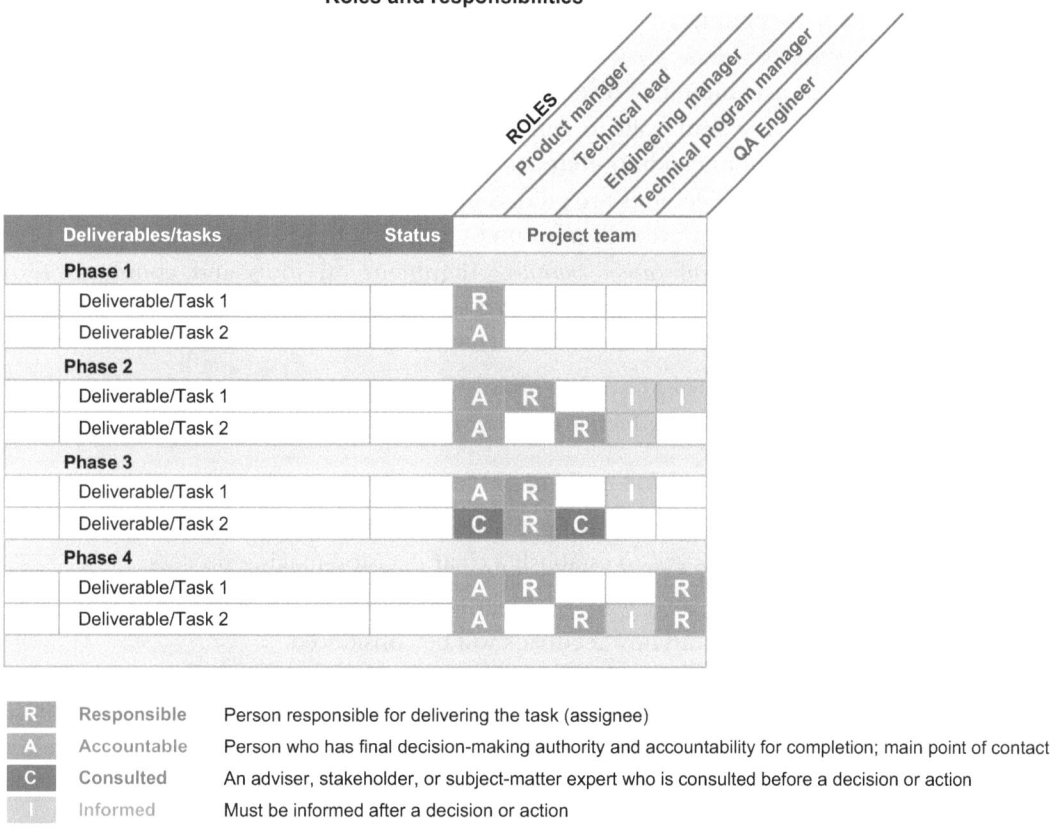

Roles and responsibilities

Deliverables/tasks	Status	Product manager	Technical lead	Engineering manager	Technical program manager	QA Engineer
Phase 1						
Deliverable/Task 1		R				
Deliverable/Task 2		A				
Phase 2						
Deliverable/Task 1		A	R		I	I
Deliverable/Task 2		A		R	I	
Phase 3						
Deliverable/Task 1		A	R		I	
Deliverable/Task 2		C	R	C		
Phase 4						
Deliverable/Task 1		A	R			R
Deliverable/Task 2		A		R	I	R

R	Responsible	Person responsible for delivering the task (assignee)
A	Accountable	Person who has final decision-making authority and accountability for completion; main point of contact
C	Consulted	An adviser, stakeholder, or subject-matter expert who is consulted before a decision or action
I	Informed	Must be informed after a decision or action

Figure 9.2 A sample RACI matrix

9.2.3 *Establishing a communication framework*

Effective communication is essential for the success of cross-functional team and for better working relationships. Establishing a communication framework involves deliberate planning and coordination. Here are key steps you can follow:

- *Understand varied communication practices.* Different teams may follow distinct communication practices (such as a daily scrum or weekly updates). Achieving alignment is crucial, considering the diverse preferences within a cross-functional team.
- *Define essential elements.* It is important to define key elements such as the following:
  - Clearly articulate project goals, milestones, and deliverables.
  - Understand dependencies and how they interconnect.
  - Specify communication channels (such as Slack, email, or Microsoft Teams).
  - Clearly define roles, using a RACI model.

- Set the frequency of updates for the working team and relevant stakeholders.
- Identify project management tools (such as Jira and Asana) to help plan projects better.
- *Accommodate diverse perspectives.* Diversity helps bring more perspectives to the table. To accommodate diverse perspectives,
  - Use surveys and polls to gather team input on meeting frequency, timing, and communication preferences.
  - Ensure that decisions are guided by poll results to accommodate varied perspectives and prevent imposition of unpopular procedures.
- *Establish a communication channel.* Alignment on tools and communication cadence is critical for building a cross-functional team. You will learn in detail about communication channels in chapter 10.

By incorporating these steps, you'll enhance communication within the team, ensuring clarity, alignment, and effective collaboration.

9.2.4 *Establishing a clear decision-making process*

Establishing a clear decision-making process is vital for smooth collaboration and workflow. Follow these steps to establish a clear decision-making process:

- *Define the decision-making process.* Clearly outline how decisions will be made, who holds authority, and how feedback will be considered.
- *Address key questions.* Define team members' roles in decision-making, including input, final calls, and necessary notifications. Also outline the decision criteria based on project goals, deadlines, budget constraints, and customer requirements.
- *Specify decision-making methods.* Clearly define methods such as consensus, delegation, voting, and consulting on different types of decisions.
- *Set timelines.* Establish clear timelines for decision-making to balance efficiency with thorough consideration.
- *Schedule regular meetings.* Conduct recurring decision-making meetings with a defined agenda and ensure that relevant stakeholders are present.
- *Create a conflict management protocol.* Acknowledge potential conflicts and establish a protocol for resolving disagreements. Encourage constructive debate and consensus-building. You will learn more about this in section 9.3.2.
- *Create documentation.* Maintain a written document capturing team agreements to prevent confusion and serve as a reference.

By addressing these elements, you'll create a structured decision-making framework, fostering a collaborative environment within the cross-functional team.

9.2.5 *Establishing an open and continuous feedback mechanism*

In cross-functional projects, managing diverse expectations is a challenge due to varying priorities among partners. Open communication and continuous feedback are crucial for addressing these differences and ensuring efficient collaboration. As an EM, consider the following:

- *Regular one-on-one meetings*—Conduct frequent one-on-one meetings with stakeholders to gather feedback, establishing a continuous feedback loop.
- *Retrospective sessions*—Organize periodic retrospective sessions with the entire cross-functional team to reflect on successes, areas for improvement, and actionable steps.
- *Collaboration with other EMs*—Work with other EMs to collect feedback from their teams, providing a comprehensive perspective on cross-functional collaboration.
- *Anonymous survey questionnaire*—Implement an anonymous survey questionnaire for immediate team members, specifically addressing cross-functional collaboration to encourage honest and open feedback.

Maintaining this continuous feedback loop supports ongoing improvement, fostering a transparent culture where team members feel comfortable sharing thoughts. If conflicting or emotional responses arise, addressing concerns through open conversations builds trust and alignment within the team.

9.2.6 *Measuring success*

Measuring the success of a cross-functional engineering team involves assessing key aspects related to team performance, collaboration, and project outcomes. Consider the following metrics and approaches:

- *Timely milestone achievement*—Evaluate whether the team is meeting milestones within the specified time frames.
- *Quality standards maintenance*—Check whether the team is maintaining the quality standards set at the project's outset.
- *Customer and stakeholder satisfaction*—Assess feedback from customers and stakeholders to gauge overall satisfaction.
- *Team velocity*—Gauge team velocity over time to understand the capacity for delivering work per sprint.
- *Collaboration and communication*—Evaluate how team members collaborate and communicate, ensuring transparency about risks and mitigations.
- *Optimal resource use*—Assess whether all team members are used to their full potential, avoiding waste of resources.
- *Innovation and upskilling*—Check whether members are innovating or upskilling themselves within the team.
- *Knowledge sharing*—Measure the team's commitment to sharing knowledge, preventing single points of failure.
- *Return on investment (ROI)*—Evaluate ROI by understanding the resources spent and comparing them with expected benefits and effect.

These metrics provide a comprehensive view of the team's success, covering various dimensions of performance, collaboration, and development. Next, let's explore strategies for maintaining ongoing collaboration within the cross-functional team.

9.3 *Collaborating with cross-functional teams*

Making cross-functional collaboration work requires harmonious work among different aspects of the system. Let's look at some common strategies for working well together.

9.3.1 *Fostering trust and transparency*

Building trust and maintaining transparency are pivotal for the success of cross-functional projects, given the unique challenges posed by various processes and the involvement of new team members. Trust development in such contexts requires time, particularly to understand each team member's strengths and opportunities. Trust breakdown in cross-functional projects can result from various factors, including the following:

- *Lack of transparency*—Decisions lack sufficient insight, eroding trust among project participants.
- *Ineffective communication*—Misunderstandings due to poor communication can lead to missed deadlines and increased stress.
- *Poor work quality*—Consistent failure to meet commitments and doubts about competence can diminish trust.
- *Lack of accountability*—Trust is undermined when there's a failure to take responsibility and resolve problems.
- *Personal and professional conflicts*—Conflicts, personal animosity, and blame-shifting can complicate collaboration and affect trust.

In practical scenarios, trust breakdown may occur if decisions are made independently without incorporating relevant team feedback. Additionally, unfamiliarity with cross-functional setups might hinder team members from expressing opinions. Establish an inclusive environment where every team member feels valued.

Transparency is key in building trust, requiring intentional efforts to foster a culture of openness and honesty, even in challenging situations. It also acts as a quick feedback loop when you're proceeding to stakeholders. As an EM, consider taking the following actions:

- *Assess trust levels.* Evaluate the established trust level among team members to identify bottlenecks. For this purpose, observe team interactions during meetings, collaborations, and informal discussions to assess the level of openness, respect, and cooperation among team members. Also observe your manager to understand their perspectives. Signs of trust include active listening, free sharing of ideas and feedback, and offering of support and assistance without hesitation. Regular feedback sessions offer a window into team dynamics and the level of trust among members. By conducting anonymous surveys or assessments specifically addressing trust and team dynamics, you can glean valuable insights from team members' perspectives and experiences. Building individual relationships with team members is a good way to gauge trust levels on a personal level. One-on-one conversations are great forums for building relationships and trust.

- *Conduct team-building activities.* Promote engagement and collaboration through activities such as FigJam sessions (https://www.figma.com), involving UX, engineering, and product teams in creating collaborative feature mockups.
- *Hold regular team meetings.* Conduct frequent team meetings to maintain high transparency levels, ensuring that all members are well informed and understand decision rationales in various scenarios.
- *Make presentations to leadership.* Engage with leadership by frequently sharing project dashboards, sprint burndown charts, sprint demos, project updates, and enablement sessions. Prepare a launch plan to get a go or no-go decision from leadership.
- *Have a scrum of scrums.* The sprint ceremony serves as a valuable mechanism for enhancing transparency with leadership. By consolidating updates from individual team scrums, it offers a holistic view of how various components integrate within the project framework. This comprehensive perspective aids in identifying and addressing dependencies and risks effectively, ensuring smooth progress without encountering blockers along the critical path of the project.

9.3.2 Managing conflicts

Conflicts between individuals and teams are inevitable in the workplaces. Managing conflicts requires taking a flexible approach that emphasizes long-term project goals and team members' commitment to the project. A kickoff meeting led by the EM or PM can establish the collaboration's direction and shared goals. Referring to this road map during conflicts prevents escalation and keeps the project on track.

> *There's a myth that you have to be best friends to win championships. We only have to have one thing, and that's respect.*
>
> —Shaquille O'Neal

We learned in detail about managing conflicts within a team in chapter 3. Revisit that chapter if you want a refresher. Apart from following the strategies discussed in chapter 3, you could designate directly responsible individuals (DRIs) to collaborate with the cross-functional team, address conflicts, and take end-to-end ownership of the project. Their say is final in times of conflict.

As an EM overseeing a product launch, I found myself in a challenging situation while collaborating with a cross-functional partner on writing the operational readiness document. As part of the product launch, this document was essential for ensuring a smooth rollout, detailing key metrics such as availability, latency, and mitigation plans in case of downtime.

Given the tight deadlines and resource constraints, my team faced significant pressure to deliver on various aspects of the launch, including the operational readiness document. As we began working with our partner, however, it became evident that we had differing expectations and priorities regarding the scope and level of detail required for the document. Whereas I prioritized thoroughness and precision in drafting the document, my cross-functional partner requested additional details, including plans, that I deemed unnecessary. This difference in perspective led to tensions and conflicts as we worked to find a compromise.

Recognizing the need to address the conflict and find a resolution, I initiated a series of discussions with our cross-functional partner. We engaged in open, honest dialogue, articulating our respective concerns and constraints while actively listening to one another's perspectives. Through constructive negotiation and collaboration, we eventually reached a consensus on a trimmed-down version of the operational readiness document. We focused on capturing the essential metrics and mitigation plans necessary for ensuring the product's stability and resilience during the launch while acknowledging the need to prioritize timeliness and efficiency.

The experience taught me valuable lessons on effective communication, compromise, and partnership. By approaching the situation with empathy, flexibility, and willingness to find common ground, we were able to overcome the conflict and deliver on our shared objectives for the product launch. Ultimately, the experience strengthened our working relationship with our cross-functional partner, fostering a spirit of collaboration, trust, and mutual respect. It also underscored the importance of adaptability and pragmatism in navigating complex challenges and achieving collective success on cross-functional teams. Managing conflict requires careful disentanglement, an open mind, a conducive discussion environment, objective decision-making, and respect for everyone's opinions.

9.3.3   *Providing additional support when needed*

Projects involving cross-functional partners often present unique challenges, and recognizing situations that demand extra support is crucial for effective project management. Considerations for additional support may include managing remote team members or addressing challenges faced by individuals. Here's how an EM can provide extra support:

- *Coordinate for remote team members.* When the team has remote members, consider those members' time zones and provide necessary support to ensure their involvement in recurring progress-update meetings.
- *Make tailored decisions.* Make decisions with individual circumstances in mind. Remote work, for example, requires a different mindset and approach. Encourage open communication to address concerns.
- *Use a pinch-hitter engineer.* Bring in a pinch-hitter engineer during challenging periods to support the team and maintain project progress.

- *Provide training and coaching.* Offer training on relevant topics to the cross-functional team, and provide coaching for members who may be struggling with certain aspects of their work.
- *Offer stress relief and appreciation.* Organize breaks for stress relief, and express appreciation to the team. Simple gestures such as organizing lunches, bringing in coffee, and sending gift cards to remote employees can foster a positive team environment.
- *Hold one-on-one chats.* Engage in one-on-one chats with team members who may need additional support, sharing learning resources to help them upskill.

Open communication with team members is key to understanding when additional support is needed, ensuring their well-being and productivity. Providing a supportive environment contributes to a positive team dynamic and successful project outcomes.

9.3.4   *Reasoning about technical work with nontechnical partners*

Nontechnical partners can include business development teams, sales and marketing staff, product managers, and sometimes senior executives. This list will vary depending on your company. Aligning nontechnical partners and stakeholders with project goals is essential in cross-functional setup. Effective communication is essential for conveying the importance of addressing technical debt for long-term gains. Here's how you can reason about technical work with nontechnical partners:

- *Communicate importance.* Clearly communicate the significance of addressing technical debt in the short term for long-term gains, emphasizing the benefits that this approach brings to the overall project.
- *Simplify problems.* Engage nontechnical stakeholders by simplifying technical problems into concrete problems, assessing effect through metrics and adopting a data-driven mindset.
- *Gather and present data.* Collect relevant data and communicate findings in non-technical terms, bridging the gap with nontechnical stakeholders.

Suppose that you manage a team that is overseeing a graph database platform. Despite its rapid adoption, the platform's onboarding process is inefficient, requiring two days of manual work for each new customer. This technical debt—a consequence of launching the minimum viable product—has not been prioritized. When you have limited time during quarterly prioritization, you should effectively communicate the need to address tech debt, as well as the effect of doing so. Simplify the problem into concrete problems and assess the effect by using the following metrics:

- *Platform reliability*—Evaluate whether the platform's reliability has declined, identify the root cause, and determine the resulting effect.
- *Service-level agreements (SLAs)*—Identify any SLA violations that affect agreements with users of the platform.

- *Product effect*—Measure the direct effect on customers by using various product metrics tied to the platform.
- *Cost analysis*—Assess the increased cost of maintaining the service in terms of both personnel and performance.
- *Short-term versus long-term cost*—Perform a cost analysis comparing short-term and long-term implications.

Conveying benefits in simple nontechnical language, such as demonstrating potential cost savings through addressing technical debt, enables nontechnical partners to understand the tangible advantages. By projecting engineering days saved and associated cost reductions, you create a clear picture of the benefits. Consistently measuring and communicating such effects ensures informed decision-making, fostering effective collaboration among stakeholders.

9.3.5   *Fostering a culture of recognition*

Fostering a culture of recognition is essential for successful cross-functional projects. Extend the practices of acknowledging and rewarding commendable efforts beyond your immediate team. Consider taking the following actions to cultivate a culture of recognition:

- *Extend recognition practices.* Apply the recognition processes used within your team to cross-functional collaborations, ensuring that outstanding contributions from partners in different departments are acknowledged.
- *Offer active appreciation.* Encourage members of the cross-functional team to actively appreciate one another's accomplishments, creating a positive and collaborative work environment.

For a deeper understanding and tools to cultivate a culture of recognition, refer to chapter 6. Recognizing the efforts of cross-functional partners contributes to a collaborative and appreciative atmosphere, enhancing the overall success of projects.

In the realm of software engineering management, collaboration with cross-functional partners is a crucial theme. Mastering the art of working seamlessly with diverse teams is not just a managerial skill but also a strategic imperative. The journey toward effective collaboration is ongoing, with each partnership and project offering valuable lessons.

What do other leaders have to say?

One of the major benefits of collaborating with cross-functional partners is the exposure to diverse perspectives. Each team brings unique expertise and knowledge to the table, leading to more comprehensive problem-solving and innovative ideas.

—Sanjay Gupta, General Manager at HCL Technologies

The most frequent pushback I see from cross-functional stakeholders is timelines. I keep referring to work visibility, but that has been the best tool to reach cross-functional alignment. By being able to show all upcoming items, ask where they believe their item slots in, and then having the cross-functional stakeholder own some of the negotiations for effect to other stakeholders, you build better ownership from that cross-functional stakeholder and reduce the likelihood of a loud stakeholder flippantly always asserting that his/her work is most important, as this now adds personal cost. An example of this was a recent sales conversation where a feature that was considered nice to help sell would have consumed the same resources as a must-have for the product to be marketable. By requiring the sales and marketing stakeholders to align and own any possible escalation around lack of alignment, we removed key resources from being in the middle of product discussions.

—Nathan Bourgoin, Chief Technology Officer at Alakazam, Inc.,
Technical Adviser, and Engineering Leader

Treating partners and your team as the same has proved to help in my teams. Everyone who contributes to the common objective has to be included in all the forums, including team dinners and celebrations.

—Rajakumar Sambasivam, Delivery Manager at Microsoft

I believe cross-functional partners are key to our success. Not only can their contributions lead towards us reaching our goal, but they are a great source for ideas and best practices that they observe in other teams., I intentionally try to create opportunities to stay connected with my peers via frequent cadences and corporate social events.

—Sumit Kumar, System Engineering Manager at Cisco

To convince cross-functional partners to prioritize nonproduct work items like operational excellence over product asks, it is important to highlight the need [to allocate] capacity on operational excellence for regular maintenance and improve platform capabilities by making cross-functional partners understand the benefits that customers, product or marketing partners, and development team will have from such investments. The effort to convince cross-functional partners to prioritize nonproduct work reduces once the return on investment is understood.

—Saurabh Gandhi, Senior Director, Software Development at Audible,
formerly with American Express

9.4 Stop and think: Practice questions

1 Who are your key cross-functional partners? How would you describe your working relationship with them?
2 What are the biggest challenges you face working with those partners?
3 Think about when you received pushback from a member of a cross-functional team. What was the reason for the pushback?
4 How would you persuade your cross-functional team to prioritize nonproduct work items such as operational excellence features over product features in a balanced manner?

5   How do you receive and provide feedback to your cross-functional team partners?

6   Do you see effective communication across all your projects? If you don't feel that your communication is effective, what are your plans to address that problem?

Summary

- Mastering effective cross-functional collaboration is crucial for an EM.
- Effective cross-functional collaboration is a hard problem. Studies have shown that roughly 75% of such teams are dysfunctional.
- Cross-team collaboration can be challenging for various reasons, some of the key ones being
  - Competing priorities between teams and ill-defined goals
  - Inefficient communication and coordination
  - Unclear roles and responsibilities for the individuals and teams involved in the project
  - Individual and team conflicts
  - Geographical constraints
  - Lack of support from cross-functional or cross-team partners who are overwhelmed with work
- Building a cross-functional team is a pivotal task for any software EM, requiring a thoughtful and strategic approach that involves the following tasks:
  - Clarifying and aligning on goals
  - Identifying key skills and roles
  - Establishing an effective communication framework
  - Establishing a clear decision-making process
  - Establishing an open and continuous feedback mechanism
  - Measuring the success of the team through metrics
- To collaborate efficiently in a cross-functional team setting, do the following:
  - Bring trust and transparency to the decision-making process by giving everyone a voice.
  - Manage conflicts by working with the individuals or the teams that are involved. Provide additional support in different situations. Be ready to anticipate and provide such support.
  - Ensure alignment of nontechnical partners and stakeholders with project goals, which is crucial in cross-functional setups. Clear communication is vital for highlighting the significance of addressing technical debt for long-term benefits.
  - Foster a culture of recognizing team members.

Project management, execution, and delivery

This chapter covers

- The five stages of the project life cycle
- How EMs are involved at each stage
- Tools and templates for navigating every phase of the life cycle

Those who plan do better than those who do not plan, even though they rarely stick to their plan.

—Winston Churchill

Whether you've played sports or watched them closely, you understand the precision and teamwork they demand. Achieving excellence in sports requires individual skill as well as collaboration within a team, with each member fulfilling a unique role. This teamwork involves rigorous training and preparation spanning weeks or months to refine strategies and ensure flawless execution. Timing is crucial, and successful teams excel at adapting to unexpected situations.

In project management, the sports analogy holds true. The entire project team—which might include the engineering manager (EM), product manager (PM), and technical program manager—functions as a cohesive unit, much like a team of athletes preparing for a game. Success hinges on meticulous planning, including creating a project plan with clear timelines and priorities, identifying risks and dependencies, establishing sprint ceremonies, ensuring leadership visibility, and tracking milestones diligently. The team must also demonstrate agility in the face of changing circumstances and iterate on the plan while managing workload and resources. Ultimately, effective coordination and collaboration are crucial for achieving shared objectives. Throughout this chapter, we'll explore the various phases of the project life cycle and key considerations for EMs as the project progresses.

10.1   Project life-cycle phases

Understanding the various phases of a project life cycle is crucial for effective project management and execution, as well as successful project delivery. Each phase represents a distinct stage in the project's journey and is characterized by specific activities and objectives. By exploring these life-cycle phases comprehensively, you can gain insights into effective ways to plan, execute, and monitor projects, ultimately leading to improved project outcomes and stakeholder satisfaction.

> **Did you know?**
>
> Project portfolio management (PPM) is the concept of managing a set of projects as a collection or portfolio. The goal is to identify the right set of projects, prioritize, and ensure that the business makes the right investments. PPM is a step higher than project delivery and execution, encompassing several projects and processes. Each project is part of the portfolio and can be managed from this centralized portfolio. The company's strategy feeds into portfolio management to identify areas for businesses to invest in. An EM might be tasked with leading three projects simultaneously, two of which involve developing new products; the third helps improve existing legacy systems. Learn more about PPM at https://mng.bz/DdME.
>
> PPM directly influences engineering management decisions by providing tools and methodologies for resource allocation, risk management, prioritization, performance monitoring, and decision support within the project portfolio context. When used effectively, PPM can optimize project outcomes, mitigate risks, and align project activities with organizational goals. The various steps involved in PPM are

- *Resource allocation*—With PPM, you assess the resource requirements for each project in the portfolio, including manpower, equipment, and budget. By having a clear overview of resource demands across all projects, you can make informed decisions about resource allocation. If one of the new product development projects requires specialized machine learning skills, you can adjust resources to assign senior machine learning engineers to it, thereby preventing bottlenecks and delays.

- *Risk management*—PPM enables you to evaluate the risks associated with each project and prioritize them accordingly. Some projects may have higher risks due to technical complexity, tight deadlines, or external factors. By identifying and assessing these risks within the portfolio, you can implement risk mitigation strategies such as allocating additional resources, adjusting project timelines, and diversifying project scopes. If the new product developments give your company an edge over competitors, it is OK to focus on them and put improving legacy systems in the background, thereby adjusting project timelines.

- *Prioritization*—Not all projects in the portfolio may be equally important or aligned with the company's strategic objectives. PPM helps you prioritize projects based on factors such as return on investment (ROI), strategic fit, market demand, and regulatory requirements. If a new government regulation requires updates to existing infrastructure, you might prioritize projects that address compliance over other discretionary projects.

- *Performance monitoring*—PPM provides tools and metrics for tracking the performance of individual projects as well as the overall portfolio. This approach allows you to identify underperforming projects and those that are at risk of missing deadlines or exceeding budgets. Using real-time data on project progress and key performance indicators, you can take proactive measures such as reallocating resources or renegotiating project scopes to keep the portfolio on track.

- *Decision support*—PM equips you with the necessary information and analysis to make data-driven decisions. Whether you're evaluating project proposals, assessing tradeoffs between competing projects, or deciding whether to terminate, defer, or accelerate projects, PPM provides insights into the potential effect on the overall portfolio and business objectives. If a new project proposal emerges midyear, you can use PPM to assess its alignment with strategic goals, resource implications, and potential effects on existing projects before making a decision.

Successful project outcomes require the collaboration of various stakeholders working toward a shared objective. Figure 10.1 shows the various phases of the project life cycle: project discovery, preplanning, planning and project kickoff, execution, and postexecution.

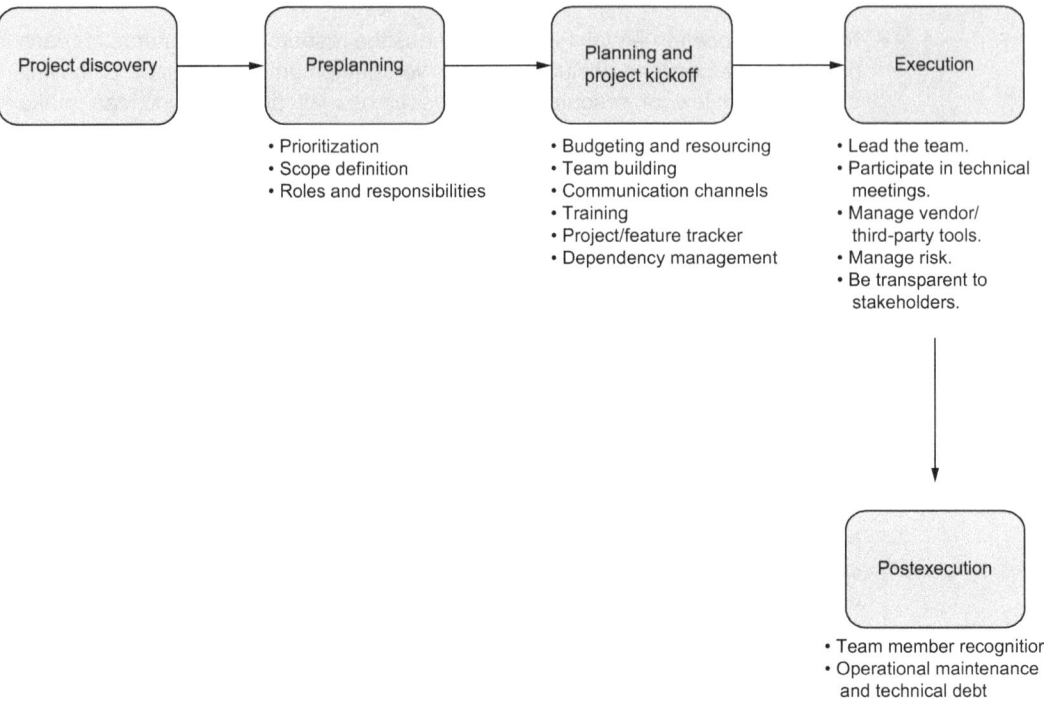

Figure 10.1 The five phases of a project life cycle

10.1.1 *Project discovery*

In the project-discovery phase, the product road map (usually created by the PM in collaboration with the EM) outlines new features or changes. As an EM, you'll also craft the technical road map, aligning it with strategic goals. Key steps in identifying projects from an engineering perspective include the following:

- *Identifying pain points and bottlenecks*—Address customer complaints or technical debts, such as insufficient load testing before a launch.
- *Conducting market research*—Conduct customer studies, analyze competitors, and gather feedback from customers to innovate and stay ahead.
- *Brainstorming with the team*—Involve the team in brainstorming sessions, using their insights for both product and technical ideas.
- *Staying updated on technology trends*—Keep abreast of the latest tech trends to seize opportunities such as implementing cost-saving measures or introducing innovative technologies such as generative AI.

The emphasis in this phase is on innovation and feasibility testing through proof of concept. It's crucial to highlight the value proposition of each project, such as time saved through automation. With projects identified, we'll explore each stage of project management and execution in more detail.

10.1.2 Preplanning

The preplanning phase of the project life cycle lays the groundwork for the project launch. This stage involves identifying the project, assessing feasibility, determining its priority within the company or team, aligning with the company's vision, defining scope, and identifying key stakeholders. Efficient preplanning is crucial for smooth project kickoff and execution. If PMs will be part of the team, typically they are assigned during this phase, when all the pieces of the project puzzle start coming together.

> **Did you know?**
>
> Objectives and key results (OKRs) project execution is a powerful tool for prioritizing and setting organizational goals. This approach helps you identify the highest priority for the business by using clear success metrics or results against each objective. Key performance indicators (KPIs) measure the success criteria for the projects and keep them objective. OKRs serve as a framework for setting clear and measurable goals; their integration with project management methodologies amplifies the process by directing attention to efficient delivery and precise execution, ultimately translating goals into tangible outcomes. Imagine a company that deals in e-commerce. A sample OKR for that company might look like this:
>
> - *Objective 1—Enhance user experience.*
>   - *Key result 1*—Increase user satisfaction score from 80% to 90% in customer feedback surveys by the end of the quarter.
>   - *Key result 2*—Reduce average page-load time from 5 seconds to 3 seconds.
>   - *Key result 3*—Achieve a 20% increase in daily active users of the mobile app.

Let's use the example of Company XYZ, which sells toys for infants and toddlers. Facing increased competition, the company decides to launch a new line of accessibility-friendly toys for specially abled kids, dubbed Project Accessible. As the EM, you're assigned to build a new website for selling this product line. Starting with the preplanning phase, we'll use this example to walk through the project life cycle.

FEASIBILITY ANALYSIS

In this phase, we conduct a preliminary assessment of project expectations, aiming for an objective evaluation of its realism and viability within the expected time frame. Large companies often engage third parties to perform feasibility analyses for critical projects, aiming to identify any fundamental flaws—business, technical, financial, or otherwise. For Project Accessible, you, the PM, and stakeholders should identify answers to the following types of questions:

- Could any legal implications of selling the new product line on the market stop us from making sales?
- Does the hardware team that will build the toys to be sold on the website have a green light from leadership?
- Do we have or can we create the technology to develop the website?
- Do we have enough people in the company and a high-enough budget for this project?

Budgeting involves assessing the costs associated with project execution, including resources, software/hardware expenses, and time allocation. It helps leadership plan for project costs and understand the expenditure involved in delivering the project. Considering budgeting as part of the feasibility phase is crucial for ensuring adequate funding and preventing unexpected delays.

Involving senior engineers in feasibility analysis helps you address technical aspects of your analysis. When confidence in project feasibility is established, proceed to the next stage. If doubts arise, the business may choose to defer the project pending further details or to cancel it.

PRIORITIZATION

When a new project's feasibility is established, assessing its priority compared with that of other planned projects for the year is crucial. Most companies operate with a three- or five-year vision plan, though start-ups and small companies may still be defining their market targets. During the preplanning phase, teams must understand where the new project stands in terms of priority. Prioritization (or stack ranking) of projects is vital for setting expectations and ensuring consistency and alignment across teams. Conflicts may arise, particularly with cross-functional dependencies, necessitating company-wide prioritization to determine precedence. Ultimately, prioritization aligns teams with the company's primary goals, ensuring concerted effort toward them.

> ### Did you know?
> A famous approach to tackling requirements prioritization is the MoSCoW technique (https://mng.bz/wxm2). *Moscow* stands for
>
> - *M (must-haves)*—These non-negotiable product items are necessary for the launch of the product. Examples are product features and security.
> - *S (should-haves)*—These essential product items add value to the product. Examples include performance, low latency, and the authentication system.
> - *C (could-haves)*—These good-to-have items also affect the launch, although at a small scale. A feature for comments to add as a journal for users is not necessary for a product launch but can have a small effect and make customers happy.
> - *W (won't-haves)*—These items are a wish list, and the launch doesn't hinge on them. Examples are features that are not priority 0 or 1 and can be implemented in later iterations or versions.
>
> The MoSCoW technique helps teams prioritize what features and launches are most important to the company and helps PMs to do stack ranking for the features. This approach can be used in new-product launches and existing-feature enhancements alike. It is especially useful in situations that involve constraints in resources, bandwidth, budget, competing priorities, and so on.

Returning to Project Accessible, team members (including you) convene with stakeholders to define the project's priorities. Following extensive discussions and analysis of ROI by business and executives, the project is categorized as a must-have and designated as the company's primary focus. This alignment ensures that all teams are on the same page regarding prioritization, allowing progression to the next phase.

SCOPE DEFINITION

In the scope-definition phase, team members take another step forward by defining and documenting the scope of the project. Here are some sample questions to address at this stage:

- What is the aim of the project, and why are we doing it?
- What is the project charter?
- Is this project going to solve a customer problem or bring in more revenue?
- What value proposition does the project bring to the table?
- What are the exact product requirements and acceptance criteria?
- Who are the customers for the product or service?
- What are the timeline and budget?
- What constraints and risks do we need to keep in mind?
- How are customers going to use this feature or product?
- For a technical solution such as a web app, will application security review be part of the scope?

This step gives you a deeper understanding of what delivering this project will involve. Key tasks at this step include the following:

- Clearly define the goals and objectives of the project, which involves gathering requirements from stakeholders.
- Document what is in scope and what is out of scope to clearly delineate the boundaries of the project.
- List any assumptions that are being made about the project.
- Note the acceptance criteria.
- List the set of functional requirements, including what a software system should do, and nonfunctional requirements such as performance, reliability, security and scalability.
- Create the success metrics for the project to help everyone understand what defines success for it. Section 10.1.5 covers the success criteria in detail.

A business-requirements document, or BRD (https://mng.bz/1MYy), generally is used to lay out the scope of the project. A BRD is a formal document that outlines the requirements and objectives of a project from a business perspective. It serves as a communication tool for stakeholders, PMs, and the engineering team to ensure a common understanding of what needs to be accomplished, and it helps build a shared understanding of the project. By clearly defining the project scope, we can minimize scope creep, reduce project risks, and ensure that the project stays on track and within budget. The project management triangle (https://mng.bz/qOzJ) is an excellent way to understand project constraints and take appropriate action.

For Project Accessible, you, as the EM, set up the meeting to define the scope. You invite all the stakeholders, including the product, program, engineering, and business teams. To define the scope, these team members go through a long whiteboarding session to break the high-level goal into smaller components. Following are some of the components identified during scope definition:

- The product should cater to specially abled students from age groups 0 to 5, so the website should be accessible.
- The website must incorporate functionality enabling users to add items to their cart and proceed to the checkout process seamlessly.
- The website should include a feature that enables users to add custom text to products as desired.

This component is out of scope:

- For the first iteration, the product will be available only in the United States because of foreign certification problems, so sales outside the United States are out of scope for the project.

Given the competitive landscape, stakeholders determine that Project Accessible must be launched within the next three months to maintain a competitive edge. Prioritizing testing and security of the website, stakeholders underscore the importance of those aspects. The next step involves defining the responsibilities of each team member as project execution commences.

10.1.3 Planning and project kickoff

The third phase of the project life cycle is project planning and kickoff. During this phase, the wish list generated in the preplanning phase is transformed into a comprehensive project plan. Planning can occur at various intervals, such as in program increments, quarterly, or semiannually. The objective now is to establish the project plan with milestones, assemble the team, equip team members with necessary skills, define communication channels, and devise a dependency management plan for projects involving multiple teams. Additionally, the EM and PM collaborate to create a project-feature tracker, facilitating transparency and progress tracking for leadership. A kickoff meeting gathers all stakeholders to align expectations. The activities in this phase can be sequenced serially or parallelized based on project requirements.

WORKING-BACKWARD PLAN

Begin by envisioning the goal—the desired outcome or product—and work your way backward to identify the steps necessary to achieve it. Start with the end in mind. What does success look like? Then break the project into smaller, actionable tasks and milestones, and add timelines against them. The way I see it, working backward is more a mindset than a plan. You start with your customer or end product and work your way backward to identify how you will reach the goal. Use tools such as Work Breakdown Structure (WBS), Gantt charts (https://mng.bz/BdXJ), and agile frameworks to map out the project timeline and dependencies. Communicate the plan clearly to the team, ensuring that everyone understands the shared responsibility of the project. In most companies, you will have a cross-functional partner such as a PM with whom you would collaborate to create such a plan. By embracing this strategic approach, even new EMs can effectively navigate the complexities of project management and drive successful outcomes.

> ## Did you know?
>
> Work Breakdown Structure (WBS) is a hierarchical decomposition of the total scope of work to be carried out by the project team. It breaks the project into smaller, more manageable components known as work packages. These work packages are organized in a structured format, typically displayed as a tree diagram, with the main deliverable of project objectives at the top and progressively detailed tasks at lower levels. Read more at https://mng.bz/d6XQ.
>
> What is the relationship between WBS and the working-backward plan? Whereas the WBS focuses on breaking the entire scope of work into manageable components, the working-backward plan helps with understanding the sequence of tasks required to achieve the objective .The WBS can provide a starting point for a working-backward project plan by providing a structured breakdown of the project scope. The tasks identified in the WBS can be sequenced in reverse order to create the working-backward plan. The working-backward plan can also help validate the completeness of the WBS by ensuring that all necessary tasks and milestones are included.

Because the project timelines in Project Accessible are three months, a good strategy would be to create a plan to detail activities. Table 10.1 shows a sample plan.

Table 10.1   A sample template for a working-backward plan

Timeline	Tasks and description	Owners	Status
T-3 months	Perform technical spikes. Create a technical-design document. Signoff by senior engineer/architect.	Engineering team	
T-2 months	Coding is implemented. QA testing is initiated.	Engineering team QA	
T-1 month	When implementation finishes, end-to-end testing is performed. Security testing is performed. User acceptance testing (UAT) is complete. Bug fixes are done. Code freeze occurs. Launch readiness is achieved.	Engineering team Security engineer	
T	Launch Postlaunch production support	.	
T+1 month	Project retrospective Measurement against success metrics	.	

ESTIMATIONS AND RESOURCING

With the project plan established, the engineering team takes charge of estimating the level of effort required for project development. Using the tasks identified in the preceding phase, the team begins by T-shirt-sizing the high-level tasks, categorizing them as Large, Medium, Small, and Extra Small, depending on the company's scale. If this metric doesn't exist in your company, you can create a simple one such as

- *Large*—12 weeks of effort
- *Medium*—8 weeks
- *Small*—4 weeks
- *Extra Small*—2 weeks

You can configure this example based on your team and its needs. Now that a high-level sense of workload is estimated, the team can deep-dive into granular tasks and estimate them. If the team follows an agile method, story points (https://mng.bz/rVKX) serve as a metric for quantifying the estimated effort needed to complete a product backlog item and a common way to estimate granular tasks.

When estimates are obtained, compare them with the developer capacity or project budget. If alignment occurs, proceed as planned. Otherwise, negotiate with stakeholders by doing the following:

- Adjusting project scope or considering a trimmed-down version that's feasible with current resources
- Negotiating timelines for implementation with the existing resources
- Allocating resources from another team to bridge the gap between estimated effort and available capacity

As an EM, your next step is handling resourcing. This task involves assigning engineers to the project, whether they work virtually, in person, or in a hybrid setup, as well as securing needed facilities and providing any necessary peripherals or hardware. Sometimes, team composition is determined above EM level by directors or vice presidents. In a start-up scenario, you may also take on roles such as product or program manager.

When you're resourcing, consider the specific skills and expertise of team members to drive the project forward. It's important to foster team cohesion by ensuring that members understand one another's roles.

> **TIP** Refer to the Forming, Storming, Norming, and Performing model in chapter 9 for insights into building effective cross-functional teams.

In some cases, external hiring may be necessary to fill specific skill gaps for the project. This process can extend the team-building timeline as you advertise roles, conduct interviews, and onboard new hires. For guidance on hiring, refer to chapter 7.

Team size and expertise will vary based on the project's size and requirements. For Project Accessible, eight full-stack engineers are allocated as resources. Your task is to recruit or select these individuals, aiming for a balanced team of senior and junior engineers. Also consider adding one or two data-engineer experts for projects that involve heavy data manipulation, and maintain at least one or two senior backend/complete stack engineers for projects that focus on backend API development, especially during the technical-design phase. Resourcing ensures that the team has the necessary balance of skills and expertise to maintain the project quality promised to stakeholders.

ROLES AND RESPONSIBILITIES

Next, it's vital to clarify the roles of key players to prevent confusion and missed requirements. Chapter 9 introduced the RACI model, a standard responsibility matrix. The Project Accessible RACI chart (figure 10.2) brings clarity to key players and their responsibilities. Explicit roles and agreements among stakeholders ensure clarity, foster collaboration, and prevent pitfalls due to blurred ownership lines. When the RACI chart is ready, be sure to run it by all stakeholders and get signoff to ensure that everyone is on the same page.

RACI matrix: Project Accessible

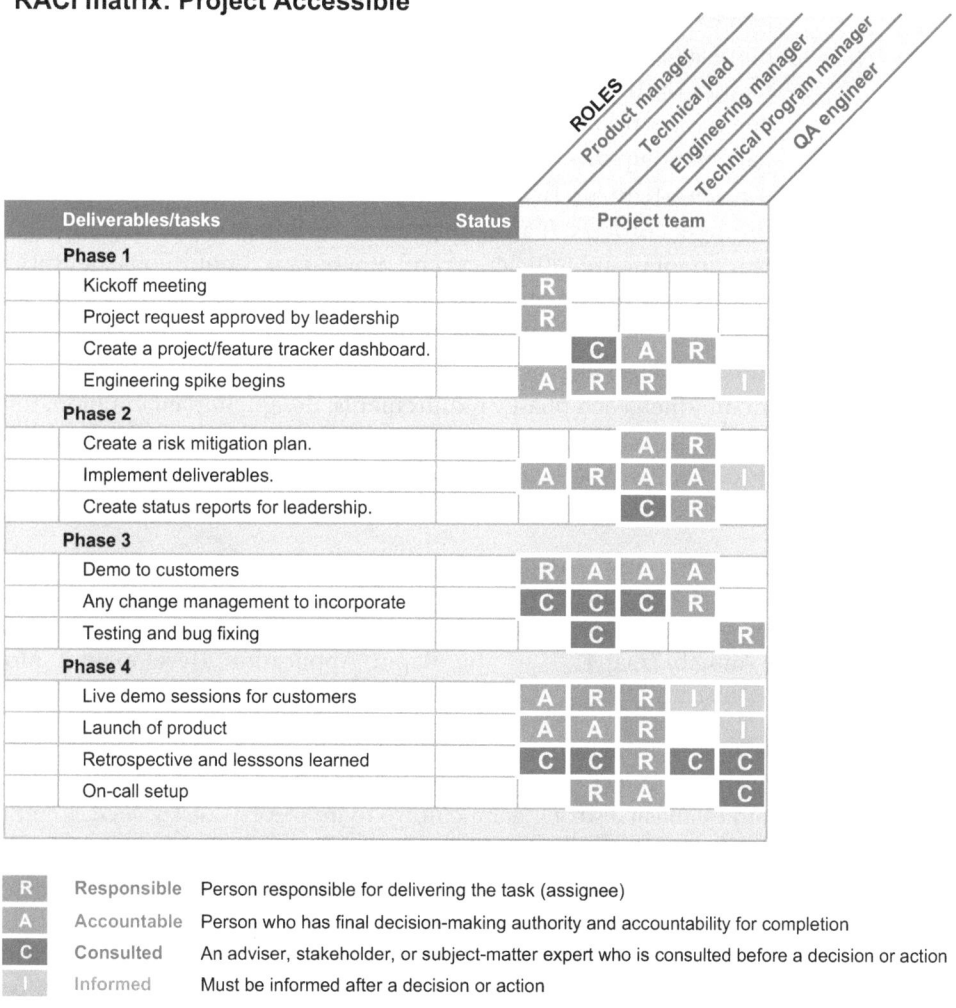

Deliverables/tasks	Status	Product manager	Technical lead	Engineering manager	Technical program manager	QA engineer
Phase 1						
Kickoff meeting		R				
Project request approved by leadership		R				
Create a project/feature tracker dashboard.			C	A	R	
Engineering spike begins		A	R	R		I
Phase 2						
Create a risk mitigation plan.				A	R	
Implement deliverables.		A	R	A	A	I
Create status reports for leadership.				C	R	
Phase 3						
Demo to customers		R	A	A	A	
Any change management to incorporate		C	C	C	R	
Testing and bug fixing		C				R
Phase 4						
Live demo sessions for customers		A	R	R	I	I
Launch of product		A	A	R		I
Retrospective and lesssons learned		C	C	R	C	C
On-call setup		R	A			C

R	Responsible	Person responsible for delivering the task (assignee)
A	Accountable	Person who has final decision-making authority and accountability for completion
C	Consulted	An adviser, stakeholder, or subject-matter expert who is consulted before a decision or action
I	Informed	Must be informed after a decision or action

Figure 10.2   A sample RACI matrix for Project Accessible defines roles and responsibilities

WORKING MODEL

In software engineering projects, the working model serves as the blueprint that guides the development process from inception to delivery. It encapsulates the methodologies, processes, and ceremonies essential for effective project management and successful product development. A well-defined working model ensures alignment among team members, fosters collaboration, and enables efficient delivery of high-quality software solutions. Key aspects to consider in a working model include

- *Methodology and framework*—The chosen methodology or framework sets the foundation for the project's working model. Common methodologies include the following:
  - *Agile*—Agile is an iterative approach to software development, emphasizing flexibility and customer collaboration. It promotes adaptive planning, evolutionary development, early delivery, and continuous improvement. Read more at https://www.agilealliance.org/agile101. Scrum is a subset of agile that focuses on breaking projects into small, manageable tasks called sprints. It emphasizes frequent communication, transparency, and adaptability through daily stand-up meetings, sprint planning, reviews, and retrospectives.
  - *Kanban*—Kanban is a visual framework for managing work as it moves through a process. It aims to balance the flow of work, limiting work in progress to optimize efficiency and encourage continuous delivery. Kanban boards typically visualize tasks in various stages of completion. Read more at https://asana.com/resources/what-is-kanban.
- *Waterfall*—Waterfall is a traditional, sequential approach to software development, in which each phase (requirements, design, implementation, testing, and deployment) is completed before moving on to the next. It follows a linear progression and is less flexible than agile methodologies. Read more at https://mng.bz/VxV5.

TIP   Although many other methodologies exist, I feel that the three basics are generally adequate. If you want to explore alternatives, check out Lean Software Development (https://mng.bz/7dMe), Extreme Programming (https://mng.bz/map4), and the Rapid Application Development Model (https://mng.bz/5lXa).

- *Project ceremonies*—The next step might be to get the team together and align on the various project ceremonies required to stay on track for the project. It is on you to establish a strong team culture to help everyone succeed, so set the foundation right. Various project ceremonies can help you set the ground rules. As EM, pick the ones that work for your team and project and decide on their cadence. Options include the following:
  - *Kickoff*—The kickoff marks the beginning of the project and serves as an opportunity for stakeholders—including clients, product owners, and development teams to align their understanding of project goals, scope, and

expectations. It sets the tone for the project and establishes communication channels and roles.

– *Grooming*—Grooming sessions, also known as backlog refinement, focus on refining the product backlog by reviewing and prioritizing user stories, adding details, and ensuring clarity and feasibility. It helps maintain a well-groomed backlog, which is crucial for efficient sprint planning and execution. It also helps ensure that the product backlog remains relevant, refined, and aligned with evolving business needs.

– *Sprint planning*—Sprint planning involves a collaborative effort on the development team to define the sprint goal and select user stories or tasks to be completed during the upcoming sprint. It requires estimating effort, prioritizing tasks, and breaking work into manageable chunks.

– *Sprint retrospective*—Sprint retrospective meetings provide an opportunity for the team to reflect on the recently completed sprint, discuss what went well, identify areas for improvement, and plan actionable steps for enhancing future sprints. It promotes continuous improvement and fosters a culture of learning and adaptation.

– *User-experience (UX) design reviews*—UX design reviews involve evaluating UX designs, prototypes, or wireframes to ensure usability, accessibility, and alignment with user needs and business goals. It encourages collaboration among designers, developers, and stakeholders to create intuitive and usercentric solutions.

– *QA meetings*—QA meetings involve coordination among QA engineers, developers, and stakeholders to discuss testing strategies, review test cases, report and prioritize defects, and ensure the overall quality of the software product. It emphasizes the importance of rigorous testing and QA throughout the development life cycle.

– *Demos*—Sprint demos involve showcasing the progress and completed work to stakeholders, including clients and product owners, to gather feedback and validate deliverables. It facilitates transparency, fosters collaboration, and ensures alignment between development efforts and stakeholder expectations.

– *Scrum of scrums*—This coordination mechanism is used in large-scale agile projects to address coordination and communication challenges across multiple scrum teams. Representatives from each team participate in regular meetings to discuss cross-team dependencies, impediments, and goal alignment. Scrum of scrums promotes transparency, collaboration, and alignment among teams, enabling them to work cohesively toward shared project objectives while maintaining agility and flexibility.

■ *Decision-making model*—The decision-making model plays a pivotal role in the project planning phase, serving as a structured approach for analyzing options, weighing alternatives, and making informed choices that align with project objectives and stakeholder expectations. A decision-making model provides a structured framework that enables project planners to define clear goals, identify potential alternatives, and establish criteria for evaluating options. See chapter 9 to learn about establishing a decision-making process.

- *Communication channel*—Open communication channels help build trust and ensure that no surprises occur later in the project development life cycle. As EM, your job is to define the communication channels that will be useful for team members to interact and unblock themselves should they hit a roadblock. Chapter 9 covered establishing a communication framework. Now let's deep-dive into the topic.

You, as EM, step up to define the communication channels, keeping the cross-functional partners involved in the process. Here are some approaches to facilitate communication:

- *Face-to-face communication*—Although they were more common before the COVID-19 pandemic, face-to-face interactions remain valuable for observing facial expressions and body language, allowing immediate feedback. Schedule significant technical discussions, such as whiteboard sessions, to happen in person and synchronously.

- *Videoconferencing*—Particularly useful during remote work periods, videoconferencing enables synchronous communication for geographically dispersed teams. Encourage the use of cameras during calls to capture visual cues and facial expressions effectively.

- *Asynchronous communication*—For nonurgent matters or during focused coding time, use nonverbal asynchronous communication methods such as email and chat messengers such as Slack or Microsoft Teams. Use tools such as Wiki and Confluence to document technical discussions and store files for future reference.

- *Escalation*—Define a clear escalation process for resolving problems that may arise. This strategy provides clarity to team members about who to contact in case of blockers or challenges. Establish service-level agreements (SLAs) for response times at each escalation level to ensure timely resolution of problems. As an example, after the product is launched, to handle customer tickets, the on-call should respond in two business days; if not, the escalation can move to level 2, where the EM has one business day to respond. Further, if no action is taken, the escalation moves to the Director level to be responded to in one business day. The process looks like this:

Person escalating > On-call (Level 1) -> EM (Level 2) -> Director (Level 3)

In addition to traditional communication methods, using a problem ticket tracking system like Jira is essential. This platform allows developers, project managers, QA, and others to communicate changes, progress, and status updates efficiently. It's vital to establish processes for communication and have action plans to address any barriers or concerns that arise.

Ensure that team members adopt the required communication channels and consider the audience when sharing information. Maintain the security of shared information, especially when dealing with sensitive data such as customer credentials. ensure that confidential information is not publicly accessible on a ticket, for example.

When you're defining a problem in the tracking system, capture all necessary details, including steps to replicate the bug, screenshots or recordings, environment and build details, and any relevant technical information or call stacks. This comprehensive approach ensures effective resolution and streamlined communication.

TRAINING

Now your focus shifts to ensuring that each team member is well prepared to contribute effectively to the project. This step involves identifying skill gaps and providing necessary resources for skill enhancement. Recognize that onboarding new team members, particularly in remote locations, may require lead time for equipment setup and training.

Begin by conducting a skills survey to assess team members' proficiency and experiences. Customize training plans based on identified gaps, understanding that each engineer may have unique needs. If the project involves cloud service development, ensure that team members are proficient in cloud computing. Tailor training to address specific requirements. One engineer may be proficient in React, but others may need training. Additionally, consider organizing sessions led by subject-matter experts (SMEs) or technical leads to guide the team through system architecture. This holistic approach ensures that each team member is equipped to excel in their role.

You can provide training opportunities such as Project Management Professional (PMP; https://mng.bz/x2ZB) or Scaled Agile Framework (SAFe; https://scaledagile framework.com) to help team members understand project models such as waterfall, agile, and scaled agile, allowing them to determine the best approach given the specific project's circumstances and constraints. Hence, it is vital to create a tailored training plan for each team member, considering their individual skill sets and learning requirements.

As the EM for Project Accessible, you find that collaboration with the team reveals the need for supporting resources to ensure success. Identified needs include accessibility training for all team members. You coordinate with the organization's training team to curate relevant resources.

Upon deep-diving into individual strengths and skill sets, you find that two engineers require additional training in frontend development. You pair them with frontend engineers from a sister team and recommend that they take online courses for skill enhancement. Additionally, two engineers volunteered to attend an upcoming technical conference/webinar on iOS application development to share insights with the team.

Training initiatives depend on project timelines and the ability to invest in skill development. For projects with tight deadlines, finding resources with requisite skills, either internally or externally, may be necessary. In such cases, sharing knowledge through shadowing experts becomes crucial.

Continuous learning is crucial in the ever-changing technical landscape. Strong foundational skills and adaptability to new technologies are essential to success.

RISK MANAGEMENT

In project management, risks are inevitable and can arise at any stage. Early identification and assessment are crucial for mitigating potential consequences. To manage risks effectively, take the following steps:

- *Identify risks.* Gather the project team to brainstorm potential risks comprehensively.
- *Categorize risks.* Classify risks based on the severity of their effects on the project.
- *Address risks.* Align on which risks to prioritize, and assign owners with timelines for mitigation.
- *Do mitigation planning.* Owners develop risk-mitigation plans to address identified risks and drive them to completion.
- *Have regular check-ins.* Conduct frequent check-ins during team sync-ups to monitor progress and ensure alignment with risk-mitigation plans.

By following these steps, the project team can manage risks proactively and minimize the effect of those risks on project outcomes.

> ### Did you know?
> A well-known lightweight model used for risk management is *ROAM*:
>
> - *R (Resolved)*—The risk has been resolved by the team and is no longer open.
> - *O (Owned)*—The risk has an assigned owner who is responsible for resolving the risk. The owner will work with the team to devise a resolution strategy in a time-boxed manner.
> - *A (Accepted)*—The team decides to accept the risk and live with the consequences, perhaps because the risk to the project is not severe.
> - *M (Mitigated)*—The team takes actions to reduce the severity of the risk. The risk is mitigated and may not be fully resolved, but the effect is reduced severity, and the team plans to live with it.
>
> The approach helps the team group the risks in categories and develop a game plan to address the open risks. It also promotes tracking risks continuously so that teams consciously consider addressing them.

The primary goal of risk management is to prevent potential problems from becoming active problems by taking proactive measures. Team decisions made throughout the project should be documented for future reference. Risks can be tracked with project tracking tools, such as spreadsheets or project trackers, and can be listed along with any resolutions. This approach allows for easy monitoring and ensures that risks are addressed in a timely manner, minimizing their effect on the project.

SPIKES AND TECHNICAL-DESIGN MEETINGS

Your involvement in technical-design discussions and spikes as an EM is paramount. This involvement encompasses engaging with the team and having sessions with enterprise architecture or cross-functional teams responsible for organization-wide security, guardrails, and strategic direction. Your role as an enabler is to collaborate closely with the team's technical lead, using your expertise to uncover potential blind spots, risks, and dependencies. By sharing insights gained from your experiences, you instill confidence in the team and demonstrate your commitment as a collaborative member. A technically adept EM fosters an environment where team members feel supported and comfortable seeking assistance when they encounter obstacles. Moreover, it's crucial to not only focus on the immediate project's design but also coach the team to prioritize maintainability and extensibility for future enhancements. Considering that team members will eventually assume on-call responsibilities for the services and features developed, emphasize ensuring operational stability. Therefore, as an EM, your role extends to ensuring that the technical design is robust and garners approval from senior engineers or, if applicable, undergoes scrutiny by an architecture board for review and signoff. This proactive approach sets the stage for successful project implementation and supports the long-term sustainability of the developed solutions.

BACKLOG AND PROJECT TRACKER

As an EM, you play a vital role in maintaining a healthy backlog of engineering tasks, collaborating with your team and potentially a Scrum lead. This task entails translating project requirements into actionable development tasks, often based on spikes and technical-design discussions.

Detailed user stories are essential, including clear descriptions, dependencies, acceptance criteria, and steps for replicating problems in case of a bug. Prioritizing tasks allows effective stack ranking, aiding engineers in task selection.

> **Did you know?**
>
> *User stories* (https://mng.bz/67yA) are descriptions of a feature or functionality from the perspective of a user or customer. They are commonly used in software development to capture requirements and communicate them to the development team in an understandable, actionable way. A user story typically follows a simple template: "As a [type of user], I want [some goal] so that [some reason]."
>
> Bill Wake, a software consultant and author known for his work in software and agile development, coined the INVEST acronym to specify the accepted criteria for evaluating the quality of a user story. When a story fails to meet any of these criteria, the team may find it necessary to rephrase the story or consider a complete rewrite, often symbolized by discarding the original story card and creating a new one. A well-crafted user story should embody the following characteristics:

(continued)

- *I (Independent)*—It should stand on its own, unaffected by other stories.
- *N (Negotiable)*—It should not be rigidly defined but open to discussion and negotiation.
- *V (Valuable)*—It should provide significant value to the user or stakeholder.
- *E (Estimable)*—It should be reasonably estimable in terms of effort and complexity.
- *S (Small)*—It should be of a manageable size to be completed within a single iteration.
- *T (Testable)*—It should be theoretically testable, even if a test hasn't been developed.

A project or feature tracker serves as a living document, ensuring team alignment with owners, status, and priorities for each feature or item. This approach facilitates transparency and serves as a source of truth regardless of project methodology. The project plan helps refine the product by stack-ranking features based on company priorities, ensuring that delivery aligns with customer needs. It also prevents overlooking critical items and provides transparency to leadership regarding project status.

Tools such as Trello, Jira, and Asana, custom in-house solutions, or Microsoft Excel worksheets are used for project tracking. These tools offer visual representations of project progress, helping the user understand the remaining work and potential blockers. Customization based on project needs and stakeholder expectations is common practice.

Let's look at a sample project tracker for Project Accessible to get a rough idea of how to make your own project/feature tracker. Figure 10.3 is a generic example; feel free to customize it to fit your project.

This sample project tracker provides a consistent blueprint from which the entire team works and holds owners accountable for the work assigned to them. In addition, QAs can use it in the testing phase to build test cases and verify traceability. Next, let's look at how to manage dependencies as part of the project.

DEPENDENCY MANAGEMENT

Dependency management involves identifying, organizing, and tracking relationships between activities that are crucial for project success. Here's how it's done:

- *Identify dependencies.* Start by identifying dependencies to uncover any missing pieces in the project plan.
- *Organize dependencies.* Arrange dependencies in a logical sequence to understand the relationships between activities.
- *Track dependencies.* Continuously monitor dependencies, ensuring that the team stays on track. If slippage occurs, consider reallocating resources or adjusting the execution plan.

A	B	C	D	E	F	G	H	I	J	K
Setup	Project feature	Goal	Priority	Assigned to	Status	Expected delivery date	Dependencies	Risks + mitigation plan	Testing complete or not	Comments/ notes
1	Design the user interface (UI) with accessibility in mind.	The goal of this feature is to ensure that the user interface is customer-friendly.	P1	Jack	Green	15-Mar-23	Yes, the feature involves collecting data from upstream accounts services to get customer accounts.	The upstream service has an active bug in production where if the customer somehow has two accounts associated with it, it randomly returns the account information for one of them. Mitigation plan: The team is actively discussing with the upstream accounts team to fix the bug and ensure consistency in the response returned.	Yes	Here, we can have a link of related documents.
2	Set up hosting and domain for the website.	Procure the domain for the website.	P1	James	Green	25-Mar-23	Not applicable	Not applicable	No	
3	Develop website functionality (product listings, shopping cart, checkout, etc.).	The goal is to provide basic checkout funtionality to the end user.	P2	Emily	Red	1-Apr-23	Yes, the feature needs to integrate a text-to-speech converter library to add the audio.	Not applicable	No	Links to text-to-speech library.
4	Test website functionality and compatibility across devices and browsers.	Focus on testing the website.	P3	Sam	Yellow	15-Apr-23	Not applicable	Not applicable	No	

Figure 10.3   A sample project tracker for Project Accessible to track a list of project items along with the priority, status, and other critical items

Dependencies can be within or across teams, related to resourcing (such as relying on engineers from other teams) or external (such as procuring tool licenses). Clear timelines for dependencies should be documented and tracked in the project/feature tracker to maintain project alignment and transparency. Figure 10.4 shows a sample dependency management scheme for Project Accessible.

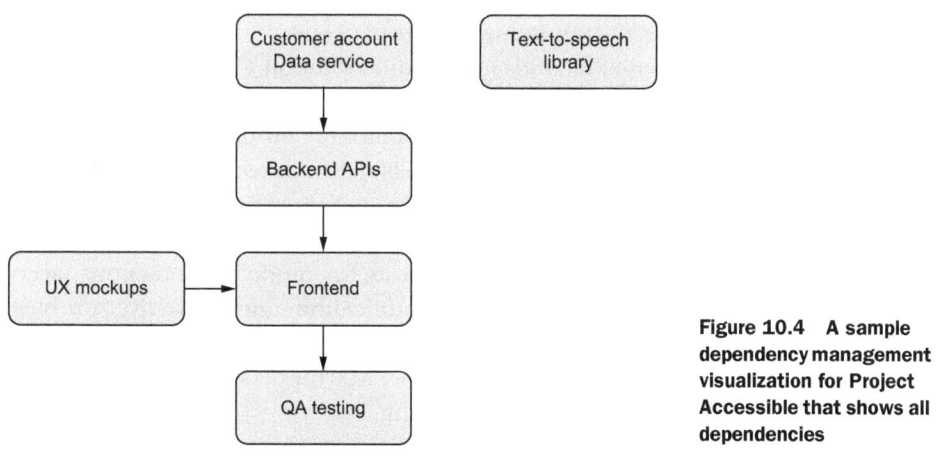

Figure 10.4   A sample dependency management visualization for Project Accessible that shows all dependencies

> **Did you know?**
> A RAID (risks, assumptions, issues, and dependencies) log (https://asana.com/
> resources/raid-log) is a project planning tool that helps you proactively identify risks
> to a project, identify any assumptions the engineering team is making, track active
> risks that need to be addressed, and lay out dependencies. This tool helps provide
> transparency, enabling the team and leadership to plan strategies to mitigate risks
> and prepare backup plans.

For Project Accessible, various dependencies are identified, ranging from backend readiness before frontend integration to reliance on upstream teams for data collection, QA for testing, and UX for mockups. Additionally, the team considered the choice between using an open-source library or building an in-house solution for a website feature, introducing a tool dependency.

To mitigate waterfall execution, frontend engineers used mock test data while backend implementation progressed. Delays in the first item of the dependency sequence could ripple through subsequent tasks.

Dependencies were organized logically and added to the feature tracker for visual representation. For an EM, collaborating with a PM (if one is assigned) involves facilitating dependency tracking through regular check-ins and providing support to unblock teams as necessary.

10.1.4 Execution

During the execution stage, the engineering team implements solutions, conducts testing, and focuses on defect/bug triage. For an EM, this phase involves juggling multiple tasks, including actively contributing to road-map execution, leading the engineering team, managing conflicts, conducting frequent check-ins with team members and stakeholders, and preparing for project release.

IMPLEMENTING AND CODING

During the implementation and coding phase of the software engineering project life cycle, the focus shifts to translating design concepts and requirements into tangible code. This critical phase demands meticulous attention to detail, adherence to coding standards, and use of appropriate programming languages and frameworks. As an EM, your role is to ensure that the development team produces clean, efficient, and maintainable code that aligns with established architecture and design principles. Version-control systems facilitate seamless collaboration and code management, enabling smooth integration of changes. Rigorous testing, including unit tests for individual components and integration tests for module interactions, accompanies the coding process. Transparent communication and proactive problem-solving among team members are crucial for overcoming challenges and progressing toward project objectives during this phase. As an EM, you play a pivotal role in supporting the engineering team by doing the following:

- *Provide technical guidance.* Offer assistance with complex technical problems and share insights based on your experience.
- *Monitor development tasks.* Ensure efficient task allocation and identify any coordination problems within the team.
- *Enforce coding standards.* Guarantee adherence to company-approved coding standards and verify the compliance of libraries and tools used in development.
- *Conduct code reviews.* Oversee code reviews to maintain code quality, provide constructive feedback, and ensure adherence to coding standards.
- *Advocate for security.* Promote high standards of security throughout the development process.

For Project Accessible, you ensure that website development aligns with defined requirements and accessibility standards. Additionally, you collaborate with the engineering team and content developer to create engaging content that highlights the benefits of the accessible-toy product line.

LEADING THE TEAM

As EM, you are the team captain, setting the foundation and culture for your team. Regular one-on-one meetings with team members are essential for addressing concerns and ensuring alignment of individual goals with project objectives. Providing guidance, support, and delegating tasks according to team members' strengths maximizes productivity and efficiency. Regular check-ins, feedback sessions, and transparent communication channels foster continuous improvement and promptly address any problems or concerns.

Chapter 9 emphasizes establishing an open and continuous feedback mechanism, which is crucial for effective leadership. Time management plays a pivotal role in leading the team, especially when you face development delays. Staying calm, developing a plan to address delays, and considering options such as adding resources, simplifying design, or negotiating a trimmed-down version of requirements can mitigate delays and maintain progress.

When dependencies on other teams affect progress, communicating proactively and setting expectations are vital. Using cross-functional partners to their fullest extent can provide valuable support and assistance in overcoming challenges.

As an EM, your role extends beyond managing tasks; you also facilitate a conducive environment for the team, advocate for members, and provide direction and advice when needed. This approach fosters a high-functioning team capable of delivering exceptional results.

MANAGING CONFLICTS

Conflicts are no surprise in a workplace, especially on projects where the teams might have dependencies and everyone involved would like to move fast. The conflict can happen intrateam (among your own team members) or cross-team (such as a conflict between an engineer on your team and the technical program manager). See chapter 9 to refresh the concept.

MANAGING VENDOR/THIRD-PARTY TOOLS

As an EM, you'll often oversee integrations with third-party tools and vendors, which involves maintaining vendor relationships for optimal pricing and service. You may need to collaborate with cross-functional teams such as product management, legal, procurement, and finance to identify suitable vendors. Seek assistance from the legal team to ensure that negotiations align with regulations. Establish clear SLAs to address conflicts and ensure compliance with safety standards. Next, let's delve into conflict management during project execution.

SHIFTING PRIORITIES

In the dynamic landscape of project execution, it's common for priorities to shift as new information emerges or unforeseen challenges arise. Effective change management processes (https://mng.bz/AdGW) are essential for navigating these shifts smoothly and ensuring that the project stays on track. Suppose that for Project Accessible, initial user feedback prompts a significant change in feature requirements. In response, the project team initiates a change management process, assessing the effect on timelines, resources, and deliverables. Following are some steps to take:

- Engage your engineers and technical PM to help estimate the new effort and see whether it can be accommodated within the constraints of bandwidth and timelines.
- Reallocate resources as needed.
- Negotiate with the PM to see what can be punted out to accommodate this high-priority task, and come to a mutually acceptable solution.

Through transparent communication and collaborative decision-making, you and the team can adapt to shifting priorities while minimizing disruption and maintaining momentum toward project objectives.

BEING TRANSPARENT TO STAKEHOLDERS AND LEADERSHIP

Transparency to stakeholders and leadership is crucial for project success. Key strategies include the following:

- *Regular demos*—Showcase project progress to stakeholders, inviting feedback for alignment and quality enhancement.
- *Dashboards and reviews*—Use dashboards, weekly business reviews, and monthly business reviews to provide real-time insights into metrics, risks, and milestones.
- *Documentation*—Maintain comprehensive records of milestones, decisions, and insights throughout the project life cycle.

By promoting transparency through these methods, teams foster trust and collaboration, driving project momentum and success. Refer to chapter 9 for more tactics that apply to day-to-day EM roles.

TESTING

In the intricate web of software project execution, testing is a critical phase, ensuring the integrity, functionality, and usability of the product. Following are some strategies to raise the bar on testing:

- *Development testing*—Developers rigorously assess individual components to identify and rectify any defects early in the process.
- *Cross-functional testing*—Stakeholders and project managers engage in testing to provide rapid feedback, fostering a collaborative environment that accelerates iteration cycles and minimizes development bottlenecks.
- *Quality assurance (QA) testing*—QA testing follows development testing and encompasses comprehensive examination of the software against predetermined criteria to guarantee adherence to specifications and standards. This testing is performed by a QA expert.
- *Usability testing*—This testing focuses on UX, ensuring intuitive navigation and seamless interaction. User acceptance testing (https://mng.bz/ZE9Z) allows users to validate the software's alignment with their needs and expectations.
- *Security testing*—This testing safeguards against vulnerabilities, fortifying the software against potential threats.
- *Load testing*—Load testing (https://mng.bz/oeYp) is performed to determine a system's behavior under both normal and anticipated peak load conditions. It identifies the maximum operating capacity of an application, as well as any bottlenecks, and determines which element is causing degradation.

With the benefits of early check-ins and feedback, several companies go on to release a beta version of the apps, sometimes doing an employee release so that the product can go through internal dogfooding (https://mng.bz/RZwP) being released to the end customer. The idea is similar: gather early feedback and fix bugs before the product goes to customers.

Upon thorough testing and meticulous bug fixes, a code freeze is enacted, halting further modifications to prevent regression and uphold the integrity of the final product. Through meticulous testing protocols, software projects can confidently progress toward successful deployment, fortified by a robust foundation of quality and reliability.

LAUNCHING AND RELEASING

The launch-and-release phase of a software project marks the culmination of extensive planning, development, and testing efforts as the project transitions from the development environment to production. Before the launch, the project undergoes operational readiness reviews to ensure that all systems, processes, and resources are prepared to support the software in its operational environment. This phase involves evaluating factors such as infrastructure, support procedures, and contingency plans to mitigate potential risks and ensure a smooth transition.

Furthermore, security and compliance signoff is critical for verifying that the software meets regulatory requirements and adheres to industry standards for data protection and privacy. This step involves conducting thorough security assessments and compliance audits to identify and address any vulnerabilities or noncompliance problems before the software is released to users.

The launch also requires signoff from all stakeholders involved in the project, including representatives from business, marketing, sales, customer support, and other relevant departments depending on the organization and the nature of the project. Each stakeholder provides their endorsement of the launch based on their respective area of responsibility and expertise, ensuring that the software aligns with organizational goals and meets the needs of users.

In the context of minimum viable products (MVPs), the launch may involve releasing a scaled-down version of the software with essential features to gather feedback and validate assumptions. Subsequent development and releases build on the MVP, incorporating user feedback and adding new features and enhancements to meet evolving requirements and address user needs. This iterative approach allows for continuous improvement and innovation, enabling the software to evolve and stay competitive in the market.

Overall, the launch-and-release phase of a software project represents a crucial milestone, requiring careful coordination and collaboration among stakeholders to ensure a successful deployment that delivers value to users and aligns with organizational objectives.

10.1.5 Postexecution

Postexecution tasks encompass actions performed after a project's completion, serving as a closure protocol to evaluate goal achievement and assess success. These activities not only conclude the project but also lay the groundwork for future iterations, documenting valuable learnings. Let's delve into these postexecution activities in detail.

RECOGNIZING THE TEAM MEMBERS

As humans, we naturally incline toward feeling notable and recognized. Revisit chapter 6 on to see how you can value your team members and the people around you.

MEASURING SUCCESS

The success of a project launch is determined by comparing results with predefined success metrics. In agile development, data analysis and course corrections are crucial. Common metrics for evaluation include the following:

- *Project timelines*—Assessing adherence to timelines, resource allocation, and milestone achievement
- *Budgeting*—Evaluating whether the project stayed within the allocated budget
- *ROI*—Gauging market reception and attainment of revenue goals
- *Customer/product satisfaction*—Gathering feedback through research, surveys, and complaints analysis
- *Innovation*—Determining whether the product offers unique value in the market
- *Employee satisfaction*—Surveying employees to ensure alignment with company goals
- *User dashboards*—Analyzing user interaction data for insights and improvement
- *Code quality*—Analyzing test coverage, technical debt incurred, and DORA metrics (https://mng.bz/2K6X) to ensure continuous maintenance or improvement in code quality
- *Operational stability*—Evaluating infrastructure performance to ensure a smooth customer experience

In the case of Project Accessible, you ensured compliance with requirements and timelines while staying within the allocated budget. The PM assessed the project's ROI, with initial sales exceeding expectations. A customer satisfaction survey yielded a score of 95/100, indicating strong market reception. Despite the familiar product line, quality and price point distinguished the product from competitors. An internal employee survey revealed a 70% satisfaction rate, with valuable feedback for improvement. Retrospectives were identified as a means to address problems earlier, such as testing challenges. Multiple dashboards were implemented for monitoring sales, ticketing, and customer complaints. Although objective metrics gauge success, subjective factors such as market hype and sentiment also play a role in evaluation, guiding future improvements and technical road-map planning for the project team and leadership.

SUPPORTING OPERATIONAL MAINTENANCE AND PRODUCTION

Operational maintenance or production support becomes a significant focus in the continuous delivery process of agile development projects. This aspect garners attention from both team members and leadership, aiming to prevent service downtime and maintain optimal application latency for a seamless customer experience. A few key things to keep in mind at this stage are

- *Optimized resources*—Plan for the infrastructure cost and optimize the resources to avoid hefty cloud services use or third-party bills.
- *Monitoring and alerts*—Ensure the right set of alerts and monitoring so that the team on call can get an immediate alert if something goes wrong, which helps make on-call support efficient.
- *Defined SLAs*—Not everything will have a huge blast radius—hence, the importance of defining SLAs for the service everyone abides by.
- *On-call run books or troubleshooting documents*—To optimize response time for high-severity problems, the team can create a repository documenting common customer problems and their resolutions. All team members contribute to enhancing this living document, improving on-call efficiency. This resource grows over time as the team encounters new challenges, aiding in knowledge transfer for future handovers to different teams postlaunch.
- *Better documentation*—When new features or enhancements are added to legacy services, maintaining them can be challenging, particularly if code quality is poor and documentation is lacking. This situation often leads to reliance on tribal knowledge accumulated over the years. Consequently, making changes to these services becomes a daunting task, as any modification in one area may have unforeseen effects elsewhere. To mitigate these risks, it's essential to prioritize documentation within your team and emphasize rigorous testing before launching new features on legacy systems.

Let's understand this situation through an example. For Project Accessible, the organization followed the standard trouble ticket and SLA agreement practiced in the company, with four levels of severity for any trouble ticket or problem (table 10.2). The team defined the SLAs and turnaround times expected for trouble tickets and escalations.

Table 10.2 Different severity levels for trouble tickets

Severity 1	This level occurs when the business is affected. Everyone should stop working on anything else and focus entirely on fixing this problem as soon as possible. The blast radius, in this case, can be that each company customer is affected. Examples: order drops or a security breach of customer data. SLA can be turnaround of four to six hours.
Severity 2	This level is critical and needs immediate attention, but the blast radius, such as the number of customers affected, may be smaller (with perhaps 40% of customers affected). Example: during the order checkout, the applying code option is broken, so any customer with a discount code cannot use it and hence needs to pay the total price-. This example isn't a happy customer experience, right? SLA in this case can be 24 hours.
Severity 3	This level is not as critical as the preceding two. On-call support can take one to two days to triage the problem and get back. Example: an application needs to go through a security review before launch. Because the service has not been launched, no production effect occurs, so the SLA is two business days.
Severity 4	This level is not urgent and can wait. It has the least priority for the on-call team and will be addressed when trouble tickets of higher priority are addressed. Example: a marketing manager requests access to your internal platform to show sale numbers. In this case, SLA can be in days, such as five business days.

Sometimes, what you built might be handed postproduction to the production operations team or handed to a different engineering team. In such cases, I recommend that teams have a warranty period where they support what they built for some time until the other team takes over. These warranty periods can vary from 30 to 90 days and are excellent ways to have the two teams work together and significantly reduce stress on both teams.

Technical debt, stemming from legacy code or rushed product launches, is a critical problem that requires attention. When time constraints demand fast prototyping for a competitive edge, an agile approach may be necessary. For an EM, negotiating features and exploring alternative technical strategies with the team becomes essential. Openly discussing technical debt is vital, even if shortcuts were taken to meet deadlines. EMs should communicate openly with stakeholders, ensuring alignment on addressing technical debt postlaunch. Using tracking tools such as Jira and Asana can help you proactively manage and organize tasks related to technical debt in the project backlog. If services become unstable, planning for a rebuild may be necessary. Enterprise architecture plays a key role in managing and tracking technical debt, assisting teams in resolution over time. In summary, actively addressing technical debt is crucial for maintaining product quality and should be an ongoing discussion throughout development.

CREATING A PROJECT RETROSPECTIVE

A retrospective ceremony serves as a valuable learning opportunity to reflect on both successes and failures, identifying opportunities for future improvement. It can occur at the end of a project or as a midproject check-in to ensure alignment and steer progress in the right direction. The involvement of key stakeholders allows for comprehensive review of the project and fosters understanding of future opportunities. Figure 10.5 is a sample retrospective board for Project Accessible.

Kudos	What went well?	What could be improved?	Action items
Kudos to Jack for going above and beyond in building the volume control feature in a short span of time.	Text-to-speech API integration with UI is complete.	Too many meetings take away builder time.	Move team stand ups from daily cadence to three days a week.
Shout-out to Jessica for documenting a run book with common troubleshooting mechanism for frequently occurring customer issues.	QA testing made good progress		
…	…	…	…

Figure 10.5   Sample retrospective board for Project Accessible

Another approach to the project retrospective is a Miro sample board (https://miro .com/miroverse/project-retrospective). The project end retrospective gathers all stakeholders to discuss challenges, lessons learned, and opportunities for improvement. Action items are prioritized, and an action plan is developed for immediate benefits. As an EM, setting a positive tone fosters a learning experience rather than blame.

I recommend checking out the *Harvard Business Review Project Management Handbook* (https://mng.bz/PZwP), *Project Management for the Unofficial Project Manager* (https:// mng.bz/JZwv), and *Agile Project Management For Dummies* (https://mng.bz/wxZQ) to learn more about project management, execution, and delivery.

What do other leaders have to say?

Choosing the right tool for tracking and managing your projects is important. Getting visibility across team projects becomes much easier if you all choose one tool for progress updates. Every time you start a project with a cross-team project, you start with getting the POC from each team and setting up a weekly rhythm with them. Once you close on high-level approaches, ensure that every dependency on cross-teams is assigned to them in the tool. One important part is to share monthly progress with all stakeholders and ensure everyone is on the same page as part of those progress reports.

—Madhur Kathuria, Engineering Leader at Microsoft,
formerly with Moengage, Oracle, and IIT

(continued)

For the last three years, I have worked with small teams at small startups. Success metrics are different than when I was at larger organizations. We seek market fit and iterate quickly, sometimes faster than a two-week sprint can accommodate. My guiding principle stays the same across organizations: "Is my team executing the most valuable work for the company? In practice, at small start-ups, this usually skews to building the minimal iterable product (instead of minimum viable product) and then rapidly iterating with feedback from sales/marketing/product to hone into the MVP. This sometimes means making quality tradeoffs to answer critical market questions knowing that we will have to clean up later.

—Nathan Bourgoin, Chief Technology Officer at Alakazam, Inc.,
Technical Adviser, and Engineering Leader

The key to tracking progress on multiple projects simultaneously is establishing project leaders or product owners from the beginning. Projects can often go sideways when ownership is unclear. As a leader, we must acknowledge that one person cannot keep track of all projects simultaneously and that delegation empowers other leaders on your team. Even in the case of cross-team projects, appointing one single owner responsible for negotiating timelines, capturing dependencies, identifying risks, and managing the overall health of the initiative is my not-so-secret sauce of a successful outcome.

—Nishat Akhter, Data Product and Engineering Leader,
Amazon Web Services

For a project's success metrics, defining success criteria early before prioritizing the project is important. This usually helps in identifying the metrics that could measure success criteria. Success metrics vary from team to team and company to company; could be related to business drivers (revenue, acquisition, engagement) or technical metrics (performance, latency, errors).

—Saurabh Gandhi, Senior Director, Software Development at Audible,
formerly with American Express

10.2 Stop and think: Practice questions

1 What is your most memorable project delivery experience? Why is it most memorable?

2 What is your most forgettable project delivery experience? Why is it most forgettable?

3 How would you navigate a project with strict deadlines?

4 Share a project experience where the delivery failed in the timelines decided. How did stakeholders react? What did you do next?

5 How would you plan operational maintenance for a newly launched service by your team?

6 What are the most unique findings that came to your attention as part of a retrospective? Why was it surprising for you?

7 Have you faced difficulty managing operations for a newly released project/product? What do you think was the problem? How did the team navigate the situation?

Summary

- Coordination and collaboration are vital for achieving smooth and effective project execution, both within the team and with external partners. This process can be likened to a dance, with the EM, PM, and technical program manager as dance partners working together for a flawless performance.

- The success of a project hinges on meticulous planning, execution, and delivery, requiring the collaborative effort of various stakeholders. The project life cycle comprises five phases: project discovery, preplanning, planning and project kickoff, execution, and postexecution.

- During the project-discovery phase, the product road map, typically developed by the PM in collaboration with the EM, outlines new features or changes. Additionally, as an EM, you'll craft the technical road map to align with strategic goals.

- Preplanning establishes the project foundation, involving assessing priority, defining scope, and identifying key stakeholders. The planning and project kickoff phase transforms the preplanning wish list into a detailed project plan, incorporating budgeting, resource allocation, team building, communication channels, training, and establishing a project/feature tracker.

- Execution involves the actual implementation, testing, and defect triage, with the EM leading the team, participating in technical discussions, managing third-party relationships, facilitating check-ins and feedback loops, and overseeing risk management.

- Postexecution tasks encompass recognizing team members, evaluating success metrics, addressing operational maintenance and technical debt, and conducting a project retrospective for continuous improvement.

- In essence, project management is a synchronized dance requiring careful planning, execution, and reflection to achieve success and continuous improvement.

Managing expectations

This chapter covers

- Setting and managing expectations
- Facing common challenges in expectation management
- Using a framework to manage expectations
- Managing expectations at all levels

If you do not know where you are going, any road will get you there.

—Lewis Carroll

Filmmakers employ storyboarding as a crucial bridge between a script and actual filming, providing a visual road map for scenes. Similarly, setting and managing expectations early in any process is vital for success. Initiating this process involves clarifying expectations and adjusting them proactively as discussions unfold, aligning with ground realities. Expectation management acts as a collaborative agreement, defining inputs, outputs, and processes to guide efforts toward common goals.

Distinguishing between realistic and unrealistic expectations is crucial. Realistic ones, grounded in data and meeting SMART criteria (chapter 3), ensure attainable goals. Unrealistic expectations, lacking a factual basis, can lead to confusion and misalignment.

Explicit and implicit expectations further complicate the landscape (figure 11.1). Explicit expectations are clearly defined and often outlined in job descriptions, whereas implicit expectations involve proactive efforts to enhance skills and contribute effectively. Striking a balance and aiming for a win–win situation is crucial in setting expectations.

Figure 11.1   Expectations can be different from what is perceived versus what is expected.

Beyond setting and managing expectations lies the crucial task of managing perceptions. Human psychology forms judgments, influencing future expectations based on past experiences. Addressing misperceptions is vital for nurturing positive relationships.

This chapter explores the importance of managing expectations, as well as common challenges in that process and a framework for effective expectation setting and management. This discussion underscores the significance of managing expectations across all levels—from managers and peers to team members.

11.1   Importance of managing expectations

Managing expectations effectively is a critical aspect of fostering a shared understanding among stakeholders and your team members, promoting realistic and achievable goals. As a manager, it's important to cultivate a collaborative, positive work environment by guiding and influencing the team's goals and working culture. This skill not only prevents misunderstandings and disappointments but also enhances communication, collaboration, and project success. The importance of managing expectations is multifaceted, involving various aspects addressed in the following sections.

11.1.1   Clarity

Setting expectations in advance offers the key benefit of eliminating ambiguity, preventing multiple interpretations of a problem statement, and hence providing clarity. Clearly articulating tasks, expectations, and the level of support provided serves as an agreement to align both parties. This clarity aids in prioritizing tasks, disentangling thoughts, and minimizing ambiguity.

Suppose that Alice expects Bob to deploy a set of code changes to production. Bob, who is relatively new to the team, has never handled a deployment. Unless Bob gets detailed information, this scenario can lead to various consequences based on his interpretation of Alice's expectations. The lack of clarity raises questions such as the following:

- Can Bob simply push the changes forward?
- Does Bob need to do a specific testing set before changes are deployed?
- Do we need to involve any quality assurance (QA) engineers for this deployment?
- Do changes need to go through some specific staging environment?
- After changes are deployed, do we need to inform any team members?

The absence of clear expectations results in multiple interpretations, causing frustration, slowing the process, and yielding less effective results. Striking a balance between being overly prescriptive and taking a hands-off approach is crucial for an EM. Establishing expectations early, aligning with team members, and providing guidelines help prevent rework and enhance overall efficiency.

11.1.2 *Relationship building*

Clear, explicit communication of expectations contributes to the establishment of robust relationships between the individual who sets the expectations and the one who is tasked with execution. This transparent alignment increases the likelihood of successful task completion, fostering trust and rapport. Such clarity leads to higher engagement, creating an environment conducive to growth. In the Alice-and-Bob example, Alice's expression of trust by sharing expectations and support builds rapport. In turn, Bob feels engaged, reciprocates the trust, and seeks assistance, fostering clear communication channels between him and her.

11.1.3 *Risk mitigation*

The process of setting and managing expectations facilitates proactive planning for contingency measures in the event of challenges. Open discussions between the expectation setter and the executor allow them to explore potential scenarios and devise a Plan B in case Plan A encounters obstacles. This approach not only addresses potential risks but also cultivates a growth mindset.

Continuing with the Alice-and-Bob scenario, suppose that Bob communicates his lack of confidence in executing the production deployment, because he's carrying out this task for the first time. This open communication allows both parties to state their expectations clearly. Alice can have another team member shadow Bob during the deployment, offering support and creating a learning opportunity. This proactive approach ensures trust and verification, establishing a plan for risk mitigation if the original plan faces challenges.

In contemporary agile methodologies, the consistent delivery of valuable outcomes to customers is a primary objective. This approach involves a continuous cycle of establishing initial expectations, delivering a portion of the product, incorporating feedback through iterations, and then managing expectations again. This iterative approach encourages experimentation, quick recognition of failures, and rapid learning, ensuring the continual delivery of value. Section 11.2 explores common challenges that engineering managers (EMs) encounter in establishing and maintaining expectations.

11.2 Challenges in managing expectations

Setting and managing expectations is a nuanced process, far from a straightforward interaction. Although it may seem simple on the surface—a directive is given, and an action is taken—we must acknowledge our human nature. Unlike robots, humans exhibit a range of responses even to seemingly straightforward tasks. If you ask that someone open a door at home, one person may do so directly, another might peer through the window first, and a third might seek further clarification before taking action. Human beings naturally harbor diverse perceptions of what is expected, making it imperative to address potential misunderstandings. This section delves into common challenges that arise during the establishment and maintenance of expectations.

11.2.1 Ambiguity

Ambiguity is a prevalent challenge in setting and managing expectations. When the individual who assigns a task provides inadequate or unclear information, the result is open-ended questions and ambiguity. The Alice-and-Bob example illustrates how a seemingly straightforward directive—asking Bob to deploy code changes—unfolded into a multitude of questions and interpretations. Particularly for newcomers who are navigating the company or role, the lack of clear instructions during expectation setting is not uncommon.

Another misstep is not considering the skill sets of the individuals involved. The task at hand may require expertise in React, but because of ambiguity or lack of knowledge, you assign a developer who has never used React. Clearly, this error could lead to misaligned expectations. Similarly, if information about the priorities of stakeholders is ambiguous, you could be setting wrong expectations to begin with. Always be clear about the priorities of the project and what should be tackled first, keeping realistic expectations in mind.

On the other hand, all these challenges present an opportunity for the executor to seek clarification and ask pertinent questions to dispel assumptions. Formulating precise queries is crucial for obtaining accurate details. Here are some clarifying questions to ask:

- Does the task involve prerequisites or dependencies?
- What is the expected outcome?
- What is the timeline for completion?
- Is supporting documentation available?
- Who is the best person to consult regarding this task?
- Does the task necessitate regular progress reports?
- If one person will be handling multiple tasks, do they know who to ask for assistance in prioritizing those tasks?

Clarifying ambiguity helps the executor understand the comprehensive set of expectations. It also prompts the expectation setter to clarify how they will provide support and to specify the expected time frame, ensuring effective time management.

11.2.2 *Inability to say no*

Reluctance to say no is a common human trait, especially in the workplace. Suppose that your manager requests your attendance at a technical talk on iOS development, even though you are a QA manager with limited interest in the topic. Your reluctance to decline politely may stem from concerns about repercussions on professional relationships. Many individuals, especially early in their careers, aim to remain likable, earn respect, and avoid conflict by accepting all that tasks that their superiors assign or invite them to take.

For an EM, understanding when and how to say no is crucial. It helps prevent burnout, allows individuals to focus on tasks that genuinely interest them, and preserves bandwidth for meaningful contributions aligned with broader company goals. Also, saying no showcases leadership skills and the ability to prioritize effectively. Although there is no one-size-fits-all approach, you can navigate these situations by following practical tips such as these:

- *Acknowledge the opportunity.* Express gratitude for being considered.
- *Reflect before responding.* Take time to reflect, and craft a thoughtful response.
- *Prioritize and evaluate.* Assess how the new responsibility aligns with broader objectives and personal goals.
- *Communicate objectively.* Clearly articulate the rationale behind your response, whether that be time constraints or misalignment with career goals.
- *Collaborate on solutions.* Engage with your team to identify alternative resources or individuals who are better suited for the task. Collaborate in a constructive negotiation with the requester if necessary.

Mastering the art of saying no at the right time fosters personal well-being and contributes to a more productive and better-aligned workplace. For engineering leaders, navigating these situations is essential, especially when they have to decline requests from customers while maintaining positive relationships.

11.2.3 *Tendency to take things personally*

A common challenge in expectation management is tending to take things personally, leading to misunderstandings and strained relationships. Personalizing interactions occurs when inappropriate comments are made; individuals interpret meanings differently, leading to feelings of offense and hurt that can create tension and negatively affect collaboration.

Suppose that David, during a project kickoff meeting, presents the business requirements document. Julie raises questions about the project's feasibility, given limited resources and engineering constraints. David, feeling attacked, responds defensively, turning the meeting into a heated argument. Julie walks out, creating an uncomfortable atmosphere. In such a situation, try these strategies to navigate personalization:

- *Take a step back.* Gather your composure before responding.
- *Move to a separate session.* Conduct a detailed discussion in a separate, focused session.
- *Seek understanding.* View conflicts as learning opportunities, and seek to understand perspectives without blame.
- *Explore alternative communication.* Foster understanding through different communication methods.
- *Strive for common ground.* Focus on finding common ground rather than placing blame. Remember that the situation isn't about you.

For an engineering leader, it is crucial to avoid personalizing conflicts and intervene when necessary to maintain a positive team dynamic. It's also essential to coach your team members not to take mistakes personally. Introducing a bug in an application doesn't define someone as a bad engineer; it simply signifies that an error occurred due to various factors. As managers, it's our responsibility to guide our team through mistakes, encouraging them not to internalize them excessively but to learn from them. This process is integral to everyone's professional development. Encouraging respectful communication fosters collaboration, acknowledging that individuals have different perspectives and ensuring collective ownership of team outcomes.

11.3   Framework for managing expectations

Managing expectations is one of the core competencies of an EM, like a recipe that needs to be mastered over time to make it perfect by learning from past experiences. Let's look at a step-by-step framework that guides you through the process (figure 11.2).

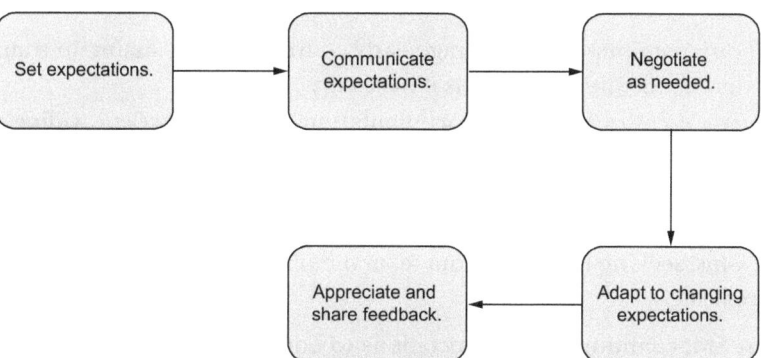

Figure 11.2   A five-step framework for managing expectations

The following sections explore these five steps: setting expectations, communicating expectations, negotiating if necessary, being agile with the expected changes, and appreciating and sharing constructive feedback with the team.

11.3.1 Setting expectations

The initial step in the expectation-management process involves a clear understanding of what is expected from all involved parties, eliminating assumptions and ambiguity. Before engaging with others, take a moment to map out realistic expectations for the other person(s), much as you would create a storyboard. When you are conveying expectations, it is important to provide the following:

- *Clear understanding*—Clearly define inputs, expected outcomes, and necessary resources and support.
- *Time-boxing*—Set time limits for tasks, avoiding open-ended commitments.
- *Mutual understanding*—Establish a shared understanding of expectations, including guidance and resources.
- *Consideration of individual strengths and weaknesses*—This step helps ensure that you set realistic expectations for the team member.

Expectations can span work-related tasks, behaviors, team guidelines, and work–life balance considerations. Jason, an EM overseeing a full-stack team, is planning a road map for the next three months. During a kickoff meeting, he communicates the need for a quarterly planning process, outlines the collaborative approach, and shares details on the sizing scale to gauge effort for each feature, setting clear expectations for the upcoming planning phase. This foundational step is crucial for effective management and collaboration.

11.3.2 Communicating expectations

The next crucial step is effective communication—sometimes overcommunication—to prevent misunderstandings and ensure clarity. This step is akin to reinforcement learning, in which repeated communication aligns everyone with a consistent interpretation of desired outcomes. Some key practices to follow are

- *Hold early conversations.* Encourage early conversations to maintain transparency and devise risk-mitigation plans if necessary.
- *Maintain documentation.* Use documentation as a reference, providing a written record for agreements, especially for projects that involve multiple teams or extended durations.
- *Perform review and validation.* Regularly review and validate expectations through check-ins, seeking feedback from team members or mentors to ensure that they are realistic.

Jason, as an EM, communicates expectations to both his team members and product leadership. The team needs clarity on the overall road map, and the product team requires confirmation based on the sizing. Jason aligns everyone through a meeting, takes detailed minutes, and shares those notes with everyone through a follow-up email, ensuring clear communication of expectations. This practice nurtures understanding and alignment throughout the team and beyond.

11.3.3 *Negotiating*

Not everything unfolds as anticipated, emphasizing the need to prepare to react to unexpected situations with a composed, calm approach. Mistakes are inherent to human nature, whether they occur during initial work estimations or technical-design overengineering, or even when defective code makes its way into production. When you face unexpected or conflicting situations, your focus should be on dissecting the root cause and devising a solution or a path forward. Employing tools such as the 5 Whys approach (https://www.mindtools.com/a3mi00v/5-whys) for root-cause analysis can be effective. It is imperative to foster an environment where team members refrain from engaging in a blame game, concentrating instead on correcting and learning from their mistakes.

Moreover, not all expectations align precisely with predefined criteria. This situation is an opportunity to delve into the reasons behind any deviations and collaborate on devising solutions. Introducing a minimum viable product can aid negotiations by allowing team members to present a draft version early in the process, gathering feedback to prevent surprises later. This approach not only benefits the customer but also enables developers to refine their estimations and assumptions regarding the workload.

Returning to Jason's scenario, assume that he received a list of ten product features from product leadership and an additional two efficiency-focused features from his engineering team. During a sizing-and-planning meeting, each of the 12 features underwent detailed discussion regarding scope and effort required to completion. Then the features were categorized as S (one or two sprints), M (three or four sprints), or L (five or six sprints). Figure 11.3 shows the full feature-request list.

Stack ranking	Feature/initiative	Priority	Sizing	Translation in # of days
1	Feature 1	P0	M	4 sprints * 2 weeks * 5 days = 40 days
2	Feature 2	P0	L	6 sprints * 2 weeks * 5 days = 60 days
3	Feature 3	P0	L	6 sprints * 2 weeks * 5 days = 60 days
4	Feature 4	P1	M	4 sprints * 2 weeks * 5 days = 40 days
5	Feature 5	P1	L	6 sprints * 2 weeks * 5 days = 60 days
6	Feature 6	P1	M	4 sprints * 2 weeks * 5 days = 40 days
7	Feature 7	P1	S	2 sprints * 2 weeks * 5 days = 20 days
8	Feature 8	P2	M	4 sprints * 2 weeks * 5 days = 40 days
9	Feature 9	P2	L	6 sprints * 2 weeks * 5 days = 60 days
10	Feature 10	P2	L	6 sprints * 2 weeks * 5 days = 60 days
11	Feature 11	P3	M	4 sprints * 2 weeks * 5 days = 40 days
12	Feature 12	P3	M	4 sprints * 2 weeks * 5 days = 40 days
Total				**560 days**
		S	1-2 sprints	
		M	3-4 sprints	
		L	5-6 sprints	

Figure 11.3   A sample feature-request list with estimated developer sizing from the team

Subsequently, the team estimated its capacity for the upcoming quarter, considering factors such as holidays, buffer days, planned vacations, on-call responsibilities, and meeting time. This approach provided accurate estimates of available development capacity, as you can see in the capacity-planning sheet in figure 11.4.

Total company working days (excluding holidays)	100
Meetings buffer (in days)	10
On-call capacity buffer (in days)	60 (Assuming 12 weeks in quarter, 5 working days each week, so 12*5 = 60 days)

Team member	Planned vacation	Available capacity
Alex	4	100-4 = 96
Bob	2	100-2= 98
Charlie	8	100-8 = 92
Daniel	4	100-4 = 96
Engo	5	100-5 = 95
Farley	3	100-3 = 97

Total capacity for the team	574 - 10 (meeting) - 60 (on call) = 504 days
Miscellaneous 10% buffer (sick day, unplanned days, and so on)	~50 days
Total available capacity for the team	**454 days**

Figure 11.4   A sample capacity-planning sheet

During the review of estimates, Jason identified a significant overcommitment: the anticipated workload for 12 features exceeded the team's capacity by 106 days. In response, he initiated negotiations with cross-functional partners to strategically defer less critical features to the next quarter, aligning the commitment with the team's available engineering capacity. In this scenario, Jason made sure to follow a few key practices:

- *Transparent evaluation*—Jason conducted a transparent evaluation of the estimates, acknowledging the capacity constraints and potential risks of overcommitment.
- *Cross-functional collaboration*—Engaging in negotiations with cross-functional partners allowed for a collective decision on deferring features, considering priority and stack ranking.
- *Appropriate commitment*—The negotiation process ensured realistic commitment to the work, preventing overcommitment and fostering a planned approach aligned with available engineering capacity.

This scenario highlights the crucial recognition that engineering capacity and estimated work hours operate in a zero-sum game, emphasizing the need for adaptability when unforeseen challenges arise.

11.3.4 *Adapting to changing expectations*

In an evolving landscape, change is inevitable. For engineering leaders, the ability to adapt to shifting expectations is crucial. Many companies have transitioned from traditional waterfall models to iterative/agile approaches, facilitating early feedback and allowing for iterative adjustments. Being flexible and accommodating to evolving requirements and expectations is paramount. Just as personal expectations evolve with time, business expectations are subject to change.

Jason is confidently navigating a negotiation on a technical road map. When a competitor's feature gains traction, strategy shifts, and Jason's team pivots swiftly to support a new product. Adaptability, clear communication, and understanding the business value behind changes are key. Embrace change; it brings new opportunities for learning and growth.

11.3.5   Appreciating and sharing feedback

Acknowledging that change is inevitable, it is essential to welcome change openly. After you successfully adapt to shifting expectations, two key actions come into play: feedback and appreciation. You can positively reinforce achievements and facilitate improvement among team members by providing constructive feedback. Regular check-ins provide opportunities for feedback, offering insights into what worked well and areas for improvement. Reflecting on these experiences helps you identify strengths and growth opportunities through the perspectives of peers.

Consider using the 360-degree peer feedback approach described in chapter 4. Expressing gratitude and recognizing efforts are equally crucial. Appreciate team members and cross-functional partners who go above and beyond. Frequent recognition not only boosts morale but also strengthens team bonds.

In Jason's scenario, his team successfully adapted to changing expectations for a new product launch. Two standout engineers and a technical program manager played crucial roles. Jason publicly appreciated their efforts through team and leadership channels, using appreciation tools such as Lattice (https://lattice.com), aligned with the company's leadership principles. This practice not only recognizes exceptional work but also fosters a positive, collaborative team environment.

Managing expectations is an ongoing task that demands skill and patience. The step-by-step framework considers both team and cross-functional partners. Section 11.4 shows you how to manage expectations at all levels, including your boss, peers, and team members.

11.4   How to manage expectations at all levels

Understanding expectations at all organizational levels—both vertically (managing up and down) and horizontally (managing peers)—is crucial for success in personal and professional realms (figure 11.5). Poor expectation management can lead to confusion, misinterpretation, and unsatisfactory outcomes. Conversely, effective expectation management, with clearly defined expectations, promotes engagement, inspiration, and increased chances of success. It contributes to a positive work environment, minimizing the risk of misunderstandings.

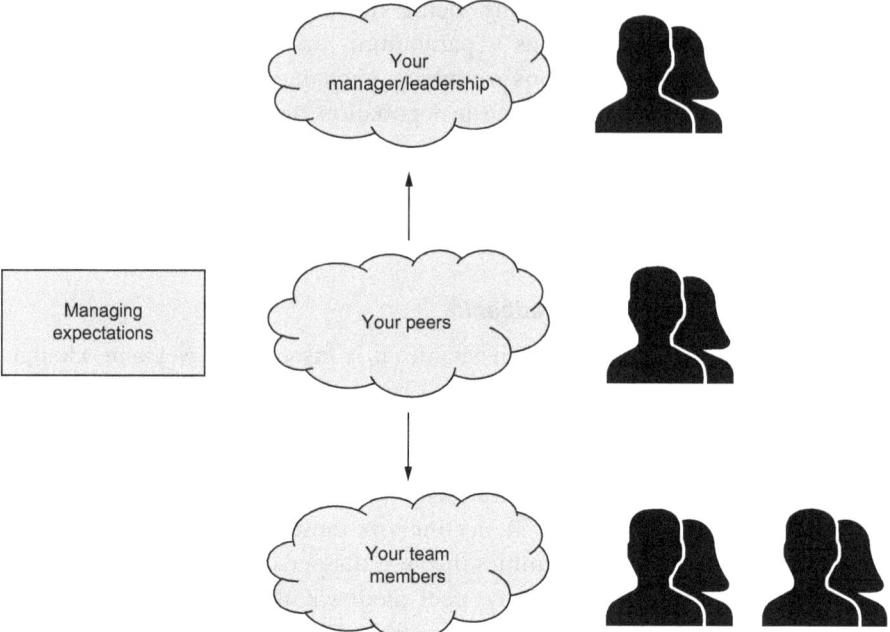

Figure 11.5   It is important to manage expectations at all levels (horizontally and vertically).

11.4.1 *Your manager/leadership*

The EM role demands versatility and self-awareness, especially when you're managing expectations from your leadership—notably, your manager. Clear, realistic expectations ensure clarity about what is expected and why, and how it should be done. These expectations encompass team deliverables, strategy, hiring goals, and the support you seek from your leadership. Consider the following guidelines:

- Establish clear expectations and realistic goals with your manager. Regular communication is vital for expectation management.
- Schedule regular check-ins to discuss progress and address any emerging problems promptly.
- Foster open communication in which constructive feedback is given proactively.
- Talk about your performance with your manager and seek feedback.
- Understand your management's preferences and adapt your communication style accordingly.
- Keep the leadership informed about roadblocks to maintain transparency and facilitate effective planning.
- Learn to say no when necessary, providing objective data to support your decisions.
- Don't hesitate to ask for help or delegate tasks when you're feeling overwhelmed.
- Recognize and appreciate your leadership. Expressing gratitude can boost team morale.

Sydney, an EM at an e-commerce firm, was excited about a crucial project introduced by her supervisor, Charlie. But she realized that without additional support, managing this project along with her team's tasks would compromise her work–life balance. Sydney declined the assignment and negotiated for an alternative project, using the company's priority list. During negotiations, she identified a low-priority project for exchange, discussed the execution plan with Charlie, and documented the agreement to prevent misunderstandings. Sydney highlighted a potential risk and agreed to biweekly check-ins on project progress. Despite initial challenges, Sydney navigated the situation adeptly, securing a mutually agreeable solution through effective communication and negotiation.

Clarifying expectations, addressing risks early, and gaining alignment before execution are critical steps in successful expectation management. Next, let's explore how to manage expectations with peers.

11.4.2 *Your peers*

When you're managing expectations with your peers, collaboration and cooperation are crucial due to the absence of a direct reporting structure. Although the fundamental framework for expectation management remains consistent, dealing with peers from different teams requires acknowledging and being realistic about each team's road map. Tools such as the RACI matrix (chapter 9) and customer demos provide clarity about roles and responsibilities, facilitating cross-collaboration and iterative product development.

Alice and Bob, EMs overseeing different product teams, find that their teams need to collaborate on a critical project, but they recognize a discrepancy in expectations regarding the project timeline. The project involves integrating a new feature into the product, which requires coordination between Alice's team (responsible for frontend development) and Bob's team (in charge of backend infrastructure). Alice believes that the frontend work can be completed within two weeks, whereas Bob anticipates that the backend modifications will take at least four weeks.

Alice's team is unable to start development until the backend tasks are completed. This dependency places them at risk of project delays due to the potential for unforeseen technical issues to arise at the 11th hour. Recognizing the importance of aligning their expectations to ensure a successful project outcome, Alice and Bob schedule a meeting to discuss their concerns and find a compromise. During the meeting, they share their perspectives and the rationale behind their estimated timelines, considering factors such as technical complexity, resource availability, and potential dependencies.

As they delve deeper into the discussion, Alice and Bob identify areas where they can streamline the development process and optimize resource allocation. They agree to prioritize certain tasks, such as API endpoint definitions and data modeling, to enable parallel development and reduce overall project duration.

Moreover, they decide to allocate additional people from both teams to work on the project, ensuring that they have the necessary personnel to meet the accelerated timeline without compromising quality. Alice offers to lend a frontend developer to Bob's team to assist with accelerating the endpoint definition, and Bob commits to providing backend support for any integration challenges that may arise on the frontend.

To formalize their agreement and maintain transparency, Alice and Bob document their decisions in a shared project tracker and also send a follow-up email to the teams, outlining the revised project plan, resource allocation, timelines, and expected deliverables. Through open communication, collaboration, and compromise, Alice and Bob successfully manage their expectations and achieve alignment on the project. Their proactive approach not only resolves potential conflicts but also strengthens their working relationship and fosters a culture of collaboration and mutual support within their teams. Managing expectations with peers is a partnership, requiring mutual understanding for shared goals. In section 11.4.3, we'll explore considerations unique to managing expectations on your own team.

11.4.3 *Your team members*

Effective management of your team's expectations is crucial for both team success and individual motivation. Clear expectations foster a supportive work environment, promoting a sense of belonging and teamwork. Recognize that expectations can originate within the team—not just from you, the EM—and emphasize mutual understanding. Key considerations for managing team expectations include the following:

- *Setting bidirectional expectations*—Provide support to the team through training, resources, and guidance, avoiding one-directional expectations.
- *Communicating openly*—Maintain open communication channels, sharing goals to build trust and encouraging team members to ask questions and seek help. As an EM, you typically possess more information than individual team members do. Therefore, it's essential to distinguish between what needs to be communicated and what you want to share, ensuring effective and relevant communication.
- *Acting as a shock absorber*—Be a shock absorber for the team, allowing them to focus on their day-to-day work and building trust for streamlined workflow.
- *Breaking down expectations*—Assist team members, especially those who are early in their careers, in breaking expectations into actionable items aligned with SMART criteria and individual goals.
- *Seeking continuous feedback*—Seek continuous feedback through surveys and regular check-ins, addressing concerns promptly and providing necessary support.
- *Leading by example*—Set a leadership example by promoting work–life balance and avoiding sending late-night emails to reinforce the desired team culture.
- *Reinforcing expectations*—Regularly reinforce expectations with the team to maintain alignment and prevent divergence from agreed-on goals.

If you expect team members to develop new skills, for example, lead by example. If you're aiming for SMART goals, define specific, measurable, achievable, relevant, and time-bound criteria:

- *Specific*—Team members should build at least one new skill tailored to their interests (such as gaining AWS or security certification or learning React).
- *Measurable*—Certifications provide measurable goals, and practical application through a project reinforces theoretical knowledge.
- *Achievable*—Ensure that goals are realistic, and provide the necessary support for team members to work toward achieving them.
- *Relevant*—Goals should be directly relevant to both the team member and the company's objectives.
- *Time-bound*—Set a clear time limit for achieving the goal, avoiding open-ended discussions.

When I was confronted with a similar challenge, I transparently shared my experience with the team during a meeting. I detailed how I dedicated time to acquiring a new skill and attaining AWS certification, providing insights into the resources that aided my learning. This approach fostered open communication, leading to a collaborative brainstorming session among team members.

In another scenario, excessive meetings, stemming largely from the product team, burdened both the engineering team and me. During a sprint retrospective, my team and I collaboratively addressed this problem, devising strategies to set appropriate expectations. We introduced a meeting bill of rights, advocating for clear agendas and expected outcomes in every meeting invite. Responsibility for this bill of rights was placed on the meeting organizer. We championed the idea internally, successfully regaining control of meeting fatigue and ensuring effective use of our team's time. This experience highlights the effectiveness of transparent communication and collaborative problem-solving in managing expectations within a team.

Managing expectations effectively, regardless of the level, involves establishing clear goals and assumptions while devising a viable path to attain them. This process requires constant collaboration to collectively strive for a shared objective. The framework provided serves as a valuable guide, helping you navigate challenges and ensuring satisfaction for those who are involved. It also helps you foster a collaborative environment, align efforts, and proactively address hurdles to maintain overall team satisfaction and success.

What do other leaders have to say?

One tip I keep in my back pocket is to make sure that stakeholders see what is being delivered at a regular cadence so that when difficult conversations need to happen about a slip or an increase in scope, stakeholders consider it to be an exception. When stakeholders only interact when there is a scope problem and are only involved in escalations, they start to believe that all work is misscoped and escalated.

(continued)

On a previous team, this meant a "this week in engineering" email to the entire company to discuss what had been accomplished and frequent messages in Slack. When a stake-holder sees general progress all the time, it's much easier to negotiate when a smaller set of items is off track. Additionally, make sure to communicate early. You have missed a communication opportunity if you wait until a project is way off track or at the missed date. Communicate that a project is trending off track or something is at risk of being off track.

—Nathan Bourgoin, Chief Technology Officer at Alakazam, Inc., Technical Adviser, and Engineering Leader

Managing expectations is key to everything we do. We need to be clear about what we can or cannot achieve given the resources, time, and budget. Setting expectations with our customers allows them to negotiate tradeoffs and ultimately helps us build an optimal solution. Setting expectations with your team provides clarity on team culture, creates a positive workplace, and also helps inform their career paths. Finally, establishing expectations with your leaders builds transparency and trust between you and your leadership.

—Nishat Akhter, Data Product and Engineering Leader, AWS

The biggest challenge when managing expectations is identifying your stakeholders. If you identify new stakeholders later in the project, then it's already too late as the ship has sailed. The other common challenge is being realistic while setting expectations. Often-times, best-guess estimates are used for initial prioritization due to urgency of ask, lack of time or resources. Later, these are not revised, resulting in project delays.

—Saurabh Gandhi, Senior Director, Software Development at Audible, formerly with American Express

11.5   *Stop and think: Practice questions*

1 How important is managing expectations for you?

2 Do you understand how your work or role fits into the bigger picture of the organization/company?

3 Think about a time when you had a conflict with a manager, peer, or cross-functional partner because of unclear expectations. What could you have done differently?

4 What are the most common challenges you have faced when setting and managing expectations?

5 Think about a time when you helped someone on the team get to the finish line by providing support and resources. What was the outcome?

6 Can you think of a time when you failed to set expectations clearly? What was the outcome?

Summary

- Setting expectations is like storyboarding in filmmaking, providing a visual sequence for alignment. Similarly, setting and managing expectations early is crucial for task success, establishing a solid foundation for execution.

- Differentiating between realistic and unrealistic expectations is vital. Realistic ones are based on data and past experiences; unrealistic ones lack a factual basis, often leading to frustration.

- Perception management plays a critical role in expectation management, addressing biases and past experiences that may influence future predictions.

- Expectation management is a key skill for an EM, and a framework helps you navigate challenges. Key steps include setting clear expectations, communicating effectively, negotiating, adapting to change, and appreciating feedback.

- Several challenges come with expectation management:
  - *Ambiguity*—When the setter of a task expects the doer to do something but provides inefficient information, open-ended questions arise, and ambiguity creeps in.
  - *Inability to say no*—We humans are reluctant to say no at the workplace and end up overcommitting to work, which often leads to burnout and job frustration.
  - *Making it personal*—People sometimes interpret comments inappropriately or misunderstand their meaning, which can lead to offense and hurt feelings between the parties.

- Managing expectations is one of the core competencies of an EM. A framework for managing expectations can help you navigate some of these difficult situations:
  - *Setting expectations*—The first step is understanding what is expected from the other person(s) and setting the expectations clearly. Stay away from assumptions and ambiguity. Clearly state what you are doing and why; sometimes ask "How are we doing?" to set the context.
  - *Communicating expectations*—The idea here is to communicate and sometimes overcommunicate. Communication provides clarity, preventing throwaway work. Place emphasis on documentation.
  - *Negotiating as needed*—In human endeavors, errors are inevitable, such as errors in initial estimations, technical designs, or code deployment. When we're faced with unexpected or conflicting situations, it's crucial to analyze the root cause and collaboratively determine a solution or path forward. This situation underscores the necessity for collaborative negotiation.
  - *Adapting to changing expectations*—Because change is the only constant, we engineering leaders need to hone our muscles so we can adapt to the changing expectations and be agile.

    – *Appreciating and sharing feedback*—Show appreciation for team members and cross-functional partners who go beyond their roles. Take the opportunity to express your gratitude to them, and provide constructive feedback to support their growth in their roles.

- Clear understanding of expectations at all organizational levels is essential for personal and professional success. This approach involves managing expectations with managers, peers, and team members through clear communication, collaboration, and goal setting.

Part 3

Learn the process

The final part focuses on processes. From the seamless integration of engineering best practices to the intricate dance of organizational change management, each chapter is a key to unlocking the true potential of your engineering endeavors.

Chapter 12 teaches the importance of engineering and operational excellence, introduces the tools that get you started, and emphasizes the importance of treating the process as continuous and iterative.

Chapter 13 offers insights into reorganizations, provides a framework to follow for organizational change management, and shows how to handle leadership changes.

Chapter 14 discusses the importance of time management, providing tips for better time planning and insights into the famous Eisenhower Matrix.

Chapter 15 extends beyond engineering projects, recapping what you've learned so far. It covers the importance of continuous learning and growing your skill set, offering valuable tips and strategies for nurturing your own development. When the final page turns, you'll be armed with both technical prowess and the wisdom to elevate yourself and those around you.

This last part is more than a conclusion; it's a call to action. It beckons you to apply the knowledge you've gained within these pages and set out on a perpetual journey of learning and growth.

Engineering and operational excellence

This chapter covers

- The importance of engineering and operational excellence
- Tools to get you started
- Engineering and operational excellence as a continuous process
- How to navigate resistance and establish engineering best practices

It is not the strongest of the species that survives, nor the most intelligent that survives. It is the one that is the most adaptable to change.

—Charles Darwin

As an engineering manager (EM) for a team of eight engineers, you have observed struggles in meeting customer expectations and delivering on time. The code deployment frequency—once every two weeks—is slow, causing delays in getting changes to production. Additionally, the code shipped by the team is often buggy, causing effects on customers. Over the past month, your team has experienced four critical problems affecting company revenue, which suggests potential problems with operational procedures, communication among team members, coding standards, and quality assurance (QA) testing. This situation is where engineering excellence and operational excellence—two distinct but connected concepts in the context of software development and management—come in.

Engineering excellence refers to the quality of the technical work performed by a software development team. It encompasses a range of factors that contribute to the effectiveness, efficiency, and sustainability of the engineering process and the resulting software product, including key aspects of code quality, test coverage, technical debt, and application security.

Operational excellence (OE) focuses on optimizing the processes, practices, and workflows within an organization to achieve efficient and reliable delivery of products or services. In the context of software engineering management, OE involves creating an environment that enables the development team to work effectively and efficiently. Key aspects of OE include effective communication, capacity planning, risk mitigation, and service-level agreements (SLAs).

If synergy exists between engineering excellence and OE, teams and organizations tend to be on a successful path. For an EM, both engineering excellence and OE are essential because they are critical factors in the success of software projects and the overall performance of the organization.

12.1 *Importance of engineering excellence and OE*

Understanding the importance of both engineering excellence and OE is vital for an EM for several reasons. This understanding facilitates the following:

- *Delivering high-quality products*—Engineering excellence ensures that the software products developed by the team meet high standards of quality, reliability, and performance. OE ensures that the development processes are efficient, streamlined, and well coordinated, leading to timely delivery of products.
- *Building trust and credibility*—Maintaining high engineering and operational standards correlates directly with improved customer satisfaction. When software consistently meets or exceeds user expectations, customers are more likely to remain satisfied, leading to positive reviews, referrals, and repeat business and ultimately contributing to the organization's success. Consistent delivery of high-quality products fosters trust and credibility for the engineering team both internally and externally, demonstrating their reliability and capability to deliver results consistently. This OE further enhances trust and confidence among stakeholders.
- *Minimizing risks and costs*—Engineering excellence helps mitigate technical risks such as bugs, security vulnerabilities, and performance problems, which can lead to costly rework, downtime, or reputation damage. OE helps identify and mitigate process-related risks such as delays, bottlenecks, and inefficiencies, reducing costs and improving resource use. By adhering to best practices, conducting

thorough testing, and implementing robust monitoring and support processes, software managers can identify and address problems early, reducing the likelihood of costly errors, outages, and security breaches.

- *Retaining and recruiting talent*—Engineers are attracted to organizations that prioritize engineering excellence. A culture of quality, innovation, and continuous improvement encourages talented individuals to join the team and motivates existing team members to stay. EMs who invest in creating an environment that fosters both engineering excellence and OE are more likely to attract and retain top talent.

- *Fostering innovation and continuous improvement*—Engineering excellence encourages a culture of innovation, creativity, and learning within the team, driving continuous improvement and adaptation to new technologies and market trends. It helps eliminate waste, inefficiencies, and bottlenecks, creating opportunities for process optimization and enhancement.

- *Maintaining a competitive advantage*—Engineering excellence and OE can be significant differentiators in the marketplace. Organizations that consistently deliver high-quality, reliable software products gain a competitive edge over their competitors. Customers are more likely to choose products and services from companies known for their commitment to excellence and reliability.

- *Driving organizational success*—The collective pursuit of engineering excellence and OE significantly affects the organization's success and competitiveness. By delivering high-quality products, optimizing processes, and ensuring customer satisfaction, the organization can boost revenue, market share, and profitability, establishing a foundation for long-term growth and sustainability. Investing in engineering excellence and OE is crucial for the organization's long-term viability and success. By consistently enhancing processes, embracing new technologies, and staying responsive to market shifts, EMs can effectively position their teams and organizations for ongoing success and adaptability.

Realizing the significance of engineering excellence and OE equips you, the EM, with the knowledge and tools you need to lead your team effectively, deliver high-quality products, and drive organizational success.

12.2   Tools and tips to get you started

Establishing a culture of engineering excellence in which long-term development decisions are valued over short-term gains is key to sustained success and the ability to launch products quickly in the long run. For engineering leaders, it's essential to advocate for and ensure the practice of engineering excellence and OE at both the team and organizational levels.

Although numerous online resources offer detailed information on tools and best practices, I'll share practical insights from my own experiences to kick-start your journey toward engineering excellence and OE. Let's explore some useful tips for introducing small guardrails and cultivating a culture of engineering excellence within your team.

12.2.1 *Raise the bar on code*

An EM can raise the bar on the team's code by implementing various strategies and best practices aimed at improving code quality, consistency, and maintainability. Here are some effective approaches for raising the coding bar:

- *Establish and enforce coding standards.* Get together with the team to establish clear coding standards and best practices, including conventions for naming variables, formatting code, commenting, and error handling. Enforce these standards through peer code reviews and automated tools to ensure consistency and ownership of the codebase.

- *Encourage code reviews.* Implementing a robust code review process is vital for maintaining code quality and fostering collaboration within the team. Encourage team members to review each other's code before merging it into the main codebase. Active participation in code reviews, whether in person or asynchronously through software tools, helps identify potential problems and provides valuable feedback. This process enhances code quality, facilitates knowledge sharing, and ensures that any blind spots are addressed before code is pushed to production.

- *Invest in training and skill development.* Provide opportunities for team members to enhance their coding skills through training programs, workshops, conferences, and online resources. Encourage continuous learning, and stay updated on the latest technologies, programming languages, and best practices in software development.

- *Promote modularity and reusability.* Encourage the development of modular, reusable code components that can be integrated into different parts of the system easily. This approach helps reduce duplication, improve maintainability, and facilitate scalability and flexibility in the codebase. You can ask the senior engineers on the team to do a knowledge-sharing session so that team members can learn best practices for coding. At the same time, take care not to reinvent the wheel.

- *Foster collaboration and knowledge sharing.* Create a collaborative environment where team members can share ideas, discuss solutions, and learn from one another's experiences. Active design and UX reviews with the engineering team can ensure that all opinions are heard. Encourage pair programming, code walk-throughs, and mentorship programs to facilitate knowledge transfer and skill development on the team.

- *Monitor code metrics and quality.* Use code analysis tools to measure code metrics such as cyclomatic complexity (https://mng.bz/wxRq), code duplication, and code coverage. Monitor these metrics regularly and address any areas of concern to improve code quality and maintainability.

In a previous role as an EM, I led a team responsible for maintaining two critical legacy services within our company, both of which were written nearly 20 years ago and exhibited significant code smells (https://mng.bz/qOlw). Upon joining the team, I conducted a thorough review of the codebase myself and engaged in discussions with team members to understand their pain points.

One major challenge we faced was reliance on tribal knowledge, which often led to short-term fixes being applied whenever production problems arose, further exacerbating the deterioration of code quality over time. To address this problem, I collaborated with the team to devise a strategy for gradually improving our coding standards. As a first step, we decided to use tools like SonarLint (https://mng.bz/QZ7G) to proactively identify and address code smells and bugs. Because we integrated SonarLint into our development workflow, every team member could catch potential problems early in the development process, reducing the likelihood of introducing new defects into the codebase.

Additionally, I recognized the need to establish a culture of code reviews within the team. Despite initial resistance, I enforced a policy requiring all code changes to undergo thorough reviews by at least two team members before being deployed to production. This policy not only helped improve code quality by providing additional eyes on the code but also fostered collaboration and knowledge sharing among team members.

Over time, these initiatives proved to be successful in raising the bar on the team's code quality and mitigating the risks associated with maintaining legacy systems. By prioritizing continuous improvement and fostering a culture of accountability, we were able to make significant strides in enhancing the reliability and maintainability of our critical services.

12.2.2 *Test coverage*

Test coverage plays a crucial role in identifying defects and bugs early in the development process. High test coverage gives developers confidence that their code behaves as intended across various scenarios, helping EMs assess the team's code quality. Although having coverage does not guarantee bug-free code, lacking test coverage poses definite risks. Monitoring test coverage helps EMs track progress and reveals areas for improvement or potential problems; it also facilitates early bug detection during development. Coverage metrics typically include line, branch, and method coverage, ensuring thorough testing of code functionality and execution paths. Following are some common types of testing:

- *Unit testing*—These tests are written to test the functionality of the smallest unit, such as the method or function block. Unit tests should be required and should be part of the definition of "done" for a task assigned to a developer.
- *Integration testing*—Integration tests are a type of software testing in which individual software modules or components are combined and tested as a group. The purpose of integration testing is to ensure that interactions between components work correctly and integrate smoothly to fulfill the requirements of the system.

- *End-to-end testing*—End-to-end testing examines the extensive codebase encompassing the entire application. By simulating real-world production functionality, it validates the system's behavior as a whole. This type of testing, however, comes with the highest maintenance costs and operates at a comparatively slower pace than other testing approaches.

- *Load testing*—In load testing, loads from sample customers are generated on the system to mimic production-like traffic. This testing helps the development team understand whether the system is scaled well to handle peak traffic in times of heavy use, identifies any bottlenecks or single points of failure in the system, and prepares the system for better scalability and reliability.

NOTE   Some companies call load testing *game-day testing* (https://mng.bz/X1ov).

- *Performance testing*—Performance testing is somewhat related to load testing, in which the load generated in the system focuses on the performance aspect of the software application. Suppose that you generate a load of 1 million customers coming to your application and downloading a short video. Now you want to measure how this load affects the system's performance, such as latency, responsiveness, and download speed. Performance testing reflects the code quality of the system and whether it is optimized for heavy use of the system.

- *Regression testing*—Regression testing ensures that new code changes do not affect or break the existing functionality of the system. It can include both functional and nonfunctional tests that are done to verify the new changes. These tests are essential have before any big new changes go to production and are usually done by a combination of software engineers and the QA for the team.

- *User acceptance testing* (UAT)—UAT is a phase of software testing in which end users or stakeholders test the software to determine whether it meets the specified requirements and is ready for deployment. In UAT, the focus is on validating the software from the perspective of users to ensure that it meets their needs and expectations.

Implementing these testing methodologies acts as a safeguard and QA measure for changes your engineering team makes before they reach users. Although you may worry about the increased scope that these methods bring to your project, automation testing is emerging as a solution. As an EM, advocate for automation testing, allowing the creation of test cases that can subsequently be rerun using test tools and frameworks. Despite the initial development investment, the advantages lie in repeatability and reusability with minimal manual intervention. Integrate testing into the development workflow, and use continuous integration (CI) tools to run tests automatically with each code commit.

A famous industry example of test coverage is the Netflix tool Chaos Monkey, which uses the concept of chaos-testing engineering (https://netflix.github.io/chaosmonkey). The Chaos Monkey tool randomly terminates production machines to test resilience

Did you know?

The testing pyramid (https://mng.bz/y8DB), shown in the following figure, is an industry-wide framework for developing robust, high-quality software. It helps define the types of tests that should be included in the automated test suite, plays a critical role in regression testing, provides time and cost savings due to automation, and removes human error.

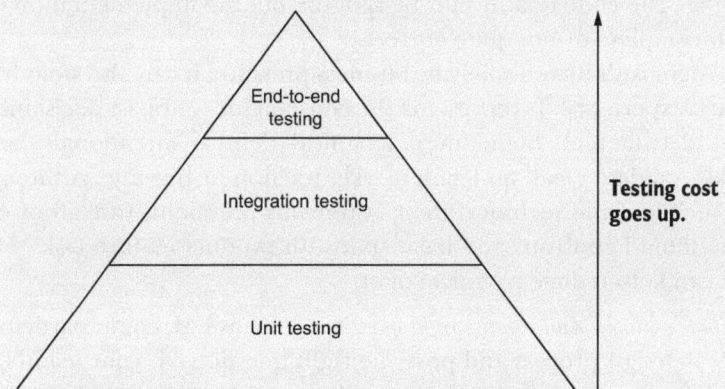

The test automation pyramid helps the engineering team produce high-quality software. It works at three levels: unit testing (base step), integration testing (middle step)m and end-to-end testing (top).

and failover mechanisms in the applications. This tool needs a controlled environment and engineers to execute it, as it takes place directly in production. But it helps prepare the development team to identify problems earlier and prepare for unexpected large-scale outages.

In start-up culture, test coverage often plays a dynamic and adaptable role compared with its use in big tech firms. Start-ups, which typically operate under lean and agile principles, prioritize rapid development and iteration to meet evolving market demands. Consequently, although test coverage remains crucial for ensuring product reliability and stability, start-ups may prioritize speed and agility over achieving 100% coverage. Instead, they often focus on testing critical functionalities and key user flows to validate hypotheses and deliver minimum viable products (MVPs) efficiently. By contrast, big tech firms, with their established processes and resources, often place greater emphasis on comprehensive test coverage across all codebases. They invest heavily in automated testing frameworks, CI pipelines, and robust QA practices to maintain high levels of code reliability and scalability. Despite these differences, both start-ups and big tech firms recognize the importance of test coverage in delivering quality software, albeit with varying approaches influenced by their respective contexts and priorities.

12.2.3 Acknowledge and reduce technical debt

Technical debt (https://mng.bz/7da9) refers to short-term decisions made in favor of expediency, often at the expense of code quality, to meet immediate needs such as time constraints, cost, and convenience. It can result from tight project deadlines or pressure to deliver with limited resources. When shortcuts are taken during design and implementation, the overall architecture suffers, necessitating future revisiting and refactoring. The code quality may be spot-on, but the implementation of the feature itself is incomplete or not quite correct.

Technical debt isn't driven solely by business pressure; it can also stem from developers who lack experience. It represents the consequences of past decisions, whether beneficial or detrimental. Sometimes, technical debt is intentionally accrued to launch quickly, validate ideas, and gain market traction or revenue. Although organizations may seek to avoid technical debt, it remains prevalent. Instead of evading it, organizations should confront and balance it with product feature tasks. Here are a few ways you can help reduce technical debt:

- *Participate actively, and ask the right questions.* You, as EM, could participate in the technical-design process and pose the right questions to your team(s) to guide them. A few questions to get you started are
  - How can we ensure that we're avoiding duplicate code?
  - How can we make the code more modular and extensible for future needs?
  - How do we ensure that the code has received thorough review by senior engineers?
  - What other design implications or blind spots do we need to consider?
  - How can we ensure that we've prioritized the appropriate tasks and implemented measures to uphold code quality?
  - How can we emphasize the importance of test coverage within our development process?
  - What steps can we take to ensure that we're creating comprehensive documentation for knowledge sharing and future reference?
  - How might our feature changes create additional latency or friction for our customers?
  - How much time do we estimate it will take to implement changes to this code and deploy it into production?
  - What potential negative effects might arise elsewhere in the system as a result of this decision?
  - How can we address frequent code changes within the same area?
  - What actions can we take to ensure that we're actively refactoring code to improve its cleanliness?
  - Could any immediate financial implications associated with this decision worsen over time?

- *Treat tech debt as another product task.* Tech-debt tasks should be treated like any other product tasks, with a specifically assigned capacity kept aside in each sprint to work on the prioritized OE backlog. This approach ensures that the entire team is aligned and working toward reducing technical debt. An easy method is a prioritized backlog of tasks from which the team members can pull a few tasks per sprint. An effective strategy I've implemented is allocating a percentage of our capacity in the road map specifically to address technical debt. By reserving x% of our resources for this purpose, we ensure that we prioritize the ongoing enhancement and maintenance of our services. Each sprint, we deliberately select one or two technical-debt tasks to tackle, enabling us to improve our systems steadily while advancing our primary objectives. This approach allows us to maintain a balance between innovation and stability, ensuring the long-term health and sustainability of our products and infrastructure.
- *Create an architecture board.* Another thing that I have seen work well is forming an architecture board at the organizational level, composed of senior engineers from multiple teams. If any team plans to work on a new feature or component, it can present the technical design to this board of senior engineers and get proactive feedback before getting into the implementation phase. This approach helps ensure that all teams are following best practices and the consistency bar.

When your team is tasked with adding a new dynamic pricing feature to the e-commerce department, you face a choice between integrating the feature into the existing monolithic legacy system or creating a new dynamic pricing microservice for future extensibility. The decision depends on factors such as resources and potential effect on delivery timelines. Opting for the microservices route allows for easier future enhancements, reducing technical debt in the legacy system. Conversely, choosing to integrate with the monolithic architecture adds technical debt.

This example highlights how technical debt and OE intersect. Making the right choices promotes OE, whereas poor decisions can lead to accumulation of technical debt. Technical debt serves as a health check for the team's performance, and it's our responsibility as engineering leaders to ensure that it's recognized, addressed, and minimized to maintain OE.

12.2.4 Manage deployments

Deployments play a critical role in transitioning code from implementation to production. Although CI and continuous deployment are often regarded as the ideal, prioritizing safer deployments is paramount. Safer deployments ensure bug-free, regression-free, and secure releases within an efficient time frame. Achieving higher code test coverage naturally contributes to safer deployments by identifying and addressing potential problems before release. As the EM for the team(s), you can try a few of the tools in the following list and see what works best for you and your team(s):

- *Deploy in phases.* Implementing a phased approach to production deployments enhances safety and stability. This involves deploying code initially to early staging environments like alpha/beta, followed by pre-production environments resembling production, and finally to production itself. Between stages, incorporating bake time, such as a 24-hour period in pre-production, ensures stability before moving to production. Additionally, Canary deployments (https://mng.bz/5lyB), in which changes are released gradually to a subset of users before full deployment based on feedback and stability, offer another avenue for safer deployments.

- *Use feature toggles where possible.* Feature flags (https://mng.bz/67Mo), also known as toggles or switches, are a valuable software development technique that allows for the control of features in production by enabling or disabling them as needed. This approach is particularly beneficial for understanding customer use trends and experimenting with different UXes. By toggling features, the engineering team can easily control aspects of the product, such as showing or hiding specific buttons. Feature flags also serve as kill switches to deactivate a feature if it's not functioning as intended. This technique empowers the development team, reduces risks, enables iterative feature launches, and facilitates analytics on customer behavior.

  Feature flags are often integrated with A/B testing (https://hbr.org/2017/06/a-refresher-on-ab-testing), directing different percentages of users to different feature states for further analysis. It's important to clean up unused feature flags regularly—a task that the EM can prioritize and include in the team's sprints.

- *Communicate effectively.* Effective communication is essential for any change being made to production, whether small or significant. Teams should proactively communicate with all members, cross-functional partners, and stakeholders about planned deployments, including dates and expectations, such as potential downtime. Some organizations designate a release manager who is responsible for coordinating overall communication and deployment for production, ensuring that everyone is informed and knows whom to contact in case of problems. After deployment, another communication can be sent to share the outcome (success or failure) and reasons, along with release notes for the changes. Additionally, creating chat rooms during deployment cycles allows faster attention to any bugs, ensuring that the product team is not caught off guard or left unaware during the rollout process.

- *Use deployment checklists.* A deployment checklist is a comprehensive document that outlines planned modifications for production, including code or infrastructure changes; responsible individuals; deployment date and time; and preparatory measures, in-progress tasks, and postdeployment actions. It encompasses testing procedures to ensure confidence in the alterations before implementation. The checklist serves as a reference for aligning team members and can undergo approvals for oversight. Integration into problem-tracker systems, such as embedding checklists within Jira, ensures accountability and prevents progression if tasks are incomplete. Given the gravity of production deployment, thoroughness is crucial for preventing oversights and ensuring a smooth process.

- *Monitor dashboards.* Dashboards play a crucial role in providing transparency and insights for all stakeholders involved in managing deployments. They allow teams to monitor changes in metrics as code progresses to production, enabling effective deployment management. Additionally, alerts should be set up to notify on-call engineers promptly of any suspected problems with newly deployed changes. Section 12.2.5 offers detailed explorations of dashboards and alerts.
- *Use quality gates/pipeline blockers.* Introducing quality gates and blockers in the pipeline can help ensure deployment of high-quality code to production. These blockers may include test coverage rules, date and time restrictions, and product launch-date constraints. Quality gates act as guardrails, preventing changes from being deployed if they're not ready or if the timing is inappropriate. You might read about the following things:
  - *Software composition analysis* (SCA)—An application security methodology that enables development teams to swiftly monitor and examine every open source component integrated into a project.
  - *Software application security testing* (SAST)—Static automated code analysis, compiled or uncompiled, conducted to detect security vulnerabilities. It parses the code to look for vulnerabilities.
  - *Dynamic application security testing* (DAST)—Actively interaction with your operational application to discover and handle any potential vulnerabilities it may possess.
- *Rollback procedure.* A predefined set of actions to revert a production deployment to its previous state in the event of unwanted customer effects. These procedures should be included in the deployment checklist and made readily accessible before deployment begins to facilitate prompt action if necessary. If a deployment affects customers, the rollback procedure is triggered to restore system stability. If a deployment leads to duplicate records in the customer table, for example, the rollback procedure might involve executing database queries to identify and delete these duplicates.
- *Automated deployments.* Mistakes are inevitable, especially in tasks that require manual execution. Automated deployments through CI and continuous deployment eliminate human errors and facilitate faster, safer deployments to production. Setting goals to enhance automated deployment capabilities can benefit engineering teams significantly. Additionally, automated change control provides valuable insights into failed deployments and potential breakdowns on teams, allowing businesses to gain visibility and make informed decisions.

- *Maintain a regular deployment cadence.* Pushing changes to production frequently offers several advantages, primarily preventing the accumulation of changes in preproduction environments and eliminating the need for a big-bang deployment. Big-bang deployments often lead to confusion when problems arise, making it challenging to isolate the cause. Collaborating with your team to establish a regular cadence for deploying changes to production promotes a smoother, more efficient deployment process.

A former boss of mine shared an intriguing perspective on software deployments. He believed that deployments should be boring. When asked what he meant, he said that a truly robust system should make deployments so smooth and seamless that they become mundane—almost automatic. Click a few buttons, and voilà—your changes are live, without any fuss or drama.

12.2.5 Use logging, monitoring, and dashboarding

Logging and monitoring systems are essential components of any software development process, providing transparency and visibility into the overall health and performance of the system. These systems play a crucial role in identifying bottlenecks and tracing problems that affect customers. Logging systems store detailed information about actions including time stamps, user activities, and system errors, aiding in troubleshooting and problem resolution. Monitoring tools detect outages and enable proactive measures to mitigate effects on customers, ensuring the reliability and availability of the system. Here are some tools that can come in handy:

- *Alerts and dashboards*—Dashboards play a crucial role in providing insights into service health and customer use trends; they also help in setting up monitoring and alerting systems. They identify problems and facilitate root-cause analysis, ensuring timely mitigation of problems. When problems resolved, dashboards ensure that values return to expected ranges and that the system is restored to a healthy state.

    WARNING It's important to be aware of false positives, however; alerts that frequently trigger without action may need reevaluation or adjustment. Tweaking alerts is an ongoing effort for development teams to ensure effective monitoring and alerting systems.

- *Run books and documentation*—Comprehensive documentation, including detailed service and feature descriptions and technical-design diagrams, provides valuable insights into system components' interactions. Run books complement this documentation by specifying ownership and detailing procedures for system maintenance and problem resolution, particularly when components are owned by different teams. Integrating alerts from monitoring systems into run books facilitates faster debugging by providing immediate access to relevant information during incidents.

- *Service-level agreements*—SLAs (https://mng.bz/MZKW) help define expectations on services expected, such as turnaround time in case of customer problems, mean time to resolution, or the number of days taken to respond to a code review. An SLA helps set a clear agreement between the parties involved and is especially useful when the team is working with third-party vendors. The agreement also involves ensuring that each party maintains an agreed-upon standard of procedures and a bar for the services provided for quality control. The article at https://mng.bz/aEz7 is an interesting read that provides more information about defining SLAs.

- *Reporting summaries*—Transparency is crucial at all levels of an organization, both on the team and in leadership. Sharing progress updates with the team fosters a sense of cohesion and motivation, and providing visibility to leadership ensures that the team's efforts are recognized and supported. Reporting summaries (figure 12.1) serve as valuable tools in these scenarios, offering snapshots of progress and individual achievements. These summaries give leadership visual representations to analyze areas for focus and investment, promoting informed decision-making and alignment with organizational goals.

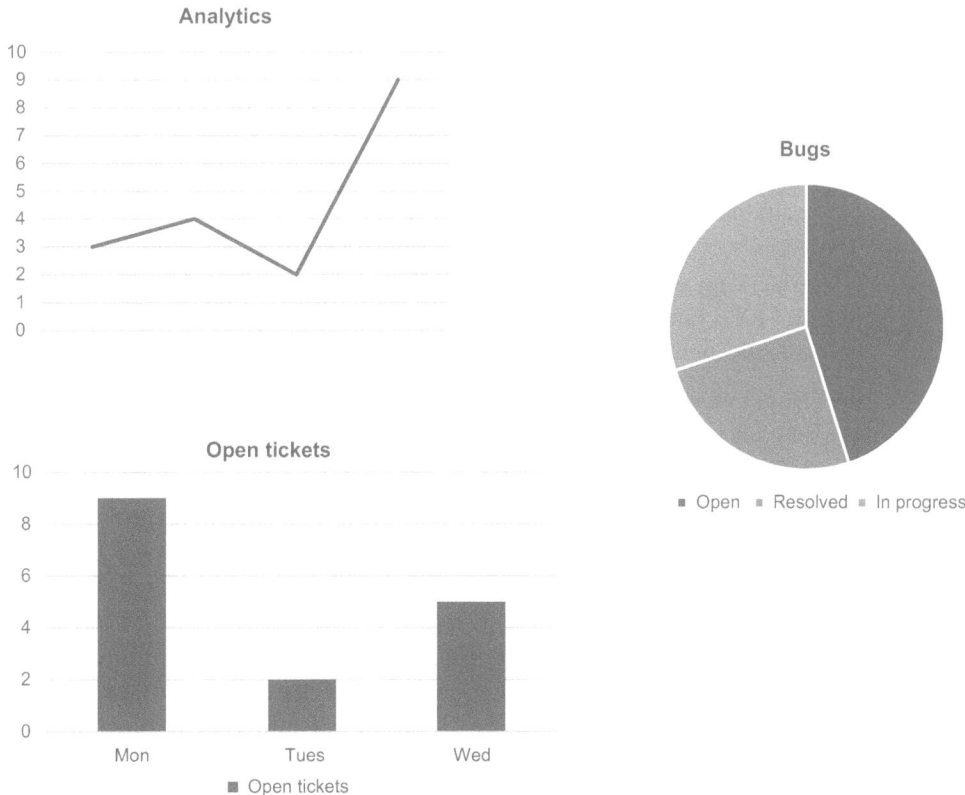

Figure 12.1   Monitoring and dashboarding help provide visibility into the health of systems.

Efficient logging, monitoring, and dashboarding allow engineering teams to make data-driven decisions to enhance security, reliability, and customer experience. Some tools that teams can explore are Opsgenie (https://www.atlassian.com/software/opsgenie), Splunk (https://www.splunk.com/en_us/home-page.html), AWS X-Ray (https://aws.amazon.com/xray), PageSpeed Insights (https://pagespeed.web.dev), New Relic (https://newrelic.com), Veritas (https://www.veritas.com), and AppDynamics (https://mng.bz/gvDV), depending on the use case.

12.2.6   *Improve on-call and production support*

EMs play a crucial role in improving on-call support and production stability for software systems. They provide leadership and direction to the team in implementing best practices for on-call support and production stability, which helps reduce failures in production, keeping employees and customers happy. This approach also ensures that team members can focus on things that are important and need immediate attention by root-causing the failures to prevent them from recurring. Some standard incident metrics to be aware of during production problems are

- *Mean time to recovery* (MTTR)—Represents the average time it takes to recover a system from failure. The lower the MTTR, the more stable the system is.
- *Mean time between failures* (MTBF)—Represents the average duration between repairable failures in an application. This metric serves to monitor the product's availability and reliability. A longer MTBF indicates a more dependable system, reflecting a higher time interval between failures.
- *Mean time to failure* (MTTF)—Represents the average duration between nonrepairable failures in a technology product.
- *Mean time to acknowledge* (MTTA)—Represents the average duration between triggering an alert and work commencing on the corresponding problem. MTTA is valuable for monitoring your team's responsiveness and evaluating the effectiveness of the monitoring system in place.

Apart from everything else you've learned so far in this chapter, you can implement a few other key practices, including the following:

- *Weekly operations and engineering meetings*—Facilitate regular meetings between operations and engineering teams to discuss ongoing problems, upcoming deployments, and areas for improvement. Use these meetings to share insights, discuss incident trends, and collaborate on preventive measures to enhance production stability.
- *On-call handoff meetings*—Conduct thorough handoff meetings between outgoing and incoming on-call engineers to ensure seamless transition and knowledge transfer. Document key information and recent incidents, and share learnings so that your team can tackle incidents better in the future. Solicit feedback from on-call engineers on the effectiveness of existing processes, tools, and support mechanisms. Iterate on feedback to refine on-call practices,

address pain points, and continuously improve the overall on-call experience for the team.

- *Troubleshooting guides*—Encourage team to document comprehensive troubleshooting guides and playbooks for common production problems and critical systems. Ensure that these guides are readily accessible and updated regularly with new learnings and best practices.
- *Escalation paths*—Establish clear escalation paths for escalating critical incidents, including defined criteria on when to escalate and whom to escalate to. Train team members on when and how to escalate effectively, emphasizing the importance of timely communication and collaboration during incidents.
- *Incident postmortems*—Schedule regular postmortem meetings following major incidents to analyze root causes, identify areas for improvement, and implement corrective actions. Encourage a blame-free culture where team members feel comfortable sharing their perspectives and contributing to the postincident review process.
- *Cross-training and skill development*—Encourage cross-training among team members to ensure broader coverage and expertise across different systems and technologies. Provide opportunities for skill development through workshops, training sessions, and certifications relevant to on-call support and production stability.
- *Continuous improvement*—Foster a culture of continuous improvement where teams regularly evaluate and iterate on their on-call processes and production support practices, which allows them to adapt to changing requirements and evolving technologies effectively.

Overall, the engineering team can have higher confidence when releasing new changes to production and focus on faster time to market with improved production support. I recommend checking out the book *Accelerate* (https://mng.bz/eojQ).

12.2.7 *Reduce operational cost*

Operational expense (OPEX) is a critical aspect of OE, encompassing infrastructure costs, employee compensation, office space, and third-party tools. Conducting a detailed audit of expenses with the expenditure team helps identify areas for cost reduction or optimization, such as renegotiating contracts or optimizing cloud spending. Advocating for cost optimization raises awareness and encourages team members to volunteer for initiatives. This focus on optimizing operational costs enables teams to prioritize automation over manual processes, eliminate resource waste, and identify areas for improvement to save money. Additionally, planning for third-party tools and infrastructure resources, such as choosing between cloud and on-premises solutions, contributes to cost-effective decision-making. Although not all questions may have immediate answers, keeping these considerations in mind supports overall operational efficiency within the engineering team.

12.2.8 *Identify ambassador(s)*

Engineering excellence and OE are crucial for team success, but as an EM, it's essential to recognize that you can't manage everything alone. Likewise, it's unrealistic to expect a single engineer to bear the burden alone. Instead, appoint an OE ambassador or champion within the team to help distribute responsibilities and ensure that progress is made consistently. The OE ambassador collaborates with the EM to prioritize the OE backlog and maintain progress sprint by sprint. Additionally, smaller OE tasks can be assigned to the on-call person, enabling faster resolution of backlog items and promoting continuous improvement. As an EM, you can do the following:

- Help identify an OE ambassador/champion for the team, and offer comprehensive coaching and mentoring to that person.
- Work with the OE ambassador to keep a prioritized OE backlog with some tasks picked up every sprint.
- Implement a culture of regular operational reviews with the team to align all members and collect feedback.
- Review team success metrics and assess progress.
- Hold retrospectives to review and improve in a continuous manner.
- Eliminate roadblocks to successful execution.

12.2.9 *Employ DevOps and DevSecOps*

The tech industry has experienced a significant cultural shift with the advent of DevOps, which aims to integrate development and operations functions. DevOps promotes collaboration and communication between development and deployment teams to prevent friction and ensure smoother application delivery. In simple terms, DevOps combines software development and operations to maintain stable systems proactively rather than address problems reactively. It emphasizes identifying root causes to prevent recurring problems and encourages continuous improvement. DevOps initiatives encompass various practices, including enhancing the on-call process, documenting run books, prioritizing security in development, adhering to coding best practices, optimizing services, conducting defect triage exercises, and improving reporting.

Although DevOps is not a one-size-fits-all solution, it underscores the importance of being transparent, setting goals, and advocating for continuous improvement within the organization. Additionally, DevOps recognizes the need to balance maintaining existing systems with building new ones, ensuring that improvements are made where necessary. Two sources I suggest reading are *The Phoenix Project* (https://mng.bz/oeld) and the Amazon Web Services (AWS) blog post about DevOps at https://aws.amazon.com/devops/what-is-devops.

DevOps practices ensure that systems degrade gracefully under unexpected or unprepared loads, providing operational ease in the present and aiming for faster recovery times in future outages. When services are equipped with OE tools that are capable of analyzing memory dumps, teams can swiftly troubleshoot problems such as full disk space and low availability by examining logs and memory-dump analysis. By integrating such practices into regular development cycles, teams enhance stability and maturity in service development and operations, resulting in quicker problem resolution. Additionally, as security threats continue to rise, developers must prioritize application security from the outset of the development process to mitigate risks. Gartner suggests that the majority of cloud security failures until 2025 will be due to customer error, emphasizing the importance of taking proactive security measures to safeguard enterprises and their customers against potential attacks (https://mng.bz/OZjE).

Did you know?

The Open worldwide Application Security Project (OWASP; https://owasp.org) is a not-for-profit organization that focuses on the security aspect of applications and software. It publishes top security threats and ideas on how to combat them to make your web applications more secure. Check out OWASP (at least the OWASP top 10) to learn more about the security aspect of applications and how you can ensure that your own applications have no loose ends.

DevSecOps (figure 12.2) extends the principles of DevOps by integrating security considerations throughout the software development life cycle. This approach, often referred to as *shift-left security*, emphasizes proactive security measures during the earliest stages of development rather than reacting to security problems later. Security testing and bug fixes are incorporated into the development cycle, enabling early detection and mitigation of security vulnerabilities. By prioritizing security from the outset, DevSecOps promotes innovation, enhances developer velocity, and facilitates rapid release cycles while ensuring that robust security practices are maintained.

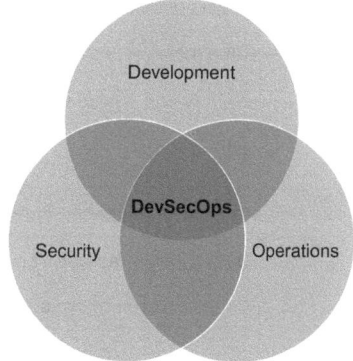

Figure 12.2 **DevSecOps combines security with DevOps to ensure development of a secure product.**

One way to address security threats in code proactively is to use security tools such as Fortify (https://mng.bz/maPr) or Veracode (https://mng.bz/Y7MA) early in the development cycle. Implementing static application security measures during the development phase enables early detection and mitigation of security threats. Some companies develop internal tooling integrated into their code deployment pipelines to address security vulnerabilities efficiently. Additionally, conducting comprehensive application security reviews before launching any production service, often performed by security engineers, helps identify and address potential loopholes, ensuring the protection of customer data. Adopting DevOps practices is a gradual process that spans several years, and initiating it early can yield long-term benefits for the organization.

12.2.10 Follow the away-team model

The away-team model (https://mng.bz/GZmO) involves an agreement between engineering teams in which one team, known as the *away team*, implements features in the codebase owned by another team, referred to as the *host team*. This approach addresses resource or time constraints that may hinder the delivery of critical projects. Although the initial preference is for the host team to handle the work due to its expertise, differing road maps and resource constraints may necessitate the use of the away-team model. This model is commonly used in companies like Amazon, where independent teams own different services and may have interdependent work dependencies. With the power of the away team comes responsibility, as the away team must respect the codebase of the host team and not make changes without proper collaboration and authorization. Table 12.1 shows a sample agreement.

Table 12.1   A sample away-team model agreement

Host team+point of contact (POC)	Team Alpha POC: Dave Chen
Away team+POC	Team Beta POC: Frank Ruth
Project/initiative	Project X
Timelines	January 15, 2023–April 6, 2023
Architecture design document	<Link to document>
Changes to expect in codebase	The away team will implement a new API in service ABC to return a list of items ordered by a particular customer.
SLA for response from host to away team	2 business days
Coding best-practices document	<Link to document>
Code deployment ownership	Away team and host team will have joint ownership for deployment, led by on-call host team.
On-call handoff	The handoff will include knowledge transfer sessions conducted in the end week of March. The away team will be part of a secondary on-call for two weeks before a full handoff to the host team.
Escalation route	Software development engineer (SDE) > Team on-call > EM > Director
Meeting-notes trail	January 22, 2023 - Architecture design document started January 15, 2023 - Kickoff meeting conducted to align on away-team model

When you're implementing the away-team model, it's essential to establish a clear agreement between the two teams involved. This agreement should be documented, detailing agreed-on work, timelines, expected changes to the codebase, access permissions for the away team, code review processes, and architecture-design review procedures. These guardrails ensure that the away team's work aligns with the code quality standards set by the host team and maintains code/service integrity. The away-team model empowers engineering teams to execute their road map without being hindered by dependencies on other teams. Knowledge transfer remains crucial, however, as the ownership and on-call responsibilities for the service still lie with the host team. Detailed documentation of code changes and troubleshooting procedures helps ensure smooth operations in case of high-severity problems. Introducing the away-team model can be beneficial for companies that face frequent dependencies on other teams, as it enables faster progress and fosters collaboration among teams to overcome roadblocks.

One of my team was tasked with implementing a crucial feature that relied on a service owned by another sister team. The owning team didn't prioritize our request. Despite the importance and complexity of our initiative, we couldn't rely on the host team's immediate support. Following the away-team model, we first attempted to align our requirements with the host team's roadmap. After failing to reach an agreement, we knew that it was time to take ownership of the process.

Embracing the away-team mindset, my team took charge and decided to take on implementation of the feature. We initiated the conversation with the host team, using a template similar to the one in table 12.1. We outlined the context of the project, stated who would be the point of contact, and maintained open communication with the host team, seeking advice and guidance where possible. Although the host team wasn't obligated to commit time to support our project, its insights were invaluable for navigating the intricacies of the service.

With determination and collaboration, my team successfully implemented the required changes. Then we handed ownership of the code to the host team and delivered knowledge-sharing sessions and troubleshooting guides along with responsibility for ongoing support and maintenance.

12.2.11 Improve accessibility

Accessibility ensures that individuals, regardless of their abilities, can access software products tailored to their needs. By identifying and eliminating barriers or friction points, accessibility empowers every user, including those with disabilities, to use the product effectively. Improving accessibility not only demonstrates commitment to inclusivity but also enhances customer trust in the product. Despite often being deferred or overlooked during software development, accessibility is crucial for reaching a broader audience and upholding engineering excellence standards. Accessibility encompasses various abilities, including vision, hearing, motor skills, and speech (figure 12.3).

As an engineering leader, advocating for accessibility is essential, whether by providing training resources for your engineers or using forums to raise awareness. When you're building a web application, for example, it's crucial to adhere to accessibility laws and regulations. From a product perspective, consider implementing features such as screen magnifiers and screen readers to assist visually-impaired users. Accessibility not only expands your audience reach but also represents a vital aspect of software

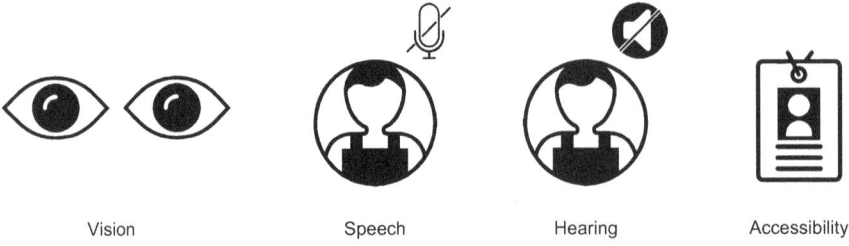

Figure 12.3 Accessibility can come in various shapes and sizes and is a critical component for customers.

development. To learn more about web-accessibility initiatives, visit the W3C Web Accessibility Initiative (WAI) website at https://www.w3.org/WAI/resources.

12.2.12 *Learn from mistakes*

When you face unexpected problems such as customers being unable to render a web page after a planned production deployment, it's crucial to take the following steps:

1 Inform stakeholders and users about the problem's existence.
2 Conduct a root-cause analysis immediately to identify the underlying problem.
3 Assess the effect on customers by determining the blast radius.
4 Work on implementing a fix, which may involve making code changes.
5 Inform customers and stakeholders when the problem is resolved, and provide a summary of the resolution.
6 Document the troubleshooting steps taken for future reference and learning purposes.

Most companies advocate learning from mistakes and creating incident documentation to understand the root cause of the problem, using the 5 Whys approach (https://www.mindtools.com/a3mi00v/5-whys). This approach feeds into the next set of action items the engineering team can take to avoid repeating this problem in the future. The idea is to avoid playing blame games, as shown in figure 12.4, and instead focus on the learning aspect of the problem at hand. So go for a fail-fast, learn-fast mindset.

Figure 12.4 Stay away from playing the blame game; focus on learning from mistakes.

Did you know?

The 5 Whys approach is a famous iterative approach to root-cause analysis that helps you get to the bottom of the problem. It is generally considered sufficient to go to five levels of "why" to get to the cause, although you can go deeper if necessary.

Suppose that a critical production problem arises, causing the system to crash unexpectedly. Let's apply the 5 Whys approach to conduct a root-cause analysis.

- *Problem*—The system crashed unexpectedly, leading to downtime and affecting UX.
  - *Why did the system crash?* The system crashed because the database server became unresponsive.
  - *Why did the database server become unresponsive?* The database server ran out of disk space on the primary storage volume.
  - *Why did the primary storage volume run out of disk space?* The disk space was consumed by large log files generated by a database backup process that failed to rotate or clean up old logs.
  - *Why did the database backup process fail to rotate or clean up old logs?* The backup process encountered an unexpected error due to misconfigured backup settings, causing it to halt without cleaning up the log files properly.
  - *Why were the backup settings misconfigured?* The backup settings were not properly validated or updated during a recent system upgrade, leading to discrepancies between the new configuration and the existing backup process requirements.
- *Root cause*—The system crashed due to a misconfiguration in the backup process settings, resulting in the accumulation of large log files that consumed all available disk space on the primary storage volume.

By applying the 5 Whys approach, we were able to trace the problem back to its root cause and identify the underlying problem that led to the system crash. This approach allowed us to implement corrective actions, such as updating and validating backup settings, to prevent similar incidents from occurring in the future.

12.3 *Engineering excellence and OE as a continuous process*

Engineering excellence and OE involve an ongoing journey of improvement and refinement within organizations. The process involves consistently delivering high-quality products and optimizing operational efficiency and reliability; fostering a culture of innovation, accountability, and continuous learning; and empowering teams to identify and implement solutions for improvement. By embracing this mindset, organizations can adapt to market demands, address customer needs, and stay competitive. Achieving excellence requires dedication, collaboration, and relentless pursuit of improvement at all levels. It's a journey without a final destination, emphasizing continuous growth and innovation. Providing resources for learning industry trends and skill development is crucial to ensure that team members are fit not only or their team but also for the organization and the industry as a whole.

Let's explore an example that illustrates the concept further. Suppose that your engineering team implements a practice in which two engineers review code before it's merged into production. As part of a team initiative, a group develops a plug-in that's integrated with a free, open source, static code analysis tool. This plug-in aims to detect code bugs and smells during the code implementation phase, enhancing the development process. All tools must undergo approval from the infosec team to ensure compliance with security standards.

After a month of using the plug-in, feedback reveals that it generates false positives, detecting nonexistent code problems. This situation adds friction to the development process, as developers must sift through these false positives before sending code for review. In response, you collaborate with the engineers to address the pain points through continuous improvement (figure 12.5).

The engineers devise a solution in which developers can flag detected false positives in the plug-in's user interface, preventing them from appearing in subsequent iterations. This simple yet effective fix significantly enhances efficiency and resolves the identified pain point. It highlights how continuous improvement in engineering excellence and OE involves refining and adapting processes, even for seemingly minor enhancements.

Figure 12.5   Engineering excellence and OE are continuous and iterative steps to create a better experience for users.

12.4   *How to navigate resistance*

In the dynamic landscape of software development, engineering teams often navigate a complex web of competing priorities, particularly when they must balance product requirements with engineering excellence and OE initiatives. Many times, the product team differs in ideology because they want all the product features, even though limited engineering capacity is available. Here are some strategies for navigating these challenges:

- *Alignment and communication*—Promote open, transparent communication among engineering, product teams, and stakeholders to align goals and priorities. Regular discussions help everyone understand the rationale behind product requirements and how those requirements align with engineering best practices and OE objectives. Establishing a shared understanding of priorities can mitigate conflicts and promote collaboration toward common goals. Emphasize how investing in quality engineering practices and operational efficiency leads to better product outcomes, improved UXes, and long-term sustainability. Building awareness, highlighting current system problems, and gaining buy-in for these principles can prioritize engineering best practices alongside product requirements.

- *Prioritization*—Develop clear prioritization methods that consider both product requirements and engineering considerations. Evaluate each requirement against criteria such as effect on customers , technical complexity, and alignment with OE goals. By establishing a systematic approach to prioritization, you can make informed decisions that balance short-term product needs with long-term engineering excellence.

- *Collaborative decision-making*—Involve cross-functional teams in decision-making processes to ensure that diverse perspectives are considered. Encourage engineers to provide input on product requirements early in the planning phase, and involve product managers in discussions of engineering best practices and technical debt. By fostering collaboration and inclusivity, you can use collective expertise to find solutions that satisfy both product and engineering priorities.

- *Iterative improvement*—Embrace an iterative approach to establishing engineering best practices and OE initiatives. Start small by identifying low-hanging fruit and gradually implement changes over time. Monitor outcomes, gather feedback, and iterate based on learnings to continuously improve processes and practices. By taking incremental steps and demonstrating tangible results, you can build momentum and support for broader initiatives.

- *Negotiation and compromise*—Recognize that compromise may be necessary at times to address conflicting priorities. Engage in constructive negotiation with stakeholders to find mutually acceptable solutions that balance competing interests. Focus on shared objectives and explore creative alternatives to resolve conflicts without compromising the overall quality or integrity of the engineering process. Sometimes, you have to follow the Disagree and Commit principle (chapter 3) while managing conflicts with team members.

In a recent role overseeing a project, I needed to navigate challenging situations within the company to raise the bar of engineering excellence while aligning with business requirements. Our team was tasked with addressing abuse on returns of the company product initiated through the web app, particularly among users who treated the platform like a "rent and return" service.

As my product partner and I strategized on how to tackle this problem, I recognized the opportunity to advocate for engineering excellence early in the discussions, during the formulation of the product road map. The current system had return limits hardcoded in a configuration file, requiring code changes and deployments for every adjustment. The same limit applied uniformly across all markets, regardless of their unique characteristics.

I saw an opportunity to enhance the system by making the return limit configurable and flexible per marketplace. To convey the value of this proposal to nontechnical stakeholders, I explained the benefits by using simple terms and analogies. I emphasized the fact that by making the limit configurable per marketplace, we could facilitate faster changes to the limits, enabling us to respond more effectively to evolving market dynamics. Furthermore, we would have the opportunity to conduct A/B testing, recognizing that not all markets are equal; customers might have different behaviors and preferences depending on their geographic location.

In the interest of transparency, I also discussed the tradeoffs involved, including the additional development effort required to implement this change. I explained that accommodating this flexibility would necessitate allocating extra time, equivalent to an additional sprint. Through effective communication and collaboration with my product partner and nontechnical stakeholders, I was able to secure buy-in for the proposed changes. Ultimately, by aligning engineering excellence with business requirements and effectively navigating the resistance within the company, we were able to implement a solution that not only addressed the immediate challenge but also laid the groundwork for future scalability and adaptability.

What do other leaders have to say?

I believe in automation as much as possible. Any work which [you do] every week/month and takes your 5% of total capacity should be automated ASAP.

—Madhur Kathuria, Engineering Leader at Microsoft, formerly with Moengage, Oracle, and IIT

I've been lucky to build trust with my leadership so that when I say "This is a business risk we need to address," I'm usually respected in that opinion. What helps me here is to think in thin interactions of improvement as I advocate for thin interactions on products. I find leaders are able to stomach an overhaul if it's done in smaller stages mixed with other business priorities. I would also say that as I've matured in my career, I tend to be more critical of what is considered debt. Some engineers have a tendency to want to work with the newest framework, the newest pattern, but hardened code in an old framework may carry less risk than new code even if that new code would be considered better practice.

—Nathan Bourgoin, Chief Technology Officer at Alakazam, Inc., Technical Adviser, and Engineering Leader

Since I primarily own data products versus a traditional high-availability system, OE isn't confined to generic metrics like latency and availability. Our metrics revolve around the quality and freshness of our data. Ultimately, we work backward from our customers to understand what will matter to them most and tie that to our operational tenets and our operational excellence.

—Nishat Akhter, Data Product and Engineering Leader, AWS

To prioritize operational excellence, encouraging teams to focus on challenges/problems of their respective teams. As leaders, spending more time aligning on the problem statement and effect, prioritizing OE enhancements based on highest return on investment (infrastructure cost, performance, productivity improvement, developer time, etc.).

—Saurabh Gandhi, Senior Director, Software Development at Audible, formerly with American Express

> *Monitoring is part of a DevOps transformation, but that means alerts and lots of them.*
> —Larry Gordan, Managing Director at Emtec, Inc.
>
> *If there is one skill or practice that all engineers should add to their repertoire, it is a thorough understanding of practices of DevOps and site reliability. These are integral parts of any modern development effort and should never be considered a "toss it over the wall" situation. The success of a good DevOps/SRE engagement is in collaboration and a shared understanding of goals. Learn about the tooling, techniques, and integrations and how they work together with your development efforts to improve reliability, efficiency, and performance.*
> —Bruce Bergman, Manager at Lytx

12.5   *Stop and think: Practice questions*

1   How will my team/organization benefit from DevOps?
2   What are the current pain points on my team(s) that focusing on DevOps might solve? Are the goals tangible?
3   Can I identify OE ambassadors/champions on my team(s) to help advocate for OE?
4   Does my team have a road map for OE items?
5   What channels in the company can I use to create awareness about the adoption of DevOps?
6   How does my organization recognize and/or track technical debt?
7   How is technical debt measured and reviewed in my team and organization?
8   Do we have an opportunity to introduce OE tools to help with OE?
9   What are my thoughts about success metrics to capture for OE efforts?

Summary

- Engineering excellence and OE are two distinct but interconnected concepts in the context of software development and management. Engineering excellence refers to the quality of the technical work performed by a software development team.
- To facilitate the journey toward excellence, EMs can employ strategies including raising the coding bar, focusing on test coverage, managing deployments, logging and monitoring, identifying champions to advocate for these practices, fostering away-team collaborations, prioritizing accessibility, and learning from mistakes as part of an iterative process.
- Engineering excellence and OE are not a destination but a continuous journey of improvement and refinement within any organization. The process encompasses commitment to consistently delivering high-quality products and services while optimizing operational efficiency and reliability.

- It's crucial to acknowledge that implementing these best practices may create resistance and require navigating internal politics and resistance within the team.
- By understanding and navigating these dynamics, EMs can establish a culture that embraces and prioritizes engineering excellence and OE, ultimately leading to greater efficiency, reliability, and innovation within their organizations.

Organizational
change management

This chapter covers

- Reasons for reorganizations
- A framework for managing organizational change
- How to handle a change in leadership
- The aftermath of changes in the workforce and how to deal with them

Change is the law of life, and those who look only to the past or present are certain to miss the future.

—John F. Kennedy

In today's fast-paced business world, change is inevitable for organizations aiming to remain competitive and relevant. Despite the natural inclination to resist change, it's crucial for individuals and organizations to embrace it. Ultimately, profitability is key for a company's survival, regardless of its stated mission. Understanding this fact is essential for effective leadership as an engineering manager (EM).

This chapter explores organizational change management, highlighting the reasons behind reorganizations and strategies for navigating change successfully. It underscores the importance of collaboration, communication, and a shared vision in achieving collective goals.

Organizational change can be incremental or transformational. Shifting from on-premises servers to cloud computing, for example, can be approached incrementally. Similarly, cost-cutting measures like layoffs can be executed incrementally over time, but they may also take place through a single transformational event.

In times of organizational change, the effect on individuals who experience layoffs or disrupted career growth can be profound. EMs play a crucial role in guiding their teams through such transitions, serving as a transparent link between upper management and staff. They maintain morale, provide support, and advocate for their team members. EMs also facilitate training and collaboration to ensure smooth integration and mitigate adverse effects. By approaching change with empathy and a focus on minimizing the human cost, EMs can foster a supportive environment and influence the success of the reorganization.

13.1 *Motivations for reorganizations*

Reorganizations are necessary in the fast-paced world of technology companies, driven by the need to outpace competitors and stay relevant. These changes, which can involve moving teams or business units or laying off staff, are essential for companies striving to innovate and meet customer demands. Although reorganizations may be daunting, they offer advantages such as increased agility, discouragement of complacency, and the opportunity to try new ideas and processes. Embracing these changes and focusing on their positive aspects is crucial. In this section, we'll delve into the various motivations behind company reorganizations, exploring both their benefits and challenges. Understanding these reasons is key to aligning with the company's mission and remaining competitive in the industry.

13.1.1 *Market conditions or external factors*

Market conditions and external factors such as evolving customer preferences, technological advancements, and emerging competitors significantly influence a company's operations. Shifts in these conditions may necessitate realigning and reorganizing the execution model to remain competitive. If Company XYZ in the audiobook industry experiences a revenue decline due to increased competition, it may introduce new features or diversify its offerings, such as adding podcasts or entering the video-streaming market. These strategic moves often require organizational realignment to refocus efforts and adapt to changing market dynamics. Moreover, the threat of disruption caused by new products or technologies intensifies the need for swift realignment. Ultimately, companies must continually adjust to market conditions to remain aligned with their vision—an adjustment that often results in reorganizations.

13.1.2 Need to streamline operations

Reorganizations aim to optimize company operations by identifying and eliminating redundancies, consolidating functions, and improving communication channels. If multiple teams are independently creating similar infrastructure stacks, a reorganization may broaden the scope of the original team to support a wider range of use cases efficiently, ensuring sharing of resources and enhanced maintainability.

As an EM, you play a crucial role in identifying redundancies and aiding in the streamlining of operations. Reorganizations can also bring clarity to the organizational structure, clarifying roles and responsibilities and improving communication channels. Additionally, they may facilitate faster decision-making and boost overall performance.

Another benefit is improved proximity of teams, which enhances communication and enables faster execution of new features related to specific products or services. Although reorganizations optimize operations and enhance competitiveness, they also require sensitivity toward those who are affected by changes, as valuable talent may be lost, leading to knowledge gaps.

Layoffs within a company, often conducted to streamline operations and eliminate redundancies, can profoundly affect the individuals affected. Facing unexpected job loss, they may experience uncertainty, stress, and emotional turmoil. Beyond financial instability, they may struggle with feelings of rejection and uncertainty about their future. The sudden disruption to their routine and sense of identity tied to their work can leave them feeling vulnerable. Practical concerns such as health-care coverage and financial obligations further exacerbate the burden. Recognizing the human aspect of layoffs is crucial, as is providing support, understanding, and resources to aid those who are navigating this challenging transition. (Section 13.3 provides guidance on handling such scenarios.)

13.1.3 New opportunities

Reorganization can enable companies to seize new business opportunities in various ways. First, it allows companies to allocate resources more effectively, consolidating investments in existing products to free resources for new initiatives. This redistribution of funds enables companies to support multiple initiatives simultaneously.

Second, reorganizations facilitate the creation of organizational structures explicitly tailored to support new initiatives. Companies might establish dedicated business units focused on developing and integrating technologies for these new investment areas, ensuring that they have the necessary support and expertise to succeed. Conversely, companies may reorganize by eliminating business units in response to market conditions or technological changes. Witness the recent ChatGPT (https://openai .com/blog/chatgpt) explosion, which is already killing some small companies. Marketing communications companies, for example, are losing contracts because now users can ask ChatGPT to write press releases for them.

TIP   *Crossing the Chasm* (https://mng.bz/z8DQ) is a marketing book by Geoffrey A. Moore that delves into the challenges involved in putting innovative products on the market, paying particular attention to the critical chasm (adoption gap) between early adopters and the mainstream market. The book offers guidance on selecting a target market, understanding what makes a comprehensive product, positioning the product appropriately, developing a marketing strategy, determining the optimal distribution channel, and establishing suitable pricing strategies.

Third, reorganizations help companies become leaner, more efficient, and agile—essential qualities needed for setting up and scaling new business units. By creating flexible organizational structures, companies can respond to market shifts swiftly, make quicker decisions, and adapt to changing circumstances.

Overall, reorganizations enable companies to align their technical departments with their strategic visions and goals, facilitating the pursuit of new business opportunities. This alignment ensures that companies can adjust their vision based on emerging opportunities and present a cohesive picture to consumers.

13.1.4 Change in leadership

A change in leadership often prompts a company to undergo reorganization, which can involve transitioning to a flatter organizational structure or redistributing teams if a director departs without a replacement. Other reasons for leadership changes include pivoting to new technologies or services, integrating newly acquired companies, or implementing enterprise systems. Such changes have far-reaching effects and require careful handling, considering factors such as the new leadership's management style.

Section 13.3 provides further insights on managing changes in leadership. For now, let's delve into a framework for managing organizational change.

13.2 Framework for managing organizational change

Managing organizational change is a multifaceted endeavor requiring careful planning, strategic execution, and effective leadership. In this section, I introduce a framework for managing organizational change based on my own experiences in the hope that it will serve as a guiding tool to help other EMs navigate the complexities of change. This framework outlines key stages, strategies, and considerations necessary to minimize resistance, maximize employee engagement, and achieve successful outcomes. By applying this structured approach, leaders can foster agility, resilience, and continuous improvement, positioning their organizations for long-term success.

13.2.1 Understanding the need for change

Understanding the need for change is the initial step in handling any organizational transformation. This step involves comprehending the rationale behind the change, the required investments from both employees and the company, and the anticipated outcomes or benefits. It's crucial to explore all alternatives and time-box the change management process to anticipate potential friction or pushback. Additionally, it is helpful to assess whether the changes that results from the strategy will be reversible or irreversible.

Lewin's change management model

Lewin's change management model (https://mng.bz/0GJ6) is widely used because it clearly outlines the steps and the role of management. The three phases of this model are as follows:

- *Unfreeze*—People generally have a natural inclination to resist change, so the initial phase of the change management process focuses on initiating change by motivating employees to embrace it.
- *Transition*—The organization goes through a transitional period when the change process is initiated. During this time, it is crucial for the company's leadership to provide strong guidance and continual reassurance.
- *Refreeze*—After the change has been implemented and accepted by the organization's workforce, everyone begins to view the new guidelines as the norm, and the organization regains stability. This phase involves solidifying the new state and ensuring that its integration becomes established practice.

A software company might need to upgrade its legacy systems to enhance performance and security in response to customer demands and competitive pressures. Recognizing the importance of champions in driving organizational change is vital for success. What do I mean by *champions*? Read on to find out.

13.2.2 *Recruiting champions for change*

Recruiting a team of passionate individuals, known as *champions* or *ambassadors*, is essential for implementing organizational change successfully. These champions act as advocates for the change, spreading awareness of it and driving its adoption within the company. As an EM, your key responsibilities in planning organizational change include identifying and onboarding these champions from existing employees. Look for self-driven, high-performing individuals who align with the mission of the change and possess effective communication skills. Involving champions early in the process, such as during the brainstorming phase, ensures their commitment and motivation to carry out the change. Chapter 4 discussed how to identify high performers; perhaps making them champions is a good opportunity to keep them challenged.

Providing the necessary training resources further supports champions' success in leading the change during the execution phase. This approach not only keeps champions challenged but also fosters a sense of ownership and motivation to achieve the change's vision.

The ADKAR change management model

The ADKAR change management model (https://mng.bz/KZzO) is a famous model that involves educating employees about the significance of the changes being introduced and their effects on their daily routines, as well as providing continuous support and reinforcement. This support enables them to comprehend and wholeheartedly accept the value of the change. The ADKAR model encompasses the following five stages:

- *Awareness*—Make team members aware of the change.
- *Desire*—Encourage their desire to change and to join the mission.
- *Knowledge*—Pass on knowledge and share how the change will take effect.
- *Ability*—Demonstrate the skills and abilities required for the change and provide desired resources for support.
- *Reinforcement*—Recognize those who embrace the change to reinforce the change and sustain its effect.

Suppose that a company called ABC wants to move from third-party project management software to an in-house tool for use across the organization. The company decides to use the ADKAR model to guide the change process, as follows:

- *Awareness*—ABC starts by creating awareness about the need for the capabilities that are missing in the current project management software. Leaders send a company-wide email explaining the current system's limitations and the new software's benefits. They also organize a town-hall meeting where the head of engineering addresses the importance of improving project management efficiency and encourages employees to embrace the change.
- *Desire*—To create desire for the new software, ABC showcases success stories from other companies that implemented similar tools in-house and the financial savings that came with the change. The company highlights how the new software will streamline processes, improve collaboration, and simplify employee jobs; it also emphasize the fact that training sessions and resources will support learning and using the new software.
- *Knowledge*—ABC provides comprehensive training programs to ensure that employees have the necessary knowledge to use the new software. The company offers online tutorials, in-person workshops, and access to a dedicated support team. It also creates a knowledge base with frequently asked questions (FAQs) and step-by-step guides to addressing common challenges.
- *Ability*—ABC understands that simply knowing is not enough; employees also need the ability to use the software effectively. Leadership assigns project mentors to each team to guide and assist during the initial implementation phase.
- *Reinforcement*—To reinforce the change and make it stick, ABC recognizes individuals or teams that use the new software effectively. The company creates a feedback loop where employees can share their experiences, suggestions, and challenges related to the software. ABC considers this feedback and makes continuous improvements to the software and support processes.

By following the ADKAR model, ABC successfully implemented the in-house solution, ensuring that employees were aware of the change, desired its benefits, had the knowledge and ability to use it effectively, and were reinforced for their efforts. The ADKAR model is a valuable tool that helps set the foundation for enterprise change management.

13.2.3 Crafting a strategy and road map for change management

Crafting a strategy and road map for change management is crucial for translating organizational change into actionable steps. Here's a breakdown of key components to consider:

- *Define the tenets.* Establish the fundamental principles and best practices that form the basis of the change. If updating privacy policies is part of the change, a tenet could be stakeholder involvement, ensuring transparency and early engagement.
- *Align on metrics and success criteria.* Set measurable goals and objectives for the change initiative, considering resources and time constraints. Define what success looks like and how it will be measured. Success criteria for a software upgrade could include a 35% performance improvement and security-standards compliance that reduces security incidents by 50%.
- *Create an execution strategy.* Determine the implementation approach, whether it's a comprehensive big-bang approach or an iterative process. Prioritize changes based on effect and complexity; identify dependencies, risks, and mitigation plans. You might roll out software upgrades in phases, starting with less critical systems.
- *Define stakeholders.* Clearly identify and align all parties involved with and affected by the change.
- *Develop a communication plan.* Develop an effective communication model to promote adoption and minimize rumors, including the following points:
  - Stating how communication will be shared with stakeholders, such as through emails or team meetings
  - Clearly communicating the change, reasons, timelines, and expected benefits
  - Establishing forums or channels for employee questions and feedback
  - Communicating available training resources, such as self-paced learning, hands-on training, and documentation

The SWOT analysis

The SWOT analysis (https://www.investopedia.com/terms/s/swot.asp) is a technique for evaluating a business and developing a strategic plan. The analysis involves four dimensions:

- *Strengths*—Areas where an organization demonstrates exceptional performance and distinguishes itself from competitors. These areas may include a strong brand, a devoted customer base, a solid financial position, and innovative technology.
- *Weaknesses*—Areas that hinder the growth of the organization and need improvement.

(continued)

- *Opportunities*—Advantageous external circumstances that have the potential to provide a competitive edge to an organization.
- *Threats*—Factors that have the potential to harm an organization. If a company that manufactures phones procures the chips from a foreign country and trade between the companies stops, the company is at risk of not being able to meet demand based on supply.

A SWOT analysis aims to enable an objective, evidence-based evaluation of an organization, its initiatives, and its industry, highlighting its strengths and weaknesses. To ensure accuracy, the analysis should avoid preconceived notions or ambiguous aspects and instead concentrate on practical, tangible situations.

When you're crafting the strategy and road map for organizational change, it's vital to understand existing pain points and organizational strengths and weaknesses. This comprehensive understanding ensures that the strategy encompasses both immediate improvements and long-term alignment with the overall vision. Getting buy-in from the leadership team is crucial, so present the strategy effectively.

13.2.4   *Executing the plan*

The next step is focusing on executing the change effectively. Execution is the pivotal stage of organizational change, when plans are put into action. Begin by implementing the strategy in phases, and remain open to early feedback, which will shape the execution plan and demonstrate receptiveness to input. Expect initial friction and pushback; address this response by holding data-driven discussions and keeping lines of communication with stakeholders open. Strategies for handling pushback include

- Maintaining objectivity
- Fostering open feedback channels
- Asking clarifying questions
- Providing training resources and support to team members

In cases of deadlock, negotiation is key to finding common ground, though enforcement may be necessary for the benefit of both individuals and the organization. Demonstrating feasibility through proof of concept and early product demos can help validate ideas and garner support. Next, let's explore monitoring and measuring outcomes to assess the effectiveness of the change efforts.

13.2.5   *Monitoring and measuring success*

Monitoring and measuring success is a critical stage in change management. Results are assessed against predetermined success criteria established during strategy development. Actively seeking feedback through surveys and retrospectives helps identify successes and areas for improvement. Recognizing and appreciating the efforts of ambassadors and champions is important. Cultural and mindset changes are crucial, requiring patience, as adoption and results take time to manifest.

WARNING   It's important to remember that organizational changes can fail, leading to loss of trust in leadership as well as wasted resources and missed opportunities for innovation or growth. Failed changes affect morale, performance, and the organization's viability. For all these reasons, it is essential to practice careful planning, execution, and evaluation to minimize the risk of failure and maximize the likelihood of success.

13.2.6   *Iterating on opportunities*

After monitoring and measuring success, the next phase is iterating on opportunities, which involves identifying gaps, consolidating feedback, organizing retrospectives, and iterating on future opportunities. If changes are needed, return to crafting the strategy and road map for change management (section 13.2.3), incorporating adjustments as necessary. Evaluate strengths, weaknesses, and trends from feedback, and adjust or pivot accordingly.

Iteration is an ongoing process, emphasizing continuous improvement and agility. By iterating on opportunities, you can optimize potential, address challenges, and discover new growth avenues.

13.2.7   *Change management case studies*

Let's delve into some case studies to glean insights. For each one, I'll provide key takeaways and references for further reading.

NETFLIX'S ADOPTION OF DEVOPS

Netflix, one of the leading streaming services, adopted DevOps practices and revolutionized its software delivery capabilities and infrastructure management. My key takeaways from the company's organizational change (https://mng.bz/9dE1) to move to the cloud and adopt DevOps include

- *Automation*—Netflix invested heavily in automation tools and processes such as centralized release coordination to streamline software deployment and infrastructure provisioning. This emphasis on automation enabled the company to innovate at a faster pace.
- *Resilience*—Netflix prioritized building resilient systems that are capable of handling failures gracefully, reducing downtime and enhancing user experience. The company embraced the concept of "failure as a constant" and implemented tools such as Chaos Monkey (https://mng.bz/Bdy8) to randomly disrupt instances in production, testing system resilience and fault tolerance.
- *Iterative approach*—Netflix adopted an iterative approach, initially transitioning to the cloud before implementing tools such as Chaos Monkey and the Netflix Simian Army (https://mng.bz/d69O), a suite of tools for enhancing system reliability. This iterative approach highlights the importance of continuous improvement and incremental changes.

These strategies underscore the importance of automation, resilience, and iterative development in facilitating organizational change and driving innovation within companies.

AMAZON'S DIVERSIFICATION

Amazon's journey from a book-selling website to a technology disruptor has been interesting. The company came up with products such as the Amazon Web Services (AWS) cloud, digital streaming, Prime Video, and a grocery business. Some key highlights that drove Amazon's diversification are

- *Customer obsession*—Amazon prioritizes a customer-first mindset that drives product development and service offerings. This focus on understanding and meeting customer needs has been a foundational principle guiding the company's diversification efforts.
- *Innovation*—Amazon's willingness to experiment and take risks fueled its diversification into various initiatives. Although some ventures, such as the Fire phone, faced challenges, the culture of innovation persists.
- *Scalability*—As Amazon's customer base expanded, scalability became a critical focus. Investments in infrastructure and technology, particularly through AWS, enabled Amazon to meet growing demand and scale operations effectively.
- *Automation*—Automation plays a significant role in Amazon's operations, streamlining processes across AWS cloud services and warehouse operations. This emphasis on automation enhances efficiency and enables Amazon to deliver services such as Prime with fast, reliable deliveries.

These principles underscore Amazon's approach to change management, emphasizing customer-centricity, innovation, scalability, and automation as drivers of successful diversification and growth. Read more about Amazon's change management at https://mng.bz/jXDP.

MICROSOFT'S FOCUS ON CLOUD

Microsoft's journey to focusing on cloud technologies, particularly Azure, showcases several key lessons in change management:

- *Adaptability*—Microsoft's ability to adapt to changing market dynamics and customer needs has been crucial to its success. By recognizing the growing importance of cloud computing, Microsoft shifted its focus and invested heavily in Azure, aligning its offerings with emerging trends and technologies.
- *Leadership changes*—The appointment of Satya Nadella as CEO marked a significant turning point for Microsoft. Under Nadella's leadership, the company embraced a cloud-first strategy and accelerated its investment in cloud technologies. Nadella's vision and leadership played a pivotal role in driving Microsoft's transformation and success in the cloud market.
- *Customer obsession*—Like Amazon, Microsoft prioritizes a customer-centric approach to innovation. By listening to customers' feedback and understanding their evolving needs, Microsoft has been able to develop and enhance its cloud offerings, ensuring that they meet the requirements of businesses and organizations worldwide.

These key takeaways underscore the importance of adaptability, visionary leadership, and customer-centricity in driving successful organizational change and transformation, as demonstrated by Microsoft's strategic shift toward cloud technologies. Read more about Microsoft's change management at https://mng.bz/WEX1.

13.3 Changes in the workforce

Navigating changes in the workforce, such as reductions and mergers or acquisitions, requires careful planning, communication, and empathy to mitigate negative effects and use opportunities for growth and resilience. Let's look at the ramifications and how to handle them.

13.3.1 Change in leadership

When leadership changes, whether that's due to a new boss's taking over or becoming the new boss of a team, it's natural for employees to feel apprehensive. However, it's important to approach this change thoughtfully and embrace it effectively. By applying the change management framework discussed earlier, you can work towards achieving a seamless transition.

WHEN YOUR LEADERSHIP CHANGES

When you're facing a change in leadership that affects you directly, the following steps can help you and your team adapt:

- *Recognize and understand the change.*
    - Acknowledge how the change will affect your daily activities, including timelines, expectations, plans, and milestones.
    - Understand the reasoning behind the change, and share pertinent information with your team.
- *Learn about your new leadership.*
    - Initiate meetings with the new leader to understand their motivations, expectations, and management style.
    - Assist the new leader in transitioning by familiarizing them with the team's structure and core principles.
- *Share with your team.*
    - Communicate the changes transparently and assure your team of your support.
    - Set up a team meeting and be direct about the reasons for the change.
    - Encourage participation, address concerns, and convey your viewpoint while being a patient listener.
- *Take ownership and accountability.*
    - Don't simply repeat what you were told; actively participate in the change process and earn the trust of your team members.
    - Emphasize communication, and create channels for candid communication.
    - Lead by example, demonstrating your alignment with the new expectations.

- *Maintain a growth mindset.*
  - View the change as an opportunity to explore new perspectives and acquire new skills.
  - Reinforce the team's mission, vision, and goals to maintain focus and motivation.
  - Collect feedback to understand what is working well and make necessary adjustments.

Following these steps will help you communicate leadership changes to your team effectively and navigate the transition period with clarity and confidence.

WHEN YOU ARE THE NEW LEADER FOR A TEAM

As the new manager joining an existing team, follow these steps for a smooth transition:

- *Assess the current situation.*
  - Understand team dynamics, strengths, weaknesses, and existing practices before considering making changes.
- *Build relationships.*
  - Schedule one-on-one meetings to understand team members' aspirations, concerns, and expectations.
  - Establish trust and rapport to foster positive working relationships.
- *Communicate transparently.*
  - Clearly communicate your vision, goals, and expectations.
  - Encourage open communication, and address any questions or concerns promptly.
- *Collaborate on a transition plan.*
  - Work with outgoing and incoming leaders to create a detailed transition plan.
  - Define key responsibilities, timelines, and monitoring mechanisms.
- *Facilitate knowledge transfer.*
  - Organize conversations to ensure a smooth handover of critical information.
  - Emphasize documentation to secure knowledge for the future.
- *Manage the people aspect.*
  - Address any commitments made by the previous leader.
  - Encourage team members' career progression, and provide empathetic support during the transition.
- *Establish clear communication.*
  - Conduct one-on-one conversations to ensure clarity.
  - Provide opportunities to answer anonymous questions to understand team members' perspectives.

- *Allow adaptation time.*
  - Give team members space to adapt to the change without setting unrealistic expectations.
  - Offer training sessions, create user-friendly documentation templates, and encourage open communication channels for feedback and clarification.
- *Tailor your approach.*
  - Customize your leadership approach based on the organization's needs and team dynamics.
  - Continuously monitor progress and adapt as necessary.

When I took over a team from a departing manager, I ensured a smooth transition by arranging a candid conversation with each team member, including the previous manager. This approach allowed for clarity and continuity. Also, I held one-on-one discussions with team members to align their expectations for the period following the previous manager's departure. To foster transparency, I facilitated anonymous questions from the team for the incoming leader. Aligning the team with goals, mission, and guidelines minimized ambiguity. It's crucial to adapt your approach to each unique leadership change and to consider the specific circumstances and needs of your team.

13.3.2 Reduction in workforce

Workforce reduction, also known as a *reduction in force*, involves eliminating positions within an organization without intending to hire replacements. This reduction can happen due to various factors, including unfavorable market conditions. The COVID-19 pandemic led to a surge in remote work and online activities, causing tech companies to overhire employees to meet demand. When some aspects of life returned to their prepandemic norms, the demand for tech services decreased, leading to mass layoffs (https://mng.bz/8wEw) in 2022 and 2023 to adjust to the changing landscape.

The rise of artificial intelligence (AI) has significantly affected the tech industry by introducing various working bots and tools aimed at automating tasks and boosting efficiency. This transformative technology is reshaping software development, increasing demand for experts in fields such as machine learning and data science. AI enables companies to accelerate development, cut costs, and enhance precision and accuracy, thereby affecting the jobs of some individuals.

> **TIP** X (formerly Twitter) laid off more than 50% of its workforce after Elon Musk bought the company in 2022. Also see Layoffs.fyi (https://layoffs.fyi), a website created during the COVID-19 pandemic that tracks recent layoff trends in the industry.

Internally, companies may merge teams, resulting in the redundancy of specific roles such as engineers and leaders, leading to their elimination. As an EM, you may encounter critical situations such as team, division, or company-wide layoffs. Layoffs can be emotional for you as well as for your team members.

HANDLING AFFECTED EMPLOYEES

Layoff information is typically communicated by the human resources department, but in some companies, EMs are entrusted with delivering this difficult news. I have witnessed both situations. In one scenario, more typical in big tech firms, even the EMs do not know who will be affected. In another scenario, EMs get early info about who will be let go. Regardless of how much information you have about layoffs beforehand, you play an important role as an EM. Performing that role can include the following tasks:

- *Coordinate with human resources.* Confirm with human resources the method of communication (email or one-on-one) and the company's stance on the message to be delivered.
- *Prepare for one-on-one conversations.* If you're delivering the news in person, reserve a private space such as a meeting room to allow the employee to process their emotions.
- *Approach with empathy.* Approach affected employees with empathy and respect, giving them time to absorb the news.
- *Provide background information.* Share relevant background details about the decision-making process while being mindful of legal constraints.
- *Familiarize yourself with support resources.* Understand the severance policy and other support resources, guiding affected employees to the appropriate human resources representative for further assistance.
- *Clarify timelines.* Clarify timelines or notice periods to affected employees, whether the layoff is immediate or they have time to explore alternative options within the company.
- *Offer support.* Acknowledge the difficulty of the situation, and assure employees of your availability to offer support.
- *Assist with career transition.* Offer assistance if desired by using your professional network for job-search help or providing career counseling through platforms such as LinkedIn.

> **TIP** Here are some suggested reading resources: blog posts on YourThought-Partner (https://mng.bz/NR91) and Pyn (https://mng.bz/Ddaw).

HANDLING YOUR TEAM

To support your team during challenging circumstances such as layoffs, consider employing the following strategies:

- *Conduct prompt outreach.* Immediately reach out to team members after layoff announcements to express your solidarity and offer support.
- *Keep communication lines open.* Maintain an open line of communication, encouraging team members to approach you for assistance and volunteering to serve as a sounding board.
- *Communicate clearly.* Provide clear and consistent communication throughout the process, ensuring transparency and understanding.

- *Exercise caution.* If you are involved in layoff planning, handle confidential information with caution, treating all individuals honestly and fairly while preserving confidentiality.
- *Reassure unaffected employees.* Organize team meetings to reassure unaffected employees of their status and provide a supportive environment for discussion. Maintain frequent communication to inspire them with the future vision.
- *Redistribute workload.* If the team has been affected, develop a plan to redistribute the workload to ensure that project deadlines are met. Negotiate scope or delivery timelines with stakeholders as needed.
- *Offer patience and support.* Recognize that productivity might decline initially. Be patient, giving team members time and space to cope with the situation, reset, and recover.
- *Communicate risks.* Proactively communicate any risks resulting from the reduced workforce to stakeholders, mitigating potential surprises in the future.

During a workforce reduction, maintaining professionalism and maturity is crucial for all involved. It's important to recognize that the effects of a reduction in the workforce can be felt for months afterward, and it's normal for emotions to linger. It's essential that you understand these facts and manage your team to the best of your capability with empathy and resilience.

13.3.3   Acquisitions or mergers

Company mergers or acquisitions often lead to significant changes in the workforce that affect employees. Whether leadership is changing or roles are being eliminated, it's crucial to handle the situation with sensitivity and to communicate effectively. Here are some strategies to help EMs manage acquisitions or mergers:

- *Knowledge of the context*—Understand the reasons behind the change, its effect, and how it will be executed. Maintain open communication with employees to ensure that they feel heard and understood.
- *Cultural integration*—Mergers often involve integrating different organizational cultures. Foster open communication, shared values, and mutual respect to facilitate successful integration.
- *Leadership alignment*—Ensure alignment among leadership teams from both organizations to facilitate effective decision-making and strategic alignment after the merger. Clarify roles, responsibilities, and expectations to minimize conflicts.
- *Employee engagement*—Engage employees from both organizations in the integration process to foster a sense of ownership and commitment to the shared vision. Provide opportunities for cross-team collaboration, training, and development.
- *Retention of talent*—Retain key talent during mergers or acquisitions to maintain organizational continuity and drive future growth. Offer incentives, career development opportunities, and clear pathways for advancement to retain valuable employees.

In conclusion, change management can cover the dynamic landscape of organizational transformations. The framework provided serves as a guiding light for leaders, enabling them to navigate change with strategic clarity and sensitivity to their workforce's needs.

We've explored the crucial aspect of leadership change, emphasizing empathy, transparency, and open communication to facilitate smooth transitions and foster employee resilience. Organizational change management requires a delicate balance of strategic foresight, compassionate leadership, and an understanding of the human element. As an EM, you must navigate these changes with confidence, driving meaningful transformation within your organization.

What do other leaders have to say?

Effectively handling organizational change can pose challenges, particularly when a new leader enters the company and implements immediate changes. As an engineering leader, it is crucial to invest time in understanding past practices and identifying the gaps that necessitate addressing during the reorganization process.

— Sanjay Gupta, General Manager at HCL Technologies

Mostly, developers fail to understand the motivation behind these reorgs and find them meaningless. Sharing a business aspect of how/why it aligns with a long-term plan helps them understand and grow as a contributor.

— Madhur Kathuria, Engineering Leader at Microsoft,
formerly with Moengage, Oracle, and IIT

As part of the team restructure, we had to move people around to different squads. The change was important for future projects. We started working with the leaders of each group to define the objectives for each team. The next step was delivering the message, working with the teams to gather feedback and documenting any process changes. Team members hesitated to change the existing process and let go of their squads. It was important for the leaders first to accept the change and be the proponents of the new model.

— Rajakumar Sambasivam, Delivery Manager at Microsoft

Often, pushbacks happen when there is a lot of ambiguity in the process and the effect is unknown. If we do not know who and how a change will affect us, we tend to reject the idea of the change itself. When there is pushback, I empower my team to dive in and figure out the answers to who and how and, most important, educate themselves on why the change is important.

— Nishat Akhter, Data Product and Engineering Leader, AWS

Reorgs are unavoidable in a growing organization. A team structure that made sense in the past may become less productive or dysfunctional due to interdependencies. Accepting and addressing this openly helps people understand the challenges and the need for reorg. As a leader, I feel it is most important to show my commitment to continuous growth and emphasize that individuals not lose their progress with the previous manager or team even after reorg.

— Saurabh Gandhi, Senior Director, Software Development at Audible,
formerly with American Express

Embrace change! Not only does it keep you on your toes and constantly learning, but it shows that you are adaptable and flexible, open to new ideas and new ways of achieving value for your team, your department, and your company. You have probably worked with someone who was the opposite—not open to change—and experienced how difficult that made just about any task. Don't be that person!

—Bruce Bergman, Manager at Lytx

13.4 Stop and think: Practice questions

1 What questions would you ask your manager if they told you about an upcoming organizational change?

2 What are some ways you have navigated an organizational change? If you were to go back in time, what would you change about your experience?

3 Have you gone through a leadership change in the past? If so, was the experience a positive one? Why or why not?

4 What do you think is an effective way to handle a change in the workforce professionally?

Summary

- In today's fast-paced business environment, change is constant and inevitable. Tech companies must reorganize to stay competitive, adapt to market conditions, streamline operations, and seize new opportunities. Changes in leadership also affect organizations, requiring careful management.

- To manage organizational change effectively, using a framework is essential. This process includes understanding the need for change, hiring champions for implementation, crafting a strategy, executing the strategy iteratively, monitoring success, and iterating on opportunities.

- Leadership transitions can be challenging, but approaching them with mindfulness is key. Fundamental principles include understanding the reasons for the change, communicating effectively, taking ownership, identifying risks, providing training, leading by example, and maintaining a growth mindset.

- Workforce changes such as leadership shifts, reductions, and mergers bring both challenges and opportunities. Navigating these situations successfully requires professional handling and strategic management.

- Change management is a multifaceted realm that EMs must navigate confidently to drive effective transformation.

Time management

14

This chapter covers

- Why time management is essential for engineering managers
- Tips for better time management
- Tools for managing your time better

Lack of direction, not lack of time, is the problem. We all have 24-hour days.

—Motivational speaker Zig Ziglar

Navigating back-to-back meetings and minimal breaks, especially in a remote work setting, makes finding time to cook a meal seem impossible. A glance at the calendar often reveals a packed day and a week devoid of personal work time. Despite your persevering until the day's end, overlooked planning documents with urgent deadlines can cause stress. Hastily jotting down a list of numerous tasks for the next day adds to the pressure, leading to burnout and disruptions in regular office work.

Engineering managers (EMs) commonly face these kinds of predicaments when their time management falters. Juggling diverse responsibilities, from enhancing hiring standards to balancing on-call loads, EMs find themselves dealing with constant "context switches," to use Paul Graham's term (https://paulgraham .com/makersschedule.html). Graham also points out the distinction between a manager's schedule, involving simultaneous tasks and context switches, and a maker's or engineer's schedule, emphasizing deep work and focus blocks. His insights add to the recognition that EMs need to prioritize tasks and manage their time well to ensure constant progress.

14.1 Importance of time management for EMs

It's also important for EMs to lead by example, as their productivity lapses can have a cascading effect on the entire team. Sending a late-night email conveys a message that late-night work is acceptable or maybe even necessary, potentially influencing team culture negatively. The benefits of time management reach far and wide, as we'll see.

14.1.1 Ensuring successful project delivery

One of your main responsibilities as an EM is successful delivery of your team's projects. Juggling multiple projects simultaneously can be challenging, but effective time management allows you to prioritize tasks, ensuring adequate allocation for each project. This approach minimizes procrastination, reduces stress, and mitigates the risk of burnout. See chapter 10 to learn more about project life cycles and key considerations for successful project management.

14.1.2 Facilitating team members' career goals

EMs play a crucial role in helping software engineers achieve personal goals that are aligned with organizational objectives. Beyond coding, your responsibilities involve guiding teams, collaborating on road maps, and monitoring goals, all of which can consume a significant portion of your time. Efficient time management is essential for prioritizing these diverse tasks, preventing imbalances that can lead to decreased productivity. Without proper management, periods dominated by supporting others or addressing personal tasks may arise, causing stress and a growing backlog. This cycle, if not managed, can hinder productivity and compromise both team support and personal goal achievement. See chapter 3 for more information about managing career conversations.

14.1.3 Navigating time pressures

For EMs, time is always of the essence, with tight deadlines being the norm. Various factors contribute to this perpetual time crunch:

- *Meetings*—Expectations often mandate your presence in numerous meetings, stretching your time thin.
- *Interruptions*—Frequent disruptions significantly reduce productivity, requiring more time to complete tasks. Ad-hoc interruptions, bearing the urgent message "We need you now," are common for EMs, setting back timelines.
- *Quality expectations*—Team leaders face an inherent expectation of high-quality deliverables. These deliverables serve as the team's quality benchmark, demanding the necessary time investment to meet the standard.

- *Procrastination*—When you're overwhelmed by multiple responsibilities, it's tempting to delay tasks. But this short-term strategy leads to heightened stress as deadlines approach, with substantial consequences for productivity.

14.1.4 Making decisions effectively

EMs bear responsibility for making critical team decisions and strategic plans, requiring significant time for problem analysis and data correlation. The resulting pressure can lead to challenges such as sleep deprivation and constant frustration, which in turn negatively affect decision-making. Stress management is crucial for making good decisions. To ensure effective decision-making, try these techniques:

- *Stress management*—Mitigate the effect of stress on decision quality. One effective way to tackle stress is through delegation, which chapter 5 covers in depth.
- *Communication*—Disseminate decisions promptly.
- *Decision records*—Maintain records to reference past choices.
- *Reflection time*—Schedule monthly assessments and quarterly reflections to adapt strategies and ensure continuous improvement in team performance.

14.2 Tips for better time management

We have already considered why effective time management is an important skill to master. Better time management helps you increase your productivity, keeps you involved in things that matter, and creates opportunities for others to uplevel themselves on the team. Let's look at some ways to manage your time better.

14.2.1 Declutter your calendar

For an EM, managing a cluttered calendar filled with numerous meetings is a common challenge. Given that you have full control of *your* calendar, it's imperative to manage it effectively. Streamlining your calendar offers significant advantages:

- *Simplified prioritization*—A clear calendar facilitates easy identification and prioritization of crucial tasks amid a busy schedule, ensuring prompt attention to essential responsibilities.
- *Enhanced productivity*—Decluttering your calendar gives you more time and energy to allocate to vital tasks, significantly boosting overall productivity. Effective prioritization ensures that you spend valuable time on crucial matters.
- *Efficient communication*—Contrary to intuition, skipping certain meetings can improve communication. A cluttered calendar can hinder focus on critical matters, leading to poor communication with partners.

As you can see in the sample EM calendar in figure 14.1, it's important to schedule time for breaks and focused work, as well as for meetings and collaborative work sessions.

	Monday	Tuesday	Wednesday	Thursday	Friday
9 am-10 am	Focus block	Focus block	Focus block	Focus block	Focus block
10 am-10:30 am	One-on-one	Meeting	Meeting	Meeting	Meeting
10:30 am-11 am	One-on-one	One-on-one	One-on-one	Meeting	Meeting
11 am-11:30 am	Project meeting	One-on-one	One-on-one	Meeting	Agile session
11:30 am-12 pm		One-on-one	One-on-one	Demo	Free block
12 pm-12:30 pm	Lunch	Lunch	Lunch	Lunch	Lunch
12:30 pm-1 pm	Meeting	Operational review	Security review	Office hours	No meeting block
1 pm-1:30 pm	Meeting			Free block	
1:30 pm-2 pm	Free block	Free block	Free block	Architecture review	
2 pm-2:30 pm	Free block	Team meeting	Free block		
2:30 pm-3 pm	Meeting		One-on-one	Free block	
3 pm-3:30 pm	Break	Break	Break	Break	Break
3:30 pm-4 pm	Free block	Meeting	Meeting	Agile session	Focus block
4 pm-4:30 pm	Meeting	Free block	Meeting	Meeting	Focus block
4:30 pm-5 pm	Focus block	Focus block	Meeting	Focus block	Focus block

Figure 14.1 Declutter your calendar by creating focus blocks, lunch breaks, and free time blocks.

Here are some tips for achieving calendar decluttering, taken from my experience:

- *Define clear priorities.* Use tools such as the Eisenhower Matrix (section 14.3) to focus on high-priority tasks and avoid wasting time on less critical activities. Make sure to set up reminders for all your meetings to ensure punctuality.

- *Eliminate unnecessary meetings.* Identify and eliminate unnecessary meetings to save valuable time. If you are joining a meeting simply to get a project update, see whether you can get it offline or use async communication to save meeting time. Ask yourself, "Am I needed in this meeting?"

- *Set up recurring meetings as needed.* Establish recurring meetings to prompt yourself to complete essential regular tasks, such as preparing for one-on-one conversations and crafting project-status updates.

- *Create focus blocks.* Use color-coded focus blocks on your calendar aligned with peak productivity times, safeguarding this time for crucial tasks. You can have focus blocks at the start of each day to help review the day ahead. Similarly, you can have an end-of-day focus block to reflect on how the day went, which helps set the stage for a productive next day.

- *Schedule breaks.* Allocate blocks for breaks, lunch, or quick walks to refresh and disconnect. Reflect on achievements and plan for the next workweek on Fridays.

- *Have a no-meetings day.* Designate a day with no meetings, fostering maker's time for engineers and building trust within the team. Regular surveys help you gauge team sentiments, fostering transparency and discussion of action items.

One Monday morning, my cluttered calendar—brimming with color-coded appointments, meetings, and deadlines—made me realize that I was overwhelmed as an EM, juggling meetings and deadlines. The tipping point was a crucial project deadline; I felt spread too thin, and my productivity suffered.

Determined to change, I decluttered my calendar gradually, questioning the necessity and relevance of each commitment and learning to say no. Did this meeting truly require my presence? Could this task be delegated or deferred? Recognizing redundancy in my meetings, I proposed eliminating separate one-on-one meetings with my product manager and technical program manager in which we discussed project status as cross-functional partners. Instead, I suggested consolidating our discussions into a single, more efficient tripod meeting. By streamlining our communication channels, we reduced the number of meetings on our calendars, freeing valuable time for more effective work.

I also embraced delegation, empowering my team while prioritizing deep work, creative pursuits, and self-care. Whether I took a leisurely walk in the park or spent an hour in meditation, I recognized the importance of replenishing my own well-being to sustain productivity in the long run. Also, I set up weekly and quarterly reflection blocks on my calendar for assessing the progress of my team and projects, which helped me assess achievements, setbacks, and lessons learned. Such reflection ensured that I stayed on track with long-term goals and adapted effectively to changing circumstances. This transformation wasn't instant; it was a journey of introspection and prioritization.

14.2.2 *Create a meeting bill of rights*

To ensure that meetings are efficient and valuable, consider establishing a meeting bill of rights or a meeting charter. This document outlines attendees' entitlements, setting clear expectations for meeting dynamics and preparation. Here are some sample rules:

- *Right to know attendees*—All attendees have the right to know who else will be present at the meeting.
- *Right to access agenda*—Attendees should receive the agenda before the meeting to prepare adequately.
- *Right to expect clarity*—Attendees have the right to know the expected outcomes of the meeting.
- *Right to request more details*—Attendees can ask for additional details to prepare effectively for the meeting.
- *Right to decline to attend*—Attendees can decline to attend the meeting if they believe that they are not the best person to provide input. Optional and informational attendees should be identified.
- *Right to leave*—Attendees have the right to leave the meeting if the organizer is late by a specified amount of time.
- *Right to have opinions heard*—Every attendee has the right to have their opinions heard and considered.

Establishing these ground rules prevents wasted time due to inefficient meeting procedures. Providing agendas in advance allows attendees to prepare adequately and
assess their suitability for attendance. In scenarios that require technical discussions,
empowering your team engineers to lead discussions is sensible.

> **TIP** Avoid being overly present in every meeting; instead, be available
> through initiatives such as office hours and team forums. Although you might
> not always have the authority to enforce these rules, advocating for them,
> earning trust, and gradually expanding your influence is a winning strategy,
> especially in diverse organizational settings.

14.2.3 Use the power of delegation

Effective delegation is a cornerstone skill for EMs, enabling them to use their team's
strengths and expertise to achieve collective goals while optimizing their own workload. Mastering this skill can be challenging for new EMs, however.

   Consider Jacob, a new EM who recently transitioned from a software engineering
role. Faced with a challenging problem, Jacob believed that only he could resolve it
due to his knowledge of the codebase. Although his intentions were good, the fact
that he spent two days on this problem presented two potential problems:

- Jacob's time could have been allocated for other essential EM tasks.
- Delegation provides growth opportunities for team members, and this problem
  could have been a valuable learning experience for someone else on the team,
  as shown in figure 14.2.

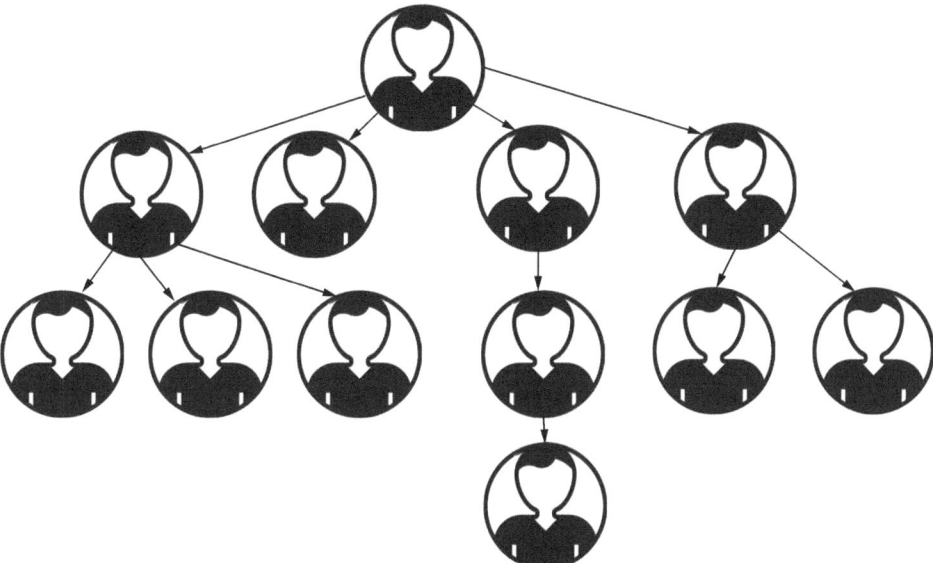

Figure 14.2   Delegation can use teams' strengths and skills.

In this scenario, Jacob overlooked the critical tool of delegation. Thoughtfully assigning tasks to his strong engineering team would have allowed him to manage his time more efficiently. For a comprehensive understanding of delegation principles, please refer to chapter 5.

14.2.4 *Learn to say no*

Recognize where your time investment is unnecessary, and hone the ability to say no. Overcommitment poses significant challenges, leading to your own underperformance and low productivity as well as heightened stress.

Timely refusals empower you to prioritize efficiently, freeing valuable time for essential tasks. Saying no to low-priority items allows you to shift your focus to core EM responsibilities: managing the team and ensuring top-notch work quality. Additionally, saying no provides precious time for introspection on the team's overall health.

On a previous job, I was leading a crucial project when my team was already stretched thin, and additional requests threatened to derail our progress. One morning, my manager approached me with yet another urgent task, asking for my team's immediate involvement. Although I understood the importance of the request, I also recognized that taking on this new task would jeopardize our current commitments and strain our resources.

I respectfully explained to my manager the current workload of my team and the potential effect of taking on additional tasks at this juncture. Instead of refusing the request outright, I offered alternative solutions to address the underlying needs while mitigating the strain on my team:

- I proposed prioritizing the new task against our existing commitments to identify any possible tradeoffs or adjustments in timelines. By aligning on priorities, we could ensure that the most critical tasks received the necessary attention without overburdening the team.
- I suggested exploring opportunities for resource allocation from other teams within the organization. By tapping available resources elsewhere, we could lighten the load on my team and still complete the new task.
- I emphasized the importance of clear communication and expectation-setting with stakeholders regarding any potential delays or adjustments in project timelines. By managing expectations proactively, we could minimize any potential fallout from reallocating resources or adjusting project plans.

It wasn't easy to push back against my manager's request, but I knew that it was essential to advocate for my team's well-being and the successful execution of our current projects. By offering constructive alternatives and maintaining open communication, I was able to navigate this challenging situation while preserving the integrity of my team's workload and commitments. My manager appreciated my candidness and strategic approach. This experience reinforced the importance of setting boundaries and advocating for the needs of my team, even in the face of challenging circumstances.

Prioritizing your calendar rigorously, identifying tasks that don't need your involvement, and confidently saying no can significantly enhance your time management. Using tools such as the RACI matrix (discussed in chapter 9) allows team members who fall into the "informed" category to skip meetings, catching up through meeting minutes and safeguarding their valuable time.

14.2.5 Keep your to-do list up to date

For an engineering leader, a surge in meetings occurs during certain periods of the year. Picture the convergence of annual planning and performance reviews, resulting in a flurry of meetings that require your attention. During such intense periods, a well-organized to-do list becomes a life-saver.

> **Did you know?**
> Getting Things Done (GTD; https://gettingthingsdone.com/what-is-gtd) is a famous time management system developed by David Allen. The idea is to identify the critical tasks and create a list with clear time-boxed limits. Each task should have an actionable item against it so you can be sure to make progress.

An updated to-do list is a powerful tool for streamlining work and optimizing time, serving as a centralized repository and making it easy to identify pending tasks. This centralized hub is invaluable for deciding the next task to tackle. Prioritizing tasks becomes seamless when you arrange them based on factors such as urgency and deadline.

To-do lists offer a range of benefits, aligning with crucial EM skills such as delegation and the ability to say no. They facilitate timely communication, promote transparency in your work, and hold you accountable for completing tasks. Using apps such as Trello, Apple Notes, and Reminders ensures that your list is constantly updated. If you favor a visual approach, sticky notes or lists written in a notebook can also be effective. Incorporating a 15- to 30-minute shutdown ritual at the end of the day helps you catch up on Slack messages and emails and to triage your to-do list, further enhancing productivity.

14.2.6 Use feature/project-tracker documents

Effective time management relies on robust project management, and tools such as Jira and Asana can play a pivotal role in helping you achieve this efficiency. These tools offer a comprehensive overview of your team's projects, encompassing dependencies, deadlines, and progress in one accessible location.

Having such a tool (or creating one if none exists) makes it effortless to check whether your team is aligned with its commitments. Early identification of potential problems, such as insufficient resources, is another key advantage. A glance at the remaining time and task progress can reveal whether additional resources are needed or plans need to be adjusted.

Although it's ideal to have this information at the project's outset, unforeseen complexities often alter initial plans. Discovering resource needs late in the game can create stress and introduce unnecessary challenges. Project management tools consolidate this information, offering holistic insights that might otherwise go unnoticed. Early attention to such areas enables proactive reprioritization, saving considerable time later. See chapter 10 for a detailed discussion of project/feature trackers.

14.2.7 *Use async communication to the fullest*

Asynchronous communication is a potent tool for enhancing time management. Unlike synchronous communication, which demands immediate attention, asynchronous communication allows flexibility in addressing problems at your own pace, within a reasonable response time defined by task priority.

The key advantage of asynchronous communication is that it significantly limits interruptions. For an EM who's juggling various responsibilities, constant context switching can affect productivity detrimentally. Research by the American Psychology Association (https://www.apa.org/topics/research/multitasking) confirms that switching among complex tasks imposes a substantial toll on productivity. Avoid the temptation to respond immediately to async chat messages; respect your time blocks unless the matter is urgent. Urgent matters can be escalated through direct messages or paging. Using async communication gives you the flexibility to respond on your own terms while still accomplishing tasks, reducing the effect of interruptions.

Beyond productivity gains, async communication mitigates FOMO (fear of missing out). A culture of diligently sharing meeting outcomes alleviates concerns about missing vital discussions.

The Pomodoro Technique

Developed in late 1980 by Francesco Cirillo, a university student who was struggling with his own time management, the Pomodoro Technique (https://www.pomodoro technique.com) relies on breaking your work time into 30-minute chunks: you spend 25 minutes working on something with complete focus and then take a 5-minute break. After four such 30-minute sessions, you take a break of 15 minutes. The following figure illustrates the technique.

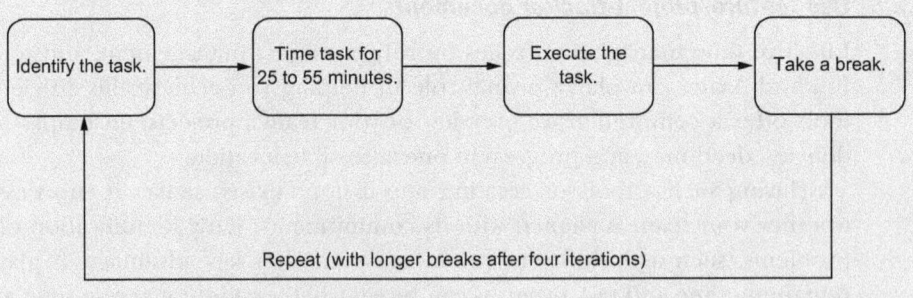

The framework of the Pomodoro technique

His technique is widely regarded as a great productivity booster because it minimizes interruptions, decreases mental fatigue, and makes you more conscious of how you are spending your time. Pro tip: try to schedule your meetings for 25- or 55-minute blocks to give attendees enough time to take a quick water or bio break, or even have a quick stretch to avoid mental and physical fatigue.

To maximize the benefits of async communication, create focused blocks on your calendar dedicated to uninterrupted work. Use Slack, work chat, or emails for nonurgent responses, reserving synchronous communication for critical, time-sensitive matters. Before scheduling or accepting meetings, evaluate whether the discussion can be handled asynchronously through team messaging apps, reducing the need for synchronous communication and enhancing overall productivity.

Although async communication offers numerous advantages, it's crucial to recognize scenarios in which prolonged back-and-forth discussions may cause more problems than they solve. In such cases, consider whether a meeting might be more effective for achieving understanding and consensus among involved parties.

14.3   The Eisenhower Matrix

I have two kinds of problems: the urgent and the important. The urgent are not important, and the important are never urgent.

—Dwight D. Eisenhower

EMs commonly find themselves caught in a perpetual state of busyness. The demands of project execution and people management can lead to constant occupation. Being consistently busy does not necessarily equate to productivity, however. Spending days multitasking may leave you feeling that you haven't accomplished enough—a feeling that poses risks to both the company and your well-being.

This cycle can result in significant stress, affecting your professional and personal lives. Often, the root cause is poor prioritization. It's tempting to focus on tasks with immediate deadlines, neglecting those with long-term benefits for yourself and your team. This reactive approach creates a continuous loop, hindering productive work.

To regain control of your time and enhance productivity, distinguish between urgent and important tasks. The Eisenhower Matrix is a valuable tool for this purpose, allowing you to break free from constant reaction to immediate problems and proactively address tasks that contribute to long-term success.

14.3.1   Meeting the requirements to use the Eisenhower Matrix

The Eisenhower Matrix serves as a straightforward decision-making tool, allowing you to prioritize tasks based on urgency and importance. To employ this matrix effectively, you must have a clear understanding of the distinction between urgency and importance.

URGENT

Tasks that fall into the urgent category demand immediate attention. The consequences of not addressing urgent tasks promptly are evident, resulting in various effects. These tasks cannot be deferred, and postponing them would escalate stress levels for both you and your team. Examples of urgent tasks include

- Resolving a critical regression in your services
- Delivering a high-priority business need with an imminent deadline
- Executing a project to enforce legal compliance for applications within the company, taking a systematic approach to ensure adherence to relevant laws, regulations, and industry standards

IMPORTANT

Although they do not require immediate attention, important tasks contribute to long-term goals and progress. Despite not being urgent, these tasks are crucial for achieving significant milestones in the future. Examples of important tasks include

- Redefining the on-call process to reduce your team's on-call load
- Strategically planning a long-term project aligned with significant milestones
- Devising a long-term maintenance strategy for the products and features supported by your team

When you have a clear grasp of the differentiation between important and urgent tasks, you can use the Eisenhower Matrix to its maximum potential, facilitating effective prioritization and decision-making.

14.3.2   *Using the four quadrants of the Eisenhower Matrix*

Confronting a lengthy to-do list can be overwhelming initially. The Eisenhower Matrix, organized into four distinct quadrants, provides a systematic approach for addressing each item on your list. The objective is to categorize each task into the appropriate quadrant, facilitating a structured and prioritized view, as illustrated in figure 14.3.

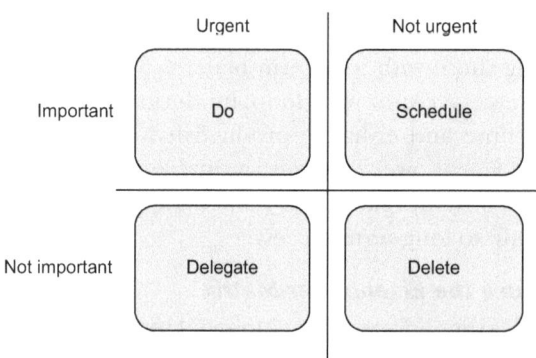

Figure 14.3   The four quadrants of the Eisenhower Matrix for time management

QUADRANT 1: DO

These tasks demand immediate attention and are both urgent and important. They possess clear consequences and outcomes, and they significantly affect long-term goals. Easily identifiable, these tasks are often top-of-mind stressors. Ideally, the presence of numerous tasks in this quadrant should prompt reflection on root causes and strategies to minimize their occurrence.

QUADRANT 2: SCHEDULE

Tasks in this quadrant are important but lack urgency. Although they don't require immediate attention, they contribute to long-term goals. Scheduling them for later execution allows for a thoughtful approach. Despite the satisfaction derived from completing tasks in this quadrant, people often neglect them due to a focus on urgent requests. Dedicating ample time to Quadrant 2 tasks, however, is essential for sustained success. Regular retrospectives can gauge the time spent in this quadrant, prompting adjustments if necessary. Delaying these tasks indefinitely can lead them to transition to Quadrant 1, introducing stress.

QUADRANT 3: DELEGATE

Tasks in this quadrant are urgent but lack importance. Commonly, individuals spend excessive time here, handling tasks that demand immediate attention but have no effect on long-term goals. The key question for tasks in this category is whether someone else can handle them. Delegating, a crucial skill, not only helps you manage your time efficiently but also helps others achieve their goals.

QUADRANT 4: DELETE

Any task that lacks urgency and importance finds its place in this quadrant. These tasks are mere distractions, hindering goal achievement. Deleting such tasks is crucial, as investing time in them serves no purpose. If a task doesn't contribute to your objectives, the best approach is to eliminate it. Figure 14.4 provides a detailed illustration of some real examples.

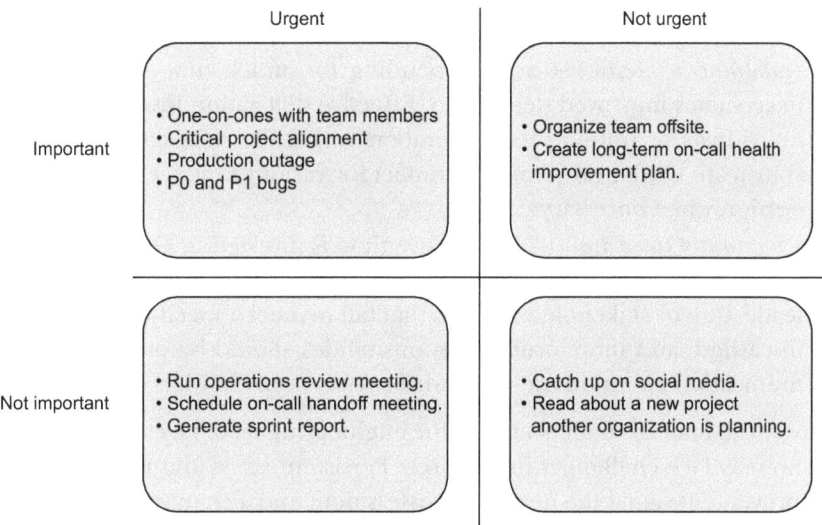

Figure 14.4   Some real examples of the four quadrants of the Eisenhower Matrix

The Eisenhower Matrix is a powerful time management tool if used correctly. It can help you evaluate the calendar, prioritize tasks, and identify tasks that you can delete or delegate so that you can focus on the most important.

14.3.3   *Spending time to find time*

Mastering the art of prioritizing your time is a valuable skill. To enhance this skill, conducting a retrospective analysis of time distribution among the Eisenhower Matrix quadrants can be beneficial. You can use either of two methods for this purpose:

- *Daily estimation approach*—At the end of each workday, assess the tasks you worked on, and roughly estimate the time you spent on tasks in each quadrant. Although this approach is time-efficient, it may lack precision due to variations in recording accuracy, and it involves a risk of missing details or miscounting time.
- *Detailed 30-minute chunking*—A more accurate method involves breaking the workday into 30-minute chunks. Allocate 25 minutes for focused work, 2 minutes to note the task, and the remaining 3 minutes for a quick break. This meticulous approach gives you clear, precise understanding of time distribution over a week or two.

Let's look at how you can rebalance your time to achieve your goals better and faster:

- *Quadrant 1 (overemphasis)*—If Quadrant 1 tasks consume excessive time, strategic planning becomes crucial. Although unexpected problems may arise, advanced planning and anticipating potential challenges can significantly reduce stress. Reducing reliance on Quadrant 1 tasks allows more time for preferred tasks.
- *Quadrant 2 (focus)*—A substantial focus on Quadrant 2 tasks is commendable, as these tasks contribute to long-term goals. Continuing this approach is advisable, as it aligns with effective time management and goal achievement.
- *Quadrant 3 (overcommitment)*—Spending too much time on Quadrant 3 tasks necessitates improved delegation. Effective delegation involves finding suitable individuals or training team members to handle such tasks. Collaborate with your team to identify points of contact for various topics, ensuring seamless delegation when necessary.
- *Quadrant 4 (time drain)*—If excessive time is invested in Quadrant 4 tasks, it signals potential wasted time. Review the importance of tasks in this quadrant with leadership or stakeholders. Tasks that fail to meet a specific threshold should be discarded, and more crucial responsibilities should be prioritized. Clear communication about this decision with relevant stakeholders is essential.

Effective time management is crucial for engineering leaders, especially for first-time EMs who may face challenges in this area. Persistent stress and time investment without improvement signal the need for reassessment and a change in approach. There's no one-size-fits-all solution, but acknowledging the importance of time and making proactive planning a habit significantly enhances productivity. Delaying effective time management is akin to compromising long-term success.

What do other leaders have to say?

I frequently say that journaling your to-do list is great (I bullet-journal) but that it's easy to fall into a trap of reducing the list size over doing the most important items on the list. It can be beneficial to cross off a few items to build psychological momentum to complete the longer and harder items.

The biggest thing is to acknowledge that there will always be more requests for your time than you can service, and you have to triage what needs to be done now and what can wait (both to take care of in the future and to see if it really is something that needs to be done), what can be delegated, and what can just be dropped or declined. Your personal bias can sneak into that prioritization (doing things you like over needed things), so be careful.

—Nathan Bourgoin, Chief Technology Officer at Alakazam, Inc.,
Technical Adviser, and Engineering Leader

I maintain my to-do [list] and reprioritize the same every day I start my day. Once a month, I retrospect my calendar to look out for no essential meetings and move them for offline discussions over live documents.

—Madhur Kathuria, Engineering Leader at Microsoft,
formerly with Moengage, Oracle, and IIT

I am a planner at heart. I review my calendar in advance and make changes as needed. Let's say I need to block time for writing, find an optimal slot, and move meetings to another day/time. Distinguishing between deep focus time versus day-to-day tasks is important and helps me prioritize my day. Finally, I recognize that not every email and Slack [message] needs to be responded to immediately and that each day will not be the same in productivity.

—Nishat Akhter, Data Product and Engineering Leader,
Amazon Web Services (AWS)

The most important aspect of time management is to ensure one spends the time on the most impactful tasks. Use a priority management tool like the Eisenhower Matrix. Block the calendar for every task to avoid distraction. Allocate the time you think each task will take you. Stop the task if you don't complete it when the time you allotted ends and come back to it later. Assess why you failed and repeat the step.

—Saurabh Gandhi, Senior Director, Software Development at Audible,
formerly with American Express

14.4 Stop and think: Practice questions

1. Do you feel that you have a grip on and control of your work time?
2. What tasks take most of your time? Can they be delegated or automated?
3. Do you feel burned out? If yes, do you feel that you are racing against time?
4. What meetings on your calendar can be canceled or deferred?

5 How many hours a day do your team members spend in meetings, and do they have sufficient uninterrupted work time?

6 What one change would you make in your office calendar, and how would you address it?

Summary

- Managing your time is probably the most important skill you need to learn to be a successful EM.
- Managing time is particularly important for EMs for the following reasons:
  - It helps you manage the successful execution of project deliverables.
  - It helps you achieve personal goals in addition to team goals.
  - You are working under a lot of constraints, such as frequent meetings, constant interruptions, and the expectation of high-quality work to be a role model for the team; so much work can be overwhelming and can lead to procrastination.
  - It contributes to effective decision-making.
- You can manage your time by
  - Decluttering your calendar and creating focus blocks for your own work
  - Establishing a meeting bill of rights so that all attendees can get the most out of the meeting
  - Using the power of delegation to both load-balance your work and provide opportunities for others to step up
  - Learning to say no when the ask is not worth your time
  - Creating a concrete to-do list, which can help you in prioritization
  - Maximizing your use of project management and project tracking tools
  - Using async communication to minimize the interruptions you face
- The Eisenhower Matrix can help you manage your time more effectively. To use this tool, you should
  - Understand the difference between important and urgent tasks. Not all urgent tasks are important, and vice versa.
  - Classify your tasks in one of the following four buckets: important and urgent (do them now), important and not urgent (schedule them for later), urgent but not important (delegate them to others), and not important and not urgent (save your time and get rid of them altogether).
  - Spend time to find more time.
  - Use retrospective sessions to understand how your time distribution looks across four buckets. At the end of the day, either make rough estimates of how much time you spent on each task or, for more accurate results, log what you have done in the past 29 minutes at 30-minute intervals. Whichever method you choose, use it for a few weeks to understand long-term trends.

- Rebalance and try to maximize working on tasks from bucket 2 (important and not urgent). These tasks tend to give you the greatest satisfaction and help you achieve your long-term goals.
- Effective time management involves a combination of strategic planning, delegation, clear communication, and prioritization. Mastering these skills will significantly contribute to your success as an EM.

Beyond this book: Grow yourself

This chapter covers

- Reviews and recaps
- The importance of continuous learning and improving your skill set
- Valuable resources for the future

Live as if you were to die tomorrow. Learn as if you were to live forever.

—Mahatma Gandhi

Welcome to the final chapter, marking the end of our enriching journey together. Our exploration has covered crucial concepts central to the engineering manager (EM) role, emphasizing commitment to fostering learning and professional growth, not only for oneself but also for the entire team. As we conclude, we'll recap key insights and provide valuable learning resources to further enhance your skills. Consider this chapter not just an endpoint but also a launching pad into a future where your leadership capabilities will shape the path to success in the dynamic realm of engineering management.

15.1 *What you've learned so far*

Our journey began with the foundational understanding that the EM role involves distinct responsibilities compared with those of individual contributors (IC) or software engineers. The book unfolded in three major parts.

15.1.1 *Part 1: Start with the people*

In this initial segment, we explored the foundational aspects of the EM role. We delved into the purpose of engineering management, distinguishing key traits that differentiate effective from less effective EMs. By examining various leadership styles, we uncovered how to align with an authentic managerial approach. The part also highlighted disparities between the EM and IC roles, aiding in the decision-making process for career aspirations. For those who are considering a transition to EM, the part discussed strategic planning and how to set individuals and teams up for success, along with pitfalls to avoid. Shifting focus to the people-centric dimension of team management, we covered motivation, handling both high performers and underperformers, and navigating performance discussions through frameworks. We explored the art of delegation, accompanied by a framework for effective implementation. Finally, the part addressed the intricacies of team building, encompassing hiring frameworks, attrition management, and proactive strategies.

15.1.2 *Part 2: Projects and the cross-functional world*

In the second part, the focus shifted to collaboration in a cross-functional landscape. We addressed questions about effective collaboration, building road maps, and communicating with both technical and nontechnical partners. Exploring the project life cycle, we detailed EM involvement in the preplanning, planning, execution, and postexecution stages. The part concluded with insights into managing expectations at all organizational levels through shared understanding, alignment, and cooperation. The part unveiled challenges related to expectation management, along with a practical framework.

15.1.3 *Part 3: Learn the process*

The final part focused on understanding DevOps and operational excellence (OE), emphasizing their continuous practice. It provided insights into organizational change management processes, covering reorganizations, change management frameworks, and ways to navigate shifts in leadership and the workforce. The part discussed the importance of time management and provided tips on practical tools, including the Eisenhower Matrix. The part concluded by stressing the significance of continuous learning and maintaining an open learning mindset. This concluding chapter will further guide us with key takeaways and additional learning resources, ensuring a well-rounded preparation for future challenges and opportunities.

15.2   *Continuously learn and hone skills*

Your journey as an EM places you in the driver's seat, steering your career toward success. In this dynamic landscape, where technological evolution is relentless, proactively and iteratively enhancing your leadership skills is crucial. Throughout this book, I've emphasized the iterative nature of learning, continual improvement, and the invaluable role of feedback. The underlying principle is clear: set well-defined goals, establish expectations, and chart a road map to your desired destination.

As you navigate this journey, the crucial step is translating your road map into actionable items. Upgrading your technological knowledge, for example, can manifest in various forms, from reading insightful books to engaging with online learning resources or even participating as a speaker at relevant technical conferences. This process is akin to taking measured steps, identifying gaps in your knowledge, fortifying those areas, and advancing persistently. I recommend exploring the Knowledge Breadth versus Depth triangle (https://mng.bz/7dRm) to tailor your learning approach; delve deep or broaden your understanding based on your goals and starting point.

During your EM journey, focus on foundational learning and the practical application of acquired knowledge. Although concepts such as delegation are familiar, true mastery comes through hands-on practice as an engineering leader. Demonstrating these practices to your team not only sets a tangible example but also instills confidence in your leadership. Maintaining an open mind to glean insights from your experiences and the collective wisdom of those around you is paramount. This mindset ensures that you optimize your efforts to expand both the breadth and depth of your knowledge and expertise. Section 15.3 places an array of learning tools at your disposal, providing you a rich inventory of resources to augment your skills and capabilities.

15.3   *Some learning resources for the future*

As we conclude this book, I'm excited to share a curated set of invaluable resources that have proved to be beneficial for EMs, including me. These resources serve as a knowledge reservoir, providing continuous learning opportunities essential for your growth in the field of engineering leadership.

15.3.1   *Mentors*

Chapter 2 emphasized the crucial role of having a mentor for your professional journey, particularly during the IC-to-EM transition. Mentors offer guidance on professional growth, assist in networking, share valuable experiences, and provide career advice. It's essential to differentiate between a manager's role in your career development plan and a mentor's function in providing an outsider's perspective. When you're seeking a mentor, follow these tips:

- Consider individuals outside your immediate leadership chain or organizational structure.
- Look for someone in a similar role, someone who is a few levels above you, or someone who has achieved what you aspire to achieve.

- Be clear about the time commitment and expectations from the mentor–mentee relationship. Discuss confidentiality and personal boundaries, and specify whether the relationship is time-boxed or open-ended.
- Having multiple mentors with unique perspectives is beneficial. You might have one mentor inside your organization and another one outside, focusing on different aspects such as technical expertise or business acumen.

You can find a mentor through various channels, such as the following:

- Company mentorship programs offer excellent opportunities for pairing.
- LinkedIn (https://www.linkedin.com) allows you to explore professionals' journeys and mentorship requests. You can find sample mentorship-request messages on the Indeed (https://mng.bz/maAP) and GrowthMentor (https://mng.bz/5lRz) websites.
- Online platforms such as PlatoHQ (https://www.platohq.com), GrowthMentor, First Round Fast Track (https://fasttrack.firstround.com), ADPList (https://adplist.org), MentorPass (https://www.mentorpass.co), and The Muse (https://www.themuse.com/coaching) specialize in mentorship connections.
- Attending technical meetups and networking events exposes you to potential mentors.

A mentor serves as a guiding force, aiding your growth, refining skills, revealing blind spots, and presenting career opportunities. If you haven't done so already, it's time to embark on the journey of finding your mentor—a trusted adviser who can illuminate your professional path.

15.3.2 Learning platforms

You can enhancing your EM skills through various learning platforms. Here are a few ways to kick-start your growth:

- *Read books (or listen to audiobooks) on software engineering, leadership, and management.* Following are a few books apart from this one that I recommend:
  - *Turn the Ship Around!: A True Story of Turning Followers into Leaders*, by L. David Marquet (https://mng.bz/gvKV)
  - *The 7 Habits of Highly Effective People: Powerful Lessons in Personal Change*, by Stephen R. Covey (https:///mng.bz/oeAM)
  - *Radical Candor: Be a Kick-Ass Boss Without Losing Your Humanity*, by Kim Scott (https://mng.bz/ngAK)
  - *The Manager's Path: A Guide for Tech Leaders Navigating Growth and Change*, by Camille Fournier (https://mng.bz/v8AM)
  - *The First 90 Days: Proven Strategies for Getting Up to Speed Smarter and Faster*, by Michael Watkins (https://mng.bz/4JRV)
  - *Your Next Five Moves: Master the Art of Business Strategy*, by Patrick Bet-David (https://mng.bz/QZ7j)

- *Good Strategy/Bad Strategy: The Difference and Why It Matters*, by Richard Rumelt (https://mng.bz/X1o6)
- *Measure What Matters: How Google, Bono, and the Gates Foundation Rock the World with OKRs*, by John Doerr (https://mng.bz/y8Aq)
- *The Making of a Manager: What to Do When Everyone Looks to You*, by Julie Zhuo (https://mng.bz/MZ7n)
- *The First-Time Manager*, by Jim McCormick (https://mng.bz/aEgB)
- *The Five Dysfunctions of a Team: A Leadership Fable*, by Patrick Lencioni (https://mng.bz/gvzE)
- *Managing Humans: Biting and Humorous Tales of a Software Engineering Manager*, by Michael Lopp (https://mng.bz/5lRB)

- *Take a manager course.* Manager courses are available on learning platforms including LinkedIn Learning (https://www.linkedin.com/learning-login), Udemy (https://www.udemy.com), Coursera (https://www.coursera.org), edX (https://www.edx.org), and Pluralsight (https://www.pluralsight.com). Such platforms usually have a subscription model with unlimited courses to test your skills. You can use them to gain technical knowledge as well as management skills.

- *Follow blogs.* Blogs are good ways to learn and also share your knowledge and experiences with others. They're also powerful tools if you are trying to build a personal brand. Medium (https://medium.com) and *Harvard Business Review* (https://hbr.org) are two of the best places to read blogs by other experts in the field; Medium also allows you to start your own blog. Other platforms you can explore include Wix (https://www.wix.com) and WordPress (https://wordpress.org). To get you started, you can share how you have learned and grown in your career and navigated challenging situations. NOREX (https://www.norex.net) is a great platform to explore.

- *Reflect on your career journey, achievements, and challenges.* This technique is an effective way to enhance leadership skills. It connects past and present experiences, providing insights for future opportunities.

- *Find an executive coach.* If you want to go one step further, you can get access to executive coaches such as those provided by platforms like BetterUp (https://www.betterup.com).

These resources offer diverse ways for you to commence your learning journey and grasp the nuances of the EM role. Recognizing that individual preferences vary, explore these options to find those that resonate with your interests and aspirations.

15.3.3 *Pet projects*

Continued learning is not limited by age, and for an EM, transitioning from coding to technical discussions is essential. Pet projects during free time involving small yet valuable initiatives focus on simplicity and foundational learning. These projects keep you updated on coding skills and industry standards, aiding in technical interviews for EM roles.

Platforms such as GitHub (https://github.com) and Taproot (https://taprootfoundation .org) offer avenues for sharing and discussing projects; Kaggle (https://www.kaggle .com/competitions) provides a gamified setting for collaborative real-world problem-solving, enhancing your learning and networking experience. Cultivating this habit not only keeps you technologically current but also instills trust within your engineering team, showcasing your sound technical leadership.

I have always been fascinated by artificial intelligence and its ability to improve user experiences, so I decided to delve into Amazon Lex by creating a chatbot in my spare time. My team faced frequent customer inquiries that could be automated, presenting an ideal opportunity to explore this technology. The goal was clear: develop a chatbot capable of understanding natural-language queries and providing relevant responses. Experimenting with Amazon Lex, Amazon Web Services (AWS) Lambda, and Amazon CloudWatch was both educational and insightful. This endeavor not only expanded my knowledge but also showcased the potential for automating repetitive tasks in the workplace, benefiting both my personal growth and organizational efficiency.

15.3.4 *Effective communication*

Effective communication is a fundamental skill for EMs, extending beyond language proficiency to articulating thoughts for both technical and nontechnical audiences. Nuances in expression can affect how messages are received, especially for new EMs who are transitioning from engineering roles. It's crucial to communicate with tact and share personal learning experiences to positively influence team morale. Consider a scenario in which a recently transitioned engineer-turned-EM discusses a technical task with a team member. If the EM, who possesses expertise on the topic, expresses concerns about the team member's pace without tact, their tactless comments can significantly affect morale. Conversely, sharing personal learning experiences and delving into the subject when the EM is a newcomer can positively influence the team member. Here are a few practical ways to refine your communication skills:

- *Join Toastmasters.* Participate in a Toastmasters group (https://www.toastmasters .org) to focus on effective communication in a supportive environment.
- *Attend and speak at conferences.* Engage in technical and leadership conferences, observing influential leaders in action. This experience gives you valuable insights into ways to break the ice and capture the audience; the forums allow you to practice and enhance your speaking skills.
- *Take online courses.* Explore online courses on platforms such as LinkedIn Learning and TEDx talks (https://www.ted.com/watch/tedx-talks) to grasp communication basics and practice effectively.
- *Publish content.* Share your insights by publishing blog posts or magazine articles or even writing a book. Platforms such as the Google Blogspot forum, Medium, and LinkedIn are common avenues for content creation.

Here are some other suggested resources for improving your communication skills:

- *Presentation Zen* (book and website), by Garr Reynolds (https://www.presentationzen.com)
- *The Back of the Napkin: Solving Problems and Selling Ideas with Pictures*, by Dan Roam (https://mng.bz/67Ro)
- *Think Faster, Talk Smarter: How to Speak Successfully When You're Put on the Spot*, by Matt Abrahams (https://mng.bz/oeAd)
- *HBR Guide to Better Business Writing*, by Bryan A. Garner (https://mng.bz/rVDD)
- *HBR Guide to Persuasive Presentations*, by Nancy Duarte (https://mng.bz/ngAa)

Taking deliberate steps to enhance communication contributes significantly to success as an EM.

15.3.5 Interviews

This advice may seem nontraditional to you, but engaging in periodic job interviews for similar roles, even when you're not actively seeking a change, can enhance your confidence in both interviewing and being interviewed. Although this advice may not be universally applicable, particularly in close-knit hiring markets, it provides valuable insights into industry expectations and helps you identify key skill sets to focus on. Regular interviews also offer an opportunity to explore potential employers that are aligned with your career goals; casual discussions can provide a nuanced match for your aspirations.

15.3.6 Feedback

Embracing feedback is a skill that fuels continuous personal and professional growth. Although our natural tendency may be to perceive feedback as negative criticism, maintaining a positive perspective allows us to see it as constructive guidance. Feedback comes in various forms, offering insights from personal connections and workplace reviews. Acknowledging imperfections and adopting a coaching mindset fosters opportunities for growth.

Prepare your own career-gap analysis document or the career-growth development plan discussed in chapter 3, and review it with your manager. This strategy will help you identify any gaps and address them early. For EMs, it's crucial to avoid defensiveness when receiving feedback; instead, we should use it to enhance our capabilities. Requesting specific instances and adopting a data-driven approach allows for targeted improvement.

Feedback can take both informal and formal forms, from casual inquiries about your performance to well-documented assessments. The book *Thanks for the Feedback: The Science and Art of Receiving Feedback Well*, by Douglas Stone and Sheila Heen (https://mng.bz/4JRw), provides valuable insights into navigating this terrain.

In essence, any feedback you receive is a golden opportunity to unveil blind spots, learn, and grow. You should seize this opportunity to propel yourself toward success.

15.4   Thank you

As we conclude this book, I express gratitude for your companionship on this exploration. We've journeyed through the vital realm of effective people management, explored the intricacies of project delivery, and navigated collaboration and organizational changes. The final part unveiled processes such as DevOps, operational excellence, and time management—a crucial skill for EMs.

Whether you found insights, practical frameworks, daily lessons, or camaraderie in your journey from a software engineer to an EM, I hope that this book added value. Best wishes for your career, and feel free to connect with me on LinkedIn (https://www.linkedin.com/in/akankshaguptamgr). I'm confident that you'll excel in your endeavors.

Thank you!

What do other leaders have to say?

I'm a lifelong learner and spend a lot of time on learning, besides access I'm a continuous reader of HBR (Harvard Business Review), Medium, and LinkedIn. I'm an avid listener to podcasts and YouTube. ChatGPT is on top of my favorites on my phone and computer. I frequently use it to understand technologies and assist with day-to-day work. I would recommend Coaching Habit: Say, Less, Ask More and Change the Way You Lead Forever, written by Michael Bungay Stanier. It provides valuable insights and practical advice for becoming a more effective coach and leader by asking the right questions.

—Sumit Kumar, System Engineering Manager at Cisco

There are two books I seem to be referencing a lot lately. The first is a novel, The Phoenix Project: A Novel about IT, DevOps, and Helping Your Business Win, by Gene Kim, Kevin Behr, et al. When working in an office, I had a stack of this book and would hand it out to anyone who would listen. It packages a lot of concepts that I care about into a story that resonates with nontechnical stakeholders in a way that works. I had a previous CEO ask me "Am I [a character who randomizes the team and then complains when the team misses deadlines]?" It led to a valuable conversation. The second is Patrick Lencioni's The Advantage. In "we have to do everything" organizations, the six critical question exercises have teased out what is the best bang for the buck for the business. It also helps raise flags when an organization doesn't know what it is, putting a magnifying glass on that question needing to be answered before we can reason about what work to do.

—Nathan Bourgoin, Chief Technology Officer at Alakazam, Inc.,
Technical Adviser, and Engineering Leader

Do not stop learning. Stay humble, and understand the business needs. Technology skills alone will not be enough to forge beyond a certain organizational level.

—Rajakumar Sambasivam, Delivery Manager at Microsoft

Hacker News is my main tech news source because of the high signal-to-noise ratio. If something is interesting, it's usually there.

—Jean Bredeche, Head of Engineering at Patch,
formerly with Robinhood, Quantopian, and Hubspot

(continued)

As an EM, one needs to be comfortable with playing different roles and switching between them with ease. That also means that the EM's learning path is diverse and could range from being up to speed with the latest tech to learning how to build a high-performing team. That translates to converting every moment into a learning moment and diving deeper as needed. It's amazing how much you can learn from daily interactions with your own team, stakeholders, and your customers.

—Nishat Akhter, Data Product and Engineering Leader, Amazon Web Services (AWS)

Some suggested reading resources are [the books] The 5AM Club, The Coaching Habit, and Six Thinking Hats.

—Saurabh Gandhi, Senior Director, Software Development at Audible,
formerly with American Express

Beyond finding a good mentor in your industry, find peers at the same level as yourself and one level above you. Local meetups are a great opportunity for this kind of thing. You can learn much from just a few opportunities to meet, chat, and share ideas and challenges. As you move up the ladder in your career, likewise make yourself available as a mentor and coach to aspiring EMs and those you're grooming to take your place.

—Bruce Bergman, Manager at Lytx

15.5   Stop and think: Practice questions

1   How confident do I feel about my role as an engineering leader in my organization?

2   What are some ways I continuously learn and grow myself? Are they enough?

3   Do I have a mentor or sounding board to help me improve and provide career guidance?

4   How is my attitude when my boss or peer gives me advice or feedback? Do I have an opportunity to improve?

5   What are some of my resolutions to improve and hone my EM skills continuously?

Summary

- As an EM, your core responsibility is to facilitate learning and guide others in their career development. Let's recap the three sections of this book:
  - *Start with the people*—Explored the people aspect of the EM role, including the transition from IC to EM; the challenges involved; and crucial skills such as managing teams and performance, delegating, providing recognition, hiring, and addressing attrition.
  - *Projects and the cross-functional world*—Focused on working with cross-functional partners, mastering project delivery, and managing expectations at all organizational levels.
  - *Learn the process*—Delved into DevOps and operational excellence, organizational changes, and the importance of effective time management.

- Remember that your journey as an EM involves taking control of your career. Iterative learning and continuous skill refinement are essential for effective leadership. The book explored key resources for continuous learning, including the following:
  - *Mentors*—Mentors play an invaluable role in professional growth, networking, and skill refinement.
  - *Learning platforms*—Platforms such as LinkedIn Learning, Udemy, and Medium help you grow your EM skills, emphasizing the importance of personalized learning.
  - *Pet projects*—Working on small projects in your free time enhances your coding skills and keeps you updated on industry standards.
  - *Effective communication*—Communicate clearly, extending beyond language fluency, to engage both technical and nontechnical stakeholders.
  - *Frequent interviews*—Regular job interviews, even when you're not actively job hunting, are valuable for your boosting confidence, keeping you current on industry standards, and exploring potential opportunities.
  - *Feedback*—Embracing feedback is a skill that offers continuous improvement, enabling your personal and professional growth.

index

RELATED MANNING TITLES

Think Like a CTO
by Alan Williamson
Foreword by Ankit Mathur

ISBN 9781617298851
320 pages, $49.99
February 2023

Think Like a Startup Founder
by Jothy Rosenberg

ISBN 9781633438422
225 pages (estimated), $39.99
Summer 2024 (estimated)

Lead Developer Career Guide
by Shelley Benhoff

ISBN 9781633438071
325 pages (estimated), $49.99
Fall 2024 (estimated)

Cybersecurity Career Guide
by Alyssa Miller

ISBN 9781617298202
200 pages, $49.99
May 2022

For ordering information, go to www.manning.com

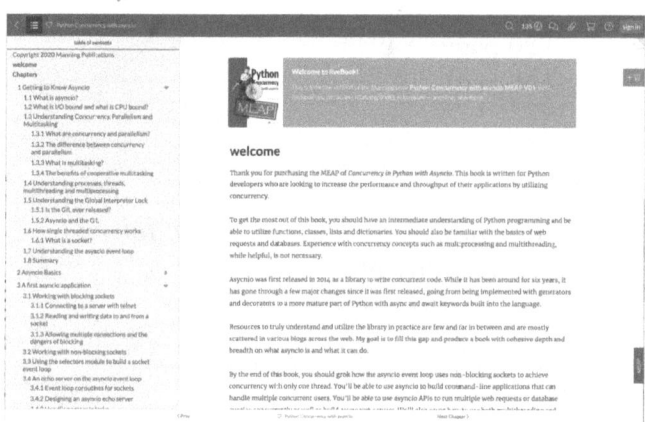

A new online reading experience

liveBook, our online reading platform, adds a new dimension to your Manning books, with features that make reading, learning, and sharing easier than ever. A liveBook version of your book is included FREE with every Manning book.

This next generation book platform is more than an online reader. It's packed with unique features to upgrade and enhance your learning experience.

- Add your own notes and bookmarks
- One-click code copy
- Learn from other readers in the discussion forum
- Audio recordings and interactive exercises
- Read all your purchased Manning content in any browser, anytime, anywhere

As an added bonus, you can search every Manning book and video in liveBook—even ones you don't yet own. Open any liveBook, and you'll be able to browse the content and read anything you like.*

Find out more at www.manning.com/livebook-program.

*Open reading is limited to 10 minutes per book daily